The Idea
of Medieval Literature

New Essays on Chaucer
and Medieval Culture
in Honor of Donald R. Howard

Edited by
James M. Dean and Christian K. Zacher

DELAWARE
Newark: University of Delaware Press
London and Toronto: Associated University Presses

Associated University Presses
440 Forsgate Drive
Cranbury, NJ 08512

Associated University Presses
25 Sicilian Avenue
London WC1A 2QH, England

Associated University Presses
P.O. Box 39, Clarkson Pstl. Stn.
Mississauga, Ontario,
L5J 3X9 Canada

The paper used in this publication meets the requirements
of the American National Standard for Permanence of Paper
for Printed Library Materials Z39.48-1984.

Library of Congress Cataloging-in-Publication Data

The Idea of medieval literature : new essays on Chaucer and medieval
culture in honor of Donald R. Howard / edited by James M. Dean and
Christian K. Zacher.
    p.   cm.
  Includes bibliographical references and index.
  ISBN 0-87413-440-4
  1. Chaucer, Geoffrey, d. 1400—Criticism and interpretation.
2. English literature—Middle English, 1100–1500—History and
criticism.   3. England—Civilization—Medieval period, 1066–1485.
I. Howard, Donald Roy, 1927 .   II. Dean, James M. (James
McMurrin)   III. Zacher, Christian K.
PR1924.I34   1992
821'.1—dc20   91-58041
                                                                        CIP

Contents

6 CONTENTS

Introduction: Howard and the Idea of Medieval Literature

JAMES M. DEAN and CHRISTIAN K. ZACHER

Le style c'est l'homme même

This book is a collection of original essays, by friends and students, honoring Donald Roy Howard, Olive H. Palmer Professor in the Humanities at Stanford University, who died in 1987 at the age of fifty-nine. Howard was a premier medievalist, and Chaucerian, in an era of great students of Chaucer and medieval literature. Among Howard's friends of long standing were Francis Lee Utley, the learned and witty folklorist, to whom he dedicated *The Idea of the Canterbury Tales;* E. Talbot Donaldson, the exceptional Middle English scholar, also learned and witty, to whom he dedicated his edition of *Troilus and Criseyde;* and Morton W. Bloomfield, the eminent medievalist, Howard's colleague at Ohio State in the late 1950s and early 1960s and at Stanford twenty some years later, a collaborator and a scholar whom he often referred to as his "unofficial teacher."

Howard will be remembered for many things: his quick and clever mind, his dynamic teaching, his sense of irony, his outspokenness on issues, his sometimes controversial views on medieval literature, his fierce loyalties, and his passionate interests, which included philology, the history of ideas, poetics, stylistics, Freudian (and Gestalt) psychology, psycholinguistics, fads and trends (medieval and modern), semiotics, and, most recently and particularly, biography and the art of dying. Above all he will be remembered as an engaging, commanding writer, a stylist whose perceptions and deft turns of phrase are singular and distinctive. J. Hillis Miller characterized his unique style as, simply, "Howardian." In this respect he resembles another prominent medievalist (whom Howard much admired), the Oxford scholar C. S. Lewis, whose prose style was also distinctive. As the list of his interests suggests, he was an eclectic thinker who combined what he regarded as the best of older and newer approaches to medieval literature and culture. This collection of essays seeks to honor Howard's diversity and to exhibit his continuing influence on medieval studies through the work of friends and students. We the editors

7

are fortunate to have been able to count ourselves as both friends and students.

Howard profoundly affected medieval studies, especially the study of Chaucer. He brought something new and unique to medieval studies: a critical sensibility, well trained in older modes of scholarship, which was yet willing to entertain and sometimes to engage newer critical voices. He was a critic and intellectual who yearned to get beyond the old controversies that seemed to bog down medieval studies in unproductive wranglings. He constantly opened up or anticipated critical projects of the present moment (for example, the historicist or "New Historical" projects) and those which promised to become important future enterprises (the current concern with biography and psychoanalytic criticism, especially in feminist studies). Even those who would deny his influence have followed his lead, for he has considerably affected the scholarly climate in interesting and significant ways. Howard's growth and development as a scholar roughly parallels and helps to illuminate the development of medieval studies—and the "Chaucerian project," so to speak—over the last forty years. For Howard's career is paradigmatic—and always instructive.

Although Howard occasionally reviewed the state of scholarship on individual authors, he seldom put together his thoughts on the larger scholarly-critical enterprise—the condition of medieval studies at the present time. A little-known exception to this general rule occurred in a brief speculative essay in *University Publishing,* a newspaper-like quarterly published by William McClung, Howard's editor for *The Idea of the Canterbury Tales* and *Writers and Pilgrims.*

In this essay, entitled "The Four Medievalisms," Howard distinguished between and among four interpretations of the Middle Ages.[1] The "first medievalism" he identified as Renaissance antiquarianism, which looked to its recent past, between "antiquity" and "modernity," with nostalgia and "impatience." By the "second medievalism" he meant that modern historical scholarship, after 1680, which focused on texts and documents and which "practiced philology and diplomatics." Practitioners of the "third medievalism," building on some of the significant concepts defined by the "second medievalism," tried to discover the "authentic" Middle Ages—how the medievals actually lived, what they cared about, what they ate and drank, what, and how, they read. We are still fleshing out Howard's "third medievalism," as many of the essays in this collection (and many of Howard's writings) witness.

But Howard went on to project a "fourth medievalism," which he felt might well be the next phase of medieval studies, a "reaction—against authenticity and against strangeness." Anticipating his own biography of Chaucer, he predicted a new interest in "emotion, mentalities, and sensibilities." "This would be imaginative and speculative history, of a kind that would eschew the narrowly delimited topic and embrace generalization for its value as a heuristic device."[2] According to this medievalism, the Middle Ages exist as much or more in *us* as in the medievals, who of course never knew they lived and wrote in the "Middle Ages," between the classical and Renaissance periods. Invoking Barbara Tuchman's popular history of the fourteenth century *(A Distant Mirror),* a book Howard admired, he concludes:

> I do not mean to suggest that the study of the Middle Ages has been one trivial fashion after another, that nothing lasts in our ideas of the past, or that nothing is after all true anyway. Truth is relative and understanding always partial, and there are fashions in all things. The changing fashions of medieval scholarship have cumulatively brought us closer to knowing the Middle Ages. We would take up a Fourth Medievalism knowing, now, that if the period is a "distant mirror," we will see in it, as in all mirrors, a selective, reversed, and distorted image in which we cannot help but see ourselves.[3]

Howard's persistent concern in his writings has been to show how "they" are like "us," or how we are like them—how in fact we exist in them, and they in us. He boldly claimed to know Chaucer's intentions, to be able to see into Chaucer's mind and feelings—this at a time when critics generally believed, as many still do, that a writer's intentions can never be divined, much less articulated (the "intentional fallacy"), and that critical "mind-reading" in any event is wrong-headed. The New Criticism had driven a wedge between the text as object and the writer as creating mind. But Howard regarded this split as misleading and artificial. In answer to a famous essay by Talbot Donaldson (who was not a New Critic), he argued that we read texts not just for ideas and out of abstract interest but because we become interested in the writer, the distinct personality behind the words and ideas on the page. We want to know—insofar as we can, and fully aware of the difficulties involved in such a project—the "real" Chaucer.

> The Chaucer we know is a creation of our own response to his works. For that he is no less the *real* Chaucer. This is true for a reason which, as exegetes, we sometimes set aside, but which as humanists we always assume: that for every man who creates great poems there is an infinite truth, of grandeur and terror, in the adage *style is the man himself*—that there must be in him, and in those who would read him, all of the human possibilities which can be realized in his works.[4]

Howard pondered the relationship between medieval and modern thought in his first book, *The Three Temptations: Medieval Man in Search of the World* (1966). In this study, a revision of his University of Florida doctoral thesis on medieval contempt of the world, Howard tackled the issue of doctrinal criticism of medieval literature in an attempt to refute, or revise, D. W. Robertson's influential thesis that cupidity and charity were governing norms for medieval literature. Howard particularly objected to the assumption that medieval culture was "monolithic" and "dominated intellectually by the Church."[5] He also resisted positing a radical otherness to the Middle Ages. Robertson, for his part, had been arguing that medieval literature is accessible to modern readers but only insofar as moderns can overcome, or block out, post-Kantian ways of understanding, such as Freudian interpretations, which he regarded as especially subversive of authentic medieval modes of reading and knowing. In *The Three Temptations* Howard did not yet adopt the subjective approach of his later writings, but he clearly anticipated them in his response to Robertsonianism and the challenges posed by doctrinal or patristic historicisms.

The major distinction between Robertson's and Howard's historicisms concerns their respective stances toward the ancients and moderns, them and us. Robertson has had serious misgivings about reading "older literature in the light of modern aesthetic systems, economic philosophies, or psychological theories"[6] or about encouraging "the use of the literature of the past as a mirror for the reader's personality," which could and does lead to the reader's sympathizing with "wrong" literary characters (such as Milton's Satan).[7] Although Howard has shown the greatest respect for the historical process, he yet approached the problem of historical reading in a different way, as witnessed in the following passage from *The Three Temptations,* which begins:

> We shall misunderstand medieval poems in the gravest way if we relax into the premise that beneath their religious trappings lie our own familiar notions.

In this sentiment Howard might seem to agree with Robertson's historicism; but he continues in a characteristic Howardian turn of phrase (and of thought), which owes more to Johan Huizinga than to Robertson:

> Reading fourteenth-century poetry requires knowing the very feeling of its thought, the dimensions of its mythic and symbolic world, the reality of its underlying threats and doubts—knowing, if we can, the styles of life and thought which medieval literary styles reflect.

He turns for illustration to a favorite literary work, *Hamlet,* one of the chief Western texts on contempt of the world. "And we go to this trouble," Howard continues,

> for the same reason that we do so with *Hamlet,* or any classic: not because we want to learn all the pedantic rules of revenge tragedy or because we care anything per se about the quaint and hollow conventions of the Elizabethan

stage, but because everywhere in and behind those rules and conventions lies an act of human consciousness which still draws us to itself.

Howard concludes that the past, including its literature, has significant meaning for the present:

> We read *Hamlet* or the *Troilus* because each has something to say not only to man about humanity but to western man about western civilization. We attempt, that is, to recapture the feeling of historical styles in their fullest complexity not to escape into the past but to understand it in its relation to the present.[8]

In Robertson's brand of historicism we as readers attempt to shed or ignore our preconceptions, those distinctly non-medieval perspectives we bring with us as we read, in order to understand medieval literature in its own terms as much as possible. They—medieval people—are radically different from us; and we must be constantly vigilant lest we misread from lack of historical awareness. Howard, while acknowledging the problem of historical reading, appeared far more optimistic about the historical project; and he seemed more willing to trust modern readers to understand medieval literature without elaborate glosses or doctrinal caveats. He urged sympathetic readings from our human experience rather than only medieval ways of knowing and understanding. He became absorbed with how medieval people sought accommodations with the material world, its allures, pleasures, and distractions, rather than with how they instilled moral lessons on avoiding cupidity and promoting charity (as they so often did, of course). If Robertson constitutes something like a critical *summa* of Howard's "third medievalism," Howard looked forward to his own "fourth medievalism."

Together with Talbot Donaldson and Morton Bloomfield, Howard was a notable adversary of allegorical or scriptural interpretations of medieval literature and he seemed to reserve his most withering scorn for such approaches. In *The Idea of the Canterbury Tales,* for example, he says of the monolithic view of medieval literary tradition: "One can argue that medieval men were all reasonable zombies who held identical opinions and saw everything in moral, not psychological, terms; but to argue this one has to ignore everything they wrote about people's motives, their inner states, their dreams, their moral choices, and their souls."[9] Elsewhere in the same book he sounds almost weary of the anti-exegetical enterprise:

> Those critics who see in Chaucer only the doctrine of *caritas* preached over and over in a hundred allegories work hard to get around this [Chaucer's treatment of feelings], but they have to resort to nonsense. Medieval men, they have to claim, did not have personalities, did not feel emotions as we do, saw everything with unruffled rationality in hierarchies and signs; whence, they insist, the

feelings Chaucer raises in us are our "sentimentality," his humanity our "psychologism," the turbulence and multivalence in his works our "Hegelianism." It is all very dreary.[10]

Howard in fact forged his interpretation of medieval literature largely in response to allegorical criticism; and he often acknowledged his debt to it for helping him to clarify his own views. A good Latinist, he read the same sources as the exegetical critics—but arrived at quite different conclusions as to the meaning and applications of those sources.

Howard was a humanist scholar who sought kinship with medieval humanism. "Humanist" has become in some circles a term for a mossback who opposes curricular changes because of misguided, nostalgic, emotional ties to a rigid canon of discredited, patriarchal writers. Howard was not a humanist in this sense but rather a forward-looking, progressive scholar who relished new and interesting ideas, especially old ideas that were once new or old ideas recast as new. In this sense he might be characterized as an intellectual humanist, full of curiosity, eager to encounter *our* world through the medieval experience of *their* world. Howard's humanism, thus, was grounded in human experience and in the faith (to invoke a word that seems almost quaint) that significant acts of interpersonal communication—intersubjectivity—can occur through literature and over time. He believed, that is, that it was possible to come to know important things about Chaucer as a man through his poetry, his life, and his world. This belief—an act of acceptance in a skeptical, critical age—informed Howard's study of Chaucer's poetics.

Although Howard will probably be best remembered as a generalizing theorist—a commentator (almost, at times, a pundit) on the medieval social and literary scene—he was trained in techniques of close reading, philology, and practical criticism. But he was never a New Critic. He was a close reader and historically-oriented stylistic critic who could mount an almost anthropological approach to medieval literature and culture. He was also something of a pluralist. At one point he writes: "Is it not . . . the quality of great art that it can prompt an unpredictable and quite possibly unlimited number of valid responses?"[11] He doubtless here anticipated what he would later call the "fourth medievalism," a way of studying the era that attends to the reader's responses as well as the artist's intentions. He seemed to argue at other times, however, that just as there are great writers and great works of literature, so there are great readers—those especially suited for divining artistic purpose.

As a critic especially concerned with style and stylistics, Howard took pains to define style in general terms. In this endeavor he anticipated the current (poststructural) interests in cultural anthropology, ethnography, and comparative literature as practiced and explained, for example, by Clifford Geertz, who noted the trend—which only continues today—for disciplines once separate and discrete to borrow from one another.[12] The anthropologist Alfred L. Kroeber, whose writings Howard knew, often treated issues of style together with (among other things) civilization, history, philology, dress lengths, and evolution.[13] In *An Anthropologist Looks at History,* Kroeber defined style very broadly, but Howard could assent to this definition: "A style may be provisionally defined as a system of coherent ways or patterns of doing things."[14] In *The Three Temptations,* Howard says of "studying style":

> By "style" I do not mean, of course, mere verbal elegancies, but the whole range of forms and qualities which characterize a work. I use the word in a general sense, as when one says "a style of life" or "a style of civilization"; such styles of thought and behavior, immanent in a culture, are reflected in a literary style.[15]

Howard also quotes Meyer Schapiro's definition of style in this sense as "a system of forms with a quality and a meaningful expression through which the personality of the artist and the broad outlook of a group are visible."[16] In *The Idea of the Canterbury Tales* Howard reiterates his notion of style as a form of "communication" between writer and audience:

> The concept of style is probably the most useful way of getting at this circumstance of communication between writer and reader if we take style in its broadest sense as the whole range of forms, effects, and qualities which characterize a work: but seen this way, style in art reflects style in behavior and culture, brings form and content with it.[17]

The approaches of Howard, Kroeber, and Schapiro might be said to express, or at least to point toward, a semiotics of culture with a special focus on literature. Howard used this focus to explain the uniqueness of texts and authors, but he never lost sight of the cultures which produced those texts and authors.

Howard admired the practical criticism of the great continental philologist and theorist Leo Spitzer, who taught at The Johns Hopkins University from 1936–1960. Spitzer's method, *explication de texte,* informed by stylistics and the history of ideas, exerted considerable influence on Howard's critical thought and method. Spitzer's practice, generally speaking, was to concentrate on one or a few short works—lyric poems, for example—and to interrogate them, through close reading, for their governing stylistic norms and assumptions, somewhat in the manner of the New Critics (with whom Spitzer had much in common). But unlike some New Critics, who concentrated on the poem as an aesthetic object without regard for its historical contexts, Spitzer believed historical and cultural contexts were central to understanding any poem. For Spitzer, as for Howard, writers create works of literature in specific circumstances and within specific cultural conditions; to ignore these is to misread historical works of literature (or any writings from the past). Moreover, Spitzer, again like Howard, believed that each historical period (and its culture) brought forth works of literature in distinctive, identifiable styles—styles in which the individual writers participated with their own unique linguistic habits of mind (their stylistic *paroles,* so to speak, within their respective *langues*). Hence a Petrarch may be distinguished stylistically from a Boccaccio, and the two Italians may be differentiated from a Chaucer; and again those three, as fourteenth-century writers, may be distinguished from Montaigne or Shakespeare, as later writers, with their own cultural and literary styles.

In formulating his humanist-stylistic response to medieval writers, Howard cites Spitzer's concept of the "click" that occurs when one reads a work of literature and then forms an impression or *idea* of the work. Spitzer formulated his notion of the "click," the "mentalistic" process, in an attempt to answer what he regarded as inaccurate criticism from Wellek and Warren in their influential *Theory of Literature.* Wellek and Warren characterized Spitzer's method as "psychological and ideological," a method whose search for "linguistic confirmation" seemed, to them, "frequently strained or based on every slight evidence."[18] Spitzer responded with an explanation of his hermeneutic by means of the philological circle:

> my procedure involves two separate movements (both of which, taken together, serve to complete the "philological circle"): I first draw from one detail (which need not always be linguistic or stylistic, but may also be compositional in nature) of incontrovertible factual evidence, an inference as to the (at this stage still hypothetic) psyche of the author of the period, which hypothesis is then, in a second movement, controlled by a scrutiny of (to the degree that this is feasible) *all* other striking details (stylistic or compositional) which occur in the same author or period.[19]

Some of Spitzer's terms and assumptions seem today naive and old-fashioned—the "philological circle" (akin to Heidegger's hermeneutic circle), "incontrovertible factual evidence," "psyche." Yet he did point toward important strains of contemporary critical theory now in vogue: phenomenological criticism (with its focus on the author's mind) and reader-response criticism (with its focus on the reader's acts of reading, hence with the reader's mind). For medieval studies, Howard has been pivotal in negotiating the movement from Spitzer's stylistic criticism and the "click" to more phenomenological, intersubjective, and even semiotic cultural approaches.

As part of his concern for something like intersubjectivity, Howard posited a "leap" or "overlap of minds"[20] that must occur for any act of apprehension or critical judgment. This "leap" or "overlap" may be considered an intersubjective cousin of Spitzer's "click" in that both the "leap" and the "click" are metaphors for sudden insight, a sudden grasping of an idea:

> Reading a literary work is after all an act of awareness; it may engage the unconscious, or the affective, or the volitional aspect of the mental life, but picking up a book and experiencing it means grasping with awareness something which existed in the author's consciousness. This leap or overlap of minds is the unique event which happens whenever a work is read; so if we think of poems as a force in society, they are such a force for this reason and no other.[21]

Although Howard's interest in authorial mind can be traced at least to 1965 ("Chaucer the Man"), his special concern with phenomenology and intersubjectivity probably dated from his association with The Johns Hopkins University, beginning in 1967. Johns Hopkins, of course, had long been associated with the history of ideas from the days of Arthur Lovejoy, George Boas, and Spitzer. When Howard arrived in Baltimore from UCLA, the English graduate faculty consisted of Don Cameron Allen (called "big Don" to distinguish him from Howard, or "little Don"), Earl Wasserman, Ronald Paulson, Charles Anderson, Jackson Cope, and J. Hillis Miller. Especially influential at this time was Miller, who, together with Richard Macksey of the Humanities Center, Eugenio Donato, and René Girard, sponsored the Structuralist conference, "The Languages of Criticism and the Sciences of Man," the year before Howard arrived there. That conference attracted formidable continental (and American) theorists, including Jacques Derrida, Paul de Man, Lucien Goldmann, Tzvetan Todorov, Roland Barthes, and Jacques Lacan.[22] Another who attended, and who influenced Howard at about this time, was Georges Poulet, a member of the so-called "Geneva School," former chair of the Romance Languages Department at Hopkins and author of *Studies in Human Time* (1956).[23] At the conference, Poulet read a paper ("Criticism and the Experience of Interiority") containing sentiments with which Howard could agree. Speaking of the experience of reading a book, which as an object differs from a sewing machine or "the under side of a plate," Poulet says:

> At the precise moment that I see, surging out of the object I hold open before me, a quantity of significations which my mind grasps, I realize that what I hold in my hands is no longer just an object, or even simply a living thing. I am aware of a rational being, of a consciousness; the consciousness of another, no different from the one I automatically assume in every human being I encounter, except that in this case the consciousness is open to me, welcomes me, lets me look deep inside itself, and even allows me, with unheard-of license, to think what it thinks and feel what it feels.[24]

Howard would claim to be able to see into the mind of Chaucer, and through his literary characters, to think what he thought and to feel what he felt.

It is a curious fact—curious to us, at least—that Howard seldom acknowledged his critical sources (except in a general way) or attempted to detail his critical methodology, as Robertson did so forcefully in *A Preface to Chaucer* and some of his essays. In *The Three Temptations,* as we have noted, he argued, *contra* Robertson, that medieval aesthetic style included more than the "perspectives" of charity and cupidity. And in the Acknowledgements to *The Idea of the Canterbury Tales,* he confessed a "general" debt not only to Lovejoy for the history of ideas but also "to the writings of those who changed it [the study of ideas], especially to Leo Spitzer, Erich Auerbach, Georges Poulet, and E. H. Gombrich."[25] Howard observes that ideas arise in specific contexts—"local" contexts as Geertz might phrase it—and that they change over time. And here Howard comes close to something like reader-response criticism as he explicates his kind of affective criticism:

> In literary study it became clear that you cannot separate a literary idea from the style in which it is expressed, and that you cannot speak of style without speaking of the effect of that style on the reader or audience. This means being subjective enough to follow one's responses and intuitions unabashedly, being (in Leo Spitzer's phrase) "mentalistic." This natural way of understanding literature had been anathematized in America as a heresy, the "affective fallacy"; but those who know what a fallacy is have ignored the anathema and embraced the heresy. This has meant breaking down the traditional barrier between subject and object, inquiring in introspective or in psychological terms what happens *in us* when we experience a work of art. It has meant viewing an idea not as a pellet of intellection but as an event, something that once happened to an author, significant only in so far as it engages our interest, captures our imagination, provokes in us at least vicarious participation.[26]

This "vicarious participation" is of course exactly what Robertson objects to in *A Preface to Chaucer.* And the issue of reading for best understanding—as an (alleged or ostensible) medieval reader or as a modern reader—continues to be central to the debate about historical reading.

Later on in *The Idea of the Canterbury Tales,* in his chapter on "Style," Howard again takes up the problem of recognizing significant stylistic features through a "mentalistic" process. Those who concern themselves with style (and, we might add, with poetics) look for "a set of principles or codes, a way of seeing things, which directed and accounts for the author's stylistic choices"—in other words, for "an ethos or 'world'." Howard does not claim that the "individual [stylistic] item or variant" is the only way through which we may come to recognize the "dominant characteristics of a style." But he does affirm that certain readers may be especially well-suited for undertaking a stylistic analysis: "I think it must be true that those critics most sensitive to style have a way of grasping significant exceptional items on instinct, of getting an inner 'click' and following it up."[27]

Howard has shown little public interest in the more philosophical trends of contemporary literary theory, especially deconstruction. He was not interested in decentering the author; to the contrary, he was vitally interested in authors, their lives and times. Howard would be charged with speculation (impressionism or "mind-reading") during his career, but he never speculated on the ontological status or readability of the text (what Miller has called *"mise en abŷme"*). On the other hand, Howard the pluralist would doubtless agree with Miller that "The poem [Shelley's "The Triumph of Life"], like all texts, is 'unreadable,' if by 'readable' one means open to a single, definitive, univocal interpretation."[28] But of intersubjectivity Howard ventured the following, somewhat cautious statement:

> Criticism of this kind is often called "phenomenological," though its practitioners usually tiptoe away from the word—wisely, because one can find such criticism appealing and effective without having any interest in phenomenology as a philosophical position, or any temperamental affinity for Husserl, or Merleau-Ponty, or Sartre, or Gaston Bachelard. Criticism of this kind might have developed independently, out of stylistics or in reaction against the "new" criticism.[29]

Elsewhere he writes: "[The problem of experience and consciousness] can be and often is made a great deal more difficult by introducing an elaborate lexicon of abstractions like 'mediation,' 'intersubjectivity,' 'vision,' 'objectification,' and the like; but the poet's language, being concrete, has nothing to do with all that."[30] Howard also distinguishes between language and its alleged failures and those who use (or misuse) language. In an oblique attack on deconstructive criticism, Howard says: "the 'inadequacy' of language, about which tongues wag so much these days [1970], is nothing more than the frustrating differential between language and consciousness; but the inadequacy is in us, not in language—the failure is our failure to use language well and to cultivate our gardens of consciousness."[31]

Some of Howard's best-known essay-length work has been done on things experiential, especially on language and what Howard calls "consciousness." His interest in language and linguistics originated in traditional philology, but it was reinvigorated by his readings in Freudian psychology and psycholinguistics. These conceptual approaches converge in Howard's studies of love and sexuality in *Troilus and Criseyde*. In "Experience, Language, and Consciousness," Howard focuses on a specific poetic sequence of about three hundred lines in Book 2 of the *Troilus* to show how Criseyde falls in love. Howard especially emphasizes the role of Antigone's song in the process, as he tries to demonstrate that Chaucer "makes us know what it feels like to *be* Criseyde, from the moment she first feels love for Troilus." The scene, according to Howard, "explores a problem often discussed in abstract terms—the relationship between experience (what we do) and consciousness (what we think)."[32] Here Howard would understand Chaucer's mind through the "mind" of a fictional character, Criseyde, a product or figment of Chaucer's imagination. He enlists the aid of the psycholinguist L. S. Vygotsky to characterize the kind and quality of "inner speech"—Criseyde's reflections and musings and decision-making—to which we as readers are privy as we experience her falling in love. As Howard phrases it: "The greatest poetry is always a miracle, but the miracle here is that of evoking what is itself miraculous, the ability of one mind, closed within its little world of thought, to enter the mind of another. Chaucer makes us experience the reality Criseyde experienced—we see what she saw, hear what she heard."[33] This is a version of the "leap" or "overlap of minds," but at one remove, since Howard understands the fictional character Criseyde to have a mind of her own.

Howard was concerned with Chaucer's poetics and with poetic structures but only as these can be apprehended through *ideas,* which one comes to know through human *experience.* For Howard, ideas provide points of convergence between the culture and its styles, on the one hand, and the individual talent, on the other; and the reader appreciates the ideas and art through his or her experience of the world. Like the concepts "idea" and "style," "experience" and what it means to be human were important in Howard's critical considerations. And just as "idea" and "style" are related in Howard's thought, so "experience" is related to Howard's notions of both "idea" and "style."

Although Howard has sometimes been characterized as a "Freudian" reader of medieval literature, he was more of a psychological reader generally who occasionally turned to Freud for analogues or emphasis. He was more interested in exploring the allegories of medieval dreams or medieval faculty psychology than in applying theories about the ego, neurosis, or psychopathology to, say, The Clerk's Tale. He was especially concerned, as we have seen, with experience (broadly conceived) as manifested in style (broadly defined).

Howard's interest in psychology and experience can also be witnessed in a brief section from *Writers and Pilgrims,* where he alludes to Edmundo O'Gorman's study of Christopher Columbus and his alleged "discovery" of America.[34] Howard's students heard much about this book in the mid-1960s, for he was intrigued by O'Gorman's distinction between "discovery," the usual word for Columbus's accomplishment, and "invention," a distinction which involves the *idea* of a thing. O'Gorman points out that one cannot discover something unless one knows what to look for: the discovered object must first be *invented,* or one must have prior idea about the thing. O'Gorman's example is gold. To discover gold, to dig it out of the earth, its value must be known and appreciated; otherwise, even if you discovered gold, you wouldn't know what you had "discovered." Hence Columbus, according to O'Gorman, cannot properly be said to have discovered America simply because he believed he had found a passage to the East Indies. America had to be invented before it could be discovered—before it could be seen, like gold, as valuable.

In *Writers and Pilgrims* Howard applied O'Gorman's thesis to his discussion of Columbus's reading of Mandeville's *Travels,* which influenced the great explorer in his enterprise. But Howard gives the discussion an arch Freudian twist. Speaking of Columbus's third voyage he says:

> He believed he had arrived at the Earthly Paradise: by all authorities it was at the easternmost end of the *orbis terrarum*—"the end of the East." Mandeville, in his thirty-third chapter, approaching Paradise from the Orient, had found it "so high that it toucheth nigh to the circle of the moon," enclosed by a moss-covered wall having one entrance barred by fire, "so that no man that is mortal ne dare not enter." Columbus must have read this passage many times and thought very hard about approaching the end of the East from the west, as he had deduced he would do. For he hatched the theory, not so improbable by medieval standards, that the earth was not round after all (as everyone knew it was) but pear-shaped; that atop the earth (at the equator), closest to heaven, was a protuberance, which he compared to a woman's breast; and that the nipple of this breast was the Earthly Paradise. Let Freudians observe that he understood what paradise really is; it was, anyway, his idea of where he had been.[35]

This is typically Howardian: he combines the history of ideas (theories of the terrestrial paradise), stylistics, and his own kind of Freudianism—a neo-Freudianism or literary Freudianism—in order to explain Columbus's idea of his discovery. One of his many plans for the future, in fact, had been a lecture on Columbus's medieval heritage he hoped to be able to deliver during the Columbian quincentenary in 1992.

Throughout his career Howard maintained—and deepened—his interest in Chaucer the man. The final achievement of this interest was his biography, *Chaucer: His Life, His Works, His World.* Howard contemplated this biography for about ten years before actually beginning work on it. A fellowship from the National Endowment for the Humanities helped launch the study in 1978, and it was sustained by additional grants from the Guggenheim and Rockefeller foundations. Howard wrote this biography and its focus on Chaucer's writings and culture—he calls it "a literary biography"[36]—because he felt that Chaucer as a man, as a human being, failed to emerge in previous biographies. He came to believe that the "real" Chaucer could be glimpsed, if at all, only through his writings:

"Surely this is the real Chaucer, more real than Chaucer . . . who is said to have beaten a Franciscan friar in Fleet Street, or raped one Cecily Champain—more real because we can read him still and take the measure of his place in history."[37] As he wrote the biography, he tried to rethink the conventional wisdom about Chaucer and his life. One technique he used was to seek analogues for Chaucer's experiences in modern-day experience without resorting to the novelistic fictions of a John Gardner.

A good example of his revision, his rethinking, of conventional views occurs in his consideration of Chaucer's possible meeting with Boccaccio during his trip to Italy in 1373. Such a meeting has been a source of speculation since at least the early twentieth century, although there is not a scrap of real evidence that such a meeting took place. Some biographers of Chaucer have conjectured that Boccaccio and Chaucer, because of their mutual interests, would have become instant friends or colleagues. But Howard—rather than speculating (as did Gardner) that the two men might have laughed endlessly at bawdy tales—tries to imagine the scene had they met. We quote the passage at some length:

> Suppose, then, that such a meeting took place. Chaucer was thirty; Boccaccio was sixty. Boccaccio was in ill health, suffered from obesity, had had a "dropsical" illness, intestinal and respiratory ailments, violent abdominal pains. From these illnesses he had partly recovered, but he was still going through stages of depression. Like Petrarch, he had had scabies a year before—a most uncomfortable ailment in the Middle Ages, difficult to treat, slow in being cured or overcome, whose painful itching, worse at night, promotes sleeplessness, nervousness, and irritability. By all accounts Boccaccio was a touchy, oversensitive man, and he was worried about his own health and Petrarch's, and about approaching death. It seems quite probable that if a meeting with Chaucer took place, it was not a success. There would, for one thing, have been the language barrier. Unless you speak a foreign language very fluently, it's dreadfully frustrating to try to carry on an intellectual conversation. If Chaucer's Italian wasn't up to this, they could have resorted to French, in which Chaucer was more at home than Boccaccio, or Latin, in which Boccaccio was more at home than Chaucer.[38]

Howard goes on to imagine that they might have turned to classical authors and their writings, but Chaucer would not have been up to Boccaccio's learning on this subject. Then he treats the issue of Boccaccio's writings as a possible topic of conversation: "Perhaps Chaucer had by now read something of Boccaccio's, but it is never easy for a young writer to talk with an older one about his works, especially when he has read but few of them." Finally, Howard doubts that such a meeting could have been "cordial" or interesting to either participant. Chaucer, for his part,

> "would have found [Boccaccio] very different from the figure he might have imagined—fat, nervous, gloomy, sickly, uncommunicative. And who is to say if

in Boccaccio's eyes the young Englishman didn't seem overconfident or cheeky, or too Frenchified or courtly, or with spotty readings in the Classics. Such uneasy meetings get shelved in our memories. We do not necessarily forget or 'block' them, but they remain a source of discomfort that we manage to keep in the darker recesses of consciousness."[39]

Howard feels that such a meeting, with thwarted expectations, could account for Chaucer's substituting the name "Lollius" for Boccaccio as author of the Troilus story. He acknowledges that Chaucer never mentions Machaut or Froissart either.

"But a meeting in which Chaucer somehow felt himself demeaned, or condescended to, or disappointed—a meeting that he left with the uneasy feeling that he had met the great man at the wrong time, or had failed to put his best foot forward, perhaps a meeting in which his own embarrassment and diffidence had made him an unlikely and foolish-seeming companion—all this could explain why he admired Boccaccio's books but ignored the man himself."[40]

Boccaccio's possible meeting with Chaucer in fact resembles Howard's own meeting with Willard Farnham, a scholar who influenced him and whom Howard held in the highest regard. He wrote the influential study *The Medieval Heritage of Elizabethan Tragedy,* which Howard drew upon for his dissertation and for *The Three Temptations* as well as for one of his first published articles, "*Hamlet* and Contempt of the World" (1959).[41] Our memories fail as to the exact details of this meeting; but we do recall that Howard, on a visit to the University of California at Berkeley, decided to pay his respects to Farnhnam. Howard was a young assistant professor at the time, and Farnham was a very senior scholar. Howard, a raconteur who could tell a good tale on himself, later described how, full of enthusiasm and good will, he tried to tell Farnham how much his book meant to him and his own work. Farnham greeted Howard with more annoyance than enthusiasm, and they had little in common, little to talk about, other than Farnham's book. Howard's audience with Farnham ended rather abruptly and, for Howard, unsatisfactorily. Doubtless Farnham quickly forgot the incident, but Howard remembered it as a bruising encounter that contained certain lessons about homage, age differences, and clashes of style—lessons that may have found their way, we believe, into his biography of Chaucer.

Howard's biography won the National Book Critics Award for Biography in 1987, a prize he would have been gratified to receive personally had he lived; he also would have been pleased to learn that his biography was a Book of the Month Club selection. Howard in fact believed that medievalists (and scholars generally) should make every effort to reach larger audiences. This is why he so much admired Barbara Tuchman's *A Distant Mirror;* for despite its faults, obvious to specialists, her work reached and moved people who otherwise would have remained ignorant about Chaucer's century. This is also one reason why he admired the writings of C. S. Lewis, Johan Huizinga, and Erich Auerbach. Although they never achieved the popular acclaim of the historian Tuchman—nor did they seek it—they reached, and continue to influence, large audiences.

As part of Howard's attempt to address a general reader, he edited two normalized texts of Chaucer for New American Library (Signet): *The Canterbury Tales: A Selection* (1969) and *Troilus and Criseyde, and Selected Short Poems* (1976, with James Dean). He took as his model the normalized texts of Talbot Donaldson, in *Chaucer's Poetry: An Anthology for the Modern Reader.* Indeed, Howard hoped to publish Donaldson's actual texts, but the publisher would not allow this, so he decided to apply similar principles of normalization but to go even further than Donaldson. In doing so he sometimes stretched the boundaries of Middle English pronunciation through his spelling choices—"drought" for Donaldson's "droughte" (General Prologue line 2), "vein" for "veine" (line 3), and "course" for "cours" (line 8), to cite but a few examples. Through these choices Howard assumes that Chaucer's lines were fairly regularly endecasyllabic (something that has been often challenged) and that the final e's of manuscript "droghte" and "veyne" (as spelled in *The Riverside Chaucer*) were not pronounced because of ellision with the following words. Howard justified his choices by pointing to the varieties of Middle English spellings; his governing precept was always *accessibility,* even, if need be, at the expense of strictest accuracy. He had no interest in preserving alternate spellings—for example, "saugh" rather than "saw," both possible forms in Chaucer's London speech—that are of interest to linguists and Chaucerians. Still, he did keep some alternate spellings on the following basis: "Since perfect consistency is not possible, there remain in this text enough spelling variants to introduce the student to the mysteries of Middle English orthography."[42] Howard also wrote the introductions to his student editions with an eye toward accessibility; and the introduction to *The Canterbury Tales* edition has been cited as useful for the beginning reader of Chaucer.[43] That edition remains in print and was for many years the best seller in the Signet Poetry series.

Howard was interested in what might be called, for lack of better terms, "fads" and "trends," medieval and modern—fashions of thought that emerge and fade in cultures. He believed these trends gave significant insights into their cultures and societies; and he especially liked to note those sensibilities or tastes in medieval society—those styles—which are most out of fashion in modern culture.

Of the literary fashions Howard studied in detail, none held greater fascination for him than contempt of the world. He began his academic career with this topic; he edited Innocent III's influential treatise *De miseria humanae conditionis* for the Library of Liberal Arts (1969); and he followed through with a bibliographical listing of *incipits* of manuscripts concerning vices and virtues, in collaboration with Morton Bloomfield, Bertrand-Georges Guyot, and Thyra Kabealo. As much as he enjoyed collecting references to favorite works on contempt of the world in Europe and the United States for the *incipit* project, he probably enjoyed even more writing about *contemptus mundi* as a literary, rhetorical phenomenon. Unlike many scholars, who regard contempt of the world as a continuing theme in western literature, Howard believed medieval *contemptus mundi* was limited to specific historical periods: about the eleventh to the seventeenth centuries. In this he disagreed with a major authority on the subject, Robert Bultot, who traced the topic to Scripture. Howard acknowledged that biblical, patristic, and later medieval writings may share certain topics *de contemptu mundi* but, he argued, "these earlier works"—even when they bear the title *De contemptu mundi*— "simply do not sound like the later ones—they do not use the same language or touch upon the same topics."[44] In other words, the later writings are in a different *style,* which harmonizes with later medieval concerns, including monastic discipline, clerical reform, and the Investiture Controversy.

Indeed, Howard argues that the dominant motifs apparent in the *contemptus mundi* writings of Innocent—as well as Peter Damian, Hugh of St. Victor, Bernard of Cluny, or Serlo of Wilton—manifest a certain style or taste: a Gothic *literary* sensibility that has less to do with pathology than literary fashion shaped by medieval rhetorical conventions. He argues that Innocent's treatise, like other medieval writings, is structurally "architectonic" (or Gothic) rather than "organic" and that it reflects a broad vision of life: "If we read it as men of the Middle Ages and Renaissance did, we shall have to remember that behind its rhetoric lay a profound vision of human wretchedness and emptiness; and that behind this lay a vision, equally clear, of man's dignity as God's creature and his hope of salvation."[45]

In his pursuit of what is old and what is new in medieval fashions, Howard distinguishes between medieval and Renaissance humanisms, between what he terms the "Old Humanism" (R. W. Southern's "scientific" humanism) and the more familiar "New Humanism" of the later Middle Ages—what we think of as the Renaissance. The "Old Humanism" was in fact a new way of looking at things—in theology and philosophy (Abelard, St. Thomas, scholasticism), in government ("a human king"), law ("the revival of Roman jurisprudence"), economics (justifications for "private ownership"). This intellectual and spiritual movement gave us the rose windows of Gothic cathedrals, the *summae* of philosophers, and Dante's *Divine Comedy*. This Old Humanism, according to Howard, was waning in the time of Chaucer's grandfather, but a New Humanism was beginning, constructed on the ruins of the old and much indebted to a nostalgia for old books, especially the classics. A chief difference between the humanisms concerned the authors and their audience: "whereas the clergy and the international world of the medieval universities had been the home of the Old Humanism, the home of the new was for about a century to be the courts of noblemen. A group of friends sharing a love of learning and cultivating individual *virtu*—moral virtue and personal virtuosity combined in a cherished mystique—was the central idea of the New Humanism."[46]

In the mid-1970s, just before he began work on biographical issues, Howard devoted his attention to Renaissance versions of medieval ideas. In one essay, "Renaissance World-Alienation" (1974), he argued that there was an unappreciated strain of pessimism in Renaissance thought, a strain which he identified as a "sensibility"—"an ideology, a complex of emotion." Together with the twelfth-century "upsurge" in literature, art, architecture, theology, and law (the "Old Humanism"), there was, according to Howard, "a corresponding upsurge of pessimism and gloom."[47] At that time began in earnest the chief writings on the contempt of the world; and in the fifteenth century a special genre of writings on the art of dying *(ars moriendi)* was inaugurated. Howard finds "world-alienation" in the endings of *Troilus and Criseyde* and *Sir Gawain and the Green Knight* alongside another kind of sensibility we usually associate with the "Renaissance." In both works, he observes, a return to the "real world" occurs—he calls it a "fictive antiworld"—in which the author communicates directly with the reader.

In the very profoundest sense, this fictive antiworld is a world made out of paper. And what do we return with? A worldly experience, an intellectual grasp of its nature, the aesthetic pleasure of getting home safe, and the conviction that the enterprise confers spiritual advantages. This is the world-alienation of all those who shuffle papers; and in it is the perennial character of humanism.[48]

In a second "Renaissance" essay from the mid-1970s, "Flying Through Space: Chaucer and Milton" (1975), Howard tackled issues that Chaucer and Milton shared—touring the continent and flying through space. But by "flying through space" Howard meant not a Dantean peregrination through the cosmos but a more earthbound, worldly excursion: a journey through the mind.[49] Anticipating the Boccaccian section of his biography, Howard comes close to imagining an encounter between Chaucer and Milton: "Suppose they could have met, Chaucer and Milton: what would they have talked about?"[50] He concludes they would have discussed Italy rather than, say, politics, religion, business, literature, or women and marriage. He also believes Milton inherited a tendency toward ideas and dreams from the Chaucerian tradition: "Milton's great inheritance from Chaucer and Spenser was the 'mentalistic' quality of his epic—its tendency to traffic in mental space, to be a landscape of the mind."[51] Chaucer, according to Howard, was not an allegorical author and certainly not a writer of polysemous allegory, a literary mode which he ascribes to Renaissance rather than medieval habits of writing and reading. In the rejection of allegory and the embracing of "particular, mundane experience," Milton resembles Chaucer even more than Spenser. And though Chaucer depicts a Dantesque flight through the air in an eagle's talons in the *House of Fame,* that flight is finally comic rather than cosmic. The eagle learnedly (and long-windedly) harangues "Geffrey," his passenger, on "tydynges"—"verbal tidbits . . . which may be lies or truths filtered to posterity by capricious Fame."[52] These verbal tidbits are of course things of the world.

Although Howard's thoughts on medieval versus Renaissance constitute a relatively minor strain in his critical work, it is clear that he pondered issues of old and new, medieval and Renaissance humanism as he prepared to launch the Chaucer biography. His viewpoint on these issues remained steadfast throughout his career: more of the Middle Ages survived into the Renaissance than is generally acknowledged, even by scholars; and medieval thinkers often anticipated Renaissance ideas more than is sometimes thought. He was not especially concerned to privilege the Middle Ages—to champion the age as particularly meritorious or worthy of special attention—nor did he crusade to break down the artificially-constructed demarcations between the Middle Ages and the Renaissance. He acknowledged differences between historical periods, and he even recognized something akin to *Zeitgeists* (without the mystic overtones of a Spengler or even of Spitzer).[53] But he left the task of periodization to others.

In his writings, as part of his idea of style, Howard manifested a continued interest in what might be called popular culture; and he enjoyed juxtaposing medieval and modern styles for effect. He would often formulate juxtapositions to clarify stylistic differences and to highlight our own (modern) assumptions. For example, speaking of lyric generally—the idea of lyric—and Antigone's song in particular (*Troilus* Book 2), Howard says: "If anyone were to tell me I ought to wear a flower in my hair if I go to San Francisco I should think him mad; but the same sentiment, heard in the song popular a few years ago, managed to take on a pleasant fancy." Of the poet's role or pose he says: "poets, even 'bourgeois' ones, wrote as if they were courtly lovers, by the same kind of conventional dictate that makes present-day singers, even those who come from England and Australia, pronounce the words of songs as if they came from Tennessee." And of the medieval idea of a book he says:

If we approach *The Canterbury Tales* with, say, Dickens in mind, we see it as unfinished, diverse, unstructured. But suppose we approach it with another kind of work in mind—with the novels of Robbe-Grillet, or a collection of discrete narratives having a common theme, setting, or characters, like Hemingway's "Nick Adams" stories (D. H. Lawrence called them "a fragmentary novel"), or a poem like Crane's *The Bridge*. The right anachronism makes us see the qualities of the work, not find shortcomings in it.[54]

Although Howard admired learning, he had an almost visceral reaction to scholarship and petty academic rigamole for their own sakes. He once referred scornfully to "the customary *pompes funèbres* of footnotes" as well as "long quotations in Latin"[55]—although he himself was not beneath multiple references, even multiple exegetical citations. And he displayed his wrath (and flair for the dramatic) at bureaucracies, especially the academic sort. He compared Chaucer's frustrations in his dealings with bureaucracies to his own exasperation with the Modern Language Association, from which he resigned, publicly and noisily (at MLA talks), more than once.

Howard was an influential critic, and his influence may be observed especially in studies that emphasize Chaucer the storyteller or medieval worldliness. Glending Olson, for example, in *Literature as Recreation in the Later Middle Ages* (1982) has analyzed the significance of *recreatio* in medieval literature—that literary element which emphasizes the "lust" rather than the "profit," the game rather than the earnest. More recently, Laura Kendrick, Carl Lindahl, and Leonard Koff have stressed Chaucerian *play*, earnest *Games*, and storytelling.[56] In short, there has been renewed stress on Chaucer's poetic art in non-monastic, non-exegetical contexts, on Chaucer as a product of his culture and times, and on the art of taletelling as a pleasurable activity, worthwhile and useful in and for itself. We are not claiming of course that all these studies (and others too) derive from Howard's work as *fons et origo*, only that his writings have offered a powerful, significant voice for revising medieval studies away from biblical norms and toward humanistic values, "experience" (*Erlebnis*), consciousness, curiosity, recreation, storytelling (even fable-making), and the world.

It is neither possible nor desirable to sum up, in a few essay pages, a scholarly career as varied as Howard's. But two interrelated strands in Howard's writings might at least be highlighted—stylistic study and reader-response criticism (although Howard never championed the latter term). As he examined medieval works for style, he came to appreciate (more and more, it seems) the reader's role in creating meaning; and he was impressed with the reader's function in closing the incomplete or fragmentary (like *The Canterbury Tales* or *The Faerie Queene*) or in explaining "gaps" in meaning (as in *Levis exsurgit Zephirus*). Medieval writers composed ("made"); readers—medieval, modern, or post-modern—receive, recreate, complete, and write anew. Howard not only pointed toward the "fourth medievalism" in his essay on medievalisms, he demonstrated in all his critical work how he might strive for something positive in medieval studies: a fusing of the best of old and new, of philology, history of ideas, and postmodern critical thought. At a moment when the critical project generally seemed to have turned pessimistic and negative, Howard tried to highlight the interesting, curious, fascinating, imaginative, and human. The contributions to this volume have tried to honor him in that same spirit, for his diversity, his humanity, and his sense of style.

Notes

1. Donald Howard, "The Four Medievalisms," *University Publishing* (Spring 1980): 5–6.
2. Howard, "The Four Medievalisms," p. 6.
3. Ibid.
4. Howard, "Chaucer the Man," *PMLA* 80 (1965): 343.
5. Donald Howard, *The Three Temptations* (Princeton: Princeton Univ. Press, 1966), p. 36.
6. D. W. Robertson, "Historical Criticism," in *English Institute Essays, 1950,* ed. A. S. Downer (New York: Columbia Univ. Press, 1951), p. 4.
7. D. W. Robertson, *A Preface to Chaucer: Essays in Medieval Perspectives* (Princeton: Princeton Univ. Press, 1962), p. 41, characterizing the aesthetic theories of Jacob Bernays. Robertson denies "vicarious experience as a valid aesthetic process" (p. 45).
8. Howard, *The Three Temptations,* pp. 259–60.
9. Howard, *The Idea of the Cantebury Tales* (Berkeley and Los Angeles: Univ. of California Press, 1976) p. 356.
10. Howard, *The Idea,* pp. 50–51.
11. Howard, "Literature and Sexuality: Book III of Chaucer's *Troilus,*" *Massachusetts Review* 8 (1967): 455.
12. "Blurred Genres: The Refiguration of Social Thought," in *Local Knowledge: Further Essays in Interpretive Anthropology* (New York: Basic Books, 1983), pp. 19–35.
13. Kroeber, *Style and Civilizations* (Ithaca: Cornell Univ. Press, 1957).
14. Kroeber, *An Anthropologist Looks at History,* (Berkeley: Univ. of California Press, 1963), p. 66.
15. Howard, *The Three Temptations,* p. 5.
16. Ibid., p. 5 n. 1.
17. Howard, *The Idea,* p. 77. See also *"Sir Gawain and the Green Knight,"* in *Recent Middle English Scholarship and Criticism: Survey and Desiderara,* ed. J. Burke Severs (Pittsburgh: Duquesne Univ. Press, 1971), p. 33, where Howard speaks of style as a *"gestalt."* Here it should be noted that Robertson's long and significant chapter 3 of *A Preface to Chaucer* concerns "Late Medieval Style".
18. René Wellek and Austin Warren, *Theory of Literature,* 3rd ed. (New York: Harcourt, 1977), p. 183.

19. Spitzer, "*Explication de Texte* Applied to Three Great Middle English Poems," in *Essays on English and American Literature,* ed. Anna Hatcher (Princeton: Princeton Univ. Press, 1962), p. 194 n. See also Spitzer's remarks in *Linguistics and Literary History: Essays in Stylistics* (Princeton: Princeton Univ. Press, 1948). Howard describes this "click" in *The Idea:* "The inner click refers to the starting point at which a critic notes a discrete stylistic item and associates it with larger stylistic traits which in turn draw his attention to other discrete items. Spitzer called this process the 'philological circle' and characterized it as 'mentalistic' " (p. 78 n. 6).

20. The phrases are from R. P. Blackmur, *The Lion and the Honeycomb: Essays in Solicitude and Critique* (New York: Harcourt, 1955), p. 35; *The Three Temptations,* p. 6.

21. Howard, "Medieval Poems and Medieval Society," *Medievalia et Humanistica* n. s. 3 (1972): 113. See also "Flying Through Space: Chaucer and Milton," in *Milton and the Line of Vision,* ed. Joseph Anthony Wittreich, Jr. (Madison: Univ. of Wisconsin Press, 1975), p. 22.

22. See *The Structuralist Controversy: The Languages of Criticism and the Sciences of Man,* ed. Richard Macksey and Eugenio Donato (Baltimore: The Johns Hopkins Univ. Press, 1972).

23. Trans. Elliott Coleman (Baltimore: The Johns Hopkins Univ. Press, 1956).

24. *The Structuralist Controversy,* ed. Macksey and Donato, p. 57. Edward Said critiques Poulet (with a glance at Spitzer): "This method is not unlike Spitzer's, which is based on what he called the 'circle of understanding,' except that Poulet claims to parallel in his own writing, and therefore duplicates, the author's consciousness of totality. The difficulty with Poulet and others working in his school [Geneva critics], however, is that no realistic allowance is made for either the brute temporal sequence of an author's production or the author's shaping of the works into independent formal texts. For the Genevans, text is an underlying plentitude of consciousness which, according to Poulet, is only existentially (but not ontologically) compromised by the individual work of art." See *Beginnings: Intention and Method* (Baltimore: The Johns Hopkins Univ. Press, 1975), pp. 194–95.

25. Howard, *The Idea,* p. xi.

26. Ibid., p. 18.

27. Ibid., pp. 77, 78.

28. Miller, "The Critic as Host," *Critical Inquiry* 3 (1977): 447.

29. Howard, "Medieval Poems and Medieval Society," pp. 112–13.

30. Howard, "Experience, Language and Consciousness: *Troilus and Criseyde,* II 596–931," in *Medieval Literature and Folklore Studies: Essays in Honor of Francis Lee Utley,* ed. Jerome Mandel and Bruce Rosenberg (New Brunswick, N.J.: Rutgers Univ. Press, 1970), pp. 174–75. See also his remarks on "subjectivity" and "objectivity" in *The Idea,* pp. 16–17.

31. Howard, "Experience, Language, and Consciousness," p. 185.

32. Ibid., pp. 173, 174.

33. Ibid., p. 185.

34. O'Gorman, *The Invention of America* (Bloomington: Indiana Univ. Press, 1961).

35. Howard, *Writers and Pilgrims,* p. 108. See also *Chaucer,* p. 174 n.

36. Howard, *Chaucer: His Life, His Works, His World* (New York: Dutton, 1987), p. xv.

37. Howard, *Chaucer,* p. xv.

38. Howard, *Chaucer,* pp. 191–92.

39. Ibid., p. 192.

40. Ibid., p. 193.

41. Howard, "*Hamlet* and Contempt of the World," *South Atlantic Quarterly* 58 (1959): 167–75; and he often said that he was much influenced by Farnham's *The Medieval Heritage of Elizabethan Tragedy* (Berkeley: Univ. of California Press, 1936). See the references to Farnham in *The Three Temptations; The Idea; Writers and Pilgrims;* and Innocent III's *On the Misery of the Human Condition,* ed. Howard and trans. M. M. Dietz (Indianapolis, Ind.: Bobbs-Merrill, 1969).

42. *The Canterbury Tales: A Selection,* p. xl.

43. Larry D. Benson, "A Reader's Guide to Writings on Chaucer," in *Geoffrey Chaucer,* ed. Derek Brewer (Athens: Ohio Univ. Press, 1974), p. 327.

44. Howard, *On the Misery,* p. xxv. For Bultot's work, see *Christianisme et valeurs humaine: La doctrine du mépris du monde,* 2 vols. (Paris and Louvain: Nauwelaerts, 1963–64).

45. Howard, *On the Misery,* p. xliii.

46. Howard, *Chaucer,* p. 34.

47. Howard, "Renaissance World-Alienation," in *The Darker Vision of the Renaissance: Beyond the Fields of Reason,* ed. Robert S. Kinsman (Berkeley: Univ. of California Press, 1974), pp. 50, 53.

48. Howard, "Renaissance World-Alienation," p. 72.

49. Erich Auerbach of course has stressed the non-metaphysical element in *Dante: Poet of the Secular World,* trans. R. Manheim (Chicago: Univ. of Chicago Press, 1961).

50. Howard, "Flying through Space," p. 3.

51. Ibid., p. 15.

52. Ibid., p. 5.

53. See Wellek's discussion of Spitzer on periodization and *Zeitgeists* in "Leo Spitzer (1887–1960)," in *Discriminations: Further Concepts of Criticism* (New Haven: Yale Univ. Press, 1970), pp. 214–16. Wellek concludes that "Spitzer's great mental urge is that toward unity, of reduction to the one, which was also the great motivating power of the romantics" (p. 216).

54. Howard, "Experience, Language," p. 183; as quoted by Elliot Krieger, "New Biography Brings Chaucer to Life," *Providence Sunday Journal* (20 December 1987): p. H–13; *The Idea,* p. 61.

55. Howard, "*Sir Gawain and the Green Knight,*" in *Recent Middle English Scholarship,* ed. Severs, p. 35.

56. Kendrick, *Chaucerian Play: Comedy and Control in the Canterbury Tales* (Berkeley: Univ. of California Press, 1988); Lindahl, *Earnest Games: Folkloric Patterns in the Canterbury Tales* (Bloomington: Indiana Univ. Press, 1987); Koff, *Chaucer and the Art of Storytelling* (Berkeley: Univ. of California Press, 1988).

The Idea
of Medieval Literature

Part 1
Chaucer's Culture

Chaucer's Edwardian Poetry

ALFRED DAVID

Very possibly to the court of John of Gaunt and Richard II the high-minded sentiments of the Knight's Tale would have seemed (to borrow an applicable modern word) a bit Edwardian.[1]

Donald Howard's witty observation about The Knight's Tale suggests that generational changes took place in the tastes of Chaucer's audience just as they do in our own time. Although Chaucer frequently undercuts the predominantly ornate style of The Knight's Tale, that style and the tale's lofty Boethian idealism could, indeed, have struck, a few Ricardians as outdated ceremonialism, in the way modernists sometimes looked back on post-Victorian writing (including their own) before World War I as naïvely nationalistic and romantic. Edward III, we may suppose, would have wholeheartedly loved the chivalry of Chaucer's Theban and Athenian knights—especially in the hunting, the dueling, and the tournament scenes—and he might perhaps have seen in the "gentil duc" Theseus a mirror of his own kingly aspirations. I shall return at the end of this essay to the idea that The Knight's Tale may be, among other things, both an ironic and a nostalgic look backward at the Edwardian Age. My first concern, though, shall be with the very different sort of poetry that Chaucer was writing in the reign of Edward III, when Chaucer was a young man at court and the great king had entered his declining years.

Most of Chaucer's "Edwardian" poetry coincides with a period in his life when he was closely associated with the royal family, first with the households of Elizabeth of Ulster and her husband Prince Lionel, and then, though the dates are uncertain, with the king's own household until he assumed the Controllership of Customs and moved into the rooms above Aldgate in 1374.[2] Though of course Chaucer continued to be employed by the crown and collected his pension, he was never again to live at court, "the stremes hed / Of grace," as he said to Scogan, who was presumably dwelling there, while Chaucer was "dul as ded, / Forgete in solytarie wildernesse" (lines glossed by scribes as "Windsor" and "Greenwich").[3] Although Chaucer's London life from 1374 was certainly not "dul as ded," he probably missed the glamor that enveloped the aging king, even during his relative retirement following the Peace of Brétigny when the heady victories over the French at Sluys, Crécy, and Poitiers were remembered glory.

After John Burrow's useful concept, Chaucer, along with John Gower, William Langland, and the *Pearl*-poet, is now often thought of as a "Ricardian" poet, sharing broad thematic, narrative, and stylistic concerns with these contemporaries.[4] Burrow defined the limits of the period as 1369–1399, thereby including the last eight years of Edward III.[5] Ricardian poetry, therefore, refers not to the circumstances of Richard's turbulent reign but to common points of view and techniques of the major poets who attained maturity at that time.

The concept of "Ricardian Poetry" does not try to differentiate between the early and late works of Chaucer and the other poets, and a new reign does not always signify a change in poetic sensibility. In many respects, the troubles of the final years of Edward III continued directly into the first years of Richard II.[6] All the same, the death of a king and the crowning of his successor, especially when the one has reigned long and the other is very young, marks a boundary and causes people to look before and after and to impose distinctions, perhaps illusory ones, between past and present. In Chaucer's case, at least, we can detect a change in mood, outlook, and expression that separates Edward's court, even in decline, from Richard's, justifying the statement that The Knight's Tale might have seemed "a bit Edwardian" at the court of Richard and his uncle Lancaster.

But which of Chaucer's works comprise his Edwardian poetry? The only poem that can be dated with some assurance is the elegy for John of Gaunt's first wife, Blanche of Lancaster—1368 if it was written not long after Blanche's death and before Lancaster began negotiating for a new wife.[7] For the purpose of this essay I shall examine *The Book of the Duchess* and *An ABC, The Complaint unto Pity,* and *The House of Fame. An ABC,* because of a rubric in Speght's 1602 edition that it was written for Blanche, has usually been dated before *Book of the Duchess.* Speght's rubrics contain a lot of fantasy about Chaucer's close ties with the noble house of Lancaster, and it is hard to believe that Chaucer's earliest extant work was done in iambic pentameter and The Monk's Tale stanza.[8] Nevertheless, its French source (Guillaume de Deguilleville's religious allegory *Le pèlerinage de la vie humaine*); the formal structure, following the alphabet; and, as I shall argue, its imagery of petitioning at court link it with a courtly social environment. Allegory and exactly that scene of a formal appeal to a person of power connect *An ABC* to *The Complaint unto Pity,* which is also generally agreed to be early. An allusion to Chaucer's bookkeeping at Customs (lines 652–653) places *The House of*

Fame during Chaucer's years at Aldgate. Although no single impulse can adequately account for that remarkable poem, it was clearly meant to culminate with the tidings the Eagle promises Geoffrey he will hear at the House of Fame. It makes sense that *The House of Fame* "grew in layers," as Donald Howard says, and that Chaucer, as he worked on it, was anticipating the announcement of Richard's engagement.[9] Two prospective French brides died, and negotiations for the hand of Caterina Visconti failed in 1379. If news of the latter was to have been the promised tidings, *The House of Fame* was completed when Richard had been on the throne for almost two and a half years; but this poem, unlike *An ABC* and *The Complaint unto Pity,* also shows Chaucer's assimilation of his first Italian journey (1373) and may have been some years in the making.[10] I shall be arguing that the journey from the Temple of Venus to the Palace of Fame and its adjunct, the House of Rumor, responds to Chaucer's personal journey from court to Aldgate, not far from the Vintry where he was born, and makes a conscious break with his Edwardian poems.

French court poetry certainly provided the major sources and influences on the poetry of "the young Chaucer"—I am thinking of the original title of Wolfgang Clemen's excellent book.[11] Indeed, it was Clemen's purpose, and that of others following his initiative, to defend the originality, integrity, and artistic excellence of these poems of Chaucer's "French period" against the charges that they were conventional, unoriginal, and therefore not very interesting reworkings of language, images, themes, and motifs in the *Roman de la Rose* and the poems of Machaut and Froissart. The assumption has been, though not always explicit, that Chaucer was catering to fashions and tastes imposed by his court audience. The situation, according to Richard Firth Green, who has most fully documented and argued the case, reflects an evolution during the fourteenth century of the position of the court poet from that of a hired minstrel, paid a wage for his services, to that of a poet in residence, so to speak, a retainer of a nobleman's household who depended on patronage.[12] The poet's stance changed, Green suggests, from that of a traditional teller of tales, who got paid for such entertainment, to that of a member of an elite, sophisticated literary circle who engages in an implied social exchange with an audience, consisting mostly of his superiors, to whose judgments in delicate social and literary questions he frequently defers.[13]

The evidence for such an audience in England during the reign of Edward III is, however, as Green's exhaustive study shows, almost entirely circumstantial. Much of it is late (often fifteenth-century), continental, and literary, and in literary works the implied audience is not necessarily a true picture of the actual one. Green is the first to acknowledge the trickiness of such evidence and is cautious and sensitive in interpreting it; moreover, he never intended to focus on anything so narrow as Chaucer's Edwardian poetry, which is only a small part of the large canvas he paints. Really we have no way of knowing whether Edward, his sons, and his courts—for we cannot speak of a single "court"—fancied the "dits amoureux" that Machaut was writing for his patrons while the English made war on them. These included Jean l'Aveugle, king of Bohemia, who died a hero's death at Crécy; his daughter Bonne of Luxembourg, married to the future king Jean le Bon, who was taken prisoner at Poitiers; Charles le Mauvais, King of Navarre; and the Duc de Berry, who also spent time in England as a hostage. Indeed, one might theorize that the literary tastes of the defeated French prisoners won over the victorious English and paved the way for Chaucer to write love-visions in English. There can be no doubt, however, that in his youth Chaucer admired and drew heavily upon the works of Guillaume de Machaut, the most famous of the fourteenth-century court poets who preceded him.[14]

It is, therefore, instructive to glance at the career of Machaut and the form of the "dit amoureux," which he created. Machaut was the most successful, in a worldly sense, of the new-style court poets whom Green describes. He seems in fact to have been a friend, at least a familiar, of some of the patrons he celebrates in his poetry. The king of Bohemia, whom Machaut served as personal secretary, obtained for him a canonry at Reims, where Machaut eventually retired and wrote prolifically, both poetry and his even more distinguished music. Indeed, the music probably had as much, if not more, to do with the patronage he obtained as did the poetry. In 1361 he entertained the future Charles V, then Duke of Normandy, at his home in Reims. Machaut was rewarded with other benefices, and when his long life ended he was buried in Reims cathedral.

These facts to some extent confirm the self-portrait Machaut draws in his poems in which he assumes the character of a man of letters, well-versed in the etiquette of court life and on intimate terms with the great. The narrator of Guillaume de Lorris's part of the *Roman de la Rose* does not let on that he thinks of himself as a poet; Machaut never allows his audience to forget the fact. He places the praise of his literary talents in the mouths of his noble patrons, who appear as characters in the poems and with whom he pictures himself on easy and confidential terms. As important as his literary skill is his knowledge of the sufferings of the aristocratic heart. The Duc de Berry, who plays a leading role in *Le Dit de la fonteinne amoureuse,* asks the poet to compose a complaint for him because he knows Machaut's expertise in the art of love and his experience of love's penetrating power:

Car je say bien que la pratique
Savez toute, et la theorique
D'amour loial et de ses tours,

Et ses assaus et ses estours
Vous ont donné mainte frisson
Plus poingnant que pel d'yresson.[15]

[For I know well that you know all the theory and practice of faithful love and its permutations, and its assaults and skirmishes have given you many a tremor more piercing than a hedgehog's hide.]

The patrons appear as lovers or as arbiters who resolve questions of love. In *Le Jugement du roy de Behaigne* the king of Bohemia keeps a lavish court where he is attended by "Franchise, Honneur, et Courtoisie, / Beauté, Desir, Leece . . ., / Hardiece, / Proece, Amours, Loyauté, et Larguece, / Vouloir, Penser, Richece, avec Joinece, / Et puiz Raison, qui de tous fu maistresse."[16] Thus the allegorical figures of the *Roman* become personified aspects of an actual court and its lord. Machaut is the ambassador and spokesperson of this court of love to the world outside. Having gone for a stroll in the fields on a fine spring morning, he eavesdrops on a debate between a lady and a knight over who suffers most—the lady whose lover has died or the knight whose lady has been unfaithful—and, revealing his presence, he proposes his lord the king as judge. The movement of this and other of Machaut's poems is from the outside to the inner circle of the court where judgment is pronounced and, in the end, all problems are resolved and everyone is royally entertained. The debate proves to be mainly an occasion for celebrating both the prince and his poet.

I

The Book of the Duchess contains an eavesdropping situation that Chaucer lifted with many details from Machaut's *Jugement*. The narrator-dreamer overhears a lyric complaint by a man dressed in black about the death of his lady. The poem is an elegy for Duchess Blanche of Lancaster, but it also dramatizes the relationship between the narrator and the Black Knight, who represents the duke. Thus the expression of sympathy could not help but be at the same time an act of homage to a powerful patron and a bid for recognition. Since Chaucer had yet to establish his reputation as a poet and was, besides, taking the revolutionary step of writing in English, the bid was a bold one, but in the poem the boldness is disguised as humility. Unlike Machaut, Chaucer could not present himself in this, probably his first important work, as a renowned poet. He does not even declare himself to be a poet until the very end, where he determines "to put this sweven in ryme / As I kan best," and concludes, as though with a sense of relief: "This was my sweven; now hit ys doon" (1330–32).

In contrast to Machaut's narrator, who is entirely at home in the world of his patrons, Chaucer's dreamer seems unsure of himself and his place. In the dream, patron and poet are strangers to one another, and from their first encounter we feel the social gap that separates them. The dreamer, having removed his hood, stands awkwardly before the knight to greet him "as I best koude" (517)—the best he knew how, which is the same disclaimer he will apply to putting the dream into rhyme.[17]

"Men seyn, 'to wrecche is consolacioun / To have another felawe in hys peyne,' " Pandarus tells Troilus (I.708–709), and the narrator, who has told us of his bootless eight-year sorrow, may have that principle in mind. But Pandarus, like the Machaut-figure whom he resembles, is already on intimate terms with his prince. The dreamer here hopes for that kind of intimacy. Having overheard the knight's complaint, and encouraged by his condescension—"Loo, how goodly spak thys knyght" (529)—the dreamer is seeking just such confidential disclosure. "I gan fynde a tale / To hym," he says, to "Have more knowynge of hys thought" (536–38). In other words, he wants the knight to tell his sorrow directly to him not only because of any consolation such a statement to a sympathetic soul might afford the knight but because such a sharing of sorrow would create a bond, would make the dreamer a fellow in the knight's pain.

Looked at in this way, we can see the conversation with the knight, which takes up some 60 percent of the lines in the poem, as typical of the elegant verbal fencing, like the debate between the knight and the lady over which bears the greater sorrow, that goes on in Machaut's poems. Indeed, much of the dialogue has been lifted directly from Machaut.[18] To speak of "dialogue" is a bit misleading, for the conversation consists mainly of four long speeches by the knight (560–709, 758–1041, 1052–1111, 1144–1297) provoked by the dreamer's persistent questioning. The relief this discourse might afford the knight is problematical, but it is a tour-de-force of the colors of rhetoric, "developed with amazing artificiality," in Manly's words.[19] It is also notable for a plethora of learned allusion: the first speech alone refers to Ovid, Orpheus, Daedalus, Hippocrates, Galen, Sisiphus, Attalus, Pythagoras, and Tantalus. Chaucer demonstrates his tact not only in letting the knight, the patron-figure, speak the eulogy of Blanche but in giving him the highest style in the poem. The knight's speeches are showpieces, meant to be admired for their eloquence as well as for their feeling and would have been high points for Chaucer's Edwardian audience.

Had Machaut been the author, the dream might have ended with an exchange of courtesies and an invitation to "long castel." An obscure young esquire of Edward III, however, was in no position to represent himself as a friend of the Duke of Lancaster. In Chaucer's poem the dream starts to dissolve with the words "She ys ded!" (1309). Not only do those words undercut the rhetoric with the stark fact of death but they dispel the illusion of fellowship between the knight and the dreamer. Perhaps the poem did lead to greater familiarity, and it may have had something to do with the pension Philippa Chaucer received from Lancaster in 1372 or with Chaucer's own pension, granted in 1374.[20] Nevertheless, the contrast between Chaucer's persona and Machaut's implies a real difference in their relationships with their patrons. The French poet views himself as an insider, a valued member of his master's *familia*. Chaucer represents himself alone. His companion is the book that speaks "Of quenes lives, and of kinges" (58). In *The House of Fame, The Parliament of Fowls,* and in the Prologue to *The Legend of Good Women,* Chaucer will portray himself ironically as a bookish fellow, one who crosses into the courts and gardens of Love only through the charmed gates of sleep. In *The Book of the Duchess,* he seems to be hovering on the fringes of that bright world, looking for a way in.

In spite of the social gulf separating the knight and the dreamer, Bronson was nevertheless right in seeing them as mirroring one another's grief and isolation.[21] Deprived of his "fers," the knight can "no lenger playe" (656) his allegorical chess game with Fortune; in a larger sense all the activities of social life have lost their meaning for him. He has withdrawn into his sorrow. Similarly the sleepless narrator, who says he has "felynge in nothyng" (11), withdraws into the book with the sad tale of Alcyone, a solitary pursuit that seems to him "better play / Then playe either at ches or tables" (51).

That sense of bereavement and solitude is proper to the elegiac mode, of course. It is partly this mood and the need for a friend-patron-protector that leads me to see *An ABC, The Complaint unto Pity,* and *The Book of the Duchess* as Chaucer's Edwardian poems, the subtext of which is the poet's personal plea for acceptance in the world of the court.

Both *An ABC* and *The Complaint unto Pity* show the speaker petitioning a lady for grace. The *ABC*-lady is the greatest of all, the Queen of Heaven; the lady in the *Complaint* is 1) Pity herself, who is dead and 2) the corpse of Pity and her surviving retainers, who comprise collectively the qualities of the lady. Together, the poems illustrate not only the borrowing of religious concepts and imagery by love poets but the cross-influence of the courtly and religious lyric.[22]

In late-medieval art and literature the qualities of the medieval romance heroine are attributed to the Virgin.[23] Chaucer does not, of course, give us physical details such as a "tretys nose" or "eyen greye as glas," but he conveys her beauty in formulas of address, which include liturgical phrases like "floures flour" (4) as well as terms like "lady bright" (16), "ladi deere" (17), "noble of apparaile" (153), "freshe flour" (159), most of which found their way also into *Troilus and Criseyde.* Her crowning virtue is pity, and that is why the petitioner has fled to her protection. She is "of pitee welle" (126); when a soul falls into error, "Thi pitee goth and haleth him ayein" (68). Her "pitous eyen cleere" (88) resemble those of the lady Blanche whose "eyen semed anoon she wolde / Have mercy" (866–67).

As Queen of Heaven, Mary rules over a court imagined to be like a feudal court, only infinitely more splendid. Because the king and his barons originally received petitions and dispensed justice when they held court, the word *court* acquired its judicial sense during the evolution of the English legal system. It was natural, therefore, that poets treating of heavenly justice should borrow terminology from French and English law. *ABC* 158, "that court . . . That cleped is thi bench," is among the examples cited in the *Middle English Dictionary* under definition 10 (a), place where justice is administered. Mary is the "advocat" who defends penitent souls at the Last Judgment. Unlike human lawyers, her services are purchased "for litel hire . . . an Ave-Marie or tweye" (103, 104). From a hint in his French source, which says merely that "sinne" and "confusion" have brought an "accioun" against the petitioner (*ABC*, lines 18–20; French, line 25),[24] Chaucer has created a pattern of legal imagery. The devil, the defendant's "cruel adversaire" (8) prosecutes him under the old law at "the grete assyse" (36) where "the rightful God," the wrathful Father of the Old Testament, "nolde of no mercy here" (31). Although the Son has written the "bill," which is the petition of appeal, with His blood, the petitioner does not dare present it in his own person. He counts on Mary, whom God made mistress of heaven and earth "our bille up for to beede" (110). It is because of her pity that God "represseth his justise", and in "witnesse" thereof "He hath thee corowned in so rial wise" (142–44).

An ABC, then, makes Mary the true embodiment of the virtue addressed in *The Complaint unto Pity*. In the religious lyric, Pity is alive not only to hear the "complaint" but to present the "bill" on the petitioner's behalf against his cruel adversary.[25] In the courtly poem, Pity is "ded, and buried in an herte" (14), and the virtues, whom she should properly rule, are now "Confedered alle by bond of Cruelte" (52). The petitioner's cause and that of all men like him is futile: "Syth she is ded, to whom shul we compleyne?" (27). In a wider sense *Pity* is an indictment not merely of the lady's conventional hard-heartedness towards her lover but of the pliability and venality of earthly courts. One expects Cruelty to be cruel; what is unexpected is that all other courtly qualities, who under Pity's dominance should oppose Cruelty, have been suborned. In *An ABC* Bounte has fixed his "tente" in Mary's heart (9); in the Complaint, Bounte is the first among the virtues standing "lustely" around Pity's hearse (31–42)—an ironic tableau of a court with the retainers grouped around their lord.

These Edwardian poems foreshadow a favorite theme of Chaucer that "pitee renneth soone in gentil herte," a line that occurs in The Knight's Tale (I.1761) and in three other later works. "Pité" had been one of the personifications in the Roman de la Rose who aids the lover; Chaucer personified her in the black knight's lady and in the all merciful queen of An ABC. The death of Pity is the subject of the Complaint. In later works these idealized figures of allegory, dream vision, and lyric become rounded characters. The petitioner of the Complaint becomes fully human in the fifth book of Troilus and Criseyde:

> "Who shal now trowe on any othes mo?
> Allas, I nevere wolde han wend, er this,
> That ye, Criseyde, koude han chaunged so;
> Ne, but I hadde agilt and don amys,
> So cruel wende I nought youre herte, ywis."

(V.1681–85)

And the poem closes with a prayer that invokes the lady of An ABC:

> So make us, Jesus, for thi mercy, digne,
> For love of mayde and moder thyn benigne.

(V.1868–69)

II

The House of Fame marks a turning point in Chaucer's life and poetry. In 1374 he left the court for good to move into the apartment above Aldgate and to begin his duties as Controller of Customs. Whether or not this change signifies a wished-for entry into the hierarchy of officialdom, independence, and financial security, the post was certainly not a sinecure of the kind that supported Machaut.[26] Chaucer had to work hard for his living; he was required to keep records in his own hand and, as we know from the Eagle, to spend his days poring over the account books:

> For when thy labour doon al ys,
> And hast mad alle thy rekenynges,
> In stede of reste and newe thynges
> Thou goost hom to thy hous anoon,
> And also domb as any stoon,
> Thou sittest at another book
> Tyl fully daswed ys thy look.

(652–58)

Without reviving nineteenth-century autobiographical interpretations,[27] we are justified, I believe, in reading into The House of Fame a bit of literary autobiography. The poem's structure and many details in it point to a conscious distancing of the poet from the circle of court life and court literature, and from the ambitions engendered there. Naturally it reflects Chaucer's encounter with Italy and the ancient world as transmitted by Italian humanism, especially his reading of Dante and Dante's master, Virgil, but also with Ovid, Boethius, and with many of the historians Chaucer sees standing on pillars in the palace of Fame.

The dream begins in relatively familiar surroundings. The glass Temple of Venus, filled with gold images, rich tabernacles, curious portraits, and frescoes of the Trojan War and the love story of Dido and Aeneas could be an elaborate set for a lover's complaint overheard, just as it is in Lydgate's imitation, *The Temple of Glass*. In Chaucer, the complaint is Dido's lament over Aeneas's falseness, taken from the speaking pictures on the walls of the temple. In a word, the lyric form, instead of being pronounced by a contemporary knight or lady, has been historicized by putting it into the mouth of a classic heroine whom Chaucer and his audience believed to have lived and uttered words already attributed to her by ancient poets.

Already in this opening scene, the narrator is no longer a protagonist, the author of his own despair, as in *An ABC* or in *The Complaint unto Pity,* or the author of another's, as in *The Book of the Duchess.* Within the dream the narrator is separated from the events he describes by the distance of time and from the dead authors from which he takes them. His personal dream vision is mediated by Virgil and Ovid, who, somewhat disconcertingly, give conflicting accounts of Dido. In *The House of Fame,* the temple corresponds to the book over which the dreamer fell asleep in *The Book of the Duchess,* and the eerie emptiness of the temple heightens our sense of the dreamer's solitude.

The way into the Garden of Mirth in the *Roman* led through a wicket gate. Here the dreamer, looking for some "stiryng man" to tell him where he is, exits by a "wiket" (477–79), and finds himself not in a lush garden filled with melodious birds but in a desert. Is Chaucer the poet not self-consciously making his poetic exodus from the temples and gardens that represent the world of the court in vision poetry? In place of birdsong, we get the giant eagle's "Awak!", which in Middle English makes a rather unmelodious, though very birdlike, sound. The Eagle's word does not merely apply, however, to the poet's temporary swoon from the shock of being swept up into the air, but it is a call to Geffrey to open his eyes to a greater world. In this world the God of Love is merely the blind nephew of Jupiter, king of the gods, whose messenger the Eagle is. Jupiter is presumably not concerned with such idealized questions of love as which of the two courtly lovers suffers most but with important alliances in the political world—just such tidings as the engagement of the young heir apparent or king. The court of Fame is not an allegory of love but an allegory of historical courts where careers and reputations are made and unmade without regard to what people deserve.

Groups of petitioners appear before the throne of Fame asking "of thy grace a bone" (1537) and are granted or denied their wish arbitrarily according to the whims of Fame. She represents neither Cruelty nor Pity but simply indifference to questions of right or wrong, though, as Chaucer portrays her, she evidently enjoys the exercise of her own perversity and like her sister Fortune tends to laugh at her victims. Whether we choose to believe him or not, it is difficult to deny that Geffrey's reply to the inquisitive man who asks his name is intended to make a statement with ramifications for Chaucer's own life and art:

> Sufficeth me, as I were ded,
> That no wight have my name in honde.
> I wot myself best how y stonde;
> For what I drye, or what I thynke,
> I wil myselven al hyt drynke,
> Certeyn, for the more part,
> As fer forth as I kan myn art.
>
> (1876–82)

Machaut made a habit of signing his poems with anagrams of his name to which he carefully calls attention.[28] *The House of Fame* is the only poem that Chaucer, as it were, signed, and then only by having the Eagle patronizingly call him by his first name. His claim of anonymity in the passage cited, besides a renunciation of Fame's dubious gifts, is also a declaration of the point of view Chaucer will maintain as an artist. It asserts a new detachment and distance between himself and both his subject and his reader. It anticipates a view of courts and courtiers that professes to be historical, the result not of marvelous dreams but of reading ancient books.

The House of Fame, probably begun under Edward but completed under Richard, breaks with the spirit of the "Edwardian" poems I have discussed. The octosyllabic couplets and occasionally formulaic style sometimes make the verse sound like the English metrical romances, often like a parody of their meters;[29] but the division into three books with their poems and invocations, the motif of the celestial journey, and the density of allusion to ancient mythology and literature as well as to Dante, give the work a totally different structure and tone from *The Book of the Duchess* and the two shorter poems. Above all, the melancholy that suffuses those earlier works is gone. Instead *The House of Fame* is exuberant with joyous energy of the sort we feel in the Eagle's pleasure at his success in having explained the science of sound to his reluctant pupil:

"A ha," quod he, "lo, so I can
Lewedly to a lewed man
Speke, and shewe hym swyche skiles
That he may shake hem be the biles,
So palpable they shulden be."

(865–69)

If the keynote of the other poems is "Alas," the Eagle's "A ha" sets the tone for this one. Here is a new voice in Chaucer's poetry, anticipating Pandarus (see, e.g., I.729, 868), and, indeed, the comedy of the Eagle's one-sided dialogue with his passive pupil foreshadows the first book of *Troilus*.

III

Jusques a Londres convoierent.
Le Prince, que le festoierent.
La furent il bien festoie
Des dames et si bien veignie
Qu'onques ne fu faite tel joie,
Se li vrais Dieux mon coer esjoye,
Com il fu faite a cely tamps.
La fu li nobles Roys puissanz
Et la Royne, sa moullier,
Et sa mere, qui l'ot moult chier,
Mainte dame, et mainte dansele
Tres amoureuse, frike et bele.
Danser et chacier et baler
Faire granz festes et jouster,
Fist on com en regne d'Artus
L'espace de quatre ans ou plus.

[They escorted the prince to London, where he was given a great welcome. He was greeted by the ladies, and never were there such celebrations as then, may the true God gladden my heart, as was done at that time. The king and queen and the king's mother were there, many ladies and many lovely, gay and loving girls. They danced, hunted, hawked, jousted and feasted, just as in King Arthur's reign, for more than four years.]

So reads Chandos Herald's account of the return of the Black Prince after the battle of Poitiers.[30] The passage bears out what Richard Barber says in the introduction to his translation, "how the Black Prince was already seen as a heroic figure from some vanished golden age within a few years of his death, during the troubles of Richard's reign. . . . a lost era when England was victorious and every knightly ideal seemed to be fulfilled."[31] Such nostalgia, though richly complicated and qualified by irony, seems to me to inform Chaucer's treatment of antiquity in *Troilus*

and The Knight's Tale, the works in which, though professing to write
historically about the ancient world, Chaucer is dealing with the experience of the recent past. Hector, Troilus, and Deiphebus are relics of that
imagined golden time of chivalry, in which they have faith and whose
ideals they try to live by and enforce.[32] The Trojan War is for them what
the Hundred Years War was for Edward III and the Black Prince in the
accounts of Froissart and Chandos Herald—an arena to test and display
their chivalry. The narrator responds like Chandos Herald when Troilus
fights like a lion for his lady's sake or returns from battle, looking like
"Mars, that god is of bataille" (II.630). The Troy emerging from the history
books he professes to be translating, however, puts a different face on war
and love, discordant with chivalric ideals. The narrator and his audience
must somehow square the chivalry of Hector and Troilus with the treach-
ery of Calchas and Antenor, the schemes of Pandarus, and, finally,
Criseyde's betrayal of Troilus.

If the irony in The Knight's Tale is not so relentless or finally so
crushing, we may chiefly thank lord Theseus—"in his tyme swich a conquerour / That gretter was ther noon under the sonne" (I.862–63). A great
point is made from the first of his chivalry and courtesy. When the Theban
widows appeal to him, he dismounts "With herte pitous" (953), raises and
comforts them, and swears to avenge them "as he was trewe knyght"
(959). The word "conquerour" becomes a synonym for Theseus: "Thus rit
this duc, thus rit this conquerour" (981), "the noble conquerour" (998).
Toward the very end of his life Chaucer would with political astuteness
apply that epithet to Henry IV in the *Complaint to His Purse:* "O conquerour of Brutes Albyon."[33] One is tempted to ask if he modeled the
figure of Theseus on another English conqueror. Whether or not by
design, there are parallels between the characters of Theseus and Edward
III that should have reminded the few companions of the king still alive in
the 1380s of their old master in his days of glory.

As he did with *Il Filostrato,* Chaucer medievalized the *Teseida* and its
hero.[34] Whereas Boccaccio had tried to give his epic a distinctly classical
flavor, modelled chiefly on Statius, Chaucer, though preserving a good
many classical features (Arcite's funeral and the catalogue of trees used
for his pyre is an extreme example), gives the poem a much more contemporary feeling. The description of the knights' armor, with details like the
"Pruce sheeld," elicits Chaucer's disarming acknowledgement of the
anachronisms: "Ther is no newe gyse that it nas old" (2122–25).

For Edward III the tournament had been not only a passionately loved
sport at which he personally excelled but an important instrument of
policy to make his court appear as a reincarnation of Arthurian chivalry.
"His reign was perhaps the apogee of the tournament," writes Juliet Vale,
who has most fully documented this aspect of Edward's reign.[35] The

description of the knights arming for the tournament, though idealized, to be sure, must have taken the older generation of the 80s back to colorful scenes of the 40s and 50s:

> Ther maystow seen devisynge of harneys
> So unkouth and so riche, and wroght so weel
> Of goldsmythrye, of browdynge, and of steel;
> The sheeldes brighte, testeres, and trappures,
> Gold-hewen helmes, hauberkes, cote-armures;
> Lordes in parementz on hir courseres,
> Knyghtes of retenue, and eek squieres
> Nailynge the speres, and helmes bokelynge;
> Giggynge of sheeldes, with layneres lacynge—
>
> (2496–2504)

In the *Teseida* Theseus stages the tournament in a great Athenian theater already in place. Chaucer's Theseus summons an army of artisans to build the stadium:

> For in the lond ther was no crafty man
> That geometrie or ars-metrike kan,
> Ne portreyour, ne kervere of ymages,
> That Theseus ne yaf him mete and wages
> The theatre for to maken and devyse.
>
> (1897–1901)

Most notable are, of course, the three temples, designed like medieval chapels, which are built into the entrances of the theater, the elaborate descriptions of which are entirely original with Chaucer. In all this artistic activity and lavish expenditure, Theseus resembles Edward, particularly in the king's refurbishing of St. George's chapel at Windsor as the home of the Order of the Garter, but also in the staging and costuming of his tournaments.[36]

The most striking reminder of Edward, however, is the scene, fabricated entirely by Chaucer, in which the Queen, Emilye, and all the ladies "for verray wommanhede, / Gan for to wepe" (1748–49) and beg Theseus to spare Palamon and Arcite. The unlikelihood of these former Amazons bursting into tears and falling on their bare knees ready to kiss Theseus's feet would have appalled Boccaccio, but it does not stop Chaucer from writing this quintessentially chivalric scene that recalls one of the most celebrated moments in Froissart:

> Than the quene beynge great with chylde, kneled downe, and sore wepyng, sayd, a gentyll sir, syth I passed the see in great parell, I have desyred nothyng of you; therfore nowe I humbly requyre you, in the honour of the son of the virgyn Mary, and for the loue of me, that ye woll take mercy of these sixe burgesses.[37]

The story of the burghers of Calais, who had come with halters around their necks to offer their lives for the city which the angry king has threatened to destroy after its long and gallant resistance, is probably legend, but it perfectly captures the myth of the Edwardian age. The fierce passions of strong and violent men are tamed by the appeal to feminine "pite," the virtue which, I have tried to show, is the major theme in Chaucer's Edwardian poetry, for "pitee renneth soone in gentil herte."

Though Edward at times acted the wrathful judge, he also wished to project an image of "pite" and seems to have been merciful by the standards of the time. In 1350 he sentenced his chief justice, William Thorp, to be hanged and to forfeit all his lands and goods, for flagrant violation of a royal injunction against bribery, but, as J. R. Maddicott, who records this episode, says, it was "a curious charade." Thorp's life was spared the same day. Within four months, Edward, "compassionating from his heart his desolation," gave Thorp a full pardon and restored his property. The following year, Thorp was made second baron of the Exchequer and so began serving again on judicial commissions. "From being a man in disgrace and under sentence of death for his misdeeds," Maddicott observes, "he had risen in eighteen months to a rank not far short of that from which he had fallen."[38]

I cite the incident because, like Froissart's story of the burghers of Calais, it illustrates Edward's penchant for the theatrical gesture, a fondness for role-playing that is both spontaneous and politically motivated. That same characteristic may provide a key to the much-debated character of Theseus, who has been viewed, on the one hand, as "representative of the highest chivalric conceptions of nobility" and, on the other hand, as a calculating politician.[39] Historically there were two traditions about Theseus, one, deriving from Statius that portrays him as heroic conqueror of the Amazons and of Thebes, the other, chiefly based on Ovid, that pictures him as the deserter of Ariadne. Chaucer's Theseus, via Boccaccio, is primarily Statian with an added Ovidian side to him, but Chaucer may have had a life-model for the Duke in Edward.

Vale recounts a characteristic episode of what she calls Edward's "splendid sense of occasion, even of dramatic flair" in announcing a great plan. According to one manuscript of Murimuth's chronicle, the king gave orders for a general assembly the following day without giving a reason. Having donned his most royal robes and crown, and with the queen also dressed in state, he led his court first to mass, and finally revealed his purpose, swearing on relics and the Bible that

> He would have a round table constructed in the same fashion and state that King Arthur, one-time king of the English, had ordered it, that is, to the number of three hundred knights, and he would support and maintain its strength to the best of his abilities, always adding to the number.

"The scene," Vale comments, "betrays a masterly command of suspense, spectacle, and illusion."[40]

Duke Theseus shows the same command of suspense and spectacle in halting the duel in the grove and in presiding over the tournament, "Arrayed right as he were a god in trone" (2529). From a scaffold the herald declares "the myghty dukes wille," which is the outlawing of dangerous weapons and the end of all fighting as soon as either of the Theban knights is taken prisoner. The crowd hails his mercy:

> God save swich a lord, that is so good
> He wilneth no destruccion of blood!
>
> (2563–64)

Critics have pointed out that this acclaim hardly accords with the harshness of the lord who utterly destroys Thebes and holds Palamon and Arcite in prison without ransom. Nor, it may be said, does Edward's compassion accord well with his devastation of France in his vainglorious and vain pursuit of the French crown. For all the cultivation of his chivalric image, Edward III could be a ruthless opportunist. Indeed, he would seem to have taken advantage of any occasion to cultivate that image, and, by and large, he succeeded in impressing it on most chroniclers and historians and on the popular mind. In the seventeenth-century John Taylor, the Water Poet, still preserves his reputation:

> *Edward* the third, a brave, victorious King,
> Did *Frenchmens* Pride into subjection bring.[41]

Did Edward also impress that image on Chaucer? If The Knight's Tale offers any evidence on that score, the answer is both yes and no. The "noble conquerour" Theseus comes across as the epitome of the chivalric ruler but hardly unscathed by Chaucerian irony. The Knight's Tale commemorates the chivalry of the Edwardian era with nostalgia and admiration, but it also lets us see how very much that memory depends on pageantry, theater, and illusion. Chaucer gives us the pageantry but continually undermines it with realistic detail such as the pillagers picking over the battlefield at Thebes or hyperbole such as fighting ankle-deep in blood. He had a good time creating the atmosphere of old-time chivalry, even demonstrating, in describing the action of the tournament, that he could rum-ram-ruff it with the Northerners:

> Ther shyveren shaftes upon sheeldes thikke;
> He feeleth thurgh the herte-spoon the prikke.
> Up spryngen speres twenty foot on highte;
> Out goon the swerdes as the silver brighte;
> The helmes they tohewen and toshrede;

Out brest the blood with stierne stremes rede;
With myghty maces the bones they tobreste.
He thurgh the thikkeste of the throng gan threste; . . .

(2605–12)

The style of The Knight's Tale is Ricardian, though some Ricardians, missing the irony, might have mistaken it for something old-fashioned. Its image of man is ultimately unheroic, though I would disagree with those who characterize it as anti-heroic. It is a style that Chaucer could have acquired only with time that also brought distance—the distance of the inglorious years after Brétigny and the distance that brought Chaucer from the Edwardian court back to his roots in London. Its sources may be sought not only in French and Italian literature but in the social and political history that Chaucer lived through, which Donald Howard has so richly recounted in his biography of the poet.

Notes

1. Donald R. Howard, *The Idea of the Canterbury Tales* (Berkeley and Los Angeles: Univ. of California Press, 1976), p. 310.
2. See *Chaucer Life-Records,* ed. Martin M. Crow and Clair C. Olson (Austin: Univ. of Texas Press, 1966), pp. 13–22, 94–122.
3. Citations are from *The Riverside Chaucer,* 3rd ed., gen. ed. Larry D. Benson (Boston: Houghton Mifflin, 1987).
4. John Burrow, *Ricardian Poetry* (New Haven: Yale Univ. Press, 1971).
5. Ibid., p. 1. The elasticity of the term is shown by the fact that C. David Benson can "metaphorically" refer to Henryson as "the last of the Ricardians." See "O Moral Henryson," in *Fifteenth-Century Studies,* ed. Robert F. Yeager (Hamden, Conn.: Archon Books, 1984), pp. 215–16.
6. Charles Muscatine also deals comprehensively with this body of poetry as conditioned by the calamities and political tensions during the latter part of the century in *Poetry and Crisis in the Age of Chaucer* (Notre Dame, Ind.: Univ. of Notre Dame Press, 1972).
7. See J. J. Palmer, "The Historical Context of the Book of the Duchess," *Chaucer Review* 8 (1974): 253–61. A later date is possible (see Edward I. Condren, "Of Deaths and Duchesses and Scholars Coughing in Ink," *Chaucer Review* 10 [1975]: 87–95), but the consensus still supports the early one. Howard Schless argues that the poem must postdate 1371 because Chaucer could not have referred to John of Gaunt as "kyng" in line 1314 before that date, "A Dating for the Book of the Duchess: Line 1314," *Chaucer Review* 19 (1985): 273–76. But in the dream there may well be a conflation of the man in black with the Emperor Octovyen who leads the hunt (368).
8. On the unlikelihood of Speght's rubric, see my essay, "An ABC to the Style of the Prioress," in *Acts of Interpretation,* ed. Mary J. Carruthers and Elizabeth D. Kirk (Norman, Okla.: Pilgrim Books, 1982), p. 149 n. 9.
9. Donald R. Howard, *Chaucer: His Life, His Works, His World* (New York: E. P. Dutton, 1987), p. 233.
10. The fact that official news about the failure of the Visconti match reached

England on 10 December 1379, would explain why Chaucer's dream is set on "The tenthe day now of Decembre" (63). See Larry D. Benson, "The 'Love-Tydynges' in Chaucer's *House of Fame*," in *Chaucer in the Eighties*, ed. Julian N. Wasserman and Robert J. Blanch (Syracuse, N.Y.: Syracuse Univ. Press, 1986), pp. 3–22. That would be after Chaucer's second journey to Italy in 1378. But a good case was made out by Howard H. Schless, admittedly before Benson's evidence, that the poem was composed "closer to 1374 [after the first Italian journey] than to 1379," See *Chaucer and Dante* (Norman, Okla.: Pilgrim Books, 1984), pp. 36–42.

11. *Der Junge Chaucer* (1938), revised as *Chaucer's Early Poetry*, trans. C. A. M. Sym (New York: Barnes and Noble, 1964).

12. Richard Firth Green, *Poets and Princepleasers: Literature and the English Court in the Late Middle Ages* (Toronto: Univ. of Toronto Press, 1980), pp. 101–134.

13. Ibid., pp. 111–13.

14. On Machaut's influence, see James I. Wimsatt, *Chaucer and the French Love Poets: The Literary Background of The Book of the Duchess* (Chapel Hill: Univ. of North Carolina Press, 1968) and "Guillaume de Machaut and Chaucer's Love Lyrics," *Medium Aevum* 47 (1978): 66–87.

15. *Oeuvres de Guillaume de Machaut*, ed. Ernest Hoepffner, 3 vols., SATF (Paris: Firmin-Didot, 1908–1921), 3.196–97, lines 1505–10.

16. *Le Jugement dou roy de Behaigne and Remede de Fortune*, ed. James I. Wimsatt and William W. Kibler, The Chaucer Library (Athens: Univ. of Georgia Press, 1988), p. 161, lines 1990–95.

17. The relationship of the dreamer and the knight has always been something of a crux in the poem. G. L. Kittredge first characterized the dreamer as a naïf, who misunderstands the knight's loss, *Chaucer and His Poetry* (Cambridge: Harvard Univ. Press, 1915), pp. 45–56. Bertrand H. Bronson takes him as a sophisticated courtier who feigns naiveté in order to draw the knight into relieving his grief by expressing it, "The *Book of the Duchess* Re-opened," *PMLA* 67 (1952): 863–81. Different interpretations of the narrator are reviewed by Barbara Nolan, who argues for Chaucer's originality and independence in his adaptation of his French models, "The Art of Expropriation: Chaucer's Narrator in *The Book of the Duchess*," in *New Perspectives in Chaucer Criticism*, ed. Donald M. Rose (Norman, Okla.: Pilgrim Books, 1981), pp. 203–22.

18. Wimsatt and Kibler supply extensive tables of parallels, pp. 27–31 in their Chaucer Library edition, with full discussions in the notes.

19. J. M. Manly, "Chaucer and the Rhetoricians," *Proceedings of the British Academy* 12 (1926): 100. In the same essay he refers to the poem's "thin prettinesses" (97).

20. *Life-Records*, pp. 67–93, 271–275.

21. Bronson, "The *Book of the Duchess* Re-Opened," p. 871.

22. See Theodor Wolpers, "Geschichte der Englischen Marienlyrik im Mittelalter," *Anglia* 69 (1950): 29–32.

23. See "An ABC to the Style of the Prioress," pp. 147–48.

24. W. W. Skeat prints a French text in *The Complete Works* (Oxford: Clarendon Press, 1894), I. 261–71.

25. On Chaucer's use of legal conventions and diction in the poem, see Charles J. Nolan, Jr., "Structural Sophistication in 'The Complaint unto Pity,'" *Chaucer Review* 13 (1979): 363.

26. It is salutory to keep in mind James R. Hulbert's sober assessment of

Chaucer's fortunes: "So far as we know, Chaucer received no exceptional favours, and . . . his career was in practically every respect a typical esquire's career." *Chaucer's Official Life* (1912; reprint, New York: Phaeton Press, 1970), p. 79.

27. Theories that the poem expresses Chaucer's dissatisfaction with his life and fortunes are reviewed and refuted by Wilbur Owen Sypherd, *Studies in Chaucer's "Hous of Fame"* (Chaucer Society Publications, 2nd ser., 39 [London: K. Paul, Trench, Trübner & Co., 1907]). Although nineteenth-century critics may have erred in taking Chaucer too seriously, it seems undeniable to me that *Fame* deals with his life and art.

28. See *Jugement*, pp. 163–65, lines 2055–66, 2979; *Remede*, pp. 407–9, lines 4259–71, 4297, in the Chaucer Library edition.

29. Burrow, *Ricardian Poetry*, pp. 21–22.

30. *Life of the Black Prince by the Herald of Sir John Chandos*, ed. Mildred K. Pope and Eleanor C. Lodge (Oxford: Clarendon Press, 1910), p. 45, lines 1501–16. Translation from *Life and Campaigns of the Black Prince*, ed. and trans. Richard Barber (London: Folio Society; reprint, Woodbridge, Suffolk: Boydell Press, 1986), p. 104.

31. *Life and Campaigns*, p. 84–85. On the mixture of romance and history in the *Life*, see Sumner Ferris, "Chronicle, chivalric biography, and family tradition in fourteenth-century England," in *Chivalric Literature: Essays on relations between literature and life in the later middle ages*, ed. Larry D. Benson and John Leyerle, *Studies in Medieval Culture*, 14 (Kalamazoo, Mich.: Medieval Institute Publications, 1980).

32. Cf. Paul Strohm, *Social Chaucer* (Cambridge: Harvard Univ. Press, 1989): "Troilus' commitments are indivisible and eternal, aspiring to transcend time and circumstance" (p. 104).

33. Of thirteen instances of *conquerour* in Chaucer's poetry five apply to Theseus; one each to Alexander, Caesar, and Pompey in The Monk's Tale; one to Attila in The Pardoner's Tale; one to Jason in the *Legend;* one to Henry IV; and Diomede thinks to himself that anyone taking Criseyde away from Troilus would be a "conquerour."

34. For a comparison of the character of Theseus in Chaucer and his sources, see Walter Scheps, "Chaucer's Theseus and the *Knight's Tale," Leeds Studies in English* 9 (1976–77): 19–34.

35. Juliet Vale, *Edward III and Chivalry: Chivalric Society and Its Context 1270–1350* (Woodbridge, Suffolk: Boydell Press, 1982), p. 94.

36. For details, see Vale, *Edward III*, pp. 62–86, *passim;* also Juliet R. V. Barker, *The Tournament in England, 1100–1400* (Woodbridge, Suffolk: Boydell Press, 1986), pp. 67–69.

37. *Sir John Froissart's Chronicles of England, France, Spain, Portugal, Scotland, Brittany, and Flanders*, trans. John Bourchier, Lord Berners, reprinted from Pynson's edition of 1523, and 1525, 2 vols. (London: F. C. and J. Rivington, et al., 1812), I: 176. Derek Brewer first drew the analogy between this scene and the one in The *Knight's Tale, in Chaucer and His World* (New York: Dodd, Mead, 1978), p. 98.

38. J. R. Maddicott, "Law and Lordship: Royal Justices as Retainers in Thirteenth-and Fourteenth-Century England," *Past and Present*, Supplement 4, 1978, 48–50.

39. The ideal description is from Charles Muscatine, *Chaucer and the French Tradition* (Berkeley and Los Angeles: Univ. of California Press, 1957), p. 183;

Scheps, "Chaucer's Theseus," p. 19, provides references to negative opinions.

40. "Mensam rotundam inciperet, eodem modo et statu quo eam dimisit domi-nus Arthurus quondam rex Angliae, scilicet ad numerum trecentorum militum, et eam foveret et manuteneret pro viribus, numerum semper inaugendo." Vale, *Edward III*, p. 68. [He commissioned a round table in the same kind and state as the one Lord Arthur, the former king of England, had designed, that is to the number of three hundred knights, and he always supported and maintained its powers lavishly. (my translation)]

41. *All the Works of John Taylor The Water Poet*, facsimile of the 1630 edition (London: The Scolar Press, 1973), *The Book of Martyrs*, p. 137 [Mmm 4.1]. This work became widely disseminated for children in *The Protestant Tutor*.

Writing Amorous Wrongs: Chaucer and the Order of Complaint

LEE PATTERSON

"Death is the mother of beauty:" Wallace Stevens's dictum reminds us of the long-standing, perhaps permanent link between poetry and loss, writing and absence. We write of and out of what we lack, what we imagine to be possible (happiness, understanding) and hope, by our writing, to discover or recover: this is what Stevens meant when he described us as "natives of poverty, children of malheur" for whom "the gaiety of language is our seigneur."[1] And if Chaucer seems to us one of the least impoverished, least unhappy of poets, we should remember that he maintained a persistent, intense interest in the kind of writing he and his contemporaries called complaint.[2] This was of course a ubiquitous albeit amorphous medieval form. The voice of lament pervades Germanic and Celtic writing, is shaped by biblical and classical models and rhetorical prescription into the *planctus* of the learned tradition, and permeates both the affective piety and the sentimental amorousness of the later medieval period. Given the *murnung* of the Anglo-Saxon scop[3] and the *englynion* of the Welsh bard, the *planh* of the Provençal poet (Cercamon on Guillaume IX of Aquitaine, Bertran de Born on Henry the young king), the satirist's "complaint of the times" (Alain de Lille's *De planctu naturae*, Rutebeuf's "Complainte de Guillaume," Gower's *Vox clamantis*), and the *planctus Mariae* of pious and the *complainte d'amour* of courtly poets—it sometimes seems as if the Middle Ages must have been awash with tears.

Despite its taxonomic skill, medieval scholarship has not yet produced a full scale account of the complaint.[4] Perhaps investigators have been understandably discouraged simply by the varieties of the form and the complexities of its history. Yet there is a deeper problem as well—one clearly recognized and brilliantly solved in an analogous area by Donald Howard. In his study of the *contemptus mundi* theme, Howard recognized that an analysis of the topoi of a single generic set, however inclusive or complex, could adequately describe neither the pervasiveness with which the theme permeated medieval writing nor the profundity of its effect.[5] Consequently, he followed his discussion of the genre itself with characteristically subtle readings of three Middle English poems, thus revealing the way the theme shaped these works both directly and by reaction. In effect, Howard showed how in the later Middle Ages the *contemptus mundi* theme was not merely an element in these poems but constitutive of them, a context so enveloping as to be both invisible and unavoidable, both taken for granted and ceaselessly at issue.

Something of the same is true of the complaint: as I have suggested, it is virtually coextensive with poetry, indeed with writing itself. If language is a form of action that mediates between the subject and the world, then complaint interrogates its relation to these two presences: can language objectify the subject and/or have an effect upon the world? The first question is asked by the emotionalism that complaint takes as its special province, the claim it makes upon the affect of both speaker and audience. Complaint negotiates between feeling and form, asking a question that has been at the center of Western poetics since their inception: is poetry primarily a spontaneous expression of feeling (as the rhetor Ion tells Socrates) or an art (Aristotle's *techne*)? Is it the inspired language of the soul (the poet as *vates*) or a product of civilization at its most exacting (the *poeta doctus*)? When in 1795 Schiller distinguished between naïve and sentimental poetry, rather than initiating a new stage in literary thinking he was projecting an age-old debate upon a historical axis. Paradoxically, however, the ahistorical lyricism of the Middle Ages, precisely because of its highly stylized and convention bound nature, raised this question in larger, more unsettling terms, as Paul Zumthor has shown. Is the speaking subject of the medieval lyric created by its own discourse—a grammatical function, Jakobson's digetic shifter—or is s/he a historical being endowed with the selfhood human beings have typically taken as their own?[6] If the complaint is above all an act of self-expression, is there a self from which it issues and to which it can be referred for interpretation, or is there only a suprapersonal discourse, Zumthor's "great game of poetry?"[7]

If the affectivity of complaint raises with special urgency questions about the emotive function of language, it asks similar questions about the referential and conative functions.[8] This is not simply a matter of representation, as if that were simple at all. But representation is a question for all literary language, as for language per se: there is no reason to see complaint as privileged in its scepticism. But what is specific to complaint is that the claim it lays upon the world is virtually always self-cancelling, and that it thus raises questions about writing as a pragmatic activity. Not only does the plaintive voice typically assume the uselessness of its declarations, but its uselessness is programmatic. The *complainte d'amour*, for instance, not only presupposes the perpetual intransigence of the lady— were she to respond to the lover's request she would not be worthy of it— but is invalidated by its very articulation: the more eloquent the lover, the less truthful his plea. An implication present throughout amorous lament, this point is made explicit by Andreas Capellanus: the lover who woos with service rather than words is to be preferred, says the noblewoman, to "the man who publicises to me the secrets of his heart explicitly in words, placing all his hopes in eloquence and doubtless trusting more to the elegance of his speech and the deceit of his words [*verborum duplicate*] than to the integrity of my will."[9] Complaint is not merely ineffective, in other words, but an illegitimate attempt to change a world that will yield only to action. The poet's relation to the world is thus one of exclusion, even alienation: rather than participating, he stands to the side, claiming the privilege of irony because he lacks the efficiency of power. And again we touch one of the central issues of western thinking about literature: does writing have any effect upon the world, whether moral or practical, or is it simply ornament and compensation?

The ubiquity of complaint within the literary system, whether as a specific genre or an element present in all writing, thus stems in part from its capacity to stage questions central to literary culture as a whole. It provides, in other words, a site for theorizing, a diminutive arena in which a poetics can be concentrated. Indeed, its modest dimensions and un-prepossessing claims are part of its appeal: here radical speculation can be granted free play. And since the issues generated by the reflexivity of complaint focus upon the ground of writing, the form can be used to raise even larger questions about the foundations of cultural and even meta-physical truths. It is in this direction, at any rate, that Chaucer moves in his complaints. Put simply, he asks whether amorous wrongs can be righted by being written—whether, that is, the self can be repaired or justice can be done through poetry. In two different but related moments of lament—the *Canticus Troili* and *The Complaint of Mars*—Chaucer shows that not only can the question not be answered but that its very asking initiates a process of interrogation that has no natural stopping point.

I

After his vision of Criseyde in the temple, Troilus retreats to his room, the first of the many acts of withdrawal to be enacted in this poem of almost obsessive inwardness. His initial instinct is to continue this inward path—"Thus gan he make a mirour of his mynde" (I.365)—but he shortly turns from the pleasures of narcissism to the empirical demands of courtship. "Thus took he purpos loves craft to suwe" (379), and he begins to plot strategy, deciding "What for to speke, and what to holden inne, / And what *to arten her* to love he soughte" (387–88). The famous Petrarchan sonnet he now rehearses derives from this wish "to arten"

Crisedye, a verb derived from *ar(c)tere* and so meaning "to constrain, compel, or force" but whose phonetic form inevitably links it to the artful Ovidian "craft" (379) to which Troilus has just committed himself—a phonetic link that in fact led many of the scribes to rewrite the line so as to enforce the neologistic meaning "to manipulate."[10] In fact, the word is indissolubly, and usefully, ambiguous: Troilus will artfully coerce Criseyde, a program that links together passion and strategy.

The song he now sings is both part of this program and an expression of its central paradox. In changing the Petrarchan original—changes that commentators have usually, and mistakenly, described as errors—Chaucer renders the song not simply a display of the oxymoronic psychology of love but rather an interrogation of its ontological status.[11] For Petrarch, as we would expect, the object of scrutiny was his own emotion: "If it is not love, what then is it that I feel? But if it is love, by God, what kind of thing is it?"[12] But Troilus takes the emotion as a given and queries its source: "If no love is, O God, what fele I so? / And if love is, what thing and which is he?" (400–401). In moving the interjection from the second line to the first, and rendering it not an assertion ("by God") but an apostrophe ("O God"), Troilus makes it clear that his poem is in fact addressed to the very God of Love whose existence he is simultaneously questioning and affirming, the God from whom comes the "torment and adversite" of which he complains. But then in the second stanza Troilus poses the alternative possibility, "that at *myn owen lust* I brenne" (407); if this is the case, he asks, in another significant change from Petrarch, "How may [there be] of the *in me* swich quantite, / But if that I consente that it be?"[13] Hence when his third stanza then invokes the simile of the rudderless boat "possed to and fro . . . bitwixen wyndes two," we can see that he is caught not simply between conflicting emotions but also between two different conceptions of love: love as a transcendent deity who imposes his power upon his subjects versus love as an inward and conflicted emotion. And as the dramatic context of the song shows, these two conceptions are symmetrically related to the double impulse of coercion and submission that motivated the song in the first place: proceeding from Troilus's own conflicted motives, the song extends them into a metaphysical question. Not surprisingly, Troilus cannot sustain this conflict, and the two succeeding stanzas immediately resolve his dilemma in favor of deity.

> And to the God of Love thus seyde he
> With pitous vois, "O lord, now youres is
> My spirit, which that oughte youres be."

> (421–23)

At the very moment he begins to enact his desire, Troilus has come to question it. Although initially defining the emotion that moves him as a transcendent force by which he is wholly possessed, his plaintive song has unexpectedly led him to acknowledge that it may be in fact a merely human feeling, and hence marked with the impure complexity that by definition characterizes the human; but the uncertainty thus elicited is then hastily submerged within a commitment to a divine source so unwavering as to raise even Criseyde, at least momentarily, into the realm of the divine: "But wheither goddesse or womman, iwis, / She be, I not, which that ye do me serve" (425–26).

The dynamic enacted here is a miniaturized instance of the erotic economy that obtains throughout *Troilus and Criseyde*. The love upon which Troilus habitually calls is, whether deified or invoked simply as a guiding power, conceived as a transcendent force that possesses and transfigures those who are its devoted recipients. Deriving from the *fons et origo* of being itself, its unifying force promises to overcome the difference or "unlyklynesse" that does not merely disfigure but constitutes the *regio dissimilitudinis* of history. Not only does it claim the power to make one of two—"ye two," says Pandarus, "ben al on" (IV.592)—but it can reconcile the lover to both the largest movements of the universe and to himself, endowing him with an inner coherence that repairs man's self-alienation and makes him whole. For the true lover is by definition a being possessed of a single *entente,* an *intentio naturalis* (as Boethius would call it) wholly directed towards a unification whose enactment may be sexual but that nonetheless promises to confirm a sacramental cosmic harmony. But in fact, as Troilus's song shows *in parvo,* love serves not to overcome the lover's alienation but to enforce it. At odds with itself in its very motivation, Troilus's artful song develops into an unpremeditated acknowledgement of the complexity of a self whose initial claim upon Criseyde had been its now discredited singleness of purpose. And far from being the first step in a process of courtship, it turns back on the entangled lover and reconfirms the narcissistic self-enclosure it was originally meant to counter. Written "to arten hire to love he soughte" (388), it is a song Criseyde never hears: the linear movement of amorous communication is converted to the circularity of psychological self-reflection.

The standard critical reaction to the inability of Troilus's love to fulfill its ambitions is to measure it against the love defined by medieval theology and philosophy, whether the Christian love of "sothefast Crist" (V.1860) that the poem comes finally to commend, or the Boethian *amor conversus* that is everywhere allusively invoked. The strengths of this interpretive procedure are obvious, as is the force of the readings it produces. But it also elicits resistance, and for a number of reasons. One is that bringing these systematic intellectual structures to bear upon a multivalent textuality creates a feedback effect that destabilizes the interpretive structures themselves. Hence, for instance, efforts to apply the elaborate medieval distinctions among different kinds of love to *Troilus and Criseyde* have as one effect an awareness of just how obsessive these taxonomies are—an obsessiveness that in turn witnesses to an impeaching insecurity. So too, the invocation of Boethian standards of judgment must come to acknowledge that even the Boethian experience of *amor* is itself irresolubly ambiguous, as Boethius himself tacitly acknowledges in the famous Orpheus meter at the end of Book 3. Moreover, this interpretive strategy requires the interpreter to stand apart from and above the object of his scrutiny, and so both to disavow the sympathy that was the initial basis of understanding in the first place and, more seriously, to foreclose attention to the dynamics of that love itself. When understood as simply the negative obverse of a legitimate *amor,* in other words, Troilus's love loses its value as an object of interpretive interest. And yet it remains the subject of Chaucer's poem, and surely not simply so that it can call up its absent opposite.

These general comments have a particular relevance to the *Canticus Troili,* because Chaucer prefaces the song with a well-known stanza that shows how he is himself implicated within the divisive dynamic of Troilus's self-reflections, and implicated not as would-be lover but specifically as a writer:

> And of his song naught only the sentence,
> As writ myn auctour called Lollius,
> But pleinly, save oure tonges difference,
> I dar wel seyn, in al that Troilus
> Seyde in his song, loo! every word right thus
> As I shal seyn; and whoso list it here,
> Loo, next this vers he may it fynden here.
>
> (393–99)

Chaucer promises here to introduce into the course of his narratorial account a privileged moment of Troilian discourse. In some way apparently unlike the other instances of Troilus's speech recorded in the poem, the *Canticus Troili* is authentic: we are to be given not just the "sentence" but "every word." Just as Troilus's song begins by asserting his closeness to the very origins of love—"every torment and adversite / . . . cometh of *hym,*" the God to whom the poem is addressed—so does the song itself derive directly from Troilus. Yet here too the initial claim plays itself out to an unlooked for conclusion: as Troilus discovers that the transcendent singularity he had posited as the source of love cannot be sustained, so too is the narrator's claim to unmediated access belied by his recourse to Petrarch. And in fact, as we have seen, the univocal Petrarchan lyric—an examination of love as simply a psychological phenomenon—becomes in Chaucer's rewriting an equivocal debate between love-as-deity and love-as-affect. Neither Troilus's love nor the poet's representation of Troilus's song about love bespeaks an authoritative origin: just as Lollius is revealed upon inquiry to be a mumbling together of sources, so is the *entente* to love (as this moment suggests and as the poem as a whole demonstrates) an unfathomable mixture of appetite and idealism, self-regard and altruistic self-sacrifice.

"To write is to have the passion of the origin."[14] This Derridean dictum is above all true of he logocentric Middle Ages, which conceived of its cultural activity as an effort, however necessarily incomplete, to ground itself upon a divinely authored originality. But it is just this theology of origins—whether conceived in amorous, literary, or historiographical terms—that *Troilus and Criseyde,* and so much of Chaucer's poetry, interrogates. In writing a Trojan poem Chaucer invoked the founding moment of Western secular history. But in saturating his narrative with allusions to a Theban prehistory he let this Trojan origin give way to reveal beneath it another foundational narrative, and one in which—as the form of the Theban legend argued—beginnings are always re-beginnings, action always repetition. As the very reduplicative form of *Troilus and Criseyde* itself argues, in other words, history is not the linear *translatio imperii* medieval secular historiography asserted but rather a recursive labyrinth, an echo chamber of tragic reenactment.

The same economy controls as well the *translatio* of writing, revealing it to be subversively conditioned by an unavoidable "tonges difference." The governing assumption of medieval literary culture was that the same thing can be said in different words: the *res*—the signified that underwrites and legitimates all verbal expression—can be articulated in an infinite number of different *verba* and yet remain always the same. The task of the medieval writer is not to discover new matter—hence the withering away of *inventio* in late classical and medieval rhetorical theory—but to rewrite the original, the authoritative text bequeathed to the present by the past. This rewriting is accomplished in large part by recourse to the tropes—the *translationes*—catalogued by the rhetorical handbooks. But figuration, as the Middle Ages well knew, is never innocent: verbal *translatio* is the transfer of a word from its proper use to an improper one, a displacement that always runs the risk of vagrancy. The continuity of literary transferral, in other words, stands under the threat of the truancy of the mediatory figures by which it is to be accomplished. Just as within the economy of the individual text figuration retards the unfolding of the narrative line, so in the larger economy of literary history does it invert the linearity that connects imitation to source into a periphrastic circumlocution. That this periphrasis is a source of anxiety is shown both by the injunctions to writers to restrain figuration within the limits of propriety and the preemptive hermeneutics with which medieval exegetes sought to protect readers from the seductions of the letter. The task of the medieval reader is to rewrite the *signa translata* of figurative language back into the *signa propria* of the literal truth, a task accomplished by recourse to an extratextual source of authority able to cut through the laterally extended veil of words to the truth within. Absent such an instrument, the reader will find himself trapped within the *regio dissimilitudinis* of the letter. The anxiety, in other words, is that just as the purposive linearity of secular history cannot maintain itself, but gives way to a compulsive recursiveness that calls into question all merely historical beginnings and endings, so writing will declare its ineluctably mediatory status—its condition as a process of *translatio* undertaken without access to an authoritative source and with no guarantee of successful conclusion. And it is just this sense of writing as ceaseless rewriting that characterizes the work of the man whom Deschamps rightly designated, in a poem based on the topos of *translatio studii,* a *grant translateur.*

In writing the song with which he will "arten" Criseyde to love Troilus comes upon some disquieting facts about his own integrity—a term with ontological meanings that are at least as important as its more familiar ethical significance. Promising to make one out of two, love has had the ironic effect of introducing ambiguity into what was formerly thought to be integral. And the poem as a whole comes to define a subjectivity that is less that of identity than a site where different selves are constituted and decomposed. Nowhere is this subjectivity made more fully present than in the act of complaint. And it is also in the complaint that we can best understand Chaucer's own inscription within the economy of amorous duplication.

II

A second example that can usefully illuminate this unsettling dynamic is one of Chaucer's most innovative and enigmatic poems, the *Complaint of Mars.*[15] The poem is presided over by Venus—"þe double goddesse of love," as John Shirley called her in a notorious rubric to the poem[16]—and is itself almost obsessively equivocal. It represents its protagonists as both planets and gods, and yet has their embarrassing celestial doings described by a bird as the subject of a Valentine's Day aubade. This remarkably complex siting apparently serves to establish an opposition between the nighttime misbehavior of the planetary gods and the orthodox natural mating of the birds. But in fact it comes to present these alternative modes of lovemaking less as terms in opposition than as counterparts. For its very status as the subject of this amorous birdsong endows the adultery of Mars and Venus with a certain legitimacy, as does their enactment of an astronomically detailed celestical itinerary. Adulterous they may be, but they are tracing a course prescribed for them by a divinely established "hevenysh revolucioun" (30), and their conjunction—a celestial event designated by the astrologers a *copulatio*—is as much in the nature of things as is the love service of the birds.[17] Similarly, Venus's astrological amelioration of Mars is simultaneously a shameful unmanning and the sign of a harmonious *discordia concors:* Venus is indeed, as the mythographers and astrologers say, *duplex*—both "the mother of all fornications" and the deity whom Boccaccio called *Venus magna* and whom Bernard Silvestris described as "the harmony of the world, that is, the even proportion of worldly things, which some call Astrea, and others call natural justice."[18] The "binding" (47–48) and "knitting" (50) by which the lovers are joined is simultaneously an expression of the Boethian "byndynge" by which Nature "restreyneth alle thynges by a boond that may nat be unbownde" (3.ii.6–7) and the constraint with which "amyable Fortune byndeth with the beaute of false goods the hertes of folk that usen them" (3.8.19–21).[19]

This ambivalence is neatly expressed in the stanza that describes the consummation of the love:

The grete joye that was bitwix hem two,
When they be mette, ther may no tunge telle.
Ther is no more, but unto bed thei go;
And thus in joy and blyse I lete hem duelle.
This worthi Mars, that is of knygthod welle,
The flour of feyrnesse lappeth in his armes,
And Venus kysseth Mars, the god of armes.

(71–77)

The allusion to *Corinthians* is at once elevating and bathetic; the assertion of verbal insufficiency that is thrice repeated in the consummation scene in the *Troilus*—"I kan namore" (III.1193, 1273, 1314)—is here both invoked and transformed into a statement of sexual urgency; and the meeting of opposites promises both a moment of cosmic harmony and future discord. Indeed, even the largest of the oppositions by which the poem is structured is in fact insolubly equivocal. The mythographical narrative records the collapse of the "perpetuall" love that Mars and Venus have plighted "for evere" (47–48), while the birds are brought together to confirm that their mutual love will last "perpetuely" (20): the fickleness of Olympian adultery is set against the steadfastness of natural instinct, change against permanence. Yet from another perspective the very fact that the birds return each year to "renovel[en]" (19) their vows—and that they choose to sing this particular song—raises the prospect of reparation: if Mars and Venus are driven apart "by hevenysh revolucioun" (30) they will also be brought back together. There can, in short, be no change

without permanence, and inevitable inconstancy promises perpetual renewal. So too with the other major thematic opposition in the poem,
freedom and constraint. The act of moral judgment that the poem everywhere calls for assumes moral freedom; and yet the agents—whether
birds, gods or planets—are constrained to their acts by dispositions that
serve to constitute their very nature. The birds are engaged in a ritual that
witnesses to the ineluctable processes of nature, and yet they have come
together to *choose* their mates—an assertion that is enforced by having
the word repeated in three successive lines (16–18). For Mars and Venus
not to conjoin would require them not to be Mars and Venus; and yet the
consequences of their conjunction are represented in terms that assume
ethical judgment and presuppose freedom of choice. The point is that the
poem represents behavior as both externally compelled and self-chosen,
as an effect of both necessity and free will. Once again, then, opposites
become counterparts, and the exclusive binarism of either/or becomes the
inclusive—and destabilizing—dualism of both/and.

The most telling instance of this pervasive doubleness is Mars's complaint itself. "His nature was not for to wepe" (94), but having been first
divested of his "cruelte, and bost, and tyrannye" (37) by Venus, and then
further chastened by her loss, he has now discovered the *alter ego* of a
previously unknown plaintive self. It is this geminated, amartial self that
now engages in the quintessentially self-duplicating act of complaint. The
aporitic context thus established gives special, ironic point to the subject
of the complaint, which is nothing less than the search for a cause:

> The ordre of compleynt requireth skylfully
> That yf a wight shal pleyne pitously,
> Ther mot be *cause* wherfore that men pleyne;
> Or men may deme he pleyneth folily
> And *causeles;* alas, that am not I!
> Wherfore the *ground and cause* of al my peyne,
> So as my troubled wit may hit atteyne,
> I wol reherse; not for to have redresse,
> But to declare my *ground* of hevynesse.

> (155–63)

This initial invocation of a forensic purpose promises to endow the complaint with a secure discursive definition: Mars appears as plaintiff, appealing to a judge for redress for the wrongs he has suffered at the hands of
certain malefactors. Yet the course of the complaint itself subverts this
discursive stability, for Mars discovers that he can specify with confidence
neither the nature of the wrong done him, nor the perpetrator, nor an
audience to whom he can appeal.[20] What instead emerges from his
ruminations is the far more disturbing awareness that the economy of
desire contains at its center an apparently irremediable doubleness. As

day follows night so does need follow fulfillment, an imperative of reenactment that is emblematized in the Broche of Thebes, itself a sign of the fatal doubling back of Theban history in an endlessly frustrated return to an always absent origin.

Mars designates this economy a "double wo and passioun" (255) and recognizes his own inscription within it. But what eludes him is its source: "What meneth this? What is this mystihed?" (224) Carefully Mars exempts Venus from blame: she is, to be sure, the "verrey sours and welle . . . Of love and pley" (174–78) and as a "double goddesse" might be thought responsible for the doubleness of love. But such a thought is for Mars unthinkable, and he instead represents Venus as herself helpless before malevolent forces and in his own condition of thwarted lament: "My righte lady, my savacyoun, / Is in affray, and not to whom to pleyne" (213–14). But in shying away from Venus as *fons et origo* Mars in fact allows for a far more destabilizing thought: by a process of logical regress he now designates as the source of "double wo" the First Mover himself, "the God that sit so hye" (218). And with this assertion Mars now finds himself forced to identify this First Mover with the misshapen Vulcan, and to see both the "hevenysh revolucioun" that has brought him to this impasse and the processes of history as motivated by the jealous malevolence of a wronged husband.

Mars's speculations have thus arrived at a self-evident absurdity, and we are invited to regard them as simply the product of his "troubled wit." Constrained by his love for Venus to exempt her from responsibility for the erotic dynamic over which she herself presides, he is instead forced to impeach the basis of his own existence, the "ground and cause" of his very being. Hence he is unable to find anyone to whom to direct his bill of complaint, and concludes by instead leading "hardy knyghte of renoun" and "ladyes that ben true and stable" (272, 281) in a choral lament for the Venus whom he thinks is abandoned but who is even now being comforted by the Mercury who will father upon her the illicit Hermaphrodite. And just as Mars becomes a figure of pathetic self-delusion to the informed reader, so his benighted complaint arrives at a philosophical impasse that can be resolved only by a Christian truth to which he himself has no access. Indeed, the universal critical response to the poem is to read it as calling up by the very ambiguity of its language the absent other of Christian doctrine.[21] In effect, Mars's discovery of the doubleness that pervades experience as a whole is taken as urging upon the reader the singular truth of Christian doctrine, and the endless dissatisfaction of venerean desire as invoking the foreclosure of Christian love. Christ is the answer to Mars's questions, the love of God the means by which the unquiet heart of wayfaring man can find peace.[22]

This strategy of stabilizing an equivocal text by locating it within a univocal interpretive context is not only authentically medieval, but is clearly solicited by the religiously charged language of the poem. But the poem also casts an interrogative light upon the procedures by which the strategy is enacted. If Christian interpretation is the necessary supplement by which that which is missing from the *Complaint of Mars* can be provided, supplementarity has its own recursive habit of revealing what Derrida has called "the anterior default of a presence."[23] That such a revelation may be a function of more than simply contemporary critical fashion is in fact suggested by the poem itself, which is after all about the ubiquity of the equivocal. It delineates a world in which the either/or of singularity is subverted by a dualistic both/and, in which oppositions are revealed to be counterparts; and this must make us hesitant to endow one element of a pair with the power wholly to sublate much less to efface the other. So too does it delineate a mind engaged in a process of mental regress in order to discover a "ground and cause" for its experience, just as does the reader of the poem. Mars is of course constrained in his speculations by his avoidance of the unthinkable thought that Venus is herself complicit in the doubleness that characterizes the rest of the world. But is not the reader also constrained by the unthinkable? Is there not an orthodoxy that we too cannot transgress, a limit beyond which we cannot go, an origin (whether historical, metaphysical, or interpretive) we fear to undo?

III

Recent historians of medieval French literature have shown that in the fourteenth century previously free-standing lyrics began to be grounded within narratives.[24] This process was accomplished through both the *dit* form popularized by Guillaume de Machaut and the development of lyric collections such as the *Cent ballades* or (to take a non-French example) Petrarch's *Rime sparse*.[25] This is a process of historicization, an insistence that the abstract voice of lyric, issuing from no one in particular and received by everyone in general, must instead be situated within a specific historical context: a singular person speaks to a determinate audience. And such a practice can naturally be understood as seeking to contain the regressive irony implicit within lyricism. Chaucer is himself part of this movement: poems like *Anelida and Arcite* and *The Legend of Good Women,* as well as *Troilus and Criseyde* and the *Complaint of Mars,* locate plaintive lyricism within a narrative context.[26] But the examples we have examined suggest that lyric irony cannot be domesticated by narrative. On the contrary, the narrative context is itself ironized, becomes itself subject to the self-reflexive uncertainties of the plaintive voice. Once introduced, irony metathesizes, subverting all efforts at sequestration. As Paul de Man has suggested, "Lyric poetry . . . [is] an enigma which never stops asking for the unreachable answer to its own riddle," and an enigma whose endless quest reveals unanticipated weaknesses within the body of the host.[27]

Notes

1. The first citation is from "Sunday Morning," the second from "Esthétique du Mal", *The Collected Poems of Wallace Stevens* (New York: Knopf, 1968), pp. 68, 322.

2. The importance of the form to Chaucer's poetry has recently been stressed by W. A. Davenport. *Chaucer: Complaint and Narrative* (Cambridge: Brewer, 1988).

3. According to C. L. Wrenn, "It might almost be said that in Old English the lyric mood is always the elegiac" (*A Study of Old English Literature* [London: Harrap, 1967], p. 140).

4. There are a number of partial accounts: see especially John Peter, *Complaint and Satire in Early English Literature* (Oxford: Clarendon Press, 1956) (primarily on complaints of the times); Monika Wodsak, *Die Complainte: Zur Geschichte einer französischen Populärgattung* (Heidelberg: Winter, 1985) (primarily on postmedieval complaints of the times); Gotz Schmitz, *Die Frauenklage: Studien zur elegischen Verserzählung in der englischen Literatur des Spätmittelalters und der Renaissance* (Tübingen: Niemeyer, 1984); and Prajapati Prasad, "The Order of Complaint: A Study in Medieval Tradition," (Ph.D. diss., University of Wisconsin, 1965). See also note 26 to this essay.

5. Howard, *The Three Temptations: Medieval Man in Search of the World* (Princeton: Princeton Univ. Press, 1966).

6. Paul Zumthor, "De la circularité du chant," *Poétique* 2 (1970): 129–40; Roman Jakobson, *Selected Writings* (Paris: Mouton, 1971), 2.130–32.

7. Paul Zumthor, "A Reading of a *Ballade* by Jean Meschinot," in W. T. H. Jackson, *The Interpretation of Medieval Lyric Poetry* (New York: Columbia Univ. Press, 1980), p. 162. As Zumthor says: "The 'first person' has passed by this way. He fades away, departs along a road known only to himself, to the beyond. He is calm: he has played his part for a little while, on the stage where traditional discourses make their speeches, and also far behind the scenes, hidden in the opacity of the work which was in course of being created . . ." (ibid.).

8. For the terms "emotive," "conative," and "referential," see Roman Jakobson, "Linguistics and Poetics," in Thomas A. Sebeok, ed., *Style in Language* (Cambridge: MIT Press, 1960), pp. 350–77.

9. P. G. Walsh, ed. and trans., *Andreas Capellanus on Love* (London: Duckworth, 1982), p. 191. Even if we read the *complainte d'amour* politically, as a literary exercise designed to promote not the lover but the courtier, self-cancellation remains at its center. On the one hand the best courtier is the most eloquent (for medieval court culture, *facetus* is often synonymous with *curialis*); yet on the other, verbal facility can be both dangerous in itself and the sign of an untrustworthy personality (hence the courtly praise of taciturnity).

10. See the variants given in Geoffrey Chaucer, *Troilus and Criseyde,* ed. B. A. Windeatt (London: Longmans, 1984), p. 111. All citations are taken from *The*

Riverside Chaucer, 3rd ed., gen. ed. Larry D. Benson (Boston: Houghton Mifflin, 1987). I have upon occasion altered the punctuation of the printed text.

11. The two major discussions of the song are by Ernest H. Wilkins, "Cantus Troili," *ELH* 16 (1949): 167–73, and Patricia Thomson, "The 'Canticus Troili': Chaucer and Petrarch," *Comparative Literature* 11 (1959): 313–28.

12. "S'amor non è, che dunque è quel ch'io sento? / ma s' egli è amor, per Dio, che cosa et quale?" Robert M. Durling, ed. and trans., *Petrarch's Lyric Poems* (Cambridge: Harvard Univ. Press, 1976), pp. 270–71. I have changed Durling's translation of *per Dio* from "before God" to "by God."

13. Petrarch instead asked his emotions how they could "have such power over me if I do not consent to it." It seems clear that Chaucer changed Petrarch's assertion of the dominion of love to his own description of its inward presence because Petrarch's phrasing inadvertently invoked the very divinity of love that Troilus initially asserted but that he is now, in this second stanza, calling into question.

14. Jacques Derrida, "Ellipsis," in *Writing and Difference,* trans. Alan Bass (Chicago: Univ. of Chicago Press, 1978), p. 295.

15. An appreciation of just how original Chaucer's poem is can be gained by comparing it with the texts discussed by Benedetto Soldati, *La Poesia astrologica nel quattrocento: ricerche e studi* (Florence: Sansoni, 1906). Despite the thoroughness of Chaucerian scholarship, it has been unable to discover either sources or analogues for the poem, a fact that should encourage us to be similarly innovative in our own interpretive efforts.

16. Shirley's comments have been reprinted by Eleanor Hammond, *Chaucer: A Bibliographical Manual* (New York: Macmillan, 1908), p. 384.

17. On conjunction and *copulatio,* see Chauncey Wood, *Chaucer and the Country of the Stars* (Princeton: Princeton Univ. Press, 1970), p. 147.

18. For Boccaccio, see *Genealogie deorum Gentilium,* 3, 22–23, ed. Vincenzo Romano (Bari: Laterza, 1951), 1.142–52; for Bernardus, see *Commentum super sex libros Eneidos Virgili,* as cited and translated by Earl G. Schreiber, "Venus in the Medieval Mythographic Tradition," *JEGP* 74 (1975): 522–23. For further on *Venus duplex,* see George D. Economou, "The Two Venuses and Courtly Love," in Joan M. Ferrante and G. D. Economou, eds., *In Pursuit of Perfection: Courtly Love in Medieval Literature* (Port Washington, N.Y.: Kennikat Press, 1975), pp. 17–50; and Richard Hamilton Green, "Alan of Lille's *De Planctu Naturae,*" *Speculum* 31 (1956): 667–68 (especially on Eriugena's commentary on Martianus Capella).

Critics have virtually unanimously read Venus' effect on Mars in this poem in negative terms, and have denied or devalued the relevance of the notion of *discordia concors,* arguing that this is a classical topos that reappears only in the Renaissance. Chauncey Wood provides a forthright account:

> The fact of the matter is that Chaucer's attitude, as well as that of the audience, toward the story of Mars and Venus was rather well fixed in the direction of condemnation, and the 'good' interpretation of Mars and Venus that became common in the Renaissance was only used outside of any reference to planetary conjunction of mythological adultery in the Middle Ages and so cannot fit the situation in the *Complaint of Mars.* . . . A close inspection of the evidence suggests that while the idea that Venus could temper the fury of Mars was well-known in the Middle Ages, the more positive idea that the union of the two produced Harmony seems to be discoverable only in the Renaissance . . . (pp. 107–11).

It is quite true, of course, that Ficino's illustration of the philosophic idea of universal harmony by means of the adultery of Mars and Venus finds its precedent not in medieval tradition but in Plutarch's *Moralia*. But the idea, in however ironically inflected a form, was always implicit in the myth, and Chaucer would have found it made explicit in Book 3 of the *Thebaid*. There Venus seeks to prevent Mars from inciting the Argives against the Thebans, a race descended from their daughter Harmonia. In explaining that he is constrained by Jove and the Fates, Mars acknowledges Venus' tempering power, describing her as "my repose from battle, my sacred joy and all the peace my heart doth know: thou who alone of gods and men canst face my arms unpunished, and check even in mid-slaughter my neighing steeds, and tear this sword from my right-hand" (ll. 295–99; trans. J. H. Mozley [Cambridge: Harvard Univ. Press, 1928], 1.473). In his commentary to these lines, Lactantius Placidus describes the effect of Venus on Mars in both astrological and cosmic terms. He first glosses *sacra voluptas* ("sacred joy") astrologically: "Si enim mixtus aliis sideribus Mars fuerit, uehementior truculentiorque fit, econtra si Iouis, bonus, si Veneris, supplex fiet." And he then glosses *unaque pax animo* ("and all the peace my heart doth know") by citing an important passage from Lucretius (otherwise unavailable to the Middle Ages) that describes Venus' pacific effect on Mars:

> nam tu, sola potes tranquilla pace iuuare
> mortales, quoniam belli fera moenia Mauors
> armipotens regit, in gremium qui saepe tuum se
> reicit aeterno deuinctus [recte: devictus] uulnere amoris.

                                                                      (1.31–34)

[For thou alone canst delight mortals with quiet peace, since Mars mighty in battle rules the savage works of war, who often casts himself upon thy lap wholly vanquished by the everliving wound of love.]

Ed. Richard Jahnke (Leipzig: Teubner, 1898), pp. 157–58. [Trans. W. H. D. Rouse (New York: Putnams, 1931), p. 5.] My point is not that in the *Complaint of Mars* Chaucer presents a vision of *discordia concors,* but rather that the conjunction of Mars and Venus, both as stars and as deities, was understood in the classical world in ambivalent terms; and that the beneficial effects of the goddess Venus upon Mars would have been known to Chaucer both implicitly through the tradition of *Venus duplex* and explicitly by means of this passage in the *Thebaid* and its commentary.

The ambivalence of the specifically *astrological* conjunction is neatly articulated in Chaucer's other two uses of it, once (positively) in the Hypermnestra story of the *Legend of Good Women* and then (negatively) in the Wife of Bath's Prologue. It should also be pointed out, of course, that the *Complaint of Mars* does *not* tell the story of the humiliating entrapment of Mars and Venus by Vulcan but allows it to remain a suppressed middle: we are given the initial discovery by Phoebus Apollo and the subsequent history of the Brooch of Thebes with which Vulcan avenged himself, but not the entrapment itself—a textual fact that ought to restrain the reader from simply importing the values of that part of the myth into the poem.

For other negative readings of the conjunction of Mars and Venus, which tend to rely upon the entrapment, see Neil C. Hultin, "Anti-Courtly Elements in Chaucer's *Complaint of Mars,*" *Annuale Medievale* 9 (1968): 58–75; and Melvin Storm, "The Mythological Tradition of Chaucer's *Complaint of Mars,*" *PQ* 57 (1978): 323–35.

19. For further descriptions of the benevolent binding and knitting accomplished by divine *amor,* see 2.v.50–51; 2.viii.13–14; 3.ix.18; 5.iii.16–17; and 5.1.92–9. The ambiguous value of the Boethian concept has been well explored by Stephen Barney, "Troilus Bound," *Speculum* 47 (1972): 445–58. I have cited the *Consolation* according to the system used by commentators on the Latin text, using Roman numerals for the meters and Arabic for the prose.

20. In his important discussion, "Chaucer's *Broche of Thebes:* The Unity of 'The Complaint of Mars' and 'The Complaint of Venus,' " *Literary Monographs* 5 (1973): 3–60, 187–95, Rodney Merrill also notices the forensic nature of the complaint, but then argues, unconvincingly to my mind, that it is structured as a classically defined judicial oration.

21. The most obstrusive instance of such ambiguity is Mars' description of God as a malevolent fisherman who baits his hook with "som pleasaunce" (238) that grants the lover "al his desir, and therwith al myschaunce" (241).

> And thogh the lyne breke, he hath penaunce;
> For with the hok he wounded is so sore
> That he his wages hath for evermore—
>
> (242–44)

doubtless the wages of sin that are death. Neil Hultin has shown that didactic literature used the image of woman as the bait on the hook of sin ("Anti-Courtly Elements in Chaucer's *Complaint of Mars,"* pp. 70–72), and Rodney Merrill has persuasively argued that this image plays on the medieval trope of *amor* as a hook *(hamus)* in order to invoke not just the biblical image of Christ as a fisher of men but the iconographic representation of God as baiting his hook with Christ in order to catch Satan ("Chaucer's *Broche of Thebes,"* pp. 38–39). Merrill concludes that "this unfulfilled desire, this aching thirst for 'reste,' is the 'line' of love by which God may 'catch' his fish. Man's desire for the fleeting things of the world leads to suffering; but this 'myschaunce' may be the very best fortune possible, if it causes him to seek more lasting goods. This is a Christian commonplace: in Mars' complaint we are made to see the psychological realities upon which it is based" (p. 39).

22. Merrill provides the most complete reading of the poem—and of the *Complaint of Venus,* which he designates a companion piece—in these terms. As he says, "Ignorant of the redeeming Christ, Mars can only look forward to an eternity of desire and frustration. . . . But human lovers who are not bound to an endless repetition of their allotted spans may take from him a serious warning with regard to the lower passion which he laments" (p. 41).

23. Derrida, *Of Grammatology,* trans. Gayatri Spivak (Baltimore: The Johns Hopkins Univ. Press, 1976), p. 145. Derrida later provides a brief account of the law of supplementarity that bears a striking relevance to the *Complaint of Mars:*

> Through the sequence of supplements a necessity is announced: that of an infinite chain, ineluctably multiplying the supplementary mediations that produce the sense of the very thing they defer: the mirage of the thing itself, of immediate presence, of originary perception. Immediacy is derived. That all begins through the intermediary is what is indeed "inconceivable [to reason]" (p. 157).

24. See Jacqueline Cerquiglini, "Le nouveau lyrisme (XIVe–XVe siècles)" in Daniel Poirion, ed., *Précis de littérature française du Moyen Age* (Paris: Presses universitaires de France, 1983), pp. 275–92; Michel Zink, *La subjectivité littéraire*

autour du siècle de saint Louis (Paris: Presses universitaires de France, 1985), pp. 47–74.

25. A connection between Petrarch's *Rime* and contemporary French practice is suggested by Sylvia Huot, *From Song to Book: The Poetics of Writing in Old French Lyric and Lyrical Narrative Poetry* (Ithaca: Cornell Univ. Press, 1987), pp. 331–32.

26. In "Chaucer's *Complaint, A* Genre Descended from the *Heroides,*" *Comparative Literature* 19 (1967): 1–27, Nancy Dean claims that Chaucer's narrativization of complaint reveals the primacy of classical models; see also Edgar F. Shannon, *Chaucer and the Roman Poets* (Cambridge: Harvard Univ. Press, 1929), pp. 15–47. On the other hand, James Wimsatt locates Chaucer's usage in relation to the contemporary French *dit amoureau:* "Guillaume de Machaut and Chaucer's Love Lyrics," *Medium Aevum* 47 (1978): 66–87, and *"Anelida and Arcite:* A Narrative of Complaint and Comfort," *Chaucer Review* 5 (1970–71): 1–8. These genetic explanations are of course not exclusive.

27. Paul de Man, "Lyric and Modernity," in *Blindess and Insight: Essays in the Rhetoric of Contemporary Criticism,* 2nd ed. (Minneapolis: Univ. of Minnesota Press, 1983), p. 186.

Chaucer's Idea of a Canterbury Game

GLENDING OLSON

The *Canterbury Tales* is a collection of narratives bound together in a frame that has two central features—a pilgrimage and a game. The pilgrimage is the outer framing device, the occasion for the gathering together of the company of storytellers; the game is a second, inner, framing device, the organizing principle that brings the stories into being. Chaucer did not have to have his pilgrims play a game in order to have them tell stories. Their prologues and tales could have emerged as part of conversation or debate or advice. Chaucer knew how the *Roman de la rose* incorporated lengthy discourses representing distinct points of view within a narrative structure. He knew the familiar didactic model of Gower's *Confessio amantis* and other story collections in which narratives function more or less as exemplary illustrations of general precepts. But he took the option Boccaccio took in the *Decameron*—he made the storytelling the playing of a game. And we need to think about the implications of that choice.

There are signs that the role of play and game in the *Canterbury Tales* is beginning to garner some overdue critical attention. For decades the dominant approaches rather ignored this central structural feature of the *Tales,* and the reasons are not far to seek. The kind of psychological, tale-teller inquiry we associate with Kittredge and Lumiansky wants to read the fictions as expressions of their narrators' personalities; it would naturally not emphasize the greater mediation between pilgrim-self and performance implicit in Chaucer's choice of a game structure. The allegorical approach associated with Robertson and Huppé fixes on the larger framing device of pilgrimage and finds it convenient to neglect the more obviously sportive and secular (though as I will show, far from amoral) game frame. And I suspect that for many critics of whatever persuasion the idea of game has seemed somehow essentially trivializing, conceding too much to the ghost of Matthew Arnold.

With some newer theory has come a more playful spirit, or at least a recognition that the game itself occupies a role in the *Tales* every bit as important as the pilgrimage. In two articles, Richard A. Lanham and Gabriel Josipovici established what should have been clear all along—that the framing narrative is permeated with references to play and game (the linking passages give us no such persistent foregrounding of pilgrimage). The critical conclusions they drew were based more on modern than on medieval views of play. Recently Carl Lindahl has explored the *Tales* in light of medieval festivity and Laura Kendrick in light of Bakhtin's idea of carnival and Freudian views of humor. Such ideas came to seem important to Donald Howard, as his discussion of the *Tales* in his biography of Chaucer attests.[1]

To this interest in the Canterbury game I add my own. It is an extension of some ideas I have presented elsewhere, and I refer readers to that book for documentation of certain basic points simply assumed here.[2] Chaucer's relationship to medieval notions of literary entertainment and recreation is so rich and complicated that it needs separate treatment beyond the few pages I gave it earlier solely in order to establish its continuity with a tradition. Toward that fuller treatment I aim now—first in this essay and subsequently in longer form, with more extensive documentation and critical discussion. My orientation is historical—I think that considering medieval views of play and game will give us a more comprehensive and nuanced understanding of the inner Canterbury frame than we presently have. Not that Huizinga, say, or Bakhtin is irrelevant; but there are medieval theories of play, too, and if we are going to think about the role of game in the *Canterbury Tales* we ought not exclude some ideas demonstrably a part of Chaucer's intellectual environment.

When Harry Bailly proposes, and the pilgrims accept, the playing of a game in order to provide comfort and mirth, the *Canterbury Tales* draws on a medieval understanding of the legitimacy and benefits of recreational play. That understanding, and its role in medieval thinking about literature conceived as a form of entertainment, was the subject of my earlier book. Here I want to explore in much more detail one aspect of that understanding and its relevance to Chaucer's collection. For the beginning of the *Canterbury Tales,* what we call Fragment I, is a sequence of storytelling that parallels directly a sequence of thoughts about play and players that was commonplace in the later Middle Ages. Chaucer's idea of the Canterbury game, though it ends in something very different, begins as an enactment of some Aristotelian distinctions.

The *Nicomachean Ethics* discusses a number of virtues, one of which is a virtue in regard to play or entertainment—*ludus* in Robert Grosseteste's translation, which was standard for the later Middle Ages. Chaucer (at least according to one interpretation of *LGW* F 165–66) knew the principle by which Aristotle defined his virtues and their corresponding vices: "vertu is the mene, / As Etik seith."[3] Aristotle treats the virtues as means between extremes, one of excess, one of defect. Courage, for example, is the virtue in regard to fear—the mean between cowardice, excessive fear, and recklessness, the lack of fear even in situations where it would be appropriate. Liberality, the virtue in regard to the use of wealth, is the mean between the excess of prodigality and the defect of avarice, both of which sins Dante punishes in the fourth circle of *Inferno* and mentions again in connection with Statius in *Purgatorio* XXII. The mean in regard to play is *eutrapelia,* the excess *bomolochia,* the defect *agroica*—"wittiness," "buffoonerey," and "boorishness" are the usual modern English translations, but the first of these is particularly inadequate to convey the resonance of the concept in medieval discussion, and I will keep the transliterated Greek as a key term.

Briefly, we can chart the late medieval dissemination of Aristotle's approach to play as follows. Grosseteste's complete Latin translation of the *Ethics* was made in 1246–47, supplemented by his translation of some early Greek scholia and some notes of his own. Shortly thereafter Albert the Great wrote a long commentary on it and later wrote a second. His student Thomas Aquinas, relying heavily on Albert's work, also wrote a commentary on the *Ethics* and subsequently incorporated Aristotelian ideas into his discussion of play in the *Summa theologica* (2–2, q.168). The texts of Albert and Aquinas contain nearly all of the thinking about the mean and extremes in regard to play that appeared in later treatises; their analyses and conclusions were variously abridged and combined by subsequent commentators. Material in the *Summa theologica,* particularly, influenced not only academic thinking but a host of later medieval works on morality intended for a less specialized audience.[4] Chaucer would not have had to go to scholastic commentaries in order to learn that eutrapelia was a mean between extremes; he could have found the idea in such places as Giles of Rome's *De regimine principum,* John of Freiburg's influential *Summa confessorum,* Dante's *Convivio,* and Robert Holcot's popular commentary on the book of Wisdom. We know he read at least portions of the latter two.

Listen to Aquinas discussing the *eutrapelus,* the man who plays virtuously:

> [Aristotle says] that men who devote themselves to amusement in moderation are called witty *(eutrapeli),* as it were, good at turning because they becomingly give an amusing turn to what is said and done. . . . It is proper to men of this sort to narrate and listen to such amusing incidents as become a decent and liberal man who possesses a soul free from slavish passions. . . . it pertains to the mean habit of virtue to speak and listen to what is becoming in jesting.[5]

Moderation, propriety, decency in language—these are the features of one whose play is morally upright. Like Aristotle, Aquinas allows for some kinds of humorous insult or reproach, but it too must be "pleasing and polite" (1 370). In the *Summa* Aquinas also calls the virtue *jucunditas,* as does Giles of Rome, thereby implicitly extending the range of the virtue beyond the narrow limits of jesting. *Eutrapelia* is not simply the ability to engage in witty repartee but a properly cheerful disposing of one's words and actions in the context of social conviviality and entertainment. An alphabetical summary of the ideas of the *Nicomachean Ethics* suggests this wider implication: "*Eutrapeli* are merry people, who act appropriately and pleasantly in social play and conversation."[6] There is even the possibility of instruction via amusement: Aquinas allows that some kinds of reproach may aim at "a man's correction" (1:370), and a later commentator, Petrus de Corveheda, claims that true *eutrapeli* intend their playing to have good, perhaps even morally beneficial, effects.[7]

The person who errs by excessive play is a *bomolochus* or buffoon. "These people lie in wait," says Aquinas,

> so they can pounce upon something to turn into a laugh. On this account persons of this kind are a nuisance because they want to make laughter out of everything. They make more effort to do this than to engage in becoming or polite conversation and avoid disturbing the man they heap with playful reproach. They would rather tell scandalous stories, even at the risk of offending others, than (not) cause men to laugh. (1:368)

Later Aquinas adds two important points concerning this vice: the buffoon "spares neither himself nor others in attempting to create laughter," and his speech goes beyond what a virtuous person would say (1:370). Brunetto Latini, working in this case not from Aristotle directly but from a Latin translation of an Arabic abridgment of the *Ethics,* calls the person who plays excessively a "jangler" and says that for the sake of laughter and play he derides himself, his wife, his sons, and everyone else.[8]

Many medieval commentators stress that the excess of the buffoon lies not just in the quantity of his playing, in his failure to observe the necessary subordination of entertainment to seriousness, but also in the nature of his play, particularly the use of foul language. Nicole Oresme's French translation of the *Ethics* gives an interesting contemporary example of such excess. In his discussion of proper and improper language in play Aristotle had alluded briefly to old and new Greek comedy, contrasting the greater obscenity of the former with the more refined innuendo of the latter. His meaning was not totally clear to medieval commentators, but most recognized a moral judgment being made in regard to the decency of language in some kind of performance or composition. In a gloss on this passage Oresme explains that Aristotle's use of the term "comedies" refers to "plays such as those where one person represents St. Paul, another Judas, another a hermit," and that such plays some times include vulgar language, improper and distasteful.[9] I take Oresme's present tense

here to encompass contemporary as well as classical habits; his explication is telling not just for what it says about religious drama in his day but
for its implicit conceptualization of performance within Aristotle's moral
perspective on play; other such publicly presented narrative, whether
enacted drama or recited tale, would logically fall in the same category due
to the context of social entertainment. This passage supplements other
evidence assembled in *Literature as Recreation* that shows the discussion
of play in *Nicomachean Ethics* 4.8 to have been a central point of reference for making judgments about forms of public entertainment, some of
which we now call literature.

And what of the vice that is defect? Aquinas explains:

> . . . men who never want to say anything funny and are disagreeable to the
> people who do . . . seem to be uncultured or boorish and coarse, like those who
> are not mellowed by amusing recreation. . . . [Such a person] is useless at these
> witty conversations. He contributes nothing to them but is disagreeable to
> everyone. He is vicious in that he completely abhors jest, which is necesary for
> human living as a kind of recreation. (I. 368–70)

Latini describes the boor as one who "always appears stern, with a pained
expression, and does not enjoy himself with others, nor speak or associate
with people having a good time" (204). The vice entails not merely lacking
a sense of humor but lacking a capacity to participate in humanly necessary social pleasures. Albert the Great cites a line from Gregory's *Moralia*
to help define the boor: anyone who cannot participate in social entertainment remains alone, living "bestialiter."[10] Social conviviality here seems
to be an image of human community, as I think it is in the *Canterbury
Tales*. The nature of one's play can be a measure of the nature of one's
ability to participate in and contribute to the common good. It is significant that John Buridan discusses eutrapelia not only in his questions on
the *Ethics* but in his questions on Aristotle's *Politics* as well, concluding
that *eutrapeli* do have a place in a well-ordered community because of
their usefulness in providing necessary recreation.[11]

The treatment of play I have been delineating is certainly not the only
medieval thinking on the subject. But it is, I believe, the dominant learned
secular tradition, and its very secularity is perhaps as significant for
understanding its importance to the *Canterbury Tales* as are the more
detailed parallels I discuss shortly. The fact is that most medieval thinking
about play (granting the bias of the surviving texts) is fundamentally moral
rather than psychological or anthropological. That does not mean that
such thinking need always be intended moralistically, or that it does not
include insights into play compatible with other approaches; but it does
suggest the likelihood that medieval reflections on play would at least
work out of a conceptual framework that concerns itself less with the

nature of play than with its ethical or social propriety. In this regard Aristotle's mean and extremes fit compatibly with medieval *distinctiones* on play based on biblical usage, which generally recognized that some playing was spiritual, some was evil or diabolical, and some more neutrally human or recreational. The Aristotelian analysis could enter in to such thinking as a means for further discrimination within that third category.

Thus Robert Holcot, after a long discussion of the conditions that must obtain in order for recreational play to the virtuous, offers a typology of play based on Aquinas's *Sentences* commentary: there is a "ludus turpis et inhonestus" (such as the gentiles played in theaters and temples before their gods), a "ludus gaudii spiritualis" (such as David's dancing before the ark and Christian playing on Corpus Christi day), and a "ludus humane consolationis" whose mean is "eutropolia" [*sic*], exemplified in the Bible in Zacharias 8.5.[12] This passage is deservedly well-known because it suggests the possibility of an early date for some form of Corpus Christi drama, as Siegfried Wenzel has argued most forcefully. It is also interesting theoretically: first for its possible inclusion of the drama as a form of play judged by moral or spiritual rather than aesthetic criteria; second for the way its Christian perspective manages both to include and to delimit Aristotle's secular approach to play. Play that promotes human solace is the sphere in which the Aristotelian mean and extremes constitute a basis for judgment; beyond that sort of play lie other kinds conceived in a framework of Christian understanding. Chaucer's framing structure, the playing of a game while on a pilgrimage, establishes much the same dual focus: an arena of secular activity with its own conceptual criteria bounded by a more inclusive perspective that is spiritual rather than ethical.

The Canterbury storytelling begins as a game to provide "comfort" and "mirthe." That fact alone serves to establish an initial secular delimitation, though one with its own claims to integrity. And despite the drama of spontaneity—the Knight wins by luck, the Miller interrupts, the Reeve takes offense at the Miller's story—an ordering principle appears among the first three tales, which reveal three distinct responses to the game that correspond to the Aristotelian analysis of the mean and the extremes in playing.

Particularly when read retrospectively, the portraits in the General Prologue suggest a triangulation of Knight-Miller-Reeve in regard to their social speech. The Knight, described first, "nevere yet no vileynye ne sayde / In all his lyf unto no maner wight" (I.70–71). The spectacular quadruple negative suggests possibly some prudishness but more probably the kind of decency in social behavior that was the subject of many regimens of princes and courtesy books in the fourteenth and fifteenth centuries. That social decency will be reflected in his tale, which for all its stylistic range never lapses into the "vileynye" of speech or action that abounds in the fabliaux. The Miller and Reeve appear near the very end of the portraits, in that closing collection of moral dwarfs among whom Chaucer disconcertingly puts himself. On the Miller's use of language: "His mouth as greet was as a greet forneys. / He was a janglere and a goliardeys, / And that was moost of synne and harlotries" (I.559–61). We can see now some of the resonance of that word "janglere." In Middle English it usually means someone who talks too much, often with implications of mischievous intent—gossiping, backbiting. But in Latini's *Tresor* the French *jangleor,* from which the ME word is derived, refers specifically to the person excessive in play; and to further complicate the issue *jangleor* and *jogleor* (entertainer), though etymologically distinct, are associated in Latini and in other texts.[13] In Middle English too "janglere" can refer not just to excessive talkers but to more or less professional storytellers. "Goliardeys," with its origins back to the legendary bishop Golias, patron of all those tavern-haunting renegade clerics popularized in some of the *Carmina Burana,* also has associations with publicly performed entertainment. The Miller likes to tell dirty stories, one of which we will be hearing, and if "janglere" carries any of the resonance that it has in Brunetto Latini, then Chaucer is not only describing Robin's inclinations as a speaker but giving us a particular conceptual framework for thinking about them.

Concerning the Reeve's speech the narrator says nothing. Oswald's medium of expression is the account book, the financial reckoning. His tight-lipped manipulation inspires dread. To compare with the Knight's verbal propriety and the Miller's indecent verbal extravagance we have only, appropriately, negative evidence. The Reeve's social engagement restricts itself to matters of business. He lives apparently alone, apart from others in the shadows of the trees on the heath. He rides at the back of the pilgrimage "evere" (I.622)—an emblem not only of his opposition to the Miller, who is leading the company out of town with his noisy bagpipes, but of his alienation from the group itself and their conviviality.

These characteristics delineated in the General Prologue manifest themselves in the speech-acts that make up the bulk of the first fragment. Particularly interesting is the Knight's reaction when he discovers that he is to tell the first tale:

> And whan this goode man saugh that it was so,
> As he that wys was and obedient
> To kepe his foreward by his free assent,
> He seyde, "Syn I shal bigynne the game,
> What, welcome be the cut, a Goddes name!
> Now lat us ryde, and herkneth what I seye."
> And with that word we ryden forth oure weye,

And he bigan with right a myrie cheere
His tale anon, and seyde as ye may heere.

(I.850–58)

The Knight is first of all a good man who has agreed to play a game, and he honors that agreement. The logic of his thinking in lines 853–54 merits notice: his welcoming of the cut follows upon his selection as the one to play first. I think the most probable interpretation of these lines is that the Knight is not necessarily eager to tell the first story, but having won the cut he *then* conducts himself in a manner suitable to the sense of "disport" that is appropriate to the purposes of the game. He has agreed to play, has found himself scheduled to lead off, and thus speaks according to the proper demands of recreational play. In other words, he is eutrapelic. He takes on a "myrie cheere," becomes *jucundus.* His geniality is in fact an aspect of his moral goodness, the observation of the mean in regard to the social play that the company has committed itself to. And as we know, the Knight continues to support the game and its recreational goals subsequently—in his reconciliation of Pardoner and Host and in his cutting off of the Monk's depressing tragedies. He is as loyal in the company's play as in his lords' wars.

The Aristotelian analysis of play describes human behavior, not stories, and I certainly do not claim that the game-structure of Fragment I in any way "accounts for" all that is in the tales themselves. I do think, though, that it can and should be enrolled as a factor in interpretation, and that in the case of the Knight's Tale it suggests a rationale for some features of the story that have been found problematic. One is the pervasive amount of *occupatio,* which works to keep us aware of the Knight's solicitous concern for proper behavior as he plays the game: "I wol nat letten eek noon of this route; / Lat every felawe telle his tale aboute" (I.889–90). Places where his tone seems overly clinical or even flip may reflect a kind of detachment necessary to give this story, riddled with chaos and tragedy, a tone suitable to its final focus on the joy that can follow woe. This is not to say that the Knight's attitude is Chaucer's or is not subject to irony: it is to say that the tale, considered as the earnest effort at a morally beneficial, "cheerfully turned" contribution to the game, may not be the uncontrolled stylistic hodgepodge some revisionist criticism contends it is.

Even Harry Bailly, whose literary tastes are hardly aristocratic, appreciates that with the Knight's Tale "the game is wel bigonne" (I.3117). He turns to the Monk but gets instead the Miller, the drunken buffoon who has seen his chance to turn the ideals of the first story into laughter. The tone of The Miller's Tale is one of cheerful ridicule: Alisoun turns Absolon's earnest into a "jape," says the Miller at one point (I.3390), and later the townspeople turn John the carpenter's punishment "unto a jape"

(I.3842). The tale mocks everyone, all for the sake of laughter. The Miller also derides himself and his wife, as Latini says of the *bomolochus*, intimating humorously in his prologue that as long as he can find "Goddes foyson" at home he will not worry about whether others are being equally well nourished there (I.3158–66). All is grist for his jangling, and the jangling emerges in "cherles termes" (I.3917), the kind of vulgarity universally scorned in moral treatments of proper verbal play.

Following upon the Knight's noble entertainment and the Miller's churlish frivolity comes the Reeve's vicious retaliation. He is unable to let pass the swipe at carpenters that is merely a portion of the Miller's repertoire of what Aquinas calls "playful reproach." Though opinion is not unanimous, in general the pilgrims laugh at The Miller's Tale. Only Oswald grieves at it and then spews out a morbidly self-conscious discussion of his old age. It is the first example on the pilgrimage of "sermonyng" (I.3899), preaching, which throughout *The Canterbury Tales* indicates discourse opposed to the recreative tale-telling the pilgrims have agreed to engage in. The Reeve is a sermonizer, deadly serious about everything; amusement has not mellowed him, nor humor moderated his infinite acerbity. He really is not capable of play, and his tale is so obviously an attack upon the Miller that it seems outside the spirit of the game.

Thinking of the Miller and the Reeve as excess and defect restores a medieval perspective that Chaucer himself proclaims just before the two fabliaux are told: "The Miller is a cherl; ye knowe wel this. / So was the Reve eek and othere mo, / And harlotrie they tolden bothe two" (I.3182–84). These lines group the two together because they are equidistant from the conventionally proper attitude toward the storytelling recreation. I think Chaucer makes the Miller less distasteful than the Reeve, more in keeping with the sportive circumstances of the storytelling, in contrast to many commentaries on eutrapelia that treat the buffoon as more reprehensible than the boor since seriousness is the more proper human condition than playfulness. But we should not simply rank the first three storytellers on a descending scale of decency in language or outlook, as the prevailing critical consensus on Fragment I holds. Chaucer distinguishes them first in terms of a two-part hierarchy, mean and extremes, gentil and churls, and only secondarily in terms of the differing characteristics of each extreme. I hasten to add that I do not see this conceptual pattern as allegorically reductionistic—the Reeve, for example, is not only Aristotle's boor but is also a choleric Norfolker. But the presence of details that "explain" the Reeve's temperament in terms of occupation, or physiology, or regional stereotyping need not mean that other more philosophically and ethically charged patterns are not also present. Paul A. Olson has argued that the Knight-Miller-Reeve sequence reenacts the triangulation of Theseus-Palamon-Arcite in The Knight's Tale, which is itself an exemplification of familiar medieval moral/psychological categories: reason, concupiscibility, irascibility.[14] I think those categories probably lie behind the rather more particular pattern I suggest, which seems most germane because it operates at that precise nexus of character and storytelling that is such an important feature of the *Canterbury Tales.*

The organizing principle of virtue and vices in regard to play can help illuminate logic and motive within the first fragment. It can also help us see how the action at the beginning of the *Tales* functions as a natural introduction to the entire work. Having decided to tell stories en route to Canterbury, the pilgrims begin in a way that we can recognize as staking out, so to speak, the directions that the game can take. It would have been as natural for Chaucer to think of mean and extremes as a starting point for the Canterbury stories as it was for Dante to think of mean and extremes when he came to the subject of avarice. The first three tales open up the collection and foreshadow, broadly, the range of responses to follow. There will be those pilgrims like the Knight who play the game as decently as they can, alert to their social obligation and to the kind of pleasure it is proper for a liberal person to offer. The Clerk is one such, certainly, as are the Franklin and Man of Law—these three among Anne Middleton's "new men," self-conscious about the ways in which stories can claim to please and profit.[15] The Miller's exuberant irreverence portends the Shipman's fabliau and, more significantly, the outrageous yet compelling Wife of Bath, who as Lee Patterson has argued occupies an analogous structural position of subversive play following upon a tale of authority.[16] The Reeve's performance anticipates that of those like the Friar and Summoner, who would turn an opportunity for communal recreation into a vehicle for their own personal, private hatreds. I am certainly not trying to pigeonhole all the storytellers into these three classes, for Chaucer goes far beyond them. But they are a convenient and suggestive structure to begin with.

Nor does Chaucer's exploration of how people play end with The Reeve's Tale. Both The Cook's Prologue and his fragmentary story deal principally with questions of play and truth in a way that is intellectually related to the game structure of the first fragment. Grosseteste's Latin translation of the *Ethics* introduces a fourth type of player into its chapter on eutrapelia, even though there is no mention of such a type in Aristotle: "Bomolochus autem minor est derisore"—the buffoon, the excessive player, is less wicked than the mocker.[17] Aquinas explains: "the mocker tries to put another to shame while the buffoon does not aim at this but only at getting a laugh" (1:370).

Mockery lies just at the borderline between game and earnest. On the one hand its appearance (by mistake) in the *Ethics* seems to make it a species of excessive play. On the other, its intentions are injurious rather than playful—it uses play for (earnestly) malicious purposes. Robert Holcot links *bomolochi* and *derisores* together as improper players when he discusses play, but when he examines sins of speech he mentions *derisio* only, ignoring Aristotle's defect and excess in regard to play.[18] The interest of the commentators in the relationship between play and mockery receives dramatic illustration when the Cook and Host exchange words. And of course, as Carl Lindahl has shown, that interest is not simply an academic and theoretical one; insult, defamation, was an important legal and social issue in Chaucer's day, and it is hard to imagine anyone in a court circle not sensitive to the power of language to cast suspicion, to affect reputation, even—or perhaps especially—when it appears in the guise of playfulness.

When the Cook proposes to continue the storytelling game with a "litel jape that fil in oure citee" (I.4343), it is quite clear that he wishes to continue in the same vein as the two previous speakers of "harlotrye." At this point, though, his speech appears no more degenerate or unrefined than the Miller's or Reeve's, and in fact his request to tell the next tale is rather more polite and respectful of the rules of the game than either Robin's interruption or Oswald's grouching. It is the Host who surprises us, by telling the Cook that his tale needs to be good because his cuisine hasn't been. After sundry claims about the culinary and sanitary defects of the Cook's operation, Harry Bailly ends his gibing as abruptly as he started: "But yet I pray thee, be nat wroth for game; / A man may seye ful sooth in game and pley" (I.4354–55). To which the Cook responds with another proverb, "Sooth pley, quaad pley," and tells the Host not to be "wrooth" if he subsequently should tell a story of an innkeeper. V. A. Kolve, in an important revaluation of the Cook's performance, reads this exchange as "bantering," intended by both participants "to amuse the company, not to defame each other's person," and his interpretation is a valuable corrective to the easy identification of Chaucer's point of view with the Host's.[19] I think there is an edge to the banter that he neglects. Harry's accusations come out of thin air—nothing prepares us for them except perhaps the detail of the Cook's mormal in the General Prologue, yet that defect, unlike the Miller's garrulousness and the Reeve's irascibility, has not been emphasized in the behavior of the pilgrim himself in the framing story.

The banter is public, and it ends in the Cook's laughter. But it introduces the problem of where joking stops and insult starts, the problem that concerned commentators on Aristotle's discussion of the morality of playful speech. At this point Harry Bailly becomes, perhaps, a *derisor,* a mocker, who, as Aquinas says, under cover of play seeks to embarrass someone else; because of the privileged status of speech made in play, his victims will not actually lose their reputation (a fact the mocker understands), but they will fear such a loss since the charges have been made public and could well be reasserted outside the special context of "game" which allows them to be at once both entertained and dismissed.

Or perhaps the Host's intentions remain purely playful, and his insults meant solely for amusement. Even if this were the case, he has approached the boundary at which it becomes difficult to know whether his raillery aims at *contemptus* or *ludus,* and the Cook's response is intended to alert Harry Bailly that he is in danger of stepping over into territory where claims of play can no longer provide moral protection. The proverb he cites may tacitly acknowledge that the Host's mockery has some truthful basis, but its chief purpose is to make him understand that his own verbal play at this point is on the verge of becoming the "quaad pley," the *malus ludus,* of the *derisor;* and his threatened retaliation is a reminder of the practical consequences of turning play into insult.

The Cook's Prologue, then, tells us as much about the Host as about the Cook, and while there is no developed equation of either character with any traditional type of player of games, the issue raised in the exchange is a logical extension of the game given medieval thinking about playful speech. We have seen the mean and the extremes in regard to play, and now Chaucer brings to the fore one important aspect of excessive play not yet considered, the problem of drawing the line between game and earnest when playful language impugns someone else. The exchange occurs in a prologue that promises the telling of a "jape" in an atmosphere of "joye" and coarse hilarity, which is Chaucer's dramatic equivalent of the commentary treatment of mockery in the context of excessive play, whose chief representative in the first fragment is the Miller. The Miller has insulted the Reeve only as part of a desire to reduce everything to laughter. The Host's more pointed attack on the Cook claims similar status as "game and pley" yet is of a different order; it is what scholastic commentators, I think, would have defined as *derisio* rather than *bomolochia.*

What remains of The Cook's Tale explores in a different way the tension between play and seriousness established in the Prologue. We meet Perkyn Revelour, who at least initially seems to evoke the atmosphere of The Miller's Tale: he has something of Alisoun's coltish manner and of Absolon's tastes in entertainment—he is always singing, hopping, leaping, dancing, playing (I.4375–84). But as the story develops, Perkyn's play begins to appear both more insistent and more insidious. It usurps his work time rather than supporting it with recreational refreshment; it includes dicing, the classic evil game of medieval moral treatises, which in turn leads to the serious crime of theft. His playing becomes "revel," "riot," and finally the master victualer releases the unreliable apprentice from his service.

In only fifty-eight lines The Cook's Tale presents a view of play that is quite complex—the fragment, as Kolve has argued, is certainly not the unremitting portrait of debased life that many critics have taken it to be. A variety of terms ("pleyen," "disport," "revel," "riot") and a variety of kinds of play (dancing, singing, public merrymaking, tavern-haunting, dicing, and by implication activities "paramour") appear in a rapid sequence that in general turns progressively more disreputable but that retains a certain ambiguity throughout. The fragment's antepenultimate line says that Perkyn's friend "lovede dys, and revel, and disport" (I.4420), a strangely ameliorative sequence of nouns given the context—"disport," after all, is the term Harry Bailly uses to define the legitimate benefits of the Canterbury game, and elsewhere in Chaucer it has quite positive associations. The effect is meant to be deliberately disquieting, I think, and its implications extend beyond the tale itself to reflect on the previous fabliaux and their framing action, in which the Miller's play and the Reeve's earnest were so readily distinguishable. The Cook's Tale complicates such distinctions by presenting play action that is sometimes buoyant and recreative and other times anti-social and destructive and by making it difficult to say exactly when one sort becomes the other, when "disport" turns into "revel" or "revel" into "riot." The tale reenacts the problem that The Cook's Prologue presented in terms of playful speaking rather than playful actions. In either case, whether the playing is in words or deeds (*dicta vel facta,* in the language of the commentaries), the moral issue concerned medieval thinkers and writers because like Freud they knew that jokes express more than themselves, like Natalie Zemon Davis they knew that forms of play, even when serving overtly only to recreate or let off steam, have serious social implications.[20]

The appearance of the Cook at the end of the first fragment, then, follows logically upon the previous sequence of tale-telling if we see it in light of medieval discussions of the morality of play: after presenting the mean and the extremes, Chaucer takes up the question of distinguishing between excessive play and mockery, the point at which distinctions between play and seriousness become most difficult and yet most necessary to make. This pattern, I would stress, works more descriptively than normatively. The first fragment is proleptic: it introduces us to a range of attitudes toward the game that will become ever more complicated as the *Canterbury Tales* progresses. In this regard The Cook's Prologue and Tale in particular point toward some of the most problematic and fascinating of the Canterbury performances, as some of Chaucer's richest characters, notably the Wife and the Pardoner, force us to look very closely at the ways in which their playing and their truthtelling are related.

Throughout the *Tales* the game is usually the norm. In places Chaucer reminds us, in one way or another, that beyond the game lies the pilgrimage—perhaps most obviously in the Pardoner's performance and exchange with the Host, where the breakdown of social agreeableness occurs in a context of phony promises of what should be a goal of the pilgrimage itself, spiritual absolution. But such episodes are the exception rather than the rule, though perhaps all the more telling for their infrequency; for the most part of the linking passages are filled with the language of game and obligation, and with Harry Bailly's energetic and often overbearing presence as director of entertainment.[21] But toward the end of the work—and here I evade a variety of questions concerning order and closure—something happens to the game. At its fullest this development encompasses the last three fragments.[22] I want to mention, rather briefly, some aspects of Fragment IX only, which present a deliberately disturbing recapitulation of some of the central features of the framing action in Fragment I. Part of Chaucer's idea of the Canterbury game is its degeneration; The Manciple's Prologue enacts such debasement of social conviviality and playful speech as to make us uneasy with the game as a sufficient ordering principle, and correspondingly his tale ends in admonitions not to tell stories of any sort.

The contrasts with the first fragment are quite specific. Although drunkenness appears throughout the pilgrimage and tales, drunkenness as it relates to storytelling is foregrounded most extensively in Fragments I and IX. The Miller's interruption is clearly due in part to his inebriation, yet whatever loss of control and decorum it implies in his case, he at least remains articulate, a participant in the game. The Cook's drunkenness in Fragment IX results in silence, sleep, nonparticipation. It is a more extreme version of the loss of reason that inebriation causes. Both Miller and Cook are "pale" because of drink (I.3120, IX.20), but the physical symptoms in the Cook's case are developed further to include glazed eyes and foul breath. A single line informs us that the Miller can scarcely keep his balance on horseback (I.3121). The Cook's transportation problems get substantially more attention: first Harry's notice that he is about to fall off his horse, then the Manciple's allusion to his jousting at the quintain, and finally his response to the Manciple's insults, a wordless angry twisting of the head that sends him off his horse into the mire.

Whatever the reasons for the incompleteness of his tale at the start of the game, whatever the order in which Chaucer actually composed the scenes, the contrast between the Cook of Fragment I and the Cook of Fragment IX is striking and indicative of the substantially different view of Canterbury conviviality in the later fragments. The Cook now becomes the featured non-speaker among the pilgrims, excused by the Host from participation in the game on the grounds of inebriation. His fall from his horse is the most potent image in The Manciple's Prologue of the social behavior of the company having gone awry. In the muck lies the "hevy dronken cors" of a Canterbury pilgrim. Images of death, judgment, and hell flicker throughout the Prologue—the thief who might come upon the Cook, the association of his open mouth with hellmouth.[23] Whereas the Miller's drunkenness leads to a story that prompts laughter, the Cook's leads only to "lakke of speche" and reminders of mortality. Whereas the Host speaks disdainfully of Robin's condition in Fragment I, in Fragment IX he laughs "wonder loude" at the situation and offers a paean to alcohol: good drink will turn rancor into "accord and love"; Bacchus can "turnen ernest into game" (IX.95–100). The language here echoes, disconcertingly, what had earlier been the province of the storytelling. In Fragment I the narrator had warned us not to "maken ernest of game" (I.3186) in regard to the Miller's and Reeve's fabliaux; the pilgrims had "been acorded" (I.818) to the Host's proposal for a game of stories to provide pleasure. In Fragment IX alcohol replaces storytelling as the source of recreation and harmony, and the master of revels who scorned the Miller's drunkenness now worships at the altar of Bacchus.

In the first fragment the Cook had warned the Host about the dangers of play that comes too close to the truth and in so doing had exposed a problem in the social uses of language well known to medieval commentators and moralists. In the ninth fragment too the Cook is a victim of insult, but here with no such teasing ambiguity as in his exchange with Harry Bailly. The Manciple "openly," to use the Host's own terminology (IX.70), reproves the Cook for his drunkenness and hurls the kind of invective at him that Carl Lindahl has shown is extreme in the rhetoric of Chaucer's churls, not to mention dangerous in real life (93–96), and that the Parson condemns as fostering disaccord and anger (X.621–30). Only when the Host reminds the Manciple that the Cook might similarly defame him does he reverse himself, suddenly announce "I seyde it in my bourde," and offer more wine to the Cook to placate him. What in the first fragment is a comic but subtle exploration of the problem of determining a borderline between play and insult, in which Harry self-consciously advertises his mockery as play, becomes in the ninth an instance of insult that, only in response to someone else's warning, attempts cynically and transparently to cover itself as jest. The secular norms of play no longer function as a governing communal standard but appear now as merely a convenient excuse for verbal attack, a self-interested afterthought.

Aristotelian, recreational justifications of play are by definition self-limiting. When play becomes excessive or offensive it can no longer claim the moral or social legitimacy extended to it via the *Nichomachean Ethics*. The context for thinking about such speech and action might well then shift to a different and more familiar kind of moral perspective, one we see emerging in the course of Fragment IX—first in the degeneration and thus the delegitimizing of the secular conviviality epitomized by the playing of a game, then in the fate of the crow punished for speaking imprudently, and finally in the Manciple's concluding moralizing, a harrangue on the theme of "keep wel thy tonge" (IX.319, 333, 362). The language at the end of Fragment IX is not the language of Aristotelian commentary on play, not the language of game and social contract that has been dominant throughout the *Tales*—it is rather the language of Christian commentary on the sins of the tongue and on the virtues of *custodia linguae*.[24] The Manciple's Prologue begins with an image of the Cook's yawning open mouth that the Manciple asks him to "Hoold cloos" (IX.37), and his tale ends with an image of teeth and lips "wall[ing] a tonge" (IX.323); in a sense the whole fragment enacts the closing of a mouth, the shutting down of speech in and for "compaignye."

As we have seen, the Aristotelian framework is a view of speech that accommodates literature as a social phenomenon. Without the category of eutrapelic play, whatever Aristotle's original notions about its range of applicability, medieval thinkers found room for those kinds of lyric and narrative that give public pleasure. The Christian tradition of the sins of the tongue has no such comparable category. Playful speech, words and deeds that provide pleasure and recreation, are subsumed without a strict logic that forces all language either into words of morality and devotion or words of worldly vanity. Yet in a sense that difference, though it is thrust upon as almost brutally in Fragment IX, has been implicitly a factor all along in understanding the *Canterbury Tales* insofar as the double frame of a game played on a pilgrimage has always allowed for, and sometimes actively encouraged, reflection on the relationship of the one to the other.

This is where Chaucer, though he followed the *Decameron* in choosing to incorporate his stories into the playing of a game, parts company from Boccaccio; and Donald Howard has written acutely about this difference:

> The frame [of the *Decameron*] puts a parenthesis around the world of story: the stories are told in an aura of moral neutrality. The frame (the escape from the plague) is static, and as an image pessimistic. But in the *Canterbury Tales* the frame of the pilgrimage to Canterbury (and the Heavenly Jerusalem) is dynamic, as an image optimistic: and the inner form, the storytelling game, is not an escape—*it* is what reveals the darker side of human nature. . . .[25]

The *Decameron* begins and ends with the author's voice explaining the conditions under which his collection of fictions claims value. The stories are for idle ladies; they will provide pleasure and profit *if* they are read in the appropriate circumstances; and so on. The *Canterbury Tales* in effect makes Boccaccio's authorial commentary a part of the drama. The very efforts at isolation of a particular arena for fiction that Howard, and earlier Singleton, argued as central to the *Decameron* become themselves subject to scrutiny in Chaucer's collection. He is not content to let Aristotelian and scholastic ideas about permissible play and legitimate recreation suffice.

What he creates instead, his idea of the Canterbury game, is an image of social and secular conviviality that establishes itself as a norm for most of the pilgrimage but ultimately degenerates in a way that calls into question its adequacy as a means of communication. What he creates is an image not just of how fictions function within society but how social discourse operates within and moves between the secular and the sacred. There is no simple formula to explain how the *Canterbury Tales* enacts that movement, particularly at the end. The game as initially established provides a set of respectable social norms, though easily subject to abuse or disruption. Occasionally a passage reminds us of what lies beyond the game. In Fragment IX the behavior of the company turns cynical and offensive, and in Fragment X the Parson speaks with hostility toward the telling of fables. He seems to reject the game, to point to another kind of discourse. But his speaking too is a *tale,* and for all his self-separation from what has preceded, the pilgrims agree that he should end the storytelling; they see his particular kind of wisdom as appropriate, not discontinuous. The Parson's Tale is both somehow within and beyond the game, and in spite of what happens in Fragment IX the structure implies that there is at least some common ground between the earlier fictions and his own "meditacioun." We know that Boccaccio's brigata takes time out from storytelling to pray and reflect on religious matters, but we do not hear the prayers and meditations because they are not part of the game. The final complexity of Chaucer's Canterbury game is the difficult of knowing when it's over, of knowing, even in the face of his Retraction, how sharply to distinguish the worldly vanity from the devotion.

Notes

1. Lanham, "Game, Play, and High Seriousness in Chaucer's Poetry," *English Studies* 48 (1967): 1–24; Josipovici, "Fiction and Game in the *Canterbury Tales,*" *Critical Quarterly* 7 (1965): 185–97; Lindahl, *Earnest Games: Folkloric Patterns in the Canterbury Tales* (Bloomington: Indiana Univ. Press, 1987); Kendrick, *Chaucerian Play: Comedy and Control in the Canterbury Tales* (Berkeley and Los Angeles: Univ. of California Press, 1988); Howard, *Chaucer: His Life, His Works, His World* (New York: Dutton, 1987), pp. 421–26.

2. Olson, *Literature as Recreation in the Later Middle Ages* (Ithaca: Cornell Univ. Press, 1982).

3. All Chaucer quotations are from *The Riverside Chaucer,* 3rd ed., gen. ed. Larry D. Benson (Boston: Houghton Mifflin, 1987).

4. For the history of the Latin text of the *Ethics* and the medieval commentary tradition, see the introduction to Aristotle, *L'Ethique à Nicomaque,* trans. R. A. Gauthier and J. Y. Jolif, 2 vols. in 4 (Louvain: Publications Universitaires, 1970), 1.1.111–46, and Georg Wieland, "The Reception and Interpretation of Aristotle's

Ethics," *The Cambridge History of Later Medieval Philosophy,* edited by N. Kretzmann et al. (Cambridge: Cambridge Univ. Press, 1982), pp. 657–72. On the influence of Aquinas's *Summa* see Martin Grabmann, "Das Weiterleben und Weiterwirken des moraltheologischen Schrifttums des hl. Thomas von Aquin im Mittelalter," *Divus Thomas* 25 (1947): 3–28.

5. *Commentary on the Nicomachean Ethics,* trans. C. I. Litzinger, 2 vols. (Chicago: Regnery, 1964), 1:368–69.

6. "Iocundi uocantur eutrapeli, qui conuenienter et delectabiliter se habent in ludis et conuersacionibus hominum." *Tabula super decem libros ethicorum.* Cambridge: Gonville and Caius College MS 462/735, f. 29v.

7. "Eutrapeli ueri sunt homines intendentes ludum ad bonum et ad bonos mores." *Sententia declarata super librum Ethicorum.* Vatican City: Vatican Library MS Urbin. lat. 222, f. 251r.

8. "Gengleour est celui ki gengle entre les gens a ris et a gieu, et moke soi et sa feme et ses fiz et tous autres." *Li Livres dou Tresor,* ed. Francis J. Carmody, Univ. of California Publications in Modern Philology, vol. 22 (Berkeley and Los Angeles: Univ. of California Press, 1948), p. 204.

9. "Il entent ici par comedies aucuns gieux comme sont ceulz ou. i. homme represente Saint Pol, l'autre Judas, l'autre un hermite, et dit chascun son personnage. . . . Et aucunes fois en telz giex l'en dit de laides paroles, ordes injurieuses et deshonestes." *Le Livre de Ethiques,* ed. A. D. Menut (New York: Stechert, 1940), p. 271.

10. Albertus Magnus, *Super ethica commentum et quaestiones,* ed. W. Kübel, *Opera omnia* 14/1, fasc. 1 (Münster: Aschendorff, 1968), p. 297.

11. Johannes Buridanus, *Quaestiones super octo libros Politicorum Aristotelis* (Paris, 1513; reprint, Frankfurt: Minerva, 1969), ff. 89r–v.

12. Robert Holkott, *Super libros sapientiae* (Hagenau, 1494; reprint, Frankfurt: Minerva, 1974), lectio 172D. For a better text see Siegfried Wenzel, "An Early Reference to a Corpus Christi Play," *Modern Philology* 74 (1977): 390. I discuss *distinctiones* on play in more detail in a forthcoming article, "Plays as Play."

13. Raleigh Morgan, Jr., "Old French *jogleor* and Kindred Terms. Studies in Mediaeval Romance Lexicology," *Romance Philology* 7 (1953–54): 290–91, 304–5.

14. Olson, *The Canterbury Tales and the Good Society* (Princeton: Princeton Univ. Press, 1986), pp. 70–71.

15. Middleton, "Chaucer's 'New Men' and the Good of Literature in the *Canterbury Tales,"* in *Literature and Society,* ed. Edward W. Said (Baltimore: The Johns Hopkins Univ. Press, 1980), pp. 15–56.

16. Patterson, " 'No man his reson herde': Peasant Consciousness, Chaucer's Miller, and the Structure of the *Canterbury Tales,"* *South Atlantic Quarterly* 86 (1987): 457–95.

17. The Latin text of Aristotle is in Albertus Magnus, 297.

18. Holkott, *Super libros sapientiae,* lectiones 172D and 27A.

19. Kolve, *Chaucer and the Imagery of Narrative: The First Five Canterbury Tales* (Stanford, Calif.: Stanford Univ. Press, 1984), p. 267.

20. Davis, "The Reasons of Misrule," *Society and Culture in Early Modern France* (Stanford, Calif.: Stanford Univ. Press, 1975), pp. 97–123.

21. See Kendrick, *Chaucerian Play,* 102–15, for discussion of the Host as a master of revels and Lord of Misrule.

22. See James M. Dean, "Dismantling the Canterbury Book," *PMLA* 100 (1985): 746–62, who cites previous work on the question of closure in Fragments VIII–X.

23. Rodney Delasanta, "Penance and Poetry in the *Canterbury Tales,"* *PMLA*

93 (1978): 245; Roy J. Pearcy, "Does the Manciple's Prologue Contain a Reference to Hell's Mouth?" *English Language Notes* 11 (1974): 167–75.

24. V. J. Scattergood, "The Manciple's Manner of Speaking," *Essays in Criticism* 24 (1974): 124–46.

25. Howard, "Fiction and Religion in Boccaccio and Chaucer," *Journal of the American Academy of Religion* 47 (1979), Supplement:320. Cf. Charles S. Singleton, "On *Meaning* in the *Decameron*," *Italica* 21 (1944): 117–24.

Augustinian Poetic Theory and the Chaucerian Imagination

SHERRON E. KNOPP

> Suche fantasies ben in myn hede
> So I not what is best to doo.
> *—Book of the Duchess*

The old debates about Chaucer's poems have to do with thematic coherence (sorrow and consolation in the *Book of the Duchess,* for example), with character psychology (the relationship between the dreamer and the Black Knight), with structural unity (the juxtaposition of the narrator's "story" with Ovid's and the Black Knight's in three segments of different lengths, tones, and styles), and with the artistic self-consciousness of narrators speaking more or less in the poet's name. The new debates, by contrast, focus on the lack of thematic coherence (the inarticulateness of sorrow, the absence or failure of consolation), on characters as rhetorical voices rather than integrated personalities (and hence the lack of any psychological relationship between the dreamer and the Black Knight), on tonal, stylistic and structural discontinuities, and, finally, on a "poetics" located not in the self-conscious remarks of a narrator/poet but embodied in the self-reflexive language of the text itself.[1] In the old view, the poet of the dream visions can be seen paying uncomfortable homage to the highly rhetorical styles and limited *matere* of classical and medieval literary traditions, while showing a penchant already for the kinds of psychological and social realism that prompted Kittredge to call *Troilus and Criseyde* the first psychological novel and to see Chaucer's pilgrims as *dramatic personae* in "a kind of Human Comedy."[2] In the new view, the preoccupations of the dream poems with literary traditions and rhetorical styles culminate in a *Troilus* obsessed with the indecipherability of "olde bokes" and the insurmountable difficulties of storytelling, and in a *Canterbury Tales* which pretends to abandon the treacherous surfaces of written texts for the solid ground of empirical observation only to disappear in a world of quicksand where accidents do not point any more reliably to essences

91

than verbal signs signify, where distinctions between "life" and "art" are collapsed beyond recovery.[3]

In both views, the dream poems have been regarded as Chaucer's clearest and most explicit inquiries into poetic theory.[4] But the question remains: how *are* we going to talk about Chaucer's texts? Are we going to talk about characters and their personalities or about voices and their rhetorical strategies? Are we going to talk about social and psychological verisimilitude or about the failures of language to refer to anything outside itself at all? And where in all this do the so-called "historical" or exegetical critics fit in, whose polemical arguments for reading medieval literature as doctrinal allegory or ethical exempla Lee Patterson calls "the great unfinished business of Medieval Studies," disdained, but never adequately answered by either the New Critics of the past or those who consider themselves more theoretically sophisticated in the present?[5] The problem with efforts to answer these questions is that what we invoke as theory is either vague and subjective—thematic readings of the poet/ narrator's self-conscious remarks about art—or not poetic theory at all— grammar, rhetoric, logic/dialectic, nominalist philosophy, for example. Chaucer at his clearest and most explicit, moreover, is notoriously neither clear nor explicit. But the second part of the problem may be a function of the first.

I want to do several things in this essay. First, I want to affirm the radical bookishness of Chaucer's poems, or rather, more particularly, their radical, bookishly theoretical preoccupations with language and art, although these are not the preoccupations of either the deconstructionists or the exegetical critics. At the same time, I want to argue that the social and psychological "realism" earlier critics saw in Chaucer's poems is also there. Far from being a delusion of nineteenth-century critical naïveté, poetic "realism"—the power of language to create intellectually convincing and emotionally compelling images—is in fact the central preoccupation of medieval poetic theory. The most important and influential expression of this theory is not any of the manuals of grammar or rhetoric or any of the philosophical or theological discussions of language (including Augustine's *De doctrina christiana,* despite its elevation to near-canonical status first by D. W. Robertson, Jr., and more recently by deconstructionist critics), but Augustine's discussion of Virgil in Book I of the *Confessions.*

In a passage that contrasts his first (useful) lessons in reading and writing with his later (useless) studies of Latin literature, Augustine denounces the adventures of Aeneas as unreal and untrue, implicating them in his intellectual wanderings from the truth and reality of Scripture, and repudiates his intense emotional reponse to Dido as "fornication" against God:

[20] For those first lessons were better certainly, because more certain; by them I obtained, and still retain, the power of reading what I find written, and myself writing what I will; whereas in the others, I was forced to learn the wanderings [*errores*] of one Aeneas, forgetful of my own, and to weep for dead Dido, because she killed herself for love; the while, with dry eyes, I endured my miserable self dying among these things, far from Thee, O God my life. [21] For what more miserable than a miserable being who commiserates not himself; weeping the death of Dido for love to Aeneas, but weeping not his own death for want of love to Thee. . . . I committed fornication against Thee, and all around me thus fornicating there echoed "Well done! well done!" for the friendship of this world is fornication against Thee; and "Well done! well done!" echoes on till one is ashamed not to be thus a man. And for all this I wept not, I who wept for Dido slain. . . . And if forbid to read all this I was grieved that I might not read what grieved me. Madness [*dementia*] like this is thought a higher and a richer learning, than that by which I learned to read and write. [22] . . . Let not either buyers or sellers of grammar-learning cry out against me. For if I question them whether it be true that Aeneas came on a time to Carthage, as the poet tells, the less learned will reply that they know not, the more learned that he never did. But should I ask with what letters the name "Aeneas" is written, every one who has learnt this will answer me aright, as to the signs which men have conventionally settled. If, again, I should ask which might be forgotten with least detriment to the concerns of life, reading and writing or these poetic fictions [*figmenta*]? who does not foresee what all must answer who have not wholly forgotten themselves? I sinned, then, when, when as a boy I preferred those empty to those more profitable studies, or rather loved the one and hated the other. "One and one, two"; "two and two, four"; this was to me a hateful sing-song: "the wooden horse lined with armed men," and "the burning of Troy," and "Creusa's shade and sad similitude," were the choice spectacle of my vanity [*dulcissimum spectaculum vanitatis:* a most delightful spectacle of vanity]. (*Confessions* I.13.20–23)[6]

Stretching back behind Augustine's indictment of Virgil, of course, is Plato's magisterial indictment of poetry in the *Republic*. In the corporeal temporal world of Platonic thought, where objects are shadows of incorporeal universal forms, the images of poetry (φαντασίαι) are shadows of shadows, imitations of imitations, illusory, unreal, untrue: "Do you suppose, then, that if a man were able to produce both the exemplar and the semblance, he would be eager to abandon himself to the fashioning of phantoms and set this in the forefront of his life as the best thing he had?" (*Rep.* X.599A).[7] The emotions aroused by such images, are, in turn, unhealthy and potentially immoral: "In regard to the emotions of sex and anger, and all the appetites and pains and pleasures of the soul . . . the effect of poetic imitation is the same. For it waters and fosters these feelings when what we ought to do is to dry them up, and it establishes them as our rulers when they ought to be ruled, to the end that we may be better and happier men instead of worse and more miserable" (*Rep.* X.606D). Augustine's compelling testimony of the extent to which the most illustrious poem in classical antiquity made him "worse and more

miserable" instead of "better and happier" generated the cliché of patristic and scholastic diatribe—*inanes fabulae, figmenta vana, ineptiae
poetarum, mendaces, spectaculum vanitatis, phantasiae, dulce venenum*—and created the paradigm for subsequnt discussions of poetry in the
Middle Ages, including the dramatic opening of Boethius's *Consolation of
Philosophy* with its intellectually confused and emotionally overwrought
narrator surrounded on his sickbed by the siren Muses of Poetry.[8]

It is this theory that is at the heart of Chaucer's famous bookishness. It
motivates his clearest and most explicit theoretical preoccupations with
art as artifice, as game, as conjuring trick, as self-referential linguistic
construct, and it motivates his equally clear and explicit preoccupations
with the various doctrinal and ethical attempts to defend the artifice and
conjuring tricks of poetry by enrolling them in the language arts of the
trivium—grammar (the correct use of language), logic/dialectic (the intellectual discovery of truth), and rhetoric (emotional persuasion to moral
action). This academic strategy (which the exegetical critics take to be
poetic theory) gives poetry a share of philosophical legitimacy: it becomes
a vehicle for truth ("Al that is writen is writen for oure doctrine," the poet
declares at the end of the *Canterbury Tales*), or an impetus for moral
choice ("Repeyreth hom fro worldly vanyte," he exhorts at the end of
Troilus). But the academic strategy itself presupposes the original negative
Platonic/Augustinian attitude towards images as illusion and delusion, that
is, towards art as conjuring trick.[9] This attitude is articulated with equal
prominence in Chaucer's poetry. The devil boasts of it in The Friar's Tale,
for example:

> Somtyme lyk a man, or lyk an ape,
> Or lyk an angel kan I ryde or go.
> It is no wonder thyng thogh it be so;
> A lowsy jogelour kan deceyve thee,
> And pardee, yet kan I moore craft than he,
>
> (III.1464–68)

and the Franklin takes it for granted when he compares the magic of
Aurelius—

>   . . . swich folye
> As in oure dayes is nat worth a flyc—
> For hooly chirches feith in oure bileve
> Ne suffreth noon illusioun us to greve
>
> (V.1131–34)

to those "sciences / By whiche men make diverse apparences, / Swiche as
thise subtile tregetoures pleye" (V.1139–41). Augustinian poetic theory
and the philosophical defenses against it are more than thematic motifs for

Chaucer: he subjects both to theoretical interrogation, as I will show before I am done.

At the same time, Augustinian poetic theory, together with the classical texts that provoked it (Virgil's *Aeneid* and Ovid's *Metamorphoses* above all), is also at the heart of Chaucer's famous, if currently somewhat tarnished, psychological and social "realism." It motivates and defines Chaucer's very clear and very explicit theoretical preoccupations with art as drama and passion, that is, with art in the Aristotelian sense as mimesis and instrument for emotional catharsis. If these are not quite synonymous with "realism," they are essential ingredients in it, and they categorically distinguish the classical texts of Ovid and Virgil not only from the *Ovide moralisé* and the various allegorical readings of Virgil produced in the Middle Ages, but from other kinds of poetic compositions, both courtly and philosophical, from the *Consolation of Philosophy* to the *Romance of the Rose,* that Augustinian poetic theory made possible and that Chaucer looked to as models for poetry.

Chaucer's preoccupations with this poetic theory are evident from his earliest narrative poems, in the kinds of works his narrators read and in the ways they read them. In what follows, I want to look in particular at the Ovidian section of the *Book of the Duchess,* not in the usual (even theoretically sophisticated) way as an example of narrative manipulation, but more precisely and explicitly as a model of theoretical interrogation. A similar argument could be made about the Virgilian section of the *House of Fame,* but for the purposes of this essay I will limit myself to the earlier poem. In both cases Chaucer's narrators do not simply, and ineptly, retell Ovidian and Virgilian stories. Rather, like Augustine in the *Confessions,* they encounter the drama and passion of the real things, and their responses—fascinated, baffled, terrified, comically inappropriate—reveal as much about the constraints of Platonic/Augustinian poetic theory as they do about Chaucer's theoretical interest in the Aristotelian art of the *Metamorphoses* and the *Aeneid.* In their sporadic efforts to discover a doctrine or discern a moral—to turn poetry into philosophy like the authors of the *Ovide moralisé* and the exegetical interpreters of Virgil— Chaucer's narrators succeed only in magnifying the distance between poetry and philosophy. For the most part, they are enthralled by the drama and passion of these poems, and because they are enthralled, they are caught up in all the well-known indictments of poetry: it traffics in fantasies and illusions, it contains no truth, it arouses the passions to no moral end. What happens to them is part parody, part satire of the intellectual dangers described by Plato and Augustine and dramatized by Boethius, but their very dilemmas, together with their repeated expressions of wonder and terror in the face of an art they are unable to explain or understand, point clearly and precisely to Chaucer's own fascination with an art that defies the categories of Platonic/Augustinian theory.

Judged primarily as a retelling of Ovid, the narrative in the *Book of the Duchess* elicits adjectives like "reductive" and "solipsistic."[10] It is not just the omission of the metamorphosis or the lopsided significance Chaucer's narrator attaches to Morpheus that derails his story, although these are extremely revealing indicators of what he fails to understand about Ovid's art. It is the reductiveness. Ovid's complex dramatic plot (like Virgil's on a larger scale) unfolds swiftly, propelled by human emotions at a pitch so intense that mere summary can barely do justice to it. Ceyx's intention to travel over the sea to consult the oracles at Claros precipitates confessions of dread from Alcyone, daughter of the wind Aeolus, and reassurances of mutual love on both sides. The graphic description of the storm that destroys Ceyx's ship and its youthful crew magnifies the stark horror of his brutal death. The poignant irony of Alcyone's unwavering prayers for his safe return finally moves even a goddess to pity.[11] In the hands of the *Duchess* narrator, the rich complexity and immediacy of the Ovidian drama is compressed into a ludicrously rapid, mechanical outline of events:

> This was the tale: There was a king
> That highte Seys, and had a wif,
> The beste that mighte bere lyf,
> And this quene highte Alcyone.
> So it befil thereafter soone
> This king wol wenden over see.
> To tellen shortly, whan that he
> Was in the see thus in this wise,
> Such a tempest gan to rise
> That brak her mast and made it falle,
> And clefte her ship, and dreinte hem alle . . .

(62–72)

On the one hand, his reductive plot summary fails to capture anything like Ovid's dramatic power—in Ovid the storm is a brilliant tour de force of mimetic art, deliberately calculated to challenge comparison with Homer and Virgil. On the other hand, the narrator's reduction of the characters to rank and proper name and his reduction of the plot to a list of verbs points to his fascinated awareness that the story is not "about" allegorical truth or moral virtue; it is "about" what *happens,* and this dramatic immediacy is part of what makes Ovid's tale "a wonder thing."[12]

The story is also "about" extreme emotions, exemplified in the eyes of many critics by the metamorphosis at the end, which is itself an image for the transforming power of poetic catharsis. That Chaucer's narrator would omit the metamorphosis is not surprising: his experience of powerful emotion translates as solipsism. But his solipsism, like his reductiveness, is a direct response to the emotional power of Ovid's real-seeming fiction—to the pathos and poignance of Alcyone's plight—and it is so intense that it incapacitates him from proceeding effectively with his own summary. When he gets to Alcyone waiting at home for her drowned husband, his initial brisk pace lurches to a halt, and for almost fifty lines he wallows helplessly in vicarious identification with Alcyone's sorrow:

> . . . certes it were a pitous thing
> To telle her hertely sorowful lif
> That she had, this noble wif . . .
>
> (84–86)

> Such sorowe this lady to her tok
> That trewly I, that made this book,
> Had such pittee and such rowthe
> To rede hir sorwe that, by my trowthe,
> I ferde the worse al the morwe
> Aftir to thenken on hir sorwe.
>
> (95–100)

Having turned to the Ovidian tale in the first place to find release from the "sorwful ymagynacioun" that was making him a "mased thyng," he finds instead that his emotional surrender to Alcyone has only compounded the initial problem: "I ferde the worse al the morwe." It is hard not to hear in this confession an echo of Plato's warning about the effects of poetic imitation: it "waters and fosters" feelings that are better dried up, making one "worse and more miserable" instead of "better and happier." It is also hard not to recognize in his response to Alcyone a reenactment of Augustine's to Dido.

The Platonic/Augustinian critique of poetry as empty illusion, *figmenta vana,* is implicit in the poem from its opening, in the narrator's complaints about "so many an ydel thoght" and "[s]uche fantasies." Although critics usually see the patchwork quilt of lines lifted almost whole from French love poetry, from Froissart's *Paradys d'Amours* and Machaut's *Fonteinne amoureuse* especially, as a sign that this is early (i.e., imitative) Chaucer, the borrowed lines may in fact confirm and illustrate the severity of the narrator's "mased" condition. As one who has overdosed on the images of poetry, his senses no longer respond to the world outside him: "I take no kep / Of nothing, how hyt cometh or gooth" (6–7); his reason no longer discriminates between good and bad: "Ne me nys nothyng leef nor looth" (8); even his emotions no longer respond to external stimuli: "Al is ylyche good to me— / Joye or sorowe, wherso hyt be— / For I have felynge in nothyng" (9–11). For all the debate about whether the cause of his sorrow is love or bereavement, the answer can only be neither: it belongs wholly to the realm of "fantasies."[13] Augustine identifies his similar "mased" condition in the *Confessions* as *dementia,* and in *De musica* he describes how the imagination produces images which "react with each other, and boil up, you might say, with varying and conflicting winds of purpose" until they become merely "images of images, to which we give the name phantasms" (VI.11.32).[14] In this context, the otherwise inexplicable vagueness of Chaucer's narrator about the "sicknesse" that troubles him and the "physicien but oon" who can heal him makes perfect sense:

> But men myght axe me why soo
> I may not slepe and what me is.
> But natheles, who aske this
> Leseth his asking trewely.
> Myselven can not telle why
> The sothe; but trewly, as I gesse,
> I holde hit . . .
>
> (30–36)

The abrupt loss of forward momentum in his syntax and rhythm mirrors his apparent disorientation as he temporizes and speculates, looking in his mind for an explanation that might prove adequate: "but trewly," "I gesse," "I holde hit." Pulled from the fog of "ydel thoght" and "fantasies" he has just complained about, neither the sickness nor its physician have any concrete reality, and they do not interest him much: "Passe we over. . . . Our first mater is good to kepe" (41, 43). That "first mater" is "sorwful ymagynacioun" itself.

If Chaucer were at all allegorically inclined, the Muses of Poetry would be hovering around the narrator's bed and Lady Philosophy would appear to drive them away with a scathing diatribe against the "sweet poison" that "kill[s] the fruitful harvest of reason with the sterile thorns of the passions," that "do[es] not liberate the minds of men from disease, but merely accustom[s] them to it" (I Prosa 1).[15] For Boethius is prostrated by this same Augustinian "sickness" at the beginning of the *Consolation:* the "maladye of perturbacion" has "crept into thi thought," as Lady Philosopphy diagnoses it in Chaucer's Middle English translation (I Prosa 6.34–35), echoing Augustine's designation of the emotions as *perturbationes animae* or *mentis.* In the non-allegorical world of the *Duchess,* however, the Muses of Poetry do not assume material form outside the narrator's mind, and Lady Philosophy does not appear in response to his complaints to banish them. Instead, when Chaucer's narrator sits upright in his bed and bids an anonymous attendant, "reche me a book, / A romaunce," his unwise request is granted with prompt, unfussy compliance: "and he it me tok / To rede" (47–49).

With no Lady Philosophy to stop him, Chaucer's narrator, like the youthful Augustine, abandons himself to the seductions of fiction. The book he chooses is a "romaunce" (48), a collection of "fables" (52), about "olde tyme" (53) and the "lawe of kinde" (56), about "quenes lives, and . . . kinges, / And many other thinges smale" (58–59). There is something almost apologetic in his admission, "This book ne spak but of such thinges" (57), as though he doesn't quite know how to justify an art that is unconcerned to explicate the meaning and significance of "such thinges" in the academic fashion. It also suggests perhaps a dim anxiety that there are better things to read than a book whose only value is the world of *kinde,* and healthier motives for reading than vicarious participation in the emotions of fictional characters.[16] From the Augustinian perspective, it comes as no surprise that his grief for Alcyone causes him to "fer[e] the worse al the morwe." Nor should it come as any surprise when his assent to the seeming reality of Ovid's mimetic art leads him to fall—spectacularly—into the trap of mistaking fiction for truth. "[I]f I question . . . whether it be true that Aeneas came on a time to Carthage, as the poet tells, the less learned will reply that they know not, the more learned that he never did," Augustine warns. Chaucer saves his narrator's intellectual surrender to the "truth" of the text for last. He confides it cautiously, circumspectly, with complete innocence—the culmination of the joke that begins when no Lady Philosophy appears to stop him from reading "fables" in the first place:

> Whan I had red thys tale wel
> And overloked hyt everydel,
> Me thoghte wonder yf hit were so,
> For I had never herd speke or tho
> Of noo goddes that koude make
> Men to slepe, ne for to wake,
> For I ne knew never god but oon.

> (231–37)

Oblivious of the blame Augustine directs at Virgil's poem for his "wanderings" from the one true God, Chaucer's narrator announces with disingenuous delight his discovery in Ovid's poem of the pagan gods.

But the error is too extreme, too comical, to be taken as an indictment of Ovid. This poetic figment of a pagan god is not powerless in Chaucer's poem either: Morpheus does answer the narrator's prayer. The narrator's "intellectual" fascination with Morpheus, moreover, for all the havoc it wreaks on his story as an effective retelling of Ovid, points dead center to Chaucer's theoretical interest in Ovid's art. As I have already indicated, the dramatic immediacy of Ovid's story and the powerful emotions it generates belong to an art that impresses Chaucer's narrator as a "wonder thing" but eludes his ability to explain or duplicate it. What stymies him are the assumptions of medieval poetic theory, that "ymagynacioun" is a source of troubling "fantasies" and "ydel thoght," and passion an exercise in psychological paralysis and self-destruction. Ovid's art begins with a different set of assumptions. For him the images of imagination are like the dreams surrounding Morpheus in the Cave of Sleep:

> hunc circa passim varias imitantia formas
> Somnia vana iacent totidem, quot messis aristas,
> silva gerit frondes, eiectas litus harenas.
>
> (*Met.* XI.613–15)

> [Around him lie empty dreams, made to resemble different shapes, as many as the corn ears in the harvest, as leaves on the woodland trees, or sands scattered on the shore.][17]

Somnia vana, he calls them, "empty"—but not with overtones of "point-less," "worthless," or "vain," as in Chaucer's "ydel thoght"; rather, shimmering with potential, "varias imitantia formas," imitating various shapes. The present participle makes the dreams vibrantly alive rather than static in their relationship to reality, and "totidem quot," "as many as"—the ears of corn, the leaves, the sands—is not the dismayed measure of a problem, as in Chaucer's "I have *so many* an ydel thoght" (my emphasis), but the celebration of fertile abundance.

Chaucer's narrator is right to be fascinated with Morpheus, even though he omits Ovid's crucial theoretical discussion of dreams. By omitting it altogether, moreover, he also sidesteps the strategies of the medieval authors of the *Ovide moralisé* and of Machaut in the *Fonteinne amoureuse,* who eliminate the problematic implications of Ovid's dream theory by recasting it to accord with the values of medieval poetic theory. Where Ovid blurs the distinction between truth and illusion, the French poets reassert the medieval opposition between them. In their poems the God of Sleep is surrounded not by a single category of *somnia vana imitantia varias formas,* but by two distinct categories: "De songes et de vanitez" (*Ovide moralisé* 3473) and "Trop vanitez et songes" (*Fonteinne amoureuse* 628).[18] The *Ovide moralisé* explains further that the "songes" appear "Aus rois et aus dus solement / Et aus princes de grant renon" (3539–40). Like the divinely sent dreams and visions of Scripture and philosophical allegory, they convey "tout le voir" (3429; cf. also 3507). "Tuit li autre," the "vanitez," like literary fable and romance, simply amuse the common people "par diverses similitudes" (3544) and "par faintes illucions" (3546). Alcyone's dream functions in these works purely as a source of truthful information. In the *Ovide moralisé* Juno sends Iris to demand of Sleep:

> Qu'il face par songe assavoir
> A Alchione tout le voir

Comment ses maris perilla.

(3428–30; cf. also
3506–9, where Iris
repeats her words exactly)

In the *Fonteinne amoureuse* Alcyone herself prays for knowledge and truth: "pour savoir, ou, et pourquoy, et quant / Il fu peris" (563–64).

But Ovid's understanding of the images of imagination is more profound than this. For him the value of the dream is not simply a question of true or false content. If that were its only function, it would be superfluous, for the real body of Ceyx washes in with the waves the next morning. Ovid's language emphasizes the nature and function of the dream as fiction. Juno sends Iris to the God of Sleep to request a dream "in the image of the dead Ceyx" ("exstinctique . . . Ceycis imagine," 587), a dream "narrating the true state of affairs" ("veros narrantia casus," 588). Iris in turn commands Morpheus to send a dream to Alcyone "sub imagine regis" to "conjure up a vision of the shipwreck" ("simulacraque naufraga fingant," 628), and she expresses her admiration for such images because they "are indistinguishable from the real shapes they imitate" ("veras *aequant* imitamine formas," 626, my emphasis). The dream does not merely inform Alcyone of something true, it provides the equivalent *experience* of "veras formas," so that when the real body of Ceyx appears, the mourning already done somehow makes possible the miraculous transformation that is at once release and reenactment—i.e., catharsis.[19]

Chaucer's narrator follows neither Ovid nor the French texts, and the drastic changes he makes in Alcyone's dream reveal his theoretical ambivalence at every turn. When his Alcyone prays to Juno for some grace "my lord to se / Soone or wite wher-so he be, / Or how he fareth, or in what wise" (111–13), for "som certeyn sweven / Wherthourgh that I may knowen even / Whether my lord be quyk or ded" (119–21), he seems to be following Machaut. Alcyone wants *knowledge* that will somehow "Helpe me out of thys distresse" (110). Thus far the dream is simply a heavy-handed instrument of truth rather than the imaginative emotional experience it is first and foremost in Ovid; and because the dream effectively delivers truth, it is unnecessary for Chaucer's narrator to have Ceyx's body wash up on the shore the next day. But the surface resemblance to Machaut is misleading, because Chaucer's Morpheus does not merely assume the image of the dead Ceyx. Juno commands that he "take up Seys body the kyng, / That lyeth ful pale and nothyng rody" (142–43) and "crepe into the body / And doo hit goon to Alcione" (144–45). Morpheus actually appears before Alcyone in the "dreynte body" itself (195–99). This is not the way Ovid collapses the distinction between image and reality, but it certainly does collapse it. The narrator's clumsy and grotesque identification of the dream with brute reality, however, contains none of the cathartic possibilities of Ovid's more subtle art. Overwhelmed by the powerful emotional experience of her dream, his Alcyone simply dies "within the thridde morwe" (214).

It is not surprising that Chaucer's narrator makes a travesty of Ovid's tale in the retelling, but, as I have tried to show, the dismal failures of the story as story make it a deft comment on poetic theory. In the contrast between the "wonder thing" the narrator reads and enthusiastically responds to, and the clunky—reductive, solipsistic, confused—ways he calls attention to the elements he admires, Chaucer seems to be measuring the distance between Ovid's Aristotelian art and the Platonic/Augustinian theory so hostile to it. Meaning in the Ovidian text (like the meaning of Virgil's *Aeneid,* if one wanted to extend this argument to the *House of Fame*) is not a truth that can be extracted or a moral lesson that can be applied. It is inextricably bound up with the successful mimetic illusion of reality and the effective cathartic stimulation of passion with all its contradictory complexity and intensity. The *Duchess* narrator is clearly enthralled by these qualities, even while the assumptions of Platonic/Augustinian poetic theory frustrate his responses to and understanding of the text he admires. But if Plato and Augustine emphasize the fantasy and illusion inherent in the images of poetry, Chaucer also emphasizes their incontestable power.

As I have already remarked, Morpheus answers the narrator's prayer for sleep. In contrast to the "fantasies" and "ydel thoght" that oppress him at the beginning of the poem, he "wakes up" in the dream Morpheus sends him in a bedroom whose walls and windows are painted in "colours fyne" (332) with "al the story of Troye" (326) and "bothe text and glose, / Of al the Romaunce of the Rose" (333–34). As the sun shines through and on them, bathing him in the bright colorful images of his reading, the sound of a hunting horn draws him outside, and the boundary lines that demarcate "fantasy" from "reality" seem to dissolve as the image on his walls and windows shimmer into a landscape from the *Romance of the Rose*—and from another Ovidian story. The figure of the Black Knight, who first provokes his irritation (" 'Lord,' thoght I, 'who may that be? / What ayleth hym to sitten her?' " 448–49) and then elicits sympathetic "wonder" that "Nature / Myght suffre any creature / To have such sorwe and be not ded" (467–69), is more than a grieving alter-ego for the narrator. Leaning against an oak and reciting poetry in a grove so filled with "founes, sowres, bukkes, does" (429) and so "many roes, / And many sqwirelles" (430–31) that even Argus couldn't count them (435–42), the knight is a reincarnation of the mythic poet Orpheus constituted from the images of *Metamorphoses* X. 80–148.

While the Black Knight's passionate laments and courtly reminiscences ransack the stores of classical and medieval poetry to try to rescue Blanche from death, however, the *Book of the Duchess* still does not come down clearly on the side of poetry. Even in the classical story, after all, the achievement of Orpheus is only temporary, partial and insubstantial. In Chaucer's story, the Black Knight is not capable of resolving the theoretical issues raised in the first part of the poem about the emotional healthiness of poetry. Confronted by this Orphean figure, Chaucer's narrator retreats nervously back to the only poetic theory he knows, suggesting that the knight's condition requires treatment: "For, by my trouthe, to make yow hool / I wol do al my power hool" (553–54). In the almost parodic Boethian discussions that follow, the knight proves to be anything but "treatable," while the narrator proves to be a comically diminished and inadequate Lady Philosophy as he admonishes the knight to "Remembre yow of Socrates" (717) and to abandon his attachment to poetic metaphor: "ther is no man alyve her / Wolde for a fers make this woo" (740–41). But this Monty Python–esque version of "Lady Philosophy meets Orpheus" ends in a draw. The narrator's stalwart refusal to acknowledge the legitimacy of the knight's passionate poetry and the knight's stalwart refusal to acknowledge the relevance of the narrator's philosophical reasoning finally counteract each other simultaneously: " 'She ys ded!' 'Nay!' 'Yis, be my trouthe!' / 'Is that youre los? Be God, hyt ys routhe!' " (1309–10).

If Chaucer is using his narrator, as I think he is, to explore the stress cracks in Platonic/Augustinian poetic theory, it is also clear that he has no explicitly articulated theory to put in its place. In this respect, Chaucer shares the problem that Gordon Leff has attributed to late medieval philosophy, that it settled for "merely redefining the terms of discourse" at a time when the "very assumptions on which it was founded need[ed] redefinition."[20] Leff hastens to add that the task was "too great for any individual intellect and too daunting for any believer": it "demanded the combined effort of a religious Reformation and a scientific revolution extending over a century to bring it about."[21] For poetry it required the recovery of Aristotle's *Poetics*.

But redefining the terms of discourse is itself no small achievement, and in the case of Chaucer's poetry the activity doesn't require a disparaging "merely." As I began by saying, the terms of Platonic/Augustinian poetic theory are the source of Chaucer's fascination with art as a self-reflexive linguistic construct *and* as an intellectually and emotionally powerful projection of real-seeming illusion. While so-called New Critics have always confronted thematic tensions in Chaucer's poetry—between experience and authority, for example, new things and old, this world and the next—self-proclaimed theoretical critics have not much attended to Chaucer's conflicts with theory. Understandably, I suppose, they demonstrate that a theory works, not that it undermines the whole enterprise. Yet Chaucer notoriously undermines whole enterprises. And the enterprise he undermines ultimately is the Platonic/Augustinian system and the kinds of poems it allows. The theoretical interests I have traced in the *Book of the Duchess* extend all the way to *Troilus* and the *Canterbury Tales,* where Chaucer finally and triumphantly subverts the terms of Augustinian poetic discourse by coopting them for different ends.

Troilus, as I acknowledged earlier in this essay, ends with a seemingly Augustinian rejection of "feynede" things (V.1848) and an ethical injunction to "Repeyre[n] hom fro worldly vanyte" (V.1837). But the narrator who weeps over his characters in the beginning of the poem is not a typical Augustinian reader immersed in destructive fantasies about Dido; nor is he Boethius abandoned in his grief to the siren Muses of Poetry; and he is not at all the *Duchess* narrator incapacitated by "sorwful ymagynacioun." The *Troilus* narrator leaves his predecessors far behind when he insists that it will "best avaunce" his "sowle" to "write [the] wo" of his fictional characters, and to "lyve in charite, / And for to have of hem compassioun, / As though I were hire owne brother dere" (I.47, 48–50). By redefining the terms of Augustinian discourse, Chaucer is able to dedicate his romance to "moral Gower" and "philosophical Strode" even while he registers an unprecedented claim to poetic *virtus* that is achieved precisely through emotional identification with fictional characters.

The *Canterbury Tales* also ends with an apparent Augustinian rejection—of the poet's "translaciouns and enditynges of worldly vanitees," including those Canterbury tales that "sownen unto synne" (X.1085–86), for the *doctrine* of Christ. But like *Troilus,* it too begins with a different kind of faith and a different kind of truth:

> Whoso shal telle a tale after a man,
> He moot reherce as ny as evere he kan
> Everich a word, if it be in his charge,
> Al speke he never so rudeliche and large,
> Or ellis he moot telle his tale untrewe,
> Or feyne thyng . . .

(I.731–36)

Although "courteous" versus "villainous" style and subject matter are the immediate concerns of the narrator here, his invocation of both Scripture and Plato in the next lines to authorize the high value he places on mimetic accuracy inevitably pulls down on his head the whole weight of medieval poetic theory and its (at best) strained relations with philosophy. By redefining the terms of Augustinian discourse in the *Canterbury Tales*— "For oure book seith, 'Al that is writen is writen for oure doctrine,' and that is myn entente" (X.1083)—Chaucer is able to register an unprecedented claim for the relationship between the *veritas* of real-seeming fiction and the *Veritas* of Scripture.

I am not claiming that these are Aristotelian poems. They are not. There is far too much self-conscious drawing of attention to the mechanics of art. But there is also too much Aristotelian drama and passion to be moralized and allegorized into philosophical truth and virtue. Without overtly dismissing the only system of poetic theory available to him, Chaucer works out in his own unique and extraordinary way what is "best to doo" with the "fantasies" in his head. It is perhaps no accident that the results seem as inexhaustible to the old New Critics as they do to the contemporary practitioners of a rather medieval-seeming deconstructionist and psychoanalytic theory.

Notes

1. For a summary of the old issues see D. W. Robertson, Jr., "The *Book of the Duchess,*" in *Companion to Chaucer Studies,* ed. Beryl Rowland, rev. ed. (New York: Oxford Univ. Press, 1979), pp. 403–10; and Robert M. Jordan, *Chaucer's Poetics and the Modern Reader* (Berkeley and Los Angeles: Univ. of California Press, 1987), pp. 51–54. Jordan, pp. 51–76, makes the strongest contribution to the new debates, but see also David R. Aers, "Chaucer's *Book of the Duchess:* An Art to Consume Art," *Durham University Journal* 69 (1977): 201–5 (on the lack of consolation in the poem); Judith Ferster, "Intention and Interpretation in the *Book of the Duchess,*" *Criticism* 22 (1980): 1–24 (on the characters as solipsistic actors in their own fictions); and Stephen J. Russell, *The English Dream Vision: Anatomy of a Form* (Columbus: Ohio State Univ. Press, 1988), pp. 142–59 (on the failure of language). All quotations of Chaucer in this essay are from *The Riverside Chaucer,* 3rd ed., gen. ed. Larry D. Benson (Boston: Houghton Mifflin, 1987).

2. George L. Kittredge, *Chaucer and his Poetry* (Cambridge: Harvard Univ. Press, 1915), p. 109, and "Chaucer's Discussion of Marriage," *MP* 9 (1912); reprinted in *Chaucer Criticism,* ed. Richard Schoeck and Jerome Taylor, vol. 1 (Notre Dame, Ind.: Notre Dame Univ. Press, 1960), p. 130.

3. I don't mean to suggest a single emphasis, however. For a variety of approaches, see Jordan, *Chaucer's Poetics;* H. Marshall Leicester, Jr., "Oure Tonges *Différance:* Textuality and Deconstruction in Chaucer," in *Medieval Texts & Contemporary Readers,* ed. Laurie A. Finke and Martin B. Shichtman (Ithaca: Cornell Univ. Press, 1987), pp. 15–26; Edmund Reiss, "Chaucer's Fiction and Linguistic Self-Consciousness in the Late Middle Ages," in *Chaucer and the Craft of Fiction,* ed. Leigh Arrathoon (Rochester, Mich.: Solaris, 1986), pp. 97–119; Robert Hanning, " 'I Shal Finde It in a Maner Glose': Versions of Textual Harassment in Medieval Literature," in Finke and Shichtman, pp. 27–50; and Carolyn Dinshaw, *Chaucer's Sexual Poetics* (Madison: Univ. of Wisconsin Press, 1989).

4. Robert P. Payne, *The Key of Remembrance: A Study of Chaucer's Poetics* (New Haven: Yale Univ. Press, 1963), p. 120; A. C. Spearing, *Medieval Dream Poetry* (Cambridge and New York: Cambridge Univ. Press, 1976), p. 51; Jordan, *Chaucer's Poetics,* p. 6. On particular poems, see especially Robert Edwards, "The *Book of the Duchess* and the Beginnings of Chaucer's Narrative," *New Literary History* 13 (1982): 189–204; Robert Hanning, "Chaucer's First Ovid:

Metamorphosis and Poetic Tradition in *The Book of the Duchess* and *The House of Fame*," in Arrathoon, pp. 121–63; Leicester, "The Harmony of Chaucer's *Parlement:* A Dissonant Voice," *Chaucer Review* 9 (1974): 15–34; Russell Peck, "Chaucerian Poetics and the Prologue to the *Legend of Good Women*," in *Chaucer in the Eighties,* ed. Julian Wasserman and Robert J. Blanch (Syracuse, N.Y.: Syracuse Univ. Press, 1986), pp. 39–55.

5. Lee Patterson, *Negotiating the Past: The Historical Understanding of Medieval Studies* (Madison: Univ. of Wisconsin Press, 1987), p. 5.

6. Augustine, *Confessions,* trans. E. B. Pusey, The Modern Library (New York: Random House, 1949), pp. 15–17. The alternative translation in the last line is from *Confessions,* ed. and trans. William Watts, Loeb Classical Library, 2 vols. (Cambridge: Harvard Univ. Press, 1912) 1:43. The Latin is from *Confessionum libri XIII,* ed. Lucas Verheijen, CCSL 27 (Turnholt: Brepols, 1981).

7. Plato, *Republic,* ed. and trans. Paul Shorey, Loeb Classical Library, 2 vols. (Cambridge: Harvard Univ. Press, 1930–1935), 2 (1935): 435.

8. In the reading I have done, only Thomas H. Bestul, "Chaucer's *Troilus and Criseyde:* The Passionate Epic and Its Narrator," *Chaucer Review* 14 (1980): 374–75, connects the passage from the *Confessions* with the opening of Boethius's *Consolation of Philosophy* and identifies both as models for the weeping narrator of *Troilus.* Winthrop Wetherbee, "*Poeta che mi guidi:* Dante, Lucan, and Virgil," in *Canons,* ed. Robert von Halberg (Chicago: Univ. of Chicago Press, 1984), p. 137, sees Augustine's emotional response to Dido as a model for Dante's Paolo and Francesca in *Inferno* 5.

9. Wesley Trimpi, *Muses of One Mind: The Literary Analysis of Experience and Its Continuity* (Princeton: Princeton Univ. Press, 1983), describes the cooptation of poetry by philosophy as the recurring fate of poetry throughout its history (p. 10 especially). See also Trimpi, "The Ancient Hypothesis of Fiction," *Traditio* 27 (1971), 63–65; Richard McKeon, "Poetry and Philosophy in the Twelfth Century: The Renaissance of Rhetoric," *MP* 43 (1945–46): 217–34; and Ernst Robert Curtius, *European Literature and the Latin Middle Ages,* trans. Willard Trask (New York: Pantheon Books, 1953; Harper & Row, 1963), pp. 203–8 and 397–401. Murray Wright Bundy, *The Theory of Imagination in Classical and Medieval Thought,* Univ. of Illinois Studies in Language and Literature 2–3 (Urbana: Univ. of Illinois Press, 1927), documents the medieval suspicion of imagination.

10. Hanning, "Chaucer's First Ovid," p. 133, and John Fyler, *Chaucer and Ovid* (New Haven: Yale Univ. Press, 1979), p. 68.

11. For excellent analyses of Ovid's story emphasizing its dramatic and emotional power, see Hanning, "Chaucer's First Ovid," pp. 127–30, and Warren Ginsberg, *The Cast of Character: The Representation of Personality in Ancient and Medieval Literature* (Toronto and Buffalo: Toronto Univ. Press, 1983), pp. 56–61.

12. Hanning, "Chaucer's First Ovid," p. 133, implies that the reductiveness gets into Chaucer's narrative via Machaut, but Machaut omits the storm and shipwreck from his *Fonteinne amoureuse:* they are irrelevant to his love complaint. Fyler likewise attributes the narrator's solipsism to Machaut (and Froissart), arguing that he tries inappropriately to turn Ovid's story into a love complaint, to make it serve his own personal (romantic) concerns (p. 68). I will suggest a different role for the French poets in a moment.

13. A number of recent studies recognize this: Hanning, "Chaucer's First Ovid," p. 134; Edwards, *"Book of the Duchess,"* p. 190; Judith Neaman, "Brain Physiology and Poetics in *The Book of the Duchess,"* *Res Publica Litterarum* 3 (1980): 101–3. All three see art as the cure rather than the cause of the problem,

however. But the "therapeutic" value of Ovid's poetry (Hanning, p. 137; Edwards, p. 191; Neaman, pp. 106–7) is not so clear, either in medieval poetic theory or in Chaucer's poem.

14. Augustine, *On Musica,* trans. Robert Taliaferro, in *Writings of Saint Augustine,* ed. Ludwig Schopp, vol. 1 (New York: CIMA, 1948), pp. 151–379. Latin text: *De musica,* in Migne 32:869–904.

15. Boethius, *Consolation of Philosophy,* trans. Richard Green (Indianapolis: Bobbs-Merrill, 1962), pp. 4–5. Latin text: *Consolatio philosophiae,* ed. L. Bieler, CCSL 94 (Turnholt: Brepols, 1984).

16. Fyler, *Chaucer and Ovid,* p. 17, notes that "as a bible of the pagan gods" the *Metamorphoses* "presented a special problem" to the interpretive strategies of medieval commentators—a problem he claims Chaucer was "oblivious" to. In fact, though, the narrator's characterization of his book as being primarily about human lives goes right to the heart of Ovid's Aristotelian art. As Elder Olson notes in "The Poetic Method of Aristotle: Its Powers and Limitations," in *Aristotle's Poetics and English Literature,* ed. Elder Olson (Chicago: Univ. of Chicago Press, 1965), p. 190, the essence of Aristotelian mimetic poetry is "human beings doing and experiencing things which are humanly interesting and affecting." A. J. Minnis, *Chaucer and Pagan Antiquity* (Totowa, N.J.: Rowman & Littlefield, 1982); Donald R. Howard, *Chaucer: His Life, His Works, His World* (New York: Dutton, 1987), pp. 353–58; and Howard, "Thwarted Sexuality in Chaucer's Works," *Florilegium: Carleton University Annual Papers on Classical Antiquity and the Middle Ages* 3 (1981): 243–49, have stressed Chaucer's fascination with the accurate representation of pagan antiquity in works like *Troilus* and The Knight's Tale. The *Duchess* narrator's fascination with "olde tyme" may be part of the same impulse, an impulse that includes the Aristotelian art of pagan antiquity. But Chaucer is not "oblivious" to the implications of pagan theology either, and his narrator's enthusiastic "discovery" of Morpheus goes beyond gratuitous silliness.

17. Ovid, *Metamorphoses,* trans. Mary M. Innes (Baltimore: Penguin, 1955), p. 252. The Latin is from *Metamorphoses,* ed. and trans. F. J. Miller, Loeb Classical Library, 2 vols. (Cambridge: Harvard Univ. Press, 1916). For a discussion of the theoretical implications of Ovid's dreams that emphasizes Ovid's playfulness, see Elaine Fantham, "Ovid's Ceyx and Alcyone: The Metamorphosis of a Myth," *Phoenix* 33 (1979): 330–45.

18. *Ovide moralisé,* ed. C. de Boer, 5 vols. Amsterdam: J. Müller, 1915–1938; the tale of Ceyx and Alycone is in 4 (1936): 190–219. Guillaume de Machaut, *La Fonteinne amoureuse,* in *Oeuvres de Guillaume de Machaut,* ed. E. Hoepffner, 3 vols. SATF (Paris: Firmin-Didot, 1921), 3: 143–244.

19. On the Aristotelian understanding of emotion, W. W. Fortenbaugh, *Aristotle on Emotion* (New York: Barnes & Noble, 1975), notes that Aristotle went beyond Plato in explaining the connection between cognition and emotion: "Viewed as an affliction divorced from cognition, emotion was naturally opposed to reason and conceived of as something hostile to thoughtful judgment . . . as extra-rational enchantment" (p. 18).

20. Gordon Leff, *The Dissolution of the Medieval Outlook: An Essay on Intellectual and Spiritual Change in the Fourteenth Century* (New York: Harper & Row, 1976), p. 146.

21. Ibid.

Telling the Private Parts: "Pryvetee" and Poetry in Chaucer's *Canterbury Tales*

R. W. HANNING

"Pryvetee" is one of those words that emerges from a reading of the *Canterbury Tales (CT)*—or of any sizeable part of it—as central to the poetic enterprise. Here, we feel, is a term Chaucer was fond of, one that occupies a keystone position in the verbal edifice he constructed, and constantly reconstructed and adjusted, through all the years he worked on his framed tale collection.

If we think of *CT* (as I prefer to) as Chaucer's world of words—a poetic cosmos created out of all the rhetorical styles and verbal manipulations the poet puts in the mouths of his surrogates, the tale-telling Canterbury pilgrims—then we can say with some justice that this world, like the medieval English mystery cycles in which the playing area was presumably defined and bordered by loci representing heaven (God's throne, at one side) and hell (the famous hellmouth, at the other side), is bounded at one extreme by God's pryvetee, at the other by the devil's. (God's [or Jupiter, the First Mover's] pryvetee is ostensibly revealed by Theseus at the end of the Knight's Tale and indubitably mocked by the Miller in his answering Prologue and Tale; the Friar expounds the devil's "theological" pryvetee as part of his attack on summoners, and the Summoner responds by coopting part of Satan's physical pryvetee, his arse, in his counterattack on friars.)[1]

In between, here on earth and in the world of human experience, we find pryvetee assuming a spectrum of meanings and, in consequence, a range of functions within the overall scheme of *CT*. The present essay will examine a few of these functions, moving toward the argument that at the center of the poem, and indeed of Chaucer's sense of his own art, is a mysterious, antithetical yet symbiotic relationship between pryvetee and poetry. I offer this discussion as a token of my long-standing admiration for Donald R. Howard, whose thoughts and writings placed a generation of Chaucerians deep in his debt.

A little detail in the General Prologue portrait of the Merchant can serve as a starting point for an investigation of the interaction between pryvetee and poetry in *CT*. The narrator says, "This worthy man ful wel his wit bisette; / Ther wiste no wight that he was in dette" (I.279–80). Hidden in this apparently straightforward statement is a crucial paradox: no one knew the Merchant was in debt, but we do. That is, pryvetee in the sense of individual secrets cannot survive becoming a poetic subject; the poet, in announcing pryvetee, destroys it; poetry and pryvetee are mutually exclusive.

There is, however, more than just opposition in the relationship between poetry and pryvetee. Chaucer had already articulated the peculiarities of this relationship in characteristically oblique and comic fashion in Book Three of *Troilus and Criseyde (TC)*, where Pandarus lectures Troilus on the importance of keeping secret the latter's burgeoning affair with Criseyde, and the former's central role in obtaining his niece's love for his royal friend. Pandarus pleads with the prince, "althogh thow shuldest deye, / That privete go with us in this cas" (*TC* III.282–83), and in the course of his lengthy exhortation is brought to the following disclaimer, which amusingly sets before us the paradox that concerns me in this essay and concerned Chaucer throughout at least the last fifteen years of his career. Pandarus says,

And nere it that I wilne as now t'abregge
Diffusioun of speche, I koude almoost
A thousand olde stories the allegge
Of wommen lost through fals and foles bost.

(*TC* III.295–98)

The impulse of discourse, and by implication of poetry, is to expand, to dilate, to give examples—to betray the pryvetee of a thousand women in arguing against such betrayals. In short, it is unnatural, *agaynes kynde,* for a poet to protect pryvetee. To do so, the poet must be silent, must cease, in other words, to be a poet. Pandarus quotes the proverb, "firste vertu is to kepe tonge" (*TC* III.294), and in doing so anticipates the mother of the narrator of the Manciple's tale, who is depicted at the end of that tale lecturing her son at great length—again the paradox comically stated—on the dangers of utterance. The poet can, in fact, no more keep silent than call his/her words back once they are uttered; the Manciple's dame makes this point (IX.353–55):

But he that hath mysseyd, I dar wel sayn,
He may by no wey clepe his word agayn.
Thyng that is seyd is seyd, and forth it gooth—

in the process negating, *avant la lettre,* the Retractions with which the poet, speaking ostensibly in his own, serious voice, will shortly end the Canterbury collection.

So Chaucer shows himself aware of the problems and paradoxes inherent in the concept of pryvetee when seen from a poet's point of view. It is worth a brief digression here to supply a fragmentary cultural and poetic context for both the concept and his idiosyncratic, vocational response to it in *CT*.

Chaucer's world, though increasingly literate and possessed of the cultural attitudes that accompany literacy, was by no means as removed as is our civilization from the institutions and outlooks of a non-literate, tradition-based society, such as obtained throughout much of western Europe until his century. In traditional cultures, celebratory poetry is public—it expresses the values, recollections, and aspirations of the group in its stories of great deeds in days gone by. It belongs to everyone: "we have heard" is how *Beowulf* begins, not "I have heard." Folktales and traditional stories are also public and symbolic in nature; they embody values and situations that have broad applicability within a culture, as wisdom or folly.

As medieval European culture passed from its "heroic age" of warfare, instability, and fragmentation to a new age of greater political stability, one result was a phenomenal growth in what we call the arts of peace: travel, with the resultant exchange of goods and ideas; economic growth, based on trade and stimulating the rise of towns and cities. The relief from near-constant war (and preparation for war) also resulted in sufficient leisure to allow the cultivation of the personal sphere in spirituality and thought and the expansion of education beyond its early medieval monastic outposts to the urban and cathedral schools and ultimately the *studia generale*.

In this new cultural ambience, we find taking shape in life and literature a new idea of the private life: a set of intellectual and emotional situations, preferences, needs, and goals collectively constituting a metaphorical extension, as it were, of the physical, tangible goods and property (including servants and, if one were a man, his wife) that had traditionally (in Roman and Carolingian law) comprised the *res privata*.[2]

If one's goal with respect to private goods was their protection against the incursions of public authorities or thieves (or, in the case of a wife, violation by an intruder or lover), the analogous goal with respect to private thoughts, feelings, and aspirations—intangible possessions of the highest importance, which we denominate collectively as our "privacy"—was to maintain their secrecy, that is, to protect them from violation by intruding eyes and ears.[3]

This newly important conception of a private (indeed secret) sphere of thoughts, feelings, words, and deeds central to human happiness—or, in the case of the life of commerce, human success[4]—was to find varied expression in the major new literary genres of high medieval Europe: lyric, romance, fabliau.[5] In addition to singing (often rhapsodically) the praises of the private world—its dreams, its exquisite sorrows, its furtive caresses—this literature (often but by no means exclusively in the fabliau) articulates a negative and cynical view of privacy that embodies two major suppositions: one is that the world is full of people ready to invade or spoil your private life if you give them a chance; the other is that everyone has something to hide, a skeleton in the closet.

The first view, derived ultimately, I think, from the clannishness of European peasant culture, finds an early, splendid exemplification in Abelard's autobiographical letter, in the sequence where the brilliant young philosopher undertakes to tutor Eloise in the privacy of her uncle's house and ends up seducing her instead.[6] The second view—that the pryvetee one seeks to keep private is something wrong, something that would bring censure or worse if it were known—constitutes, I believe, a literary response to and version of the new emphasis on private confession and the importance of intention in determining sinfulness. This new theology of confession, at the center of which is Abelard's *Ethics,* stresses that only God really knows our hearts, and therefore whether or not we are sinners, because only God can pierce beyond actions to the inner intentions motivating them. Translated into the literary plot, this means characters of virtuous appearance who, however, harbor secret vices or sins. But instead of God seeing this, we all do, thanks to the mediation of the storyteller, or writer, who reveals this pryvetee from his/her privileged position as creator of the story, and therefore the analogue to God within the fictional universe created.

This second literary model brings us back to the implicit opposition between self-serving, flawed privacy and the poetry that exposes it. Put in more general terms, we intuit a larger rivalry or tension between pryvetee (henceforth I will use the Chaucerian term for ease of reference) and language. Language reveals what is hidden in pryvetee. But then there is a further implication: for language is thus the instrument of truth which cuts through the layers of appearance erected to protect pryvetee—the appearance of virtue, the deployment of rhetoric, and so on. This means that with the notion of pryvetee comes the idea of life as a fiction hiding truth— appearance hiding reality. Which, of course, is a version of the concept of *integumentum* so dear to medieval professional exegetes in their dealings with learned, Latin poetry.[7]

Such poetry of the pagans (and of Christian imitators like the philosophical poets of the twelfth century usually associated with the cathedral school at Chartres) is to be understood as a husk of fable wrapped around a kernel of truth. But where the exegete pierces through the pleasing but false fable to find the salutary truth beneath, the language of the poet

exposing flawed pryvetee pierces through pleasing but false appearances—of monks, clerics, merchants, women—to discover, expose, and
revel in the unsavory truth beneath.

It may appear that I am describing the office of the satirist, but in fact I
am not. For I am speaking here of poetry that aims not at exposing vice
with a view to correcting it, but rather at giving pleasure by piercing
through facades to lay bare pryvetee, exposing the strategic fictions that
are thereby shown to be a central part of life. By its characteristic concerns and construction, such poetry suggests that fiction-making to hide
truth and story-telling to reveal it are locked in a perpetual, symbiotic
embrace within the human condition. Each impulse, by its very existence
and strength, calls forth the other; each is deeply ingrained and gives great
pleasure, but that pleasure is somehow increased by the coexistence, and
hence the challenge, of its opposite. This is not so much a static dichotomy
in human nature as a creative rivalry operating in the world of language—
as the interaction of impulses toward *integumentum* and exegesis—and in
the world of human behavior—as the opposition between strategic self-
presentation and efforts to get at the facts that lie behind it. (I will assess
the importance of this rivalry for *CT* at the conclusion of this essay.)

Before returning to Chaucer I would like to offer one famous twelfth-
century example of the interactive paradigm I have just described. It deals
with the kind of pryvetee that provides the most enduring subject for
literature of this type, namely sexual pryvetee. Indeed, it can be argued
that the originary myth of pryvetee as a concept in our civilization occurs
in the second creation story in Genesis, when Adam and Eve perceive
their nakedness and proceed to make coverings for their genitals. Medieval stories that delight in exposing sexual pryvetee in effect constitute
reversals of this originary myth. The covering of the genitals functions as
an emblem of propriety, a covering up of one's sexual impulses by the
norms of polite or moral behavior. But beneath this covering—this *integumentum* of the respectable figleaf—are the stewing passions of sexual
pryvetee, represented by the private parts that are their focus. Adam and
Eve, as fabricators of genital coverings, are the first makers of fictions of
respectability to hide the disreputable pryvetee beneath.[8] And the poet
who exposes this fiction-making by telling stories that reveal, and revel in,
sexuality, is playing God in the sense of exposing the attempt to hide, to
stay in the garden.

The comic poetry of violated sexual pryvetee thus re-creates the expul-
sion from the garden by its derisive exposure of those who would seek to
disguise their sexuality in order to indulge it without personal or social
cost. This suggests again the antagonism of sexual pryvetee to truth
telling, and by extension to language as potentially truth telling. Such

antagonism in fact animates my example, the song *Farai un vers, pos mi somelh* by Guillaume of Poitou, the first known troubadour.[9]

Guillaume's narrator tells us how he was out walking alone one day, apparently in the guise of a pilgrim, when he met Agnes and Ermessen, the wives of two noblemen. The women greet him politely, and say that he appears to be respectable enough, although the world is full of crazies:

> E Dieus vos salf, don pelerin;
> mout mi semblatz de belh aizin,
> mon escient;
> mas trop vezem anar pel mon
> de folla gent.
>
> (20–24)

> ["God save you, my lord pilgrim,
> you look to me like a gentleman,
> as far as I can tell;
> but we all see crazy fools too often
> walking through the world."]

Reading this as a coded invitation to dalliance, the narrator replies, he tells us, not with analogously coded utterance of words like "stick" or "rod," open to sexual double entendre, but by mouthing gibberish:

> . . . anc no li diz ni bat ni but,
> ni fer ni fust no ai mentaugut,
> mas sol aitan:
> "Babariol, babariol,
> babarian."
>
> (26–30)

> ["I didn't say but or bat to them,
> didn't mention a stick or a tool,
> but only this:
> Babariol, babariol,
> babarian."]

That his strategy is correct is immediately confirmed; the women agree that they have found the man they are looking for; they will take him home with them "qe ben es mutz, / e ja per lui nostre conselh / non er saubutz" (34–36)—because "he is really mute / [and] with this one what we have in mind / will never get found out."

Here we are confronted with the central irony of the poem: the wives' sexual pryvetee, since it involves extramarital sex, must remain secret if they are to maintain the fiction of respectability—a fiction encapsulated in their polite, yet suggestive, words to the supposed pilgrim. Yet it also requires a participant if it is to take place at all; and the only safe participant is a mute one, since the power of language carries with it the threat to pryvetee. The irony here is that the chosen man, the ostensible mute, is actually the poet. And a mute poet is a contradiction in terms.

In fact, the image of the mute poet is precisely an image of the poet at work, collecting his material; his muteness is strategic, a necessary pose to allow others to speak and act so that he will have matter for his poems. The mute poet is a listening, observing poet; his lack of language is language deferred so that it can in fact later come to be, and have a subject. The poet's temporary alienation from his chosen medium marks him as dangerous—it is a sign that he will later have something to tell that will pierce integumental respectability and expose incriminating pryvetee. The mute pilgrim/poet is gathering ammunition; he is a pilgrim en route toward a poetic utterance; by the end of his sexual imprisonment with the two noble ladies, he has something to tell, and of course he tells all:

Ueit jorns ez encar mais estei
en aquel forn.

Tant les fotei com auzirets:
cen e quatre vint et ueit vetz,
q'a pauc no.i rompei mos coretz
e mos arnes. . . .

(77–82)

[Eight days and more I stayed in that oven.

I fucked them, you shall hear how many times:
one hundred and eighty-eight times. C.LXXX.VIII.
I nearly broke my breaching strap
and harness.]

Indeed, the poem opens with a warning of the poet's ability to tell unpleasant truths:

Domnas i a de mal conselh,
e sai dir cals:
cellas c'amor de cavalier
tornon a mals.

(3–6)

[There are ladies who are all wrongheaded,
and I can say who.
the ones who turn down the love of a knight
and treat it badly.]

The rest of the poem can be understood as a kind of exemplum in support of this statement; the poet can expose promiscuous women, and hence is prepared to do similar damage to the woman or women who are now taking the opposite tack, and refusing him. Of course, this in turn raises the possibility that he will get back at such hardhearted women by telling precisely the tales about them that he proceeds to tell about Agnes and Ermessen. That is, he can tar a refuser with the same brush as a seducer. He can, in short, manufacture pryvetee and call it truth.

Which raises the question, of course, has he done so here? What is the truth about his encounter with the women? We are reminded of all the versions of the biblical tale of Joseph and Potiphar's wife (Genesis 39.6–20)—versions such as that found in Marie de France's *Lanval*, where a knight at Arthur's court refuses the Queen's proposition and she, furious at being scorned, publicly accuses him of trying to rape her. Has Guillaume's poet-persona adopted this durable paradigm, reversing the genders? In sum, the mute poet speaks, but whether he speaks truth or fiction we cannot tell. His revelation of the sexual pryvetee of the two noble women may be true, or vengeful, or a macho boast.

In any case, the striking image of the mute poet serves to put before us the primal opposition of poetry and pryvetee, while also reminding us that the paradigm of penetrating a fiction to lay bare the truth it hides can itself be pressed into service as a powerful and effective poetic fiction.

And now, at last, to *CT*. Within Chaucer's tale collection, the term pryvetee, in its earthly as opposed to divine or diabolic meanings, carries many connotations. For instance, it has the traditional meaning of the *res privata*—the literal, material goods of a male head of household, and the enclosure that protects them from invasion or violation—in the Cook's comment on The Reeve's Tale: "Wel oghte a man avysed for to be / Whom that he broghte into his pryvetee" (I.4333–34).

Roger of Ware refers, of course, to the disastrous results for Simkin, the thieving Miller, when he allows the two Cambridge clerks he has just cheated of part of their grain to spend the night under his roof. In the world of his trade, the public world of mill and village, Simkin the swaggering "market-betere" (I.3936) reigns supreme, and easily foils (by the expedient of unloosing their horse) the clerks' attempt to protect their college's wheat (part of its *res privata*) from his depredations. Once inside the one-room house, however, the clerics are able to turn its cramped sleeping conditions to their advantage, slipping in and out of beds and rearranging the topography of the darkened space by the strategic moving of a cradle.

The result, of course, is that the Miller's wife and daughter—again, part of his literal pryvetee—are swyved by Alan and John, and, to make matters worse, the daughter further violates Simkin's pryvetee by revealing to Alan the location of the cake made of the stolen grain. To crown the jest (quite literally), Simkin's wife, misled by the darkness of the room, ends the vicious fight between Simkin and Alan by braining her husband, rather than the clerk, with a staff. What the clerks lost in public, they get back in private realm; they do this by ingenuity and manipulation of the scene in which they find themselves.

Furthermore, the Reeve has set up the tale in such a way as to stress Simkin's absurd pride in the social status of his wife—in fact, the illegitimate daughter of the town parson—and his consequent, even more absurd pretension that his daughter deserves to make a good marriage, given her exalted lineage. When Alan swyves the daughter, he is in effect striking a mortal blow at Simkin's social climbing pretensions. That this is the greatest effect of the violation of Simkin's pryvetee (via his daughter's sexual pryvetee, or private parts) is made indubitably clear by the Miller's first words on hearing Alan's declaration (which the clerk, having climbed into the wrong bed, thinks he is making to his colleague John) that he has "thries in this shorte nyght / Swyved the milleres doghter bolt upright" (I.4265–66). "Thow shalt be deed, by Goddes dignitee," roars Simkin, "Who dorste be so boold to disparage / My doghter, that is come of swich lynage?" (4270–72). The disparagement more than the sexual violation hurts Simkin, because it strikes him in his most sensitive part, his self-serving imaginings about his (and his daughter's) social status—self-aggrandizing fictions of the type Chaucer elsewhere denominates *fantasye*. In fact, the Miller's household pryvetee serves, in the Reeve's account of it, as the point of encounter between the clerks' manipulation of plot and setting and Simkin's imaginative vision. Alan and John effect a satisfactory story, but the Miller's self-esteem—his metaphorical pryvetee, bolstered by his imaginings about his daughter—receives a grievous wound thanks to the invasion and violation of his literal pryvetee—his household and household "goods"—by strangers whom he, to make matters worse, has invited in. The Reeve's Tale, then, stages an attack on pryvetee, both physical and mental, in the course of which Chaucer is able to arrange a comic confrontation between two aspects of his own poetic art: plot making and *fantasye*.

We move next to the sense of pryvetee as a particular private or secret component of someone's life that is better not revealed lest it result in blame or ridicule. In The Knight's Tale, the component in question is identity pure and simple: when Arcite returns to Athens from his supposedly perpetual exile in Thebes, in order to try to win Emelye, he is breaking his vow to Theseus, and thus risks certain death if he is discovered. In order to avoid detection, Arcite adopts a disguise (and the name Philostrate), a task made easier by the fact that his appearance has already been transformed beyond recognition by love sickness.

To mask and serve his pryvetee, the Theban prince plots a new career as well as a new identity for himself in Athens. He goes to the palace to offer his service as a menial laborer, "to drugge and drawe." Because of his strength and willingness to do hard work, he wins respect and then love; he becomes page of Emelye's chamber, and eventually Theseus takes a liking to him and makes him a squire of the Duke's own chamber. Chaucer's audience would presumably have recognized Arcite's adventures as Philostrate as the plot of a popular romance, *Havelok the Dane*. By this touch Chaucer emphasizes the way in which, in service of our private interests, we are constantly re-creating ourselves as fictions in our dealings with society and the public world. And in this case of disguise and indirection, Arcite's public fiction is a pleasing *integumentum* that masks a potentially damaging (and in this case physically dangerous) truth.

Arcite's uncomplicated (if potentially lethal) pryvetee and straightforward means of protecting it makes him an excellent foil for Alisoun of Bath, the character in *CT* who engages the subject and problems of pryvetee in the most complex manner possible, in the process bringing to the fore the peculiar relationship between poetry and pryvetee that, I believe, so interested the mature Chaucer.

A large part of The Wife of Bath's Prologue is given over to her *chronique scandaleuse* of her five marriages, a systematic revelation of events, strategies, and confrontations that constitute the private dimensions of marital life. In addition, she wanders by the way of this larger narrative into several local eruptions of revelation about herself and, by extension, about women in general. For in Alisoun Chaucer has created a character who claims to speak both or her own experience and that of all womankind. Thus at one moment we get a personal confession:

> For certes, I am al Venerien
> In feelynge, and myn herte is Marcien. . . .
> I folwed ay myn inclinacioun
> By vertu of my constellacioun;
> That made me I koude noght withdrawe
> My chambre of Venus from a good felawe. . . .
> For God so wys be my savacioun,
> I ne loved nevere by no discrecioun
> But evere folwede myn appetit. . . .

(III.609–23)

At another moment, we get what might be called a generic, or perhaps genderic, confession:

> We wommen han, if that I shal nat lye,
> In this matere a queynte fantasye:
> Wayte what thyng we may nat lightly have,
> Therafter wol we crie al day and crave.

Forbede us thyng, and that desiren we;
Preesse on us faste, and thanne wol we fle.
With daunger oute we al oure chaffare;
Greet prees at market maketh deere ware,
And to greet cheep is holde at litel prys;
This knoweth every womman that is wys.

(515–24)

In both cases Alisoun reveals damning evidence to her predominately male audience—evidence, to be sure, drawn by Chaucer from a well-documented tradition of mysognistic writings by males—that she might rather, within the conventions of a social fiction, be expected to conceal.

Alisoun raises the issue of pryvetee and its violation in a particularly interesting passage that comes just after the last one I quoted, and has resonances with it. She begins for the second time to speak of her fifth husband, a former Oxford cleric who was boarding with the Wife's "gossib," also called Alisoun. Our Alisoun waxes enthusiastic:

God have hir soule! Hir name was Alisoun.
She knew myn herte, and eek my privetee,
Bet than oure parisshe preest, so moot I thee!
To hire biwreyed I my conseil al.
For hadde myn housbonde pissed on a wal,
Or doon a thyng that sholde han cost his lyf,
To hire, and to another worthy wyf,
And to my nece, which that I loved weel,
I wolde han toold his conseil every deel.
And so I dide ful often, God it woot,
That made his face often reed and hoot
For verray shame, and blamed hymself for he
Had toold to me so greet a pryvetee.

(530–42)

What's being described here is the Wife's automatic betrayal of pryvetee to her female network of relatives and gossips. We find ourselves, in effect, present at the transformation of the word "gossib" from its reference to a person to its definition of a kind of discourse and storytelling. The Wife exemplifies the force that links, indeed transforms, relationship into discourse, a person into language. (We should recall in this connection that she tells us her fifth husband could "glose" her (509), as if she were a text, to get sexual response from her even after he has beaten her.)[10]

Several things about this passage deserve comment. First, Alisoun is not here, as so often elsewhere in her Prologue, talking about strategic battles with a particular husband or husbands. She's not getting even or pursuing *maistrye*. She is, in this digressive eddy in the wandering current of her monologue, telling us about doing what comes naturally: sharing her information with her network. The husband in question is what we might call the generic husband, here considered solely in his function of someone with private experiences that he wishes to keep private, because they embarrass (pissing against a wall) or threaten him ("a thyng that sholde han cost hys lyf"). These experiences become, in effect, the subject and substance of the wife's relationship with the other women, the connective tissue that binds them in an alliance. They are a storytelling community, and the matter of their stories is the pryvetee of their men folk.[11]

What Chaucer is giving us here is an image of the Wife of Bath as the embodiment of a female, oral, subliterary tradition that exists in opposition and subjection to the male, literate culture and legacy represented by Jankyn's book of wicked wives. In a literate culture, what we know and learn can be put in books, rendered abstract and impersonal, and walked away from, while we rest secure in the knowledge that the material is there ready to be used whenever a literate person takes up the book again. The process is discontinuous, fragmented, and entirely personal—a series of encounters between reader and text. By contrast, in a non-literate, tradition-based culture what is known is what is remembered and passed on from person to person and generation to generation in song and story. The human voice becomes the medium of circulation and communication—no "facts" exist in abstraction or separation from it.

Alisoun, in her dealings with her network of gossips, is performing the function of a person in a non-literate culture: listening, collecting, passing on. That she is a good listener is clear from her recall of the contents of Jankyn's book, and her ability to turn against male clerics their own exegetical techniques which she has heard them use against her and her sex in and out of church. In her role as embodiment of the oral tradition, she has also gone far afield to collect information:

> . . . therefore I made my visitaciouns
> To vigilies and to processiouns,
> To prechyng eke, and to thise pilgrimages
> To pleyes of myracles, and to mariages . . .

> (III.555–58)

It follows, then, that for the tradition and culture the Wife of Bath represents to survive, it cannot respect pryvetee, cannot leave known things untold. There can be no break in the chain, no lying fallow on a bookshelf, no selection of apposite material. What is not kept in circulation is lost forever; what is untold cannot be passed on or recalled—it dies, and some of the culture along with it.

The specific uses of this female, oral, anti-privatistic culture become clear as the wife describes her courtship of her fifth husband. As she tells us herself, in concocting her erotic dreams and her contention that Jankyn has enchanted her, Alisoun "Folowed ay my dames loore, / As wel of this as of othere thynges moore" (III.583–84). On the one hand, this is simply a dramatization of the male fantasy that women conspire together to share information on catching men. But it is also a testimony to the operation of the non-literate tradition of women side by side with male learned culture. Alisoun's dame and her lore about dealing with men are the female analogue of the patristic texts used by clerics to put down women. (It is, in my opinion, no accident that immediately after mentioning her "dames loore" Alisoun loses her place and has to stop and think before she can "have [her] tale ageyn" (586). Chaucer thus emphasizes the wife's dependence on her memory—the distillation and contingent repository of the female oral tradition—rather than on a fixed text or texts.)

So Alisoun represents the impulse to tell, to pass on information, which is the basic survival strategy of a non-literate culture. Her unwillingness or inability to keep secrets, about herself or her husbands, is a metaphor for a traditional culture's will to survive. But it is also a metaphor for the imperative to use language, rather than repress it, which is at the center of the poetic impulse. You cannot be a poet by not talking; hence, as we saw with Guillaume de Poitou, poetry—a specialized manifestation of the human impulse toward expression—is the natural enemy of pryvetee—the suppression of facts and of talk about them.

Finally, Alisoun's refusal of pryvetee as a limit to discourse is also a sign of her sometime unwillingness to buy into a culture of pryvetee, in the sense of private possession. In the realm of the *res privata,* the husband wants to keep the wife and her sexuality all to himself; it is for this reason that old John the carpenter keeps his Alisoun "narwe in cage"—"For she was wylde and yong, and he was old / And demed hymself been lik a cokewold" (I.3224–26). A wife is a possession not to be shared, not only so that you will know whose your children are, but also so that you are one up on your neighbors for having private control of a commodity (albeit a human one) they want, too.

In an expanded, metaphorical sense as well, pryvetee, in the form of a private sphere of plans and strategies, is part of a mechanism of control the aim of which is to make you compete successfully with, and be better off than, your fellows. As suggested earlier in this essay, the rise of a mercantile culture in high medieval Europe was a major factor promoting the expansion of a commercial privacy—located literally and symbolically within the merchant's home in his *countour-hous* (see VII.77)—which included records of past dealings and present assets as well as general intentions and specific schemes for future transactions, and had to be kept hidden from clients and competitors (see note 4). We recall that in the General Prologue the Merchant is full of language "Sownynge alwey th' encrees of his wynnyng," and that beneath this verbal facade "Ther wiste

no wight that he was in dette" (I.275, 280). His *semblable,* the merchant of
St. Denis in The Shipman's Tale, lectures his wife that merchants must
"dryve forth the world as it may be, / And kepen oure estaat in pryvetee"
(VII.231–32). The implication is that a merchant is never as well off as he
seems, and should the facts come out, he would lose further trade and face
ruin; indeed, this passage continues (VII.233–34), the truth should only
come out after the merchant has died, or perhaps disappeared, or gone off
on pilgrimage in a pretended exercise of piety—apparently a late medieval
equivalent of filing Chapter 11.

In the face of all this masculine hiding and repressing of information,
this hoarding of facts and goods (including her own person and sexuality)
for gain of various kinds, the Wife of Bath stands up, and stands out, for
the imperative of disclosure, sharing, giving. She says not only that she
will tell her husband's pryvetee to her gossips, but that women in general
cannot keep secrets. She inserts into her tale of the rapist knight who must
save his life by discovering what all women want a truncated, revised
version of Ovid's story of Midas's barber, here become Midas's wife, who
cannot keep the secret that her husband has asses' ears. (This tale, by the
way, assures us that the knight will find his answer sooner or later, since no
secret can be kept by women.) That Alisoun speaks as much as a figure of
the poet as of woman is underscored by the question—half rallying cry,
half challenge to those wedded to ideas of pryvetee—with which she
opens her Midas digression: "wol ye heere the tale?" (III.951).

Furthermore, the Wife proclaims that she can't hoard her sex any more
than her words—neither is to be private. We have already quoted her
admission that she can't keep her sexual pryvetee from any "good felawe"; elsewhere in her Prologue she chides one of her old husbands who
has asserted exclusive claim to her sexual pryvetee, her private parts,
saying,

> Have thou ynogh, what thar thee recche or care
> How myrily that othere folkes fare?
> For, certeyn, olde dotard, by youre leve,
> Ye shul have queynte right ynogh at eve.
> He is to greet a nygard that wolde werne
> A man to lighte a candle at his lanterne;
> He shal have never the lasse light, pardee.
> Have thou ynogh, thee thar not pleyne thee.
>
> (III.329–36)

Scorning even the more literal *res privata* of her own property, Alisoun
even says that she gave her fifth husband, the one she loved most, "al the
lond and fee / That evere was me yeven therbifoore" (III.630–31).

But, as anyone familiar with Chaucer's Alisoun of Bath knows, this is

only half her story. There is a side of the Wife which contradicts everything said thus far about her attitudes toward pryvetee, and which establishes her as a central paradox of *CT*. First of all, to counter her truthtelling impulse, with its subversion of pryvetee, there is her enormous
capacity for lying. Of the supposed transcripts of her first three husbands'
drunken tirades that she throws back at them, she tells us "al was fals"
(III.382). Of the dreams with which she beguiles Jankyn to be her fifth
husband, she confesses "al was fals" (III.582). In the latter case, she is
fabricating material of high sexual content, and ostensibly violating her
own pryvetee to reveal them to Jankyn. Furthermore, she prefaces her
entire account of her marriages, her entire revelation of marital pryvetee,
with this ambiguous disclaimer:

> But yet I praye to al this compaignye,
> If that I speke after my fantasye,
> As taketh nat agrief of that I seye,
> For myn entente nys but for to pleye.

> (III.189–92)

Where does *fantasye* end and pryvetee begin? This question surfaced in
connection with Guillaume de Poitou's account of his involvement in the
sexual pryvetee of Agnes and Ermessen, and we have already noted the
subversive link between pryvetee and *fantasye* in the Reeve's Tale; here
the issue strikes to the heart of Chaucer's enterprise, in effect. How is the
poet, and how are we, his/her audience, to disentangle truth telling from
fiction making? Is each somehow inextricably implicated in the other?

Next, in dialectic with the Wife's desire to give, share, and overflow
limits is her fully articulated desire to hoard, to deny her pryvetee strate-
gically to her husbands, and give in finally in order to get control of their
bodies, their wills, above all their goods and chattels. "For wynnyng," she
says, "wolde I al his lust endure" (III.416). In other words, the commercial
impulse, to get more while giving less, battles against the poetic impulse,
the impulse toward gratuitous outpouring, toward undamned, unrestricted
giving of words or of self. On the one hand, "I took no kep, so that he liked
me, / How poore he was, ne eek of what degree" (III.625–26); on the other,
"Wynne whoso may, for al is for to selle" (III.414).

Indeed, the Wife at one point refers to her sexual favors as "chaffare,"
merchandise or goods, which she and other women will make accessible
to men who play hard to get; the implicit model is of an unwilling buyer
who forces the salesman to come down in price, and it is said here to
govern sexual relations and games between men and women. Later, the
Host, in refusing to tell about his own wife's shortcomings, offers as an
excuse the fact that his disclosures, or violations of pryvetee

. . . sholde reported be
And toold to hire of somme of this meynee—
Of whom, it nedeth nat for to declare,
Syn wommen konnen outen swich chaffare. . . .

(IV.2435–38)

Here the Host alludes unmistakably to the Wife's earliest confession, but misreads or misapplies it not to sexual promiscuity but to indiscriminate storytelling. The result is a suggested, and suggestive, equivalency between sexuality and taletelling, between two kinds of life-affirming energy that also violate pryvetee, but an equivalency placed within a mercantile model that as often requires hiding as revealing, hoarding as giving.

We are getting close here to the central mystery of *CT* as a whole. In *CT,* most of the characters bring private worlds with them on the pilgrimage—worlds of their professional secrets, or rackets and swindles, e.g., the doctor's arrangement with his pharmacist, the Manciple's cheating of the young men of the Inns of Court whom he should serve, the Reeve's selling his master's own goods back to him and knowing everyone else's privy tricks. Yet the very existence of all these secrets cries out for exposure, and invites storytelling, not of "aventures that whilom han bifalle" (I.795; the Host's formulation) but of pryvetee violated under the licensed conditions of a holiday, whereby "A man may seye ful sooth in game and pley" (I.4355; also the Host's formulation).

Hence pryvetee and the impulse to "telle on" (to recall yet another term frequently used by the Host to keep the storytelling going) feed each other, as the impulse to hide one's own pryvetee makes one paradoxically more interested in others' pryvetee. Accordingly, the Host's refusal to tell about his wife coexists with the universal impulse to answer in the affirmative the wife's cry, "wol ye heere the tale?" The interaction between the impulses toward pryvetee and disclosure constitutes the basic transaction of Chaucer's storytelling society; words are finally that society's most important chaffare, and determining the circumstances under which to "outen" words—and which words to "outen"—are its most important business.

By mingling pryvetee and *fantasye,* truth and fiction, storytelling becomes the playful, and therefore allowable, exchange of what a society normally prefers to keep out of circulation—its secrets of desire and performance, of scandalous success and ignominious failure. Paradoxically, storytelling preserves the social fabric by reminding us of the precariousness of that fabric's integrity; it dramatizes society's construction on the fragile base of private as well as public lives, and therefore society's dependence for its survival and prosperity on all its members' lies, wishes, and dreams as well as their deeds and possessions. Perhaps

Chaucer's greatest poetic accomplishment in *CT* was to dramatize the processes of hiding and revealing—of fiction-making, fiction-breaking, and fiction disguised as revelation—that characterize, and finally define, the social enterprise as he had come to understand it.

Notes

1. Since "pryvetee" appears so frequently throughout this essay, I have refrained, after its first use, from distinguishing it by italics or quotation marks. All references to Chaucerian texts follow *The Riverside Chaucer,* 3rd ed., gen. ed. Larry D. Benson (Boston: Houghton Mifflin, 1987). Quotes from and references to *CT* are identified by fragment and line numbers; references to other works by Chaucer include an abbreviated title as well as section and line numbers. For Theseus' explication of Jupiterian pryvetee, see I.2987f. (and cf. the Knight's exposition of the pryvetee of the gods Mars, Venus, and Saturn, I.2438–78); for the Miller (in propria voce) on Goddes pryvetee, see I. 3163–66, and cf. its evocation within The Miller's Tale by John the carpenter (I.3454f.) and Nicholas the clerk (I.3558). The fiend in The Friar's Tale tells the damned Summoner that in hell he will "knowen of oure privetee / Moore than a maister of dyvynytee" (III.1637–38); Satan's arse appears as the dwelling place of friars in Hell in The Summoner's Prologue (III.1683–99). It should be noted that in *CT* both God's and the devil's pryvetee are presented as human constructs, or at least as theological truths subject to appropriation and manipulation by human beings in their attempts to gain mastery over each other. For a quite different, more philosophically and theologically based analysis of pryvetee in parts of *CT,* see E. D. Blodgett, "Chaucerian Pryvetee and the Opposition of Time," *Speculum* 51 (1976): 477–93. See now A. C. Spearing, "The Medieval Poet as Voyeur," in *The Olde Daunce: Love, Friendship, Sex, and Marriage in the Medieval World,* ed. Robert R. Edwards and Stephen Spector (Albany: State Univ. of New York Press, 1991), pp. 57–86. Spearing's elegant, perceptive essay complements but does not duplicate the approach I have adopted here.

2. My sketch of both literal and what I call metaphorical pryvetee in medieval Europe is greatly indebted to Georges Duby, ed., *A History of Private Life, II. Revelations of the Medieval World,* trans. Arthur Goldhammer (Cambridge and London: The Belknap Press of Harvard Univ. Press, 1988), hereafter *HPL.* For the basic issues of public vs. private life, see especially Duby's *Introduction,* "Private Power, Public Power" (pp. 3–31). I should note that the emphasis of this volume is on private life as a series of practices, rather than on the attitudes that underlay these practices and the strategies by which people sought to protect their privacy and, perhaps, invade the privacy of others.

3. See *HPL,* chapter 5, "The Emergence of the Individual," section titled "Solitude: Eleventh to Thirteenth Century," by Georges Duby: during the twelfth century, "the self staked a claim to an identity within the bosom of the group; it insisted upon its right to keep secrets, distinct from the secrets of the collectivity" (p. 513).

4. Duby (*HPL,* preface, p. xii) stresses "the direct impact of economic growth on the nature of private life"; he notes "a gradual transition from a gregarious to a more individualistic existence, which led to greater introspection; within the privacy of the house there developed an even more intimate preserve, an inner

privacy of the self." In addition, the affairs of merchants came to be recorded with more and more precision and fullness, but this in turn meant that this was material that had to be held in the strictest confidence. "Such a variety of information incidental to active, professional lives was recorded in these books that we are able to view from many different angles personal concerns that had to be kept carefully hidden from public sight. The book of the Valori of Florence bore on its cover the words, 'This book must not be shown to anyone'" (*HPL,* chapter five, section titled "Toward Intimacy: The Fourteenth and Fifteenth Centuries," by Philippe Braunstein, pp. 551–52). That is, in a commerce-oriented world privacy doesn't just exist as an abstract sense, but as a strategic position in the face of others—rivals, enemies—who could hurt one by knowing too much. It comes into play in one's dealings with co-citizens in a competitive situation, a commercial agon.

5. For the literary representation of the expanding private sphere see *HPL,* chapter three, "Imagining the Self: Exploring Literature," by Danielle Regnier-Bohler (pp. 311–93).

6. See J. T. Muckle, trans., *The Story of Abelard's Adversities* (Toronto: Pontifical Institute of Mediaeval Studies, 1964), pp. 26–28.

7. A convenient summary of this concept, with abundant bibliographical references, can be found in Winthrop Wetherbee, *Platonism and Poetry in the Twelfth Century: The Literary Influence of the School of Chartres* (Princeton: Princeton Univ. Press, 1972), pp. 36–48.

8. For Augustine's preaching on this subject, see the lively summary/translation in Peter Brown, *Augustine of Hippo* (Berkeley and Los Angeles: University of California Press, 1969), p. 388. On the ambiguity of clothing vis a vis the nudity (and, by extension, the sexuality) it covers, see *HPL,* pp. 366–67, 373 (Regnier-Bohler); 568, 570, 574–75 (Braunstein).

9. I follow the text and translation of Frederick Goldin, ed. and trans., *Lyrics of the Troubadours and Trouvères: An Anthology and a History* (Garden City, N.Y.: Anchor Books, 1973), pp. 26–33.

10. See R. W. Hanning, "Roasting a Friar, Mis-taking a Wife, and Other Acts of Textual Harassment in Chaucer's *Canterbury Tales,*" *Studies in the Age of Chaucer* 7 (1985): 19–21.

11. See *HPL,* chapter two, "Portraits," section titled "The Aristocratic Households of Feudal France," by Georges Duby, p. 80: "Among themselves, women were believed to exchange secret knowledge of which men had no inkling. This knowledge was passed on to younger women by the 'little old ladies' who appear in any number of stories." Cf. Regnier-Bohler, pp. 346–48, on "the functioning of collective memory within the gynaeceum," or womens' quarters of a household, the secrets of which "can only be passed from women to women," according to medieval misogynistic texts.

Part 2

Chaucer

The Textual Environment of Chaucer's *Lak of Stedfastnesse*

PAUL STROHM

Theoretical tendencies now seem to have a half-life of three or four years, and their particular terms and applications a good deal less. But, whatever their duration, current theories of textuality have had the salutary and probably permanent effect of exposing the rigidities of previous approaches to literary production and reception. When I was in graduate school, interest in the textual environment of a given work was, for example, exhausted by the discovery of the "source"—the particular precursor-text that represented the author's point of access to literary tradition. Matters of reception were usually limited to the relation of poet to patron, with an author shaping an interested utterance to the requirements of a powerful sponsor. Current theories of textuality, however, encourage us to abandon the search for the single, privileged source, in favor of an appreciation of the larger environment of texts and utterances within which a work was composed; not only may such texts be "non-literary" as well as "literary," but awareness of the material involvements of discourse suggests that such an environment may include unwritten and even nonverbal actions and gestures. The perception that both the author and the audience of a work share such an environment encourages us, in turn, to appreciate common elements in the production and reception of texts, to view the work less as a straight-line communication *from* author *to* patron than as an inscription held in common by the participants in a cultural and political situation.

This essay seeks to delineate the larger environment of precursor texts, traditions, and political actions within which Chaucer composed a poem (and within which, presumably, Richard II and others read it). This environment is more than just "background" or "world picture" or even "context." It is a productive matrix within which a variety of verbal and nonverbal political actions and gestures took place. At its center is a variety of controversial social practices founded on that dramatic expansion of opportunities for temporary and opportunistic service described by K. B. McFarlane as "bastard feudalism."[1] Lords, greater and lesser, were availing themselves of these new forms of social relation to expand their retinues and were exploring new forms of local coercion and domination. Persons at the upper range of the middle strata, including the landowning gentry and prosperous merchants who comprised the parliamentary commons, were among those most threatened by this emergent situation; themselves the beneficiaries of a moderate relaxation of social rules, they were nevertheless stimulated by local disorder to an appreciation of traditional social arrangements. Even Richard II, in his political eclipse of the later 1380s, shaped a view of his own; in fact, his policy on lawlessness and retention would be an important element of his return to power. This vital and unstable mix of interests, analyses, and activities created a field for the production and interpretation of more utterances and gestures—including a deceptively slight poem, *Lak of Stedfastnesse,* by temporarily on-the-shelf civil servant and Ricardian loyalist Geoffrey Chaucer.

As a first step in delineating this environment, I will consider an event that involved a text—or, to put it differently, a text that was implicated in an event. This text is an omnibus petition formulated and advanced by the parliamentary commons in September 1388 for discussion with the lords and ultimate action by their king.

A Petition of Commons—Cambridge, September 1388

The Westminster Parliament of 1388 had dragged on from early February through early June with just one significant recess, earning its designation as the "Merciless Parliament" by condemning Nicholas Brembre and Simon Burley and other supporters of the king and by severely circumscribing Richard's own power. By its end, all participants appear to have been in a state of stressful exhaustion and glad for a respite. Petitions advanced by commons were less comprehensive than usual, dealing mainly with matters related to the impeachments and their immediate aftermath.[2] But the commons, already looking ahead to matters ignored during the struggle between King and Appellants, called for another parliament at Michelmas "pur Amendement du Roilaume, en confort de sa Commune" (*RP* 3:246).

At this parliament, which convened in Cambridge on 10 September 1388, the commons presented a composite or "comprehensive" petition dealing with an accumulation of concerns and grievances, of which the opening sections and most or all of the rest have been preserved in the *Westminster Chronicle*.[3] Noting that this text consists of "separate petitions concerning the public interest . . . 'edited' to form a series," its most astute analyst treats it as something of a miscellany of statements on discrete matters.[4] But I find in its provisions a common productive impulse, grounded in an idea of public order based on respect for central and hierarchical authority.

The petition's concern with public order is expressed in its first provision, calling for the lords of the realm to desist in granting liveries called signs or badges ("lez liverees appeliez signes").[5] This is hardly a novel request. The parliamentary commons pleaded again and again, throughout the reigns of Edward III and Richard II and Henry IV, for restraint upon the easy exercise of temporary forms of association—affinities, congregations, confederacies, covines, and other gatherings for purposes of extortion or local domination. A statute of 1 Richard II, for example, complains of the ease of retinue formation by petty aristocracy who enlist esquires and others to maintain their quarrels. Specifically at issue is the ease of their enlistment: they can be enrolled for one hood or other livery a year, from which—the framers of the statute note in dismay—the grantors often collect full value from the recipient, or even turn a profit ("repreignantz vers eux la value de cel livere ou par cas la double value")![6] A concerted, though unsuccessful, initiative of commons occurred again in the Salisbury Parliament of 1384, framed as a complaint that locally powerful persons, supported by the signs or ornaments of lords ("per dominos regni signis quasi ornamentis diversis"), sought to oppress poor persons in the countryside (*West* 80–82).

Exemplified in these initiatives is no mere concern with apparel or ornament, but an urgent unease about the forms of appropriate relation between persons. That distress about temporary and unsanctioned associations recurs in the century after 1350 should occasion no surprise; shifting definitions of appropriate relations may be seen as one aspect of the larger transition from feudalism to capitalism, between the residue of a feudal ideal (a vertical and stable hierarchy based on land tenure and sanctified by oath) and the emergent practices of "bastard feudalism" (with its new possibilities for more flexible associations based on mutual interest and regulated by contract or informal agreement). In the 1388 petition itself, this distress—and an accompanying impulse to limit new forms of association through regulation—is manifested in a number of ways.

Anxiety over unsanctioned associations for illicit ends resurfaces, for example, in the petition's discussion of "touz manerez de meintenance, extorcions, et oppressions faitz ou affaire al poeple." The extent of its framers' concern with maintenance is revealed in their care to include an extensive definition of the practice, a definition too long to include here, but from which the following extract is taken:

Et purceo qe diverses opinions sont en quel cas meintenance doit estre ajugge et en quele nemye, declarissement ensuyt: cest assavoir quant ascun seignur espirituelle ou temporelle ou dame ou femme de religioun ou qeconqe autre de quele estat ou condicion qil soit emprent ou susteigne ascun querele dautre homme a qi il nest pas partie cosyn nalye . . . et quant ascuns soy assemblent en grantz routes et multitude de poeple outre lour degre et estat . . . en destourbaunce de la ley ou en affray du poeple, ou feignent diverses querels par autres de lour assent devers plusours lieges du roiaume. . . . (*West* 358)

[And because there are different opinions about the cases in which maintenance ought or ought not to be adjudged, the definition follows: that is to say when any lord, spiritual or temporal, lady, woman of religion, or any other of whatsoever estate or condition he be, takes up or supports another's quarrel to which he is not a party by reason of blood or marriage . . . and when any gather together in great routs and multitudes of people in excess of their degree and condition . . . to the disturbance of the law or to the intimidation of the people; or feign sundry quarrels by the agency of others in collusion with them against many lieges of the realm. . . (p. 359)]

Some of the points of particular concern here—all inimical to the stability of sworn relations—are that such associations involve alliance of persons not otherwise related ("homme a qi il nest pas partie cosyn nalye"), that they represent a temporary and voluntary association for concerted action ("par autres de lour assent"), and that they seem to involve transgression of the normal constraints of personal degree ("outre lour degre et estat"). Subject to particular condemnation, in other words, is the idea of collusion outside the boundaries of the sanctioned order for purposes of self-advancement or gain.

This same concern about illicit association and transgression for purposes of advancement underlies a number of seemingly unrelated provisions of the larger petition. One of its most puzzling sections, for example, involves the abolition of "touz lez gildes et fraternites" (*West* 356) and the expropriation of their funds. Tuck explains this proposal in terms of a desire to fleece these establishments, together with a prevailing fear of sedition, and pecuniary motives (including the capture of revenue for land held by these organizations in mortmain) almost certainly underlay an ensuing inquiry into the rules and resources of guilds, fraternities, and misteries.[7] Inspection of the details of the original petition suggests, however, a further source of unease on the part of the parliamentary commons, involving neither sedition nor finances. The original petition provides for the *exemption* of those guilds and fraternities "ordenez al honour de seint esglise et encres de divine servise, sanz livere, confederacie, meintenaunce ou riotes "(*West* 356) [ordained to the honour of Holy Church and the increase of divine service, without livery, confederacy, maintenance, or riots (*West* 357)]. Spared, in other words, are those religious fraternities and confraternities that do not aspire to political influence, and that reject the new forms and practices of short-term association for civic or economic advantage. Remaining under suspicion are two categories of organizations. The first consists of urban craft-guilds. Later fourteenth-century usage, as signaled by the language of the dual writs issued to gain information about guild structures as a consequence of the Cambridge petition, was to distinguish between "gildae et fraternitates" or *religious* guilds on the one hand and "misterae et artificia" (or, as Caroline Barron says, "mysteries of artificers") on the other.[8] The implication of the petition, and the writs subsequently issued as a result of the petition, is that the parliamentary commons regarded *all* craft-guilds (though not, presumably, the more prosperous mercantile guilds) as potential sources of economic and civil disequilibrium. Similarly under suspicion are *some* religious fraternities that refuse to confine their activities to keeping their candles lit, and that venture into organizational techniques involving livery, confederacy, maintenance, or worse.[9]

Revealed in this suspicious approach to socially innovative guilds and fraternities are several critical social divisions within the middle strata: first, between those prosperous and mercantile citizens and burgesses in parliament and the artisanal tradespersons of more middling stature who served as masters of the craft guilds, and second, between any and all guild masters and the disenfranchised journeymen or *servientes stipendiarii* who served them. Or, to put it more simply, between the prosperous merchant-capitalists who tended to dominate the parliamentary commons and other, less favorably situated artisan-workers of all categories.[10] Apparently expressed in this provision against socially unruly guildsmen is a mistrust by the parliamentary commons of those persons—whether above them or, in this case, below them on the social scale—who might benefit from unsettling practices of livery and maintenance that had proliferated so rapidly in the middle years of the fourteenth century.

A similar vision, fusing both a desire for social order and a prudent self-regard, informs the petition's treatment of those workers who wander the countryside, without official permission, seeking to better their circumstances. The proposed treatment of those arrested without letters patent is revealing: they shall not only be placed in jail but returned to a condition of servitude—bound, if claimed by no other, to the person by whom they are apprehended ("soit tenuz de servir a luy qi luy ensi prist"). An underlying element of self-regard is apparent; as Tuck points out, the commons contained many small landowners and petty capitalists who stood to gain from a clear subordination of the workforce and from control of its wages.[11] Yet the self-interested substructure of this argument would not necessarily have been evident to the commons who promulgated it, precisely because of the degree of their investment in the whole idea of social order grounded in patterns of domination and subordination. The very idea of masterless men would have seemed so evidently repugnant to the commons that its members would hardly have had to probe their motives in advancing an argument for the reinstitution of social hierarchy at every level of society.

The petition embraces other concerns that I will not examine here, including establishment of appropriate wages for laborers and servants according to their degree ("solonc lour degre"), orderly administration of justice and conduct of trade, and payment of parliamentary and judicial expenses according to schemes more favorable to the commons than to the aristocracy (with free tenants of lords to contribute to the expenses of shire knights and other charges "en supportacion del comune poeple," and with only "villeins de sanke" or hereditary villeins exempted).

However diverse, the different provisions of the petition originate within a body of propositions and assumptions favorable to civil order and to the interests of commons. The dominant proposition asserts the necessity of stable hierarchy at every level of social experience—with the centrality of "degre" everywhere asserted, and with prevailing condemnation of those seeking to operate "outre lour degre." We may notice, on the other hand, that this principle of hierarchical order is selectively imposed. Lords are to keep retinue, but the ranks of their followers are drastically limited, to tenants "de sanke" and (by inference) to lifetime retainers or retainers fully indentured to their lords. Laborers, and especially rural laborers, are bound to serve. But we are told little about the obligations of the middle strata. Aligning themselves with social stability and order, the successful merchant-capitalists serving in commons were able to assail the very configurations designed to advance the interests of others through collective action—both "bastard" retinues and those guilds and fraternities that employed the new tactics of livery and maintenance to increase their effectiveness—while leaving themselves pragmatically free, responsible only to the law and their self-evident attachment to the good of the people.

Richard on Livery and Maintenance, 1388–1390

The commons generated petitions on livery and maintenance with regularity. A crucial difference between the 1388 petition and other petitions, however, is that the 1388 petition achieved unprecedented notice, especially in the form of Richard's own support. In order to understand Richard's sudden solicitude for the commons' position on public order, we must step back from the petition itself to consider the general situation in which it was composed and within which Richard framed his response.

The Merciless Parliament had dealt severe blows to Richard's kingship. Although Gloucester and his fellow Appellants abandoned their briefly-held plan to depose Richard (*RP* 3:379), and although commons would renew homage to Richard and he his coronation oath to them (*West* 294), the parliament nevertheless ended with severe circumscription of his prerogative and with a continual council still in place "pro gubernacione regis continua" (*RP* 3:248; *West* 232). Thus began that summer of Richard's eclipse when, the Westminster chronicler tells us, the king spent June through autumn engaged in the chase ("venacioni indulsit," *West* 342). When parliament next convened in Cambridge on 10 September the king remained in a weak position, effectively barred from rule by the residual prestige of the Appellants and the continuing activities of the council. Yet the Appellants had left open the door for a reassertion of royal authority by their failure to institutionalize their own gains, to advance domestic reform, or to inspire military success.[12] Richard was set to capitalize fully, even brilliantly, on these omissions.

The Westminster chronicler's account of the Cambridge Parliament highlights the concern of commons with those very forms of retaining addressed in their petition; at this parliament, the chronicler observes, the commons complained about the badges issued by lords, since those who wear them, buoyed up by insolent arrogance, practice various extortions in the countryside:

> Item illi de communitate in isto parliamento de signis dominorum graviter sunt conquesti 'eo quod ea gestantes propter suorum potenciam dominorum in tam cervicosam superbiam sunt elati quod varias extorsiones in patria circumcirca ausu temerario committere non verentur.' (*West* 354)

The lords (as they had in 1384) responded defensively, assuring the commons that any offenders handed over to them would be appropriately dealt with. "Ista promissio illis non placuit," comments the chronicler, making clear the commons' resolution not to be so easily satisfied. And at this point Richard came forward with a surprising proposal of his own, offering for the sake of tranquillity to set an example by abandoning his own use of badges:

> Ad hec rex, affectans ut tranquillitas foret in regno pro bono pacis et ut aliis daret exemplum, optulit se deponere sua signa. (*West* 356)

Note the elements of conscious self-representation involved in Richard's performance. Whether through conscious forethought or through momentary inspiration, he chooses exactly the right moment to put himself forward as a mediator of disharmony: a moment of total standoff between the lords and commons. At this moment, he does not simply express an opinion but makes himself into an *exemplum,* an example of correct behavior. And, as if in recognition that they have witnessed a performance, the commons constitute themselves as an approving audience: "quod summe placuit communitati predicte" (*West*

256). Certainly the chronicler was converted; he emphasizes throughout that Richard's motives are of the highest order: "Ut tranquillitas foret in regno. . . . (Out of a desire for domestic tranquillity) . . . volens comune dissidium evitare (anxious to avoid a general split) . . . ut omnis materia dissencionis radicitus exstirpetur (in order to root out completely all matter for controversy) (*West* 356, 357). The extent of Richard's victory is figured in his final response to the lords, allowing them to go on using their signs until the next parliament ("concessit dominis sepedictis uti eorum signis usque in proximum parliamentum"); hitherto so enfeebled as to be excluded from affairs of state, he has now repositioned himself to make "concessions" to the lords, out of an evident reserve of civil power.

As several commentators have pointed out, this intervention marks a decisive stage in Richard's reassertion of sovereignty.[13] Richard's success at the Cambridge Parliament paved the way for his resumption of sole governance at Westminster in May 1389. His own recognition of his successful self-representation as an exponent of public order and enemy of new forms of association is embodied in his proclamation upon resumption of power. To his subjects he promised a full program of public order, including the suppression of illicit congregations and associations, for purposes of maintenance or oppression: "congregaciones, oppressiones, manutenancias, seu coventicula illicita in perturbacionem pacis" (*RP*, 3:404). Nor did Richard immediately abandon this profitable stance toward public order. He instituted new peace commissions in the fall of 1389, with members drawn not from the aristocracy but from the strata of parliamentary commons.[14] He engineered a compromise at the Westminster Parliament of January 1390, in which the lords agreed to retain only persons "de privata familia," receiving a fixed annual annuity.[15] He oversaw a comprehensive, if ineffective, council ordinance on retaining in May 1390. This ordinance was his last significant effort to woo the parliamentary commons via issues of public order. By November 1390, he had abandoned his efforts to reform the peace commissions.[16] Yet, for a period of nearly two years, he had exploited this strategy with marked success.

That Richard's opposition to abuses of retaining was more a matter of political expediency than personal conviction is evident from his own behavior before September 1388 and after May 1390. The very heart of his anti-Appellant strategy in the summer of 1387 had been the widescale retention of personal followers, in part through the activities of deputies who would distribute badges to influential citizens who were to swear to hold with the king ("jurare quod postpositis ceteris dominis quibuscumque cum ipso utpote eorum vero rege tenerent, datisque eisdem signis, scilicet coronis argenteis ac deauratis . . ." (*West* 186). Likewise, he instituted his own order of the white hart at the tournament at Smithfield in October 1390, "ubi datum erat primo signum uel stigma illud egregium in ceruo albo" ("where was first bestowed the badge or notable insignia of the white hart")[17]—a "liveray that he yaf to lordes & ladies, knyghtis and skquiers, for to know his housholde from other peple."[18] Nevertheless, at a crucial period, Richard was able to suppress his own inclination to exercise bastard feudalism on the grandest of scales, in pursuit of a longer-term, ultimately absolutist, goal.

Chaucer's Poem

Often treated as a tissue of commonplaces[19] or as an utterance so opaque that its relatedness to one or another social issue of the day can be asserted without an accompanying burden of demonstration,[20] Chaucer's *Lak of Stedfastnesse* complexly inhabits a highly specific place of its own in this continuing discussion of public order, new forms of retention, and the social responsibility of the nobles and the king. Generally and appropriately typified as a poem about "the world upside-down," it is nevertheless implicated in contemporary history at a number of points, including its explanation for contemporary malaise and its injunction to princely intervention. Here is the poem:

Somtyme the world was so stedfast and stable
That mannes word was obligacioun,
And now it is so fals and deceivable
That word and deed, as in conclusioun,
Ben nothing lyk, for turned up-so-doun   5
Is al this world for mede and wilfulnesse,
That al is lost for lak of stedfastnesse.

What maketh this world to be so variable
But lust that folk have in dissensioun?
For among us now a man is holde unable,   10
But if he can by som collusioun
Don his neighbour wrong or oppressioun.
What causeth this but wilful wrecchednesse,
That al is lost for lak of steadfastnesse?

Trouthe is put doun, resoun is holden fable,   15
Vertu hath now no dominacioun;
Pitee exyled, no man is merciable.
Through covetyse is blent discrecioun.
The world hath mad a permutacioun
Fro right to wrong, fro trouthe to fikelnesse,   20
That al is lost for lak of stedfastnesse.

Lenvoy to King Richard

O prince, desyre to be honourable,
Cherish thy folk and hate extorcioun.
Suffre nothing that may be reprevable
To thyn estat don in thy regioun.   25
Shew forth thy swerd of castigacioun,
Dred God, do law, love trouthe and worthinesse,
And wed thy folk agein to stedfastnesse.[21]

The basis of the current inversion of values in the world is, we learn at the outset, the subversion of an earlier system of "obligation," in which people were bound (*ob + ligo,* "to fasten" or "to bind") in a stable relation based on the certainty of *trouthe* or "mannes word." This system of stable obligations, presented as an object of nostalgia in the poem, may be understood to allude to the sworn hierarchy of feudal tradition, a system whose devotion to the common good is suggested by its distance from rampant individualism (or "wilfulnesse") and proclivity for social fracture (or "dissensioun"). So much an object of nostalgia is this system that its economic basis in the rents derived from proprietorship is wholly concealed; only its successor-system is described as having an economic basis, in individual greed or "covetyse" exemplified in the desire for "mede."

What might seem to be taking shape here is a sweeping claim on my part about the "transition from feudalism to capitalism," and I would not deny the broad pertinence of such a formulation—though at a level of grand abstraction still fairly remote from the actual dynamics of Chaucer's poem. The greater specificity of Chaucer's poem is that it lodges its indictment of covetousness in a contemporary social practice, a practice that might possess a few precapitalist elements but that is essentially a function of a fourteenth-century state of affairs: that of short-term "collusioun" with others for the purpose of doing "wrong or oppressioun" to neighbors. The means of this oppression—whether through force, or intimidation, or maintenance in legal proceedings—remain unspecified. But the result is "extorcioun," the act defined by the *MED* as "wresting money . . . by force, intimidation, or the undue exercise of power or authority."

This emphasis on collusion for purposes of extortion in turn draws Chaucer's poem into close association with maintenance as defined in the 1388 petition: that situation when a lord or other takes up a quarrel to which he is not party by reason of blood or marriage ("a qi il nest pas partie cosyn nalye") in order to gain reward, or colludes with others to feign quarrels ("feignent diverses querels par autres de lour assent") to assault lieges of the realm or to occupy their lands, or to maintain or retain ("mayngtenent ou retiegnent") brigands or other shady characters. The authors of the petition seek an inquiry into all forms of "meintenance, extorcions, et oppressions" practiced upon the people; the result of *collusioun* in the poem is "oppressioun" and "extorcioun" of neighbors. The emphasis on oppression and extortion within both petition and poem is explicable not because one document is a "source" for the other, but because both petition (with its condemnation of connivance in suits and quarrels) and poem (with its condemnation of collusion against neighbors) draw upon current language and concepts to address a current situation of abuse of power.

Even in the weakened condition in which he first received the parliamentary petition, Richard is its addressee; in fact, his response to the provisions on livery ("le roy voet . . .") is interpolated within the text of the petition preserved in the Westminster Chronicle. So, too, as Donald Howard pointed out, would Richard appear to be the "prince" of Chaucer's poem.[22] Not only does the poem's emphasis on public order coincide with Richard's own program, but the role imagined for the prince in Chaucer's poem coincides with a public stance Richard had already devised and enacted for himself. This role is, of course, that of princely mediator. In parliament, Richard had bound himself to an act of voluntary self-submission, in this case to the demands of commons for curtailment of lawless retinues, in order to mediate between rival factions. At once principal practitioner of lordship as head of the royal household and meek subject in voluntary submission to the wishes of commons, he possesses the prerequisites for mediation: an ability to place himself, at least imaginatively, in each camp, and a willingness to refrain from pressing his own claims. In the envoy to the poem, he is urged to do very much the same: to submit to a series of voluntary self-curtailments ("Dred God, do law, love trouthe and worthinesse") and to efface his claims, in order to serve as mediator, go-between, and priest in the wedding between his subjects and their own lost virtue ("And wed thy folk agein to stedfastnesse").[23]

That Chaucer should address Richard at such a time and in such a way is consistent with what we know of his career. In May 1388, during the last frenzies of the Merciless Parliament, Chaucer had severed his last royal and London/Westminster ties by relinquishing his exchequer annuities,[24] completing the process of prudent withdrawal to Kent that he appears to have adopted in order to ride out the emergency. But no sooner was this process complete (on 1 May) than the Merciless Parliament adjourned (on 4 May) and the condemnation, exile, and banishment of Richard's followers came to an abrupt end. Some residual prudence might have been in order, and Chaucer's situation in Kent during the summer of 1388 may be likened to Richard's decision to spend the summer apolitically, indulging in the chase. The difference, however, is that Richard had a job; Chaucer,

effectively unemployed since 1386, appears to have been in serious financial straits.[25] With tensions subsiding in the course of the summer of 1388,
and then with Richard's remarkable reemergence at the Cambridge Parliament, Chaucer's hopes of renewed preferment surely quickened. Events
now unfold with rapidity. In September 1388 Richard launched his campaign for public order. In May 1389 he resumed sole governance. In July
1389 Chaucer was among the first of the Ricardian adherents reappointed
to office, with his assumption of the clerkship of works. In May 1390
Richard's campaign for public order came to an effective end. Between
September 1388 and May 1390 Richard was an appropriate addressee of a
poem about the responsibility of the prince to preserve order in the
countryside, and Chaucer, first as petitioner and then as grateful client,
had good reason to write such a poem.

This is as specific as I wish to be about the possible timing of Chaucer's
poem, since my objective is less to "date" it than to position it within a
broad array of roughly contemporary statements and gestures. In this
sense, I am less concerned to argue that the petition is a "source" for the
poem or that the poem depends upon a specific knowledge of Richard's
parliamentary self-presentation, than that all three were created and understood within a much larger and more diffuse matrix of language, ideas,
and expectations. An advantage of the concept of the textual matrix, as
refined and extended by J. G. A. Pocock, is that it exonerates the critic
from suspicions of overingenuity or arbitrariness in asserting connections
between texts and events. Arguing that "languages are the matrices within
which texts as events occur," he observes that "if we have succeeded in
demonstrating that continuities of discourses were historically actual, that
they were recourses of language available for use . . . over periods of
historical time, then we have escaped the reproach that we are merely
reading them into the record."[26] My own objective is to overcome the
incommensurability of texts and actions, and hence to close the gap
between them, by delineating an environment within which both texts and
actions are produced and received. If the petition of commons, Richard's
intervention, and Chaucer's poem are seen to originate within a common
matrix of ideas about collusion and maintenance, extortion and oppression, and princely redress, then less conjecture needs to be focused on
their special relation to each other; at the same time, discussion of their
legitimate interrelation within a larger situation will rest on a less particular and more defensible argumentative ground. Acting in a common
environment of texts, gestures, and assumption about public order and
new forms of retaining, the commons frame a petition, Richard launches a
campaign, Chaucer writes a poem. We need not wonder that certain words
and concepts surface and resurface in each.

Chaucer, Richard, and Ideology

Chaucer's relation to Richard is, in some senses, that of poet to patron as traditionally conceived. But, in some sense, his address to Richard is not a straight-line communication from petitioner to patron at all, but is rather produced, and undoubtedly received, within this larger matrix that encloses them both. This matrix is, if I may introduce a term withheld until now, *ideological* in nature.

In my use of this term, I am rejecting the notion of ideology as distortion or false consciousness, in favor of a more neutral conception of ideology as the essential element of any form of social organization, a system of imaginary representations and enactments through which persons approach understanding of their historical situation.[27] Ideology so conceived functions as a crucial middle term in literary production, mediating between what Medvedev calls the "literary environment" upon which the text depends for its form and style and the "socioeconomic environment" that, although not necessarily represent directly in the work, exerts an absent influence upon it.[28] I would argue, as well, that it exerts a crucial iinfluence on reception, establishing the terms and expectations within which a text is assimilated to the experience of its reader or hearer.

The propositions on social order produced and sustained within this ideology are broad and flexible: the prince is responsible for maintenance of public order; society depends on orderly degrees of domination and subordination; augmentation of local authority is suspect; collusive attempts to deprive others of their rights or property are to be condemned. Such propositions are hardly the property of Richard, or Chaucer, or the commons—or for that matter any individual or class of persons. They are available throughout the later fourteenth century for varied appropriation and use in a variety of tactical situations.

For example: the 1388 petition invokes these and related propositions in its condemnation of unruly aristocratic retinues and disorder in the countryside. But, earlier in 1388, the aristocratic Appellants had made their own use of similar reasoning to indict Richard's followers, condemning the king's involvement in new-fangled practices of "covyn," "affinite," "meyntenaunce" and retinue-building ("les ditz traitours . . . firent le roy de fair grant retenue de novell' des diverses gentz et a doner a eux diverses signes autrement qu il ne soloit estre dancien temps") [the said traitors . . . caused the king to have of late a great retinue of sundry people and to give them sundry badges otherwise than was wont to be done of ancient time (*West* 257).][29] Then, the wheel having come round again, Richard and his followers at the law-and-order parliament of 1397 indicted Gloucester and the "senior" Appelants for the great number of "Extorsionibus, Oppres-

sionibus, Gravaminibus, & aliis Malefactis" visited against king and people.[30] Then, the wheel having come round *yet* again, followers of Henry IV
stripped certain lords who had profited by the death of Gloucester of their
right to give "Liverees of Sygnes," the more so because of clamor among
the people that "some of her men have done grete extorsions, wronges,
and oppressions to the poeple" (*RP* 3:452). Chaucer's poem, written 1388–
89, casts Richard as the agent of social stability, well able to castigate
disorder. But Gaunt and the great lords invoked the same principle of
princely responsibility, though at the aristocratic rather than monarchic
level, when they replied to the complaint of commons that their retinues
were oppressing the countryside, asserting that every lord was able to
punish his own dependants for any outrages (*West* 82).

Such examples testify to the broad currency of an ideology of civil
order, sanctifying old ties and deploring new and opportunistic social
arrangements. It might even be styled a "dominant" ideology, although not
in the Althusserian sense that it wholly set the terms of contemporary self-
understanding, or that it functioned in the same way for all social groups.
The varied uses to which the discourses of social order might be bent
suggest that, rather than setting the limits of self-understanding, ideology
actually produced concepts of varied applicability, available for appropriation and manipulation by different groups in their own behalf. Far from
disavowing central conceptions of social order, each of the dominant
centers of later fourteenth-century authority and power—including the
royal party, the artistocratic opposition, and those upper gentry and mer-
chant/oligarchs represented in commons—sought to advance its interests
through acts of imaginative appropriation. (Alternative discourses were
simultaneously available, and sporadic and fragmentary appeals to principles of fraternity, brotherhood, and even fair profit may be found in guild
ordinances and among the occasionally insurgent peasantry. Members of
the more secure social groups tended, however, to define themselves by
self-interested application of traditional social principles rather than by
introducing a discourse encouraging new social arrangements. New social
arrangements do surface within discourses of social order sponsored by
these dominant groups, but in highly stigmatized forms, as when new
patterns of association are branded "collusive" in Chaucer's poem or guild
activities are suspected of "riotousness" in the 1388 petition.)

In *Lak,* Chaucer performs an act of appropriation on Richard's behalf.
He assembles a body of powerfully suggestive statements linking steadfastness, sworn relations, reason and virtue and pity, and the honorable
rule of law, and opposes to it a nightmare of collusive greed, wrong,
oppression, fickleness, and extortion, associating the former with Richard
and the latter with his opponents. Part of the tact and presumed effectiveness of Chaucer's poem is its alignment with Richard's campaign to

present himself as an agent of social tranquillity, both in the Cambridge Parliament and in the following year. That is, for all its severe and hortative tone as a poem of advice, *Lak* actually flatters and supports Richard by its very consistency with his own program of self-representation. In this sense, it is the most welcome kind of advice, advice that the recipient does not really need. John Gower, in the first version of his *Confessio,* offers to Richard what he describes as "wisdom to the wise."[31] So does Chaucer offer to Richard a course of action and a rationale that he does not really need, a pretended instruction for one who—in his plentitude of power and wisdom—really needs no instruction at all.

One view of ideology—a view that I have endorsed and used—would have it as a reservoir of possible social solutions, of "answers to questions posed by the situation in which it arose."[32] Yet the dynamics of Chaucer's address to Richard in *Lak* suggest an expanded view of how ideology works, a view that treats ideology as still more broadly enclosing, as a source not only of answers but of questions as well. In their influential collective essay on John Ford, the *Cahiers* editors speak of "questions posed after the fact ('post posées'), the existence of which is made possible because their answer has already been given."[33] Chaucer's poem poses a series of questions about how to respond to the threat of retinues and collusive practices and then bases its answer on the availability of the prince to offer himself as go-between, reeffecting the union between his people and their own traditional virtue. I would suggest that the implied questions to which *Lak* is a response were to some degree made possible by the existence of this answer—not just its prior existence in Chaucer's imagination or in the ballade tradition, but its prior existence in the form of Richard's own self-representation, in and after September 1388.

Ideology saturates the materials from which texts and enactments are assembled, including vital notions of civil order, sworn association, the common good, voluntary restraint, and selfless mediation. But, more than that, it appears to shape the questions to which answers are sought— whether answers in the form of a political petition or a princely enactment or Chaucer's modest poem—since, in the absence of the materials for their solution, the questions would have been less likely to be asked at all. This sway of ideology over the production of meaning within texts and gestures holds true not only for composition but for reception as well, for it is the author's awareness of acting within a field of charged and broadly-accepted significations that fosters his or her confidence of being understood.

All this being said, my intention is not to argue for an endless recycling of ideologically charged elements in a self-enclosed process of signification. For contestants in the power struggles of 1388 represented real centers of social authority: the landed aristocracy and its attempt to expand its power through retinue formation; the monarchy and its attempt to regain the prerogatives of sole rule; the parliamentary commons with its mistrust of new forms of guild organization; journeymen seeking their own organizational base; civil servants displaced by the struggles of the previous year. For each of these groups, secure possession of the principal elements of ideology would have conferred unquestioned practical advantage.

There is a paradox here: ideological commonplaces are both the *means* of symbolic assertion (in the sense that they constitute those ideological forms by which, according to Marx, people become aware of struggle and fight it out) and the final *objective* (in the sense that their possession, by any of the major groups, would have contributed enormously to its success). The resolution of the paradox is that a group asserts its claim to possession of an ideological structure by using it effectively; by producing arguments, representations, and enactments through the apt deployment of ideological materials, the group demonstrates its right to them, their rightful place in the narrative of that group's ascendancy. In this sense, Chaucer's *Lak* renders an exceedingly valuable service. For it offers Richard, in a role he had already chosen, as the final "answer" to charged "questions" that ideology, operating within a deeply contested and incompletely resolved situation, presents.

Notes

1. McFarlane, "Bastard Feudalism," *Bulletin of the Institute of Historical Research* 20 (1943–45): 161–80.

2. *Rotuli Parliamentorum* [hereafter *RP*] 3:246–52.

3. The "comprehensive commons petition" was first described by Howard L. Gray, "Early Commons Bills," in *The Influence of the Commons on Early Legislation: A Study of the Fourteenth and Fifteenth Centuries,* Harvard Historical Studies 34 (Cambridge: Harvard Univ. Press, 1932), pp. 201–87. He commented that "it was a petition of several articles. Although each article was in itself a petition and demanded its own response, there was a certain appropriateness in enumerating in a series the commons' requests . . ." (p. 203). A. R. Myers, "Parliamentary Petitions in the Fifteenth Century," *English Historical Review* 52 (1937): 385–404, 590–613, doubts Gray's conclusion that the comprehensive petition persisted into the fifteenth century (pp. 593–610), but Gray's observations about the parliamentary processes of the fourteenth century in general, and the Cambridge Parliament in particular, retain their force. Granting Gray's point, and that of J. A. Tuck, "The Cambridge Parliament, 1388," *English Historical Review* 84 (1969): 225–43, any consistency within the provisions of the petition of the Cambridge commons must be seen to result less from any tradition or imperative or unity than from persistent elements in the larger situation within which the petition was composed.

4. Tuck, "The Cambridge Parliament," p. 230.

5. *The Westminster Chronicle 1381–1394* [hereafter *West*], ed. and trans. L. C. Hector and Barbara Harvey (Oxford: Clarendon, 1982), p. 356.

6. *Statutes of the Realm* (London: Basket, 1763), 1:335.

7. Tuck, "The Cambridge Parliament," pp. 237–38.

8. See *Calendar of Close Rolls,* Richard II, vol. 6, 1396–99 (London, 1927); Caroline M. Barron, "The Parish Fraternities of Medieval London," in *The Church in Pre-Reformation Society: Essays in Honour of F. R. H. Du Boulay,* ed. Caroline M. Barron and C. Harper-Bill (Woodbridge, Suffolk: Boydell, 1985), pp. 13–37.

9. Organization for economic and civil influence behind a screen of pious fraternalism evidently did occur in the 1380s and 1390s. Caroline Barron is currently editing a previously-undiscovered English guild return—that of the "yeomanrie of the curriers"—in which the journeyman-curriers mouth a few pieties and then launch into a series of tough-minded economic provisions: "no man of that Craft ne shall sette non vncouth man a worke . . . ," etc. That such activities did occur under guild cover is evident from a 1387 complaint of master-cordwainers that journeymen were seeking to organize contrary to the 1383 ordinance against covins, under the guise of a religious association. See *Calendar of Letter-Books . . . of the City of London: Letter-Book H,* ed. Reginald R. Sharpe (London: J. E. Francis, 1907), p. 219. Additional attempts of relatively dispossessed workers to work within religious guilds for wage-gains and other objectives are signaled in the 1396 complaints of the master-saddlemen against their own journeymen or yeomen (*Letter-Book H,* p. 311).

10. With respect to the domination of commons by a mercantile patriciate, May McKisack has observed that "during the fourteenth century the election of parliamentary burgesses was in nearly all towns the exclusive privilege of a few of the wealthier citizens." See *The Parliamentary Representation of the English Boroughs during the Middle Ages* (London: Oxford Univ. Press, 1932), p. 38. Nearly half were gentle in the first quarter of the fifteenth century, and the proportion of royal officers was growing apace. See J. S. Roskell, "The Social Composition of a Commons in a Fifteenth-Century Parliament," in *Parliament and Politics in Late Medieval England,* 2 vols. (London: Hambledon, 1981), 1:(VI) 161; and A. L. Brown, "Parliament, c. 1377–1422," in *The English Parliament in the Middle Ages,* ed. R. G. Davies and J. H. Denton (Philadelphia: Univ. of Pennsylvania Press, 1981), p. 120. In her unpublished study, Barron draws a clear distinction between the parliamentary strata and the more humble artificers or craft-guildsmen: "All the London guild certificates [issued in response to the writs of 1388–89], whether of parish or craft fraternities, emanate from the 'middle class' of London society. The royal writ specifically asked for returns from keepers of guilds and fraternities and 'misteries of artificers' and so, by implication, *excluding groupings of merchants.* If we look at the masters and wardens whose names are included in the returns printed here, the 'artisan' nature of these associations is made abundantly clear. The Virgin's guild in the Church of St. Stephen Coleman Street was [for example] founded by a mason, a brewer, a smith, a currier and a leather dyer." Despite some aristocratic and gentle membership—Edward III had, for example, been enrolled as a skinner—the craft-guilds tended to enroll those sorts of lesser entrepreneurs (described by Ruth Bird) who had joined John Northampton in his opposition to the merchant-victualing oligarchs earlier in the 1380s. See Sylvia Thrupp, *The Merchant Class of Medieval London* (Chicago: Univ. of Chicago Press, 1948), p. 73; Ruth Bird, *The Turbulent London of Richard II* (London: Longmans, 1949). See also Barron, "The Parish Fraternities of Medieval London," in *The Church in Pre-Reformation Society,* ed. Barron and Harper-Bill, pp. 29–30; Thrupp, "Medieval Gilds Reconsidered" (1942), reprinted in *Society and History: Essays by Sylvia L. Thrupp* (Ann Arbor: Univ. of Michigan Press, 1977), p. 233.

11. Tuck, "The Cambridge Parliament," p. 236.

12. Ibid., pp. 225–27.

13. Ibid., p. 235. See also Tuck's *Richard II and the English Nobility* (London: Arnold, 1973), pp. 133–37; Anthony Goodman, *The Loyal Conspiracy: The Lords Appellant under Richard II* (London: Routledge, 1971), pp. 50–51; and R. L. Storey, "Liveries and Commissions of the Peace 1388–90," in *The Reign of Richard II: Essays in Honour of May McKisack,* ed. F. R. H. Du Boulay and Caroline M. Barron (London: Athlone, 1971), pp. 135–40.

14. Storey, "Liveries and Commissions of the Peace," pp. 140–42.

15. See Thomas Walsingham, *Historia anglicana,* ed. H. T. Riley, Rolls Series 28, pt. 1, 2 vols. (London: Longman, 1864), 2:195–96.

16. Storey, "Liveries and Commissions of the Peace," pp. 149–52.

17. *Historia vitae et regni Ricardi Secundi,* ed. George B. Stow, Jr. (Philadelphia: Univ. of Pennsylvania Press, 1977), p. 132.

18. *Brut,* edited by F. W. D. Brie, pt. 2, EETS, O.S. 136 (London: Kegan Paul, 1908), p. 343.

19. The argument for conventionality has in fact been made, and thoroughly, by J. E. Cross, who demonstrates by extensive reference to classical Latin, Old French, and Old Swedish that the poem's "seemingly unique statements" are actually so "commonplace" as to frustrate any attempt to connect it with contemporary circumstances, such that it must remain "undated and unaddressed." See "The Old Swedish *Trohetsvisan* and Chaucer's *Lak of Stedfastnesse*—A Study in a Medieval Genre," *Saga-Book of the Viking Society for Northern Research* 16 (1965): 283, 302. On inspection, however, the language and conceptions of the poem turn out to be freighted with a good deal more historical specificity than Cross's line of argument would suppose. Cross argues, for example, that there is no essential difference between *Lak's* "Trouthe is putte doun" and such precedental texts as Isaiah's "Et conversum est retrorsum iudicium" and Juvenal's "Probitas laudatur et alget." But in fact the deepest historical and cultural differences separate the Hebrew/Latin emphasis on the judicial system in *iudicium* and the Latin emphasis on personal responsibility in *probitas* from the fourteenth-century concept of *trouthe. Trouthe* is deeply involved in medieval convictions about the permanence of sworn understandings and the possibility of securing sworn relations from temporal decay by associating them with the divine.

20. Cross's line of argument notwithstanding, scholars have continually sought to connect Chaucer's poem with particular, later fourteenth-century events. It has, for example, been viewed as a disapproving commentary on the Merciless Parliament, as an approving commentary on Richard's extension of his prerogative in 1397, and as a statement of dismay occasioned by the Peasants' Revolt. See, respectively, A. W. Pollard, *Chaucer,* rev. ed. (London: Kegan Paul, Trench & Co., 1912), p. 123; Aage Brusendorff, *The Chaucer Tradition* (London: Oxford Univ. Press, 1925), p. 274; D. S. Brewer, *Chaucer,* 3rd ed. (London: Longman, 1973), p. 41. The very proliferation of these proposals would seem, however, indirectly to support Cross's contention: a poem adaptable to so wide a range of contemporary events can hardly be viewed as a singular response to any one of them.

For all the earnestness with which commentators have sought to historicize the poem, they would still seem to have run afoul of what J. Hillis Miller has called "the apparent canyon between history and language"—or, in this case, between specific history and a highly conventional text. See "The Triumph of Theory, the Resistance to Reading, and the Question of the Material Base," *PMLA* 102 (1987): 291. Temporarily pursuing this metaphor of the canyon, one might observe that the conjectures with which the poem's commentators have sought to bridge it have a decidedly improvised quality, a look of not being ready to bear much weight. One response to the embarrassments posed by this canyon is simply to acknowledge them. This is why I find the most intelligent observation on this poem to be that of John Scattergood, "Social and Political Issues in Chaucer's *Lak of Stedfastnesse,*" *The Chaucer Review* 21 (1987): 469–75. He acknowledges the difficulty of moving between unique historical particulars and self-enclosed texts, reminding us that Chaucer's habitual strategy is to talk "about the particular by way of traditional genres" (p. 474). In effect, Scattergood recognizes the need for what must be considered a scholarly "leap" across the canyon between texts and circumstances. Because of his broad learning, his own conjecture—that the poem's exhortation to its addressee to maintain his "estat" alludes to Richard's defense of his prerogative in 1386–87—is more interesting and persuasive than most. That it must remain a conjecture is implicit, however, in his formulation of the problem.

21. Chaucer quotations from *The Riverside Chaucer,* 3rd ed., gen. ed. Larry D. Benson (Boston: Houghton Mifflin, 1987) p. 654.

22. Donald Howard's treatment of the poem argues that Richard is its addressee, and that it proposes a royal role while representing the poet's own views. See *The Idea of the Canterbury Tales* (Berkeley and Los Angeles: Univ. of California Press, 1976), pp. 129–130. That Richard is Chaucer's addressee is, of course, suggested by Shirley's manuscript heading, "Lenvoye to kyng Richard." See *The Minor Poems,* ed. George B. Pace and Alfred David, *A Variorum Edition of the Works of Geoffrey Chaucer,* vol. 5:1 (Norman: Univ. of Oklahoma Press, 1982), pp. 83–84. Yet Shirley's attributions are notoriously fanciful and self-serving, and can at best be taken as evidence only of one reasonably acute fifteenth-century reader's response, rather than as evidence in the usual sense. More persuasive are the coincidence of the poem's admonitions to defend the people against extortion with Richard's own campaign for public order, and the fact that Richard's campaign occurred at a point in Chaucer's own career when a flattering poem addressed to his monarch would have made most sense.

23. In fourteenth-century England the role of mediator is traditionally played by women; Richard's mother Joan of Kent and his first wife Anne of Bohemia were, of course, renowned for their intercessions. The prince as voluntary intercessor, withholding his own spousal claims in order to promote a marriage of his subjects and their own lost virtue, would have borne a strangely gendered charge for many readers of Chaucer's poem. In this sense, the highly assertive "swerd of castigacioun" that has posed interpretative temptations and difficulties for some readers of the poem might simply be thought compensatory: a visible emblem of incontestable phallacity to offset any less-than-princely elements in Richard's chosen role.

24. *Chaucer Life-Records,* ed. Martin M. Crow and Clair C. Olson (Oxford: Clarendon, 1966), pp. 336–39.

25. *Chaucer Life-Records,* pp. 384–91.

26. Pocock, "Texts as Events: Reflections on the History of Political Thought," in *Poetics of Discourse: The Literature and History of Seventeenth-Century England,* ed. Kevin Sharpe and Steven N. Zwicker (Berkeley and Los Angeles: Univ. of California Press, 1987), p. 28.

27. See, for example, Louis Althusser, *For Marx,* trans. Ben Brewster (New York: Pantheon, 1969), pp. 231–32; Clifford Geertz, "Ideology as a Cultural System," in *The Interpretation of Culture* (New York: Basic Books, 1973), p. 218; Raymond Williams, *Keywords: A Vocabulary of Culture and Society,* rev. ed. (New York: Oxford Univ. Press, 1983), pp. 153–57.

28. M. M. Bakhtin/P. M. Medvedev, *The Formal Method in Literary Schol-*

arship (Cambridge: Harvard Univ. Press, 1985), pp. 26–27.

29. *West* 256. See also pp. 242, 244, 248.

30. *Foedera,* edited by Thomas Rymer, 3 vols. (The Hague: Joannen Neaulme, 1740), 3 (iv):131.

31. *The Complete Works of John Gower,* 8, 1. 3059, ed. G. C. Macaulay, 4 vols. (Oxford: Clarendon, 1899–1902), 2:475.

32. Kenneth Burke, as cited in Geertz, "Ideology as a Cultural System," p. 230.

33. " 'Young Mr. Lincoln' de John Ford," *Cahiers du cinéma* 223 (August 1970): 33.

Chaucer, Pope, and the *House of Fame*

JOHN M. FYLER

Like any editor of a minor poem, I am no doubt inclined to magnify the importance of the *House of Fame*. Yet the poem does, I think, have what I have called a "notable speculative energy," and it is in fact "Chaucer's fullest exploration of the poet's position and responsibilities, the sources of his knowledge, and the limits of his vision."[1] Donald Howard would have agreed; indeed, he argued that the *House of Fame* "may be the greatest poetical statement in the English language about the nature of poetic influence and poetic tradition. It affords, moreover, a surprising glimpse into a poet's inner world of thought."[2] Its extended examination of poetic tradition, the nature of language, and the transmission of meaning reverberates in Chaucer's major works—in *Troilus and Criseyde* and, even more obviously, in the *Canterbury Tales,* where the tale-tellers of the House of Rumor are given names and substantial form. And the skeptical reserve of Chaucer's narrator, faced with the false allurements of Fame and the uncertain truth in his sources of knowledge, directly shapes his characteristic self-presentation in the later poems.

The *House of Fame,* so thoroughly concerned with influence and tradition, has its own place in later poetic tradition. The high point of its afterlife in English literary history is certainly in the works of Alexander Pope, who wrote a youthful imitation of Book Three entitled the *Temple of Fame*. When A. C. Cawley commented on "Chaucer, Pope, and Fame," he was largely content to point out that Pope's conception of Fame is the modern one, introduced by the Renaissance, while Chaucer's is more closely akin to Virgil and Ovid's Fama, *rumor*.[3] More recently, John E. Sitter has argued convincingly that Chaucer gave Pope useful lessons in the vision form, which he used not only in his Chaucerian imitation but even more fruitfully in the *Dunciad;* Book Four of the *Dunciad,* as Sitter points out, is in fact "an ironic, elaborately inverted version of the grand convocation in the *Temple of Fame,*" and descends, through this intermediary, from Chaucer's own presentation of Fame enthroned.[4] There is still more to be said, I think, about Pope's debt to Chaucer: in both the *Temple of Fame* and the *Dunciad,* he repeats Chaucer's central interest in language, the nature of signification, and poetic meaning, and he learns from Chaucer's way of talking about these issues.

Despite Pope's protestation, in the "Advertisement" to the Temple of Fame, that there is "nothing in the Two first Books" of Chaucer's poem "that answers to their Title,"[5] his imitation makes apparent that he has read the entire poem with attention, and assimilated the first two books in his version of Book Three. He summarizes Chaucer's aerial view of the world, repeating his counterpoint of land and ocean, desert and city, and most of all, clear sight and confusion:

> I stood, methought, betwixt Earth, Seas, and Skies;
> The whole Creation open to my Eyes:
> In Air self-ballanc'd hung the Globe below,
> Where Mountains rise, and circling Oceans flow;
> Here naked Rocks, and empty Wastes were seen,
> There Tow'ry Cities, and the Forests green:
> Here sailing Ships delight the wand'ring Eyes;
> There Trees, and intermingl'd Temples rise:
> Now a clear Sun the shining Scene displays,
> The transient Landscape now in Clouds decays.
>
> (11–20)

He also gives a brief account of the Eagle's disquisition on "kyndely enclynyng" and the wave motion of sound (428–47). These passages suggest that Sitter oversimplifies matters when he says that Pope "discards all of Chaucer's first book, and he uses the second book primarily as the source for a few extended similes."[6] Pope's imitation is certainly preoccupied with the scene of Fame's judgment. But the *Temple of Fame* and the *Dunciad* also make thorough use of Chaucer's account of significant sound in its context of babble and meaningless noise; and Pope adapts Chaucer's view of the poet's place in a poetic tradition.

In Book Three of the *House of Fame,* Chauces sums up the weight of literary tradition in his portrayal of the poets and historians on pillars, bearing up the fame of their historical subjects; and he shows that one must maintain a skeptical relation to that tradition because of its uncertainties:

> But yet I gan ful wel espie,
> Betwex hem was a litil envye.
> Oon seyde that Omer made lyes,
> Feynynge in hys poetries,
> And was to Grekes favorable;
> Therfor held he hyt but fable.
>
> (1475–80)

In Book One he exemplifies such ambiguities, and the uncertainty of the poet's knowledge, by presenting side by side the Virgilian and Ovidian versions of Dido's story, at the same time that he uses—tongue-in-cheek— their descriptions of the goddess Fama and her house as authoritative accounts. Pope's imitation internalizes these conflicts. The *Temple of Fame* makes us aware of the weight of tradition, and the uncertain place of an imitation within that tradition—paying homage to it, giving it new life, but with a risk at the same time of misappropriating it or putting it to trivial use. Pope's imitation is conspicuously allusive, even at times incorporating the poems of the past by direct quotation, as on Horace's pillar: "The polish'd Pillar diff'rent Sculptures grace; / A Work outlasting Monumental Brass" (226–27). But as so often in Pope's work echoes of the great poets, here especially Milton and Virgil, look back to an epic world, set against the triviality of the world Pope describes. In the *Dunciad,* Dulness sits "High on a gorgeous seat, that far out-shone / Henley's gilt tub, or Fleckno's Irish throne" (2.1–2) (cf. *Paradise Lost* 2.1–2); in the *Temple of Fame* the western face of the goddess' house recalls, down to its Doric pillars (76; cf. *PL* 1.714), Milton's account of Pandemonium: in place of Milton's "Anon out of the earth a fabric huge / Rose like an exhalation" (1.710–11),[7] Pope has, describing the creation of Thebes by Amphion's lyre:

> There might you see the length'ning Spires ascend,
> The Domes swell up, the widening Arches bend,
> The growing Tow'rs like Exhalations rise,
> And the huge Columns heave into the Skies.
>
> (89–92)

The demonic apparition of Pandemonium, in the background of these lines, gives Amphion's Thebes a hint of the spurious; and that hint is particularly apt here because the miraculous expansion of Thebes reminds us of the defining properties of Fame's palace. Moreover, "exhalation" in the context of windy Fame has a special pungency. When Pope compares the "promiscuous Throngs" of Fame's petitioners with swarms of bees in spring (281–87), he copies Milton's trick of turning the epic simile against itself: we remember Milton's use of the same simile to describe the assembled devils (*PL* 1.768–77), but also its originals in the *Aeneid* (1.430– 36 and 6.707–9), and Pope's later use of it in the *Dunciad:*

> And now had Fame's posterior Trumpet blown,
> And all the Nations summon'd to the Throne.
> The young, the old, who feel her inward sway,
> One instinct seizes, and transports away.
> None need a guide, by sure Attraction led,
> And strong impulsive gravity of Head:
> None want a place, for all their Centre found,

Hung to the Goddess, and coher'd around.
Not closer, orb in orb, conglob'd are seen
The buzzing Bees about their dusky Queen.

(4.71–80)

When he describes the approach to Fame's Temple—"High on a Rock of Ice the Structure lay, / Steep its Ascent, and slipp'ry was the Way" (27–28)—he inverts Dryden's translation of *Aeneid* 6.126: "Smooth the Descent, and easie is the Way" (6.193) from Avernus;[8] but there is a notable incongruity between the dark infernal depths and the mild heights of Fame.

In these instances Pope is elaborating upon Chaucer's repeated moments of anticlimax and ironic collapse. There are a number of other points at which the *Temple of Fame* embellishes Chaucer with particular aptness, revealing Pope's complex understanding of Chaucer's meaning while he pursues his own habitual concerns. In his description of Fame's icy mountain, on which the names of the famous melt or remain sharply etched according to the accident of their placement, Pope adds another category of interlopers, who end their quest for fame with uncertain success:

Criticks I saw, that other Names deface,
And fix their own with labour in their place:
Their own like others soon their Place resign'd,
Or disappear'd, and left the first behind.

(37–40)

Pope makes Fame's Temple more precisely a microcosm, by adding a description of its four sides, each of which sums up a quarter of the world's history, learning, and literature. His answer to the question "Art thou, fond Youth, a Candidate for Praise?" exhibits a Boethian awareness of the exigencies fame brings:

'Tis true, said I, not void of Hopes I came,
For who so fond as youthful Bards of Fame?
But few, alas! the casual Blessing boast,
So hard to gain, so easy to be lost:
How vain that second Life in others' Breath,
Th'Estate which Wits inherit after Death!
Ease, Health, and Life, for this they must resign,
(Unsure the Tenure, but how vast the Fine!)
The Great Man's Curse without the Gains endure,
Be evny'd, wretched, and be flatter'd poor;
All luckless Wits their Enemies profest,
And all successful, jealous Friends at best.

(500–512)

And when Pope ends the poem, he combines a reminiscence of the *Aeneid*

(3.56–57; cf. *An Essay on Criticism* 520–21: "To what base Ends, and by what abject ways, / Are Mortals urg'd thro' *Sacred Lust of Praise!*") with a paraphrase of Chaucer's words to Frend:

> Drive from my Breast that wretched Lust of Praise;
> Unblemish'd let me live, or die unknown,
> Oh grant an honest Fame, or grant me none!
>
> (522–24)

Finally, Pope repeats with great effectiveness Chaucer's perception that Fame mixes false and true, so that the poet's sources of knowledge are always problematic: "All neither wholly false, nor wholly true" (457), the true and false "strict Companions are for ever join'd, / And this or that unmix'd, no Mortal e'er shall find" (495–96). The wellspring of mortal knoweldge, with true and false forever joined, is in ever-multiplying rumor:

> Above, below, without, within, around,
> Confus'd unnumber'd Multitudes are found,
> Who pass, repass, advance, and glide away;
> Hosts rais'd by Fear, and Phantoms of a Day.
>
> (458–61)

The most interesting effect of putting Pope's version of Fame next to Chaucer's is the apparent congruence of late medieval and eighteenth-century concerns with signification. In Book Two of the *House of Fame* the Eagle's discourse reduces all meaningful sound to its merely physical dimensions—the joke being that, in his system, flatus and the *Aeneid* are essentially the same thing.[9] The closest analogue to this joke in Augustan satire is Swift's definition of the Aeolists, in *A Tale of a Tub:* "Words are but Wind; and Learning is nothing but Words; Ergo, learning is nothing but Wind."[10] Swift here expresses the satirist's universal fear that words are no longer connected to things; in a medieval expression of that fear, John of Salisbury laments: "Our age has expired and is reduced almost to nothing; not knowing the degrees of honor, it puffs itself up with honors; it is charmed by the vanity of names, while despising the truth and fruitful consequence of realities."[11] But Pope too shows himself to be well aware of the ironic possibilities here, the ways in which the world of words can alternately be one of inflation or deflation. On the one hand, as Chaucer makes evident by his emphasis on linguistic multiplication, Fame's peculiar quality—in Pope's version as well—is to expand things beyond their natural contours.

> The Wall in Lustre and Effect like Glass,
> Which o'er each Object casting various Dies,
> Enlarges some, and others multiplies.

Nor void of Emblem was the mystic Wall,
For thus Romantick Fame increases all.

(132–36)

On the other hand, especially in a satiric mode, language may suffer deflation when its referents no longer match the grandiloquence of their signifiers: Laura Brown quotes a parody of the *Temple of Fame* (436–41), *Aesop at the Bear Garden* (1715), in which this process works on the most memorable image in Book Two of the *House of Fame:*

As on the smooth Expance of Chrystal Lakes,
The sinking Stone at first a Circle makes;
So from a House of Office o'er a Lake,
A T--d falls down, and does a Circle make.
The trembling Surface by the Motion stir'd
Spreads in a second Circle, then a third;
Wide and more wide the Excrements advance,
Fill all the watry Place, and to the Margin dance.[12]

Pope follows the example of his parodist in the *Dunciad* (2.405–8), and the deflation of language is especially appropriate in Book Four, where we find, as John Sitter points out, "a poem recording the notorious 'fame' of characters so ephemeral they need footnotes."[13] This world of "Fame's posterior Trumpet" (4.71), is a world defined and constrained by language:

Then thus. "Since Man from beast by Words is known,
Words are Man's province, Words we teach alone.
When Reason doubtful, like the Samian letter,
Points him two ways, the narrower is the better.
Plac'd at the door of Learning, youth to guide,
We never suffer it to stand too wide.
To ask, to guess, to know, as they commence,
As Fancy opens the quick springs of Sense,
We ply the Memory, we load the brain,
Bind rebel Wit, and double chain on chain,
Confine the thought, to exercise the breath;
And keep them in the pale of Words till death."

(4.149–60)

The world of things beyond the pale exacts its revenge: the effect of this miseducation is the loss of substantial being in the fop who, finishing his Grand Tour,

Dropt the dull lumber of the Latin store,
Spoil'd his own language, and acquir'd no more;
All Classic learning lost on Classic ground;
And last turn'd *Air,* the Echo of a Sound!

(4.319–22)

Lo! ev'ry finish'd Son returns to thee:
First slave to Words, then vassal to a Name,
Then dupe to Party; child and man the same;
Bounded by Nature, narrow'd still by Art,
A trifling head, and a contracted heart.

(4.500–504)

In these satirical laments of a divorce between language and reality, and of a world where the Schools advance Dulness' cause by "confining Youth to *Words,* and keeping them out of the way of real Knowledge" (*Argument* to the *Dunciad,* Book Four), there is some kinship with such projects as the Royal Society's search for a scientific prose style. In Thomas Sprat's account:

They have therefore been most rigorous in putting in execution, the only Remedy, that can be found for this *extravagance* [of prolixity]: and that has been, a constant Resolution, to reject all the amplifications, digressions, and swellings of style: to return back to the primitive purity, and shortness, when men deliver'd so many *things,* almost in an equal number of *words.* They have exacted from all their members, a close, naked, natural way of speaking; positive expressions; clear senses; a native easiness; bringing all things as near the Mathematical plainness, as they can: and preferring the language of Artizans, Countrymen, and Merchants, before that, of Wits, or Scholars.[14]

The medieval analogue for this discontent is the *sermo humilis*, a plain style stripped of ornament and sophistical devices, which the Eagle comically claims to have used in his exposition of the theory of sound (*HF* 853–59). But the virtues of plain style and clear thought, as they appear in the *House of Fame,* are also undercut. The Eagle's reductiveness extends to the issue of signification itself, primarily in a running joke about the stars and constellations, the mysterious signs of our fate marked out in the heavens. Chaucer first raises the question with his comic alarm "Wher Joves wol me stellyfye, / Or what thing may this sygnifye?" (586–87). The Eagle, like Dante's Virgil a mind-reader, assures Chaucer of his insignificance, a relief no doubt, though a rather humiliating one:

"Thow demest of thyself amys,
For Joves ys not theraboute—
I dar wel putte the out of doute—
To make of the as yet a sterre."

(596–99)

As the vision progresses, its bookishness corrupts the physical actuality of what the heavens manifest; we begin to doubt the reality of any stellar apotheosis. Just as, according to the Eagle, the placing of the House of Fame verifies Ovid's description in *Metamorphoses* 13, so the constellations are apparently in heaven primarily to establish the veracity of myth. Phaethon on his ill-fated journey, which the Eagle recounts, saw "the Scorpioun, / Which that in heven a sygne is yit" (948–49). Language usurps the proper territory of the astronomer; and external, physical signs come to seem dependent on words for their proof, even their very existence. In this poem words are the roots, not the consequences of things: though the narrator says that he can now, having seen the heavens, believe Martianus Capella and Anticlaudianus, the poem implies that his vision simply recapitulates the terms of their descriptions.

The climax of this joke is the Eagle's interruption of Chaucer's reverie:

> "Wilt thou lere of sterres aught?"
> "Nay, certeynly," quod y, "ryght naught."
> "And why?" "For y am now to old."
> "Elles I wolde the have told,"
> Quod he, "the sterres names, lo,
> And al the hevenes sygnes therto,
> And which thy ben."
>
> (993–99)

As the Eagle goes on to argue, when Chaucer reads "poetrie, / How goddes gonne stellifye / Bridd, fissh, best, or him or here" (1001–3), he does not know where these constellations are located: "For though thou have hem ofte on honde, / Yet nostow not wher that they stonde" (1009–10). Chaucer replies that he willingly believes

> "Hem that write of this matere,
> As though I knew her places here;
> And eke they shynen here so bryghte,
> Hyt shulde shenden al my syghte
> To loke on hem."
>
> (1013–17)

This exchange shows that for Chaucer's eager travel guide, a name is simply a notation, a shorthand for nothing important, a synecdoche for a fiction.

In this respect, the Eagle's disquisition on sound parallels the issue the goddess Fame herself brings up: that is, what's in a name? Chaucer's lack of curiosity about the names and locations of the stars extends to a modest self-sufficiency in response to Fame's blandishments: he is, he says, content with his own valuation of himself, "As fer forth as kan myn art" (1882). His disclaimer acknowledges the central lesson of his vision, that languge implicates its users in its possibilities for corruption. Though the tendencies to logorrhea which the *House of Fame* makes so manifest are impossible entirely to resist—one form of resistance is in fact the use of names as a form of shorthand expression—the wise course is to use language with a temperate caution. After all, as Proverbs 10.19 teaches, "In the multitude of words there wanteth not sin: but he that refraineth his lips is wise." It is certainly for this reason that Chaucer refuses to pass on the one tiding he knows (2136). And his refusal to join Fame's suitors— except in the relatively austere and relatively honorable company of the poets and historians—expresss a strong awareness of the mutability of all things, including the names that Fame sees fit to perpetuate, for a time.

For the poet, dependent on speech and, willy-nilly, the servant of Fame, the implications of his vocation are not altogether pleasant ones. Chaucer comically inverts the pretensions of the *Commedia:* like Dante, he is to be rewarded with "Unkouthe syghtes and tydynges" (2010). But if Dante's vision is of the upper bounds of language, which force a redefinition of poetry and eventually its transcendence, Chaucer's is in some respects of the other extreme, the foul rag and bone shop from which the poet, like all other human beings, takes his terms of discourse. What he sees is a simulacrum, a representation of language, at least as it works in the fallen world. Its source is uncertainty, its value ambiguous; its terms are subject to arbitrary multiplication and distortion. The House of Rumor turns "as swyft as thought" (1924); indeed, it is in some sense thought itself, but thought seen as a whirling cage, ruled by contingency.[15]

Pope's imitation of Chaucer, and his reworking of that imitation in the *Dunciad,* show that he had assimilated Chaucer's troubling thoughts about the centrality and central ambiguities of language. The two poets together have a fitting modern heir, whose conspicuous debt is to Pope, but in whom traces of Chaucer's discourse remain. Vladimir Nabokov's *Pale Fire* is preoccupied with the issues Pope and Chaucer raise: the properties of language as signifier, and the rewards of immortality shared, or vied for competitively, by an author and the subjects the author commemorates. Its land of likeness Zembla is named in the *Temple of Fame,* and Nabokov quotes from *An Essay on Man* to position his work as a heroic treatment of the antiheroic modern world: "The sot a hero, lunatic a king" (2.268).[16] In one maneuver Nabokov follows Pope in his departure from Chaucer: the mad critic intervenes, claiming that Shade's poem is a disguised account of his own life, or to use Pope's phrasing in the *Dunciad:*

Let standard-Authors, thus, like trophies born,
Appear more glorious as more hack'd and torn,
And you, my Critics! in the chequer'd shade,
Admire new light thro' holes yourself have made.

(4.123–26)

But in language's multiplying power, the way in which the commentary dwarfs and subsumes the poem it is meant to comment on, the novel repeats a central Chaucerian point. Even the qualities of Fame as sound and language as moving air find their echo here. As Kinbote complains:

> [I] found in my coat pocket a brutal anonymous note saying: "You have hal.....s real bad, chum," meaning evidently "hallucinations," although a malevolent critic might infer from the insufficient number of dashes that little Mr. Anon, despite teaching Freshman English, could hardly spell.[17]

In the expansion of dashes needed to make halitosis into hallucinations and the implied connection between bad breath and faulty vision, I delight in finding if not new light, then a pale fire snatched from Chaucer's unwilling journey into the air.

Notes

1. *The Riverside Chaucer,* 3rd ed., gen. ed. Larry D. Benson (Boston: Houghton Mifflin, 1987), pp. 347, 348. All citations from Chaucer are to this edition.

2. Donald R. Howard, *Chaucer: His Life, His Works, His World* (New York: Dutton, 1987), p. 252.

3. A. C. Cawley, "Chaucer, Pope, and Fame," *Review of English Literature* 3, no. 2 (1962): 9–19.

4. John E. Sitter, *The Poetry of Pope's* Dunciad (Minneapolis: Univ. of Minnesota Press, 1971), p. 88; also see esp. p. 83.

5. All citations from Pope are to the Twickenham Edition of his works (London: Methuen): the *Temple of Fame* appears in *The Rape of the Lock and Other Poems,* ed. Geoffrey Tillotson (1940); *The Dunciad* of 1742 in *The Dunciad,* ed. James Sutherland, 2nd ed. (1953).

6. Sitter, *Poetry of Pope's* Dunciad, p. 69. Also see Tillotson, *Rape of the Lock,* p. 216, and Maynard Mack *Alexander Pope: A Life* (New Haven: Yale Univ. Press, 1986), pp. 163–64: "The ambling, somewhat garrulous (though in detail often charming) narrative with which Chaucer fills the intervening space apparently appealed to Pope as little as it does to most twentieth-century readers apart from specialists. It is therefore only on the last book . . . that Pope draws."

7. *The Poems of John Milton,* ed. John Carey and Alastair Fowler (Harlow: Longmans, 1968).

8. Quoted by Tillotson, *Rape of the Lock,* p. 247.

9. I have discussed this section of the poem at greater length in *Chaucer and Ovid* (New Haven: Yale Univ. Press, 1979), pp. 54–55. For useful remarks on the definitions of *vox* in medieval grammatical theory, see: Piero Boitani, "Chaucer's Labyrinth: Fourteenth-Century Literature and Language," *Chaucer Review* 17 (1983): 197–220 (esp. 212–14); and Martin Irvine, "Medieval Grammatical Theory and Chaucer's *House of Fame,*" *Speculum* 60 (1985): 850–76.

10. Jonathan Swift, *A Tale of a Tub,* ed. A. C. Guthkelch and D. Nichol Smith (Oxford: Clarendon, 1920), p. 153.

11. John of Salisbury, *Policraticus,* ed. C. I. Webb, 2 vols. (Oxford: Clarendon, 1909), 2:41.

12. Laura Brown, *Alexander Pope* (Oxford: Blackwell, 1985), p. 150.

13. Sitter, *Poetry of Pope's* Dunciad, p. 69.

14. Thomas Sprat, *The History of the Royal-Society of London, for the Improvng of Natural Knowledge* (London, 1667), p. 113.

15. The pillars in Fame's hall, correspondingly, may well recall the places of an art of memory, such as John of Garland's *Poetria Parisiana:* see Mary Carruthers, "Italy, *Ars Memorativa,* and Fame's House," *Studies in the Age of Chaucer,* Proceedings 2 (1987): 179–88.

16. Vladimir Nabokov, *Pale Fire* (New York: Putnam, 1962), pp. 202–3.

17. Ibid., p. 98.

The Friar and the Critics

FLORENCE H. RIDLEY

In *The Idea of the Canterbury Tales* Donald Howard defends "those who believe that a great literary work has the power to generate an indefinite number of valid critical accounts, as many at least as there are critics," and points out that "history itself prompts rival interpretations."[1] This is explained by the fact that the historical period when critics consider a complex, multilevel work, as well as the eyes with which and the point at which they look, determine what they see; and that in turn enables a work to generate as many accounts as there are critics.

Over time, from the fifteenth century to the present, the truth of Howard's generalizations has been borne out by critical commentary on Chaucer's Friar and his tale; for the section of *The Canterbury Tales* delineating that character has generated accounts, if not "indefinite" in number, at least impressively numerous. And although they represent a wide range of often contradictory opinions, most of them can be seen as "valid" to some degree, if they are understood as the responses of individuals conditioned by their own experience, knowledge, and focus upon specific aspects rather than upon the poem as a whole. In this essay I shall survey some of such commentary, then present an account of the Friar which I believe is more complete than previous ones because it is based upon more of the relevant evidence than any of them has been.

The earliest critics of Chaucer, at least those whose comments have survived, saw him "as a moralist and satirist who exposes and rebukes vices and follies."[2] Thus his much younger contemporary, John Lydgate, praised him for setting "all his entent idelnes and vices for to flee," as did Stephen Hawes for "Kindlyng our hartes, wyth the fiery leams / Of morall vertue." One wonders of whom they were thinking. Surely not the Miller or Reeve or Wife of Bath! Perhaps the Second Nun or patient Griselda? Or that Pardoner or Monk or Friar? Whoever its object, this early focus on the moral aspect of Chaucer's poetry was carried on in the sixteenth century when, as Caroline Spurgeon notes, the Reformers annexed him "as a kind of forerunner and sharer of their opinions with regard to Rome, as evidenced by his keen satirical exposure of the religious orders of his time." And that concept of Chaucer as reformer persisted well up into the eighteenth century.

For what they saw as a stand against popery, opponents of Catholicism praised the poet, and Catholic apologists condemned him. In 1584 Reginald Scot noted with approval that Chaucer had "smelt out the absurdities of poperie, found out the priests' knaverie, derided their folie and falsehood." In 1737 Charles Dodd also responded to his treatment of ecclesiastics, but with marked disapproval. "The courtiers . . . [of Edward III]," he wrote, "were disposed to buzz many thing[s] in the king's ear, that were prejudicial to the Church; in which they were encouraged by a flattering divine called *John Wickliff,* and the witty satires of sir Geoffrey Chaucer, who took all occasions to lessen the power of churchmen, and ridicule their character."

Just as the onset of the Reformation conditioned early response to figures such as the Friar, so did the debate between secular and regular clergy, which had arisen in thirteenth-century France and was at white heat in fourteenth-century England. As Robert P. Miller explains, "Tension between these regular orders [of friars] and the secular clergy arose when the former were granted papal license . . . to preach, to hear confession, and to bury the dead," for in performance of such activities they became natural rivals of the local priest or curate for revenue, and by so doing "threatened the entire secular establishment."[13]

That this tension influenced Chaucer's depiction of friars is clear enough in The Summoner's Tale, where he utilizes attacks upon them by William of St. Amour and Richard FitzRalph, attacks which must have been familiar and readily apparent to his contemporary audience of London professional men and courtiers.[4] Knowledge of the widely recognized hostility between the clerical branches has influenced the response of critics up to the present day. In fact a majority of commentators on Chaucer's poetry have taken professional antagonism between the Friar and Summoner to be their most important aspect, at times even seeing it as the only aspect of their characterization worth considering.

In the eighteenth century Thomas Tyrwhitt wrote of the two, "The ill humour which shews itself between those two characters is quite natural, as no two professions at that time were at more constant variance. The Regular Clergy, and particularly the Mendicant Friars, affected a total exemption from all Ecclesiastical jurisdiction, except that of the Pope, which made them exceedingly obnoxious to the Bishops, and of course to all the inferior officers of the national hierarchy."[5] In the nineteenth century Richard Morris and W. W. Skeat apparently agreed. They offered no original interpretation of the Friar, but simply quoted Tyrwhitt's assessment of him without further comment.[6] More recent critics have responded to The Friar's Tale and that of the Summoner as nothing more than a professional spat: Nevill Coghill as merely a "comedy of contempt" between ecclesiastical rogues; Bertrand Bronson as "a case of namecalling, with nothing much settled either way."[7]

Naturally there is a connection between medieval society and the literature which is built upon and reflects it. Chaucer not surprisingly shaped his poetry in light of his audience's knowledge of and expected response to the strife among members of the clerical hierarchy, their proper duties, improper practices, and the large body of antimendicant satire then current. As Jill Mann points out, he incorporates such satire in the General Prologue in a series of ambiguous hints as to the well-known hypocrisy of friars, their flattery, lechery, greed, and pride, rather than in explicit comments.[8] Thus Chaucer does not say that his Friar Huberd is lecherous, merely that he brings gifts to fair wives. Or that he is proud and wishes to be called "master," only that "he was like a maister or a pope." Or that he is mercenary, only that "He was an esy man to yeve penaunce, / Ther as he wiste to have a good pitaunce." And, "over all, ther as profit sholde arise, / Curteis he was and lowely of servyse." She further notes how Chaucer makes Huberd attractive, gives him twinkling eyes, white neck, and muscular build; stresses the winning nature of his speech and manner and adds, "at times the Friar need not be seen as deceiving his client, but acting as his accomplice in the aim of keeping life pleasant."

Mann is an extremely capable critic, and her explication is valid—as far as it relates to the General Prologue. But she stops short of considering the ultimate end to which Chaucer uses details he gives in that particular section. Naturally the Friar described there thinks, as she says, that he is a worthy, sociable man, well qualified for his job and well beloved by just the right sort of people. And although the audience might pick up the poet's hints of antimendicant satire, his consistent use of ambivalent words would, indeed, "make it hard to subject the Friar to moral analysis," *at this point*. But Mann goes further to suggest that the audience would have found "much in common between the approval of this 'worthy' and 'merye' Friar, and everyday standards of judgement," would have shared Huberd's opinion of himself, his values, which stress the social over the spiritual, and his notions of respectability, which rate innkeepers higher than lepers and beggars—as probably would all Chaucer's audiences, modern ones included. Systematically she stresses "Chaucer's consistent removal of moral judgement."

It is difficult to argue with this as an interpretation of the "General Prologue." Yet only to the Friar as depicted *there* can Mann's concept of the response of Chaucer's audiences to the character be considered valid. In the General Prologue Chaucer does indeed give only hints of antimendicant satire. But those hints imply corruption; and in other sections of the poem he provides ample material for generating moral judgement of the Friar. He does this in The Summoner's Tale, of course, where the promiscuity, lies, cupidity, hypocrisy, and unctuous speech of friars, ambiguously hinted at before, are assigned to a friar clearly modeled on Huberd; and in the Friar's own tale, where his venomous intent toward the Summoner is apparent almost from the start, if thinly veiled by a pose of piety.

A similar exclusive concern with one or the other aspect of *The Canterbury Tales* has occasioned various identifications of his tale's genre. For example, focus upon the relation between tellers has led a majority of critics to classify both the Summoner's and the Friar's tales as fabliaux, apparently only because the former is such an obvious example of the genre.[9] Certain fabuliau characteristics—irony, contemptuous treatment of the victim, a single, clear-cut, swift-moving plot, springing of a trap where the trickster tricks himself—do appear in The Friar's Tale, but others do not. It lacks the usual erotic themes and sexual play; the delight in obscenity designed to shock; love triangle with stock characters, lecherous wife, sensual priest or clerk, stupid, cuckolded husband; and what Per Nykrog identifies and Melissa Furrow defines as a satirical "adversarial relationship to romance" made clear by misuse of romance trappings, vocabulary, and versification.[10] In fact, only Joseph Bédier's definition of the fabliau, "des contes à rire en vers"[11] might fit this particular tale; and that is at once too broad to distinguish it from many other pieces, and too narrow to encompass the Friar's dual intent of destroying an enemy with laughter while preaching a sermon to impress the pilgrims.

Other critics focus upon its relation to the Summoner, and find The Friar's Tale to be a satirical anecdote or farcical satire; upon the deceitful appearance of the fiend, and find it a tale of magic; upon its incorporation of a German folktale, and find it a traditional or popular story; upon contemporary clerical abuses, and find it "an accurate representation of discernible historical particulars." Still others define it as a *novellino*, like those elaborated from the anecdotes of Poggio, because of its narrative structure; an exemplum because of its analogues; or more broadly as pulpit literature because of its echoes of sermons and religious images, motifs, assumptions or attitudes.[12]

Such differences of opinion arise from the fact that The Friar's Tale is all these things and more, and as a result refuses to fit into any strict generic classification—as a number of critics have discovered. Beryl Rowland groups it with the fabliaux, then acknowledges its affinities with the medieval debate and morality play. Derek Brewer describes fabliau subject matter as "indecent, concerned either with sexual or excretory functions," agrees that The Friar's Tale doesn't "fully accord" with the description, yet includes it among the fabliaux anyway, explaining in genial fashion that "Chaucer's fabliaux are the grandchildren of the originals, and must be expected to differ." And Ross Robbins simply accepts the fact that "Chaucer's fabliaux [including The Friar's Tale] go so far beyond the traditional genre as to cease being fabliaux at all."[13]

Generic classifications too narrowly applied hinder rather than help understanding of a literary piece when critics settle on a specific type, then try to make the piece fit by focusing on some aspects and ignoring or glossing over others. Yet generic terms can provide a useful way of understanding and talking about the complex, multilevel performance of the Friar. His tale is a combination of several types: fabliau, moral exemplum, sermon, satire, dramatic monologue. If none of the terms is entirely applicable, in combination they describe what the Friar does, how, why, and to what effect. The ambiguity of the tale's genre simply corresponds to the ambiguity of the teller's intent and its outcome, although this becomes apparent only if one considers as much of the evidence as possible within and without the poem as a whole.

Viewed in a comprehensive light, the Friar's multiple motives and the behavior to which they drive him can be readily perceived. Apparently he wants to have it both ways, or rather several different ways at once. As a fourteenth-century representative of the regular clergy, he wants to attack the secular clergy; as a preacher of dignity, learning, and pride, to deliver a moral sermon and impress his pilgrim audience; and at the same time as a vicious hypocrite he wants to annihilate his enemy, the Summoner. These motives, as well as the natural expectations of the contemporary audience upon which Chaucer played, explain a number of puzzling things about The Friar's Tale, including its uneven, disproportionate structure and lack of specific reflection of the Summoner portrayed in the General Prologue.

The Friar's long opening diatribe against an archdeacon and a summoner is disproportionate to his narrative proper. But it is designed to impress, and to fulfill his audience's expectations of a proper friar involved in the clerical debates, as is the didactic, sermon-like quality of his discourse. In fact when he calls it a "game," Huberd may have been thinking of a real sermon, one also called a "game," a *jocosa*, which contained the same central trickster-tricked incident as his tale.[14] His display of learning—lengthy disquisition on the form and function of evil, scattering of biblical and classical references—is also meant to impress, though again it disrupts and is out of proportion to the story's action.

Although some critics suggest that the Friar's protagonist duplicates the Summoner of the General Prologue,[15] the two figures actually resemble each other only in their greed, propensity for blackmail, and titles. And this, too, is in line with what could be expected in a tale told by a proper friar, who might well attack abuses commonly associated with archdeaconal courts, but should never spit out venom at a personal enemy. I belive it is his attempt to maintain a pose of pious concern with the sins of a general class, not an individual, which leads the Friar to say nothing about the individual traits of Chaucer's Summoner, nothing about his love of spicy food and strong wine, his lechery, disease-marred face and probably homosexuality. The Summoner, on the other hand, has no need to be, or appear to be objective, so in his tale he makes glaringly clear his enemy's corruption by depicting a Friar John who acts out the specific vices of Friar Huberd hinted at in the General Prologue. But that is only after the Friar has spoken; and at the end of his tale he could have expected his audience to be impressed, and to see him as he intended they should—the epitome of a worthy ecclesiast. Just so the Wife of Bath at the end of her tale probably expected them to see her as a worthy woman and a viable candidate for remarriage.

Critics have tried to find unity between her performance and that of the Friar by focusing on theme, and seeing their tales linked by similar treatments of "maistry," or tyranny, or magic, or "the value and significance of earthly experience in general."[16] But such themes are either too all-encompassing or too tangential to serve as effective links between the two. If one compares tellers instead of tales, it becomes apparent that the Wife of Bath and the Friar, as well as the Pardoner, are related not so much by the themes they develop as by the way in which they develop them. For all these pilgrims deliver dramatic monologues, as they speak conveying a strong sense of attempting to influence an audience and inadvertently revealing more than he or she intends to comprehends. The Wife of Bath, for example, appears to be hunting husband number six.[17] But in recalling her vehement attacks upon her five husbands she reveals arrogance, cruelty, militancy, and selfishness—it must be inadvertently, since such qualities are scarcely designed to attract another victim.

The Friar wants to appear to be a compassionate clergyman, concerned only with correction of sin, and perhaps a bit of amusement. But as he moves from his vehement opening tirade to a disdainful display of learning and final satirical prayer for a wicked summoner, he reveals more and more clearly his hypocrisy, rage, and passion for revenge. The Friar's true motivations are most clearly revealed by the thoroughness with which he demolishes *the* Summoner in depicting *a* greedy, stupid summoner whom he ultimately consigns to hell. They are most ironically revealed by his identifying himself with the devil who traps that summoner. Marshall Leicester believes that he makes the identification consciously, using the devil to display his own feelings of superiority.[18] But surely Huberd would not have intended prospective donors in his audience to see him as a devil, any more than Alice would have intended prospective husbands to see her as a shrew. It must be, then, that like Alice he inadvertently tips his hand, unwittingly assigning a devil qualities he admires and fancies are his own—makes him a gentleman and scholar, polite, learned, and scrupulously honest, a real professional whose seizing of the summoner is strictly in the line of duty, even commendable. The Friar's contempt for the summoner gradually fades into admiration for the devil, with whom by the end he completely, and I believe unconsciously, identifies;[19] and the Summoner can quite rightly say, "freres and feends been but lyte asonder" (III. 1674).

Yet there is evidence at the end of his tale that at least some scribes did not respond in this way, but accepted Huberd's view of himself as valid. In the Hengwrt and Ellesmere MSS, two of some thirty-three texts collated for the *Variorum Edition* of The Friar's Tale, the final couplet reads, "And preyeth that these summonours hem repent, / Of hir misdedes, er that the fend hem hente," (III. 1663–64).[20] The scribes of these MSS make the lines a prayer for a whole group of sinners by a pastor, apparently dedicated to saving many souls. But the scribes or editor of the other twenty-nine texts make the lines a final savage blow at the Summoner, giving "And preyeth that this somonour him repente / Of his misdedes, er that the feend him hente," which seems at least as much a wish as a prayer.

How the pilgrims felt about the Friar at the end of his tale is perhaps indicated by the responses of their Host, Harry Bailly, whose developing attitude is traced by Mary Carruthers.[21] As she notes, at first the Host is courteous to the Friar, addresses him as "sire," cuts off the Summoner, who interrupts, with a brusque, "Pees, namoore of this," and requests the Friar to "Tel fourth youre tale, my leeve maister deere." But after Huberd has told his tale, and in his turn interrupts the Summoner, Harry's polite request turns to a rude command: "Pees . . . for Cristes mooder deere!"; and he urges the Summoner to press his attack on the Friar, and "spare it nat at al." Ultimately, seeming to realize that neither man is better than the other, Harry Bailly treats them both with contempt. In at least two instances, at the end of The Knight's Tale and the begining of the Parson's, the Host reflects the opinions of the pilgrims as a group. May we not assume, then, that their attitude toward the Friar develops as his does? That when they see the Friar as he is introduced in the General Prologue they think him to be a responsible member of society; when they hear him begin his tale at first they understand him to be a worthy ecclesiastic; but as they hear his cruel attack on the Summoner unfold, like Harry they come to despise him? Certainly the idea of the Friar develops in the minds of readers as they progress through the poem, from his portrait in the General Prologue through his exchanges with the Wife of Bath, Host, Summoner, through the performance of the Pardoner, in whose light the Friar is at last completely disclosed.

There is an affinity between the Pardoner and the Friar which has not been previously explored; although early writers did occasionally link them, or confuse one with the other. John Heywood wrote a "Mery play between the pardoner and the frere." John Lydgate thought it was "The pardowner beerdless [who told] . . . / a tale to angre with the frere." And a seventeenth-century Parliament-Officer had the Friar, not the Pardoner, convert souls "with the Shoulder-bone of the lost Sheep "[22] Writers such as these seem to have connected the two men unconsciously, perhaps because both are vicious, corrupt clerics and powerful, dramatic story-tellers who preach to impress their audience. Their narratives are, moreover, quite similar in details of action, effect, and significance.

The Pardoner's begins when three wicked rioters seeking to slay Death swear to be brothers and meet an Old Man clad in black. The Friar's begins when a wicked summoner seeking to profit through extortion meets a demon-yeoman in a black-fringed hat, and they swear to be brothers. Both the yeoman and the Old Man are unfailingly courteous. Devils, it seems, are often so, the contrast between their manner and intent making them more frightening; and in light of other similarities between their tales it seems probable that the Pardoner's Old Man as well as the Friar's yeoman is an emissary of Satan, sent to trap the unwary. Both of them, at any rate, lead stupid sinners to destroy themselves, the summoner by stubborn perseverance in evil, the rioters by murdering each other for gold.

As regards effect, we might note that both narratives convey a sense of foreboding, and despite the comic stupidity of their protagonists, a sober didacticism, although in the case of The Friar's Tale this is often overlooked. Critics such as Craik and Pearsall, for example, find it to be a farce, or a comedy which demonstrates "that there are no values, secular or religious, more important than survival and satisfaction of appetite."[23] Yet in reality the tale's imagery as well as its affinities with orthodox theology and the legend of Faust give it a moral dimension as serious as that of the Pardoner's.

The sobering effect of the hunter-prey imagery has been traced by Janette Richardson, who points out how it evolves as the prey is, first, wretches hunted by the summoner, then the summoner himself hunted by the devil, and finally the pilgrims themselves, hunted by Satan, "the leoun [who] sit[s] in his awayt alway" (III 1657).[24] The tale's central irony turns on a concept crucial in penitential theology, "entente." Thus while in its analogues a victim's curse damns the villain, in The Friar's Tale the villain damns himself by his own *intent*.[25] The concluding exhortation, based as it is on Compline, the service for the seventh hour of the Breviary, further strengthens the tale's sense of orthodox ritual, as do the quotations throughout from rites of excommunication and anathema, and expressions from formal malediction such as "paines of Hell" or "body and bones."[26]

Its basic plot is the same as that of the Faust legend; and Chaucer's poem and Marlowe's play have something of the same culminating irony.[27] For in both a demon captures a soul for his master; the intended victim seeks knowledge of hell in a question-and-answer sequence with the demon; is warned, but rejects a last chance for his own salvation, Faust by despairing of Christ's power to save, the summoner by refusing to repent. Of course very few critics take the summoner as seriously as they take Dr. Faustus, some in fact finding him to be at best possessed of an "engaging dottiness."[28] Yet the totality of his destruction, borne off as he is body and soul to hell, has at least a little of the same effect as the damnation of Faust, and might well have aroused a chill in its original audience, as doubtless did the fate of the Pardoner's rioters.

If, in fact, one considers as many aspects as possible of The Friar's Tale, he will find it strikingly similar to that of the Pardoner. Talbot Donaldson even thought it would have been Chaucer's supreme achievement in an exemplum based on the supernatural, had the poet not also written The Pardoner's Tale.[29] Of course the Pardoner's is better. It has greater consistency, conciseness, and completeness; its teller reveals himself as he speaks, while the Friar is laid bare by the Summoner, after his tale is finished. Judging from the better quality of the one and the similarities between the two, we might conclude that The Friar's Tale served as a kind of work-in-progress for the Pardoner's. Whether or not that was the original relationship between them, they do have the same significance. For in both a wicked man who should be a moral guide tells a tale with wicked intent, and in doing so serves as an instrument of God, a "meenes to doon his commandementes" (III. 1484).

The Friar preaches only to impress his audience and attack the Summoner; the Pardoner preaches only from avarice, "nothyng for correccioun of synne"; yet both succeed in teaching a viable lesson: evil destroys itself. As embodiments of evil, the teachers might be expected to see the resemblance between themselves and their villains, heed their own lessons and change their ways before it is too late, but neither does so. The Pardoner continues to peddle his fake relics, ill-advisedly to Harry Bailly; the Friar continues to attack the Summoner. And Harry destroys the Pardoner; the Summoner destroys the Friar.

Donald Howard describes the Pardoner's end more effectively than anyone else has ever done, or is ever likely to do. When the Pardoner offers his relics to the Host, as the one "moost envoluped in synne," he responds with a taunt:

> . . . by the croys which that Seint Eleyne fond,
> I wolde I hadde thy coillons in myn hond

In stide of relikes or of seintuarie.
Lat kutte hem of, I wol thee helpe hem carie;
They shul be shryned in an hogges toord!

(VI. 951–55)

This brutal gibe calls to mind the Pardoner's sexual aberration, and silences him; in Howard's words, cuts off his tongue, which for one of the great proprietors of language is a kind of martyrdom.[30] When all the people laugh, it is clear that the Host has reflected their final devastating opinion of the man who tried to impress them, just as earlier he had reflected their opinion of the Friar who tried to do the same.

When the Friar drives the Summoner into a fury, he lashes out with an obscene vignette about the home of friars in the anus of Satan, then excoriates his enemy in his tale. Paul Zeitlow describes the Friar's end almost, if not quite, as vividly as Howard has done that of the Pardoner.[31] He suggests that the Summoner destroys Friar Huberd in telling of a Friar John who fumbles behind old Thomas's buttocks to grasp a bag of gold and receives a fart instead. For John's grasping, Zeitlow points out, is as gross, as insulting as Thomas's fart, and the whole action crystallizes a truth the Summoner knows very well: the pretensions, gentility, and inflated oratory of friars are all aimed at the culminating moment "when the hand grasps the loot." The final scene when John demands revenge and receives instead a recipe for dividing farts reveals to everyone the contempt in which he is held, and shatters the fastidious, genteel facade of friars within and without The Summoner's Tale. For everyone hearing it will henceforth see them all as false, debased parasites.

The ultimate irony for Chaucer's Friar as for his Pardoner seems to be that each achieves an end quite opposite from the one he had intended, and teaches a lesson whose real truth lies beyond his comprehension, though it is fully demonstrated by the fate he brings down upon his own head.

In his interpretative study of The Canterbury Tales, Howard utilizes the same technique he identifies as functioning within the poem to explain the idea behind it. In doing so he demonstrates that the "idea" is of an interlaced development of themes within a frame, whose total pattern cannot be perceived until all is past, when the reader steps out of the interlace he has experienced and suddenly comprehends the whole.[32] The idea of the Friar is a microcosm of that process. To comprehend it fully, it is necessary to be concerned, not as most critics in the past have been, with one particular facet of character or narrative, or one particular aspect of the poem's historical context, but to consider the teller and his tale in light of their original audience's intellectual, social, and theological milieu, and move through, experience, all the relevant parts of the work as a whole. When they do this, critics will, indeed, continue to construct an indefinite number of accounts of Chaucer's Friar, and they will be not only valid as creative responses of the individuals, but complete.

Notes

1. Donald R. Howard, *The Idea of the Canterbury Tales* (Berkeley and Los Angeles: Univ. of California Press, 1976), p. 4.

2. For the early commentary see Caroline F. E. Spurgeon, *Five Hundred Years of Chaucer Criticism and Allusion* (Cambridge: Cambridge Univ. Press, 1925), I, especially pp. xix, xciv (Lydgate), xviii–xix (Hawes), 124–25 (Scot), 380 (Dodd).

3. Robert P. Miller, *Chaucer: Sources and Backgrounds* (New York: Oxford Univ. Press, 1977), p. 237.

4. For discussion of St. Amour and FitzRalph and Chaucer's use of their polemics, see Miller, *Chaucer*, p. 237; Arnold Williams, "Two Notes on Chaucer's Friars," *Modern Philology* 54 (1956): 117–18; Janette Richardson, "The Friar," in *The Riverside Chaucer*, 3rd ed., gen ed. Larry D. Benson (Boston: Houghton Mifflin, 1987), p. 808; and Penn R. Szittya, *The Antifraternal Tradition in Medieval Literature* (Princeton: Princeton Univ. Press, 1986).

5. Thomas Tyrwhitt, "An Introductory Discourse," in *The Canterbury Tales of Chaucer* (1775; reprinted, New York: AMS Press Inc., 1972), p. 154.

6. *The Canterbury Tales of Chaucer*, ed. Richard Morris, new and revised ed., *The Aldine Edition of the British Poets* (London: Bell and Daldy, 1866), I, p. 229; *The Complete Works of Geoffrey Chaucer*, ed. W. W. Skeat, 7 vols. (Oxford: Clarendon Press, 1894–97), 3: 450.

7. Nevill Coghill, *The Poet Chaucer*, Oxford Paperbacks Univ. Series, Opus 23, 2nd ed. (London: Oxford Univ. Press, 1967), p. 119; Bertrand H. Bronson, *In Search of Chaucer* (Toronto: Univ. of Toronto Press, 1960), p. 84. See also George Lyman Kittredge, *Chaucer and His Poetry* (Cambridge: Harvard Univ. Press, 1915), pp. 156, 192. Some commentators, apparently seeing the tales as merely epitomizing the quarrel between Friar and Summoner, seem scarcely to have glanced at them, or to have read only the Summoner's fabliau. For example, see H. S. Bennett, *Chaucer and the Fifteenth Century* (Oxford: Clarendon Press, 1947, p. 73, and Nicholas Havely, "Chaucer, Boccaccio and the Friars," in *Chaucer and the Italian Trecento,* ed. Piero Boitani (Cambridge: Cambridge Univ. Press, 1985), p. 250.

8. Jill Mann, *Chaucer and Medieval Estates Satire* (Cambridge: Cambridge Univ. Press, 1973), pp. 37–54, 197. Quoted comments are from pp. 54, 197.

9. See, for example D. S. Brewer, "The Fabliaux," in *Companion to Chaucer Studies*, ed. Beryl Rowland, rev. ed. (New York: Oxford Univ. Press, 1979), p. 297; Albert C. Baugh, *A Literary History of England*, 2nd ed. (New York: Appleton-Century-Croft, 1967), p. 198; Janette Richardson, *Blameth Nat Me: A Study of Imagery in Chaucer's Fabliaux* (The Hague: Mouton, 1970); Charles A. Owen, Jr., *Pilgrimage and Storytelling in the Canterbury Tales* (Norman: Univ. of Oklahoma Press, 1977), p. 211; Thomas D. Cooke, *The Old French and Chaucerian Fabliaux* (Columbia: Univ. of Missouri Press, 1978), pp. 170–71; and Rossell Hope Robbins, "The English Fabliau: Before and After Chaucer," *Moderna Sprak* 64 (1970): 23. All of these critics discuss *The Friar's Tale* as one of Chaucer's fabliaux.

10. Per Nykrog, *Les Fabliaux: Étude d'Histoire Littéraire et de Stylistique*

Médiévale, nouvelle ed. (Geneva: Libraire Droz, 1973); Melissa Furrow, "Middle English Fabliaux and Modern Myth," *English Literary History* 56 (1989): 1–18. For characteristics of the genre see the critics cited in footnote 9, as well as Robert E. Lewis, "The English Fabliau Tradition and Chaucer's 'Miller's Tale,' " *Modern Philology* 79 (1982): 255; Charles Muscatine, *The Old French Fabliaux* (New Haven: Yale Univ. Press, 1986); and Beryl Rowland, "What Chaucer Did to the Fabliau," *Studia Neophilologica* 51 (1979): 205–13, among others.

11. Joseph Bédier, *Les Fabliaux: Etudes de Littérature populaire et d'Histoire Littéraire du moyen âge,* 5th ed. (Paris: Champion, 1925), p. 30.

12. Derek Pearsall, *The Canterbury Tales* (London: George Allen & Unwin, 1985), p. 270; T. W. Craik, *The Comic Tales of Chaucer* (London: Methuen, 1964), p. 53; Morton Bloomfield, "Chaucerian Realism," in *The Cambridge Chaucer Companion,* ed. Piero Boitani and Jill Mann (Cambridge: Cambridge Univ. Press, 1986), p. 187; Judson Boyce Allen and Teresa Anne Moritz, *A Distinction of Stories* (Columbus: Ohio State Univ. Press, 1981), pp. 137, 154–55; Piero Boitani, *English Medieval Narrative in the Thirteenth and Fourteenth Centuries* (Cambridge: Cambridge Univ. Press, 1982), pp. 136, 249; Thomas Hahn and Richard W. Kaeuper, "Text and Context: Chaucer's 'Friar's Tale,' " *Studies in the Age of Chaucer* 5 (1983): 69; Earle Birney, " 'After His Ymage': The Central Ironies of the 'Friar's Tale,' " in *Essays on Chaucerian Irony,* ed. Beryl Rowland (Toronto: Univ. of Toronto Press, 1985), pp. 85–86; Larry D. Benson and Theodore M. Andersson, *The Literary Context of Chaucer's Fabliaux* (Indianapolis: Bobbs-Merrill, 1971), pp. 362–63; P. Mroczkowski, " 'The Friar's Tale' and Its Pulpit Background," *English Studies Today,* ed. G. A. Bonnard, 2 (1961): 107–20; G. R. Owst, *Literature and Pulpit in Medieval England* (Oxford: Basil Blackwell, 1966), pp. 162–63, whom both R. T. Lenaghan, "The Irony of the 'Friar's Tale,' " *Chaucer Review* 7 (1973); p. 284, and A. C. Spearing, *"The Canterbury Tales IV:* Exemplum and Fable," in *Cambridge Chaucer Companion,* ed. Boitani and Mann, pp. 161, 176. cite.

13. Rowland, "What Chaucer Did to the Fabliau," pp. 205–7; Brewer, "The Fabliaux," pp. 296–97; Robbins, "The English Fabliau: Before and After Chaucer," p. 235.

14. A Latin sermon by Master Rypon of Durham, termed in the margin of the MS "a narratio jocosa," in MS Harl. 4894, fol. 103v. Cited by Owst, *Literature and Pulpit,* p. 162.

15. Paul E. Beichner, "Baiting the Summoner," *PMLA* 22 (1961): 370–71; Hahn and Kaeuper, "Text and Context," p. 76; A. C. Cawley, "Chaucer's Summoner, the Friar's Summoner, and the *Friar's Tale," Proc. of Leeds Philological and Literary Soc.* 8 (1957): 173–80; Craik, *Comic Tales of Chaucer,* pp. 98–99; Janette Richardson, "Friar and Summoner: The Art of Balance," *Chaucer Review* 9 (1974–75): 231; Penn R. Szittya, "The Green Yeoman as Loathly Lady: the Friar's Parody of the Wife of Bath's Tale," *PMLA* 90 (1975): 390.

16. Szittya, "Green Yeoman," pp. 386–94, especially pp. 389, 391; N. F. Blake, "The Wife of Bath and Her Tale," *Leeds Studies in English* 13 (1982): 53; Allen and Moritz, *A Distinction of Stories* pp. 137, 154–55; William E. Rogers, *Upon the Ways: The Structure of the 'Canterbury Tales,'* no. 36 (Victoria: Univ. of Victoria, 1986), p. 52.

17. Her tendency to plan ahead seems clear in the ejaculation, "Yblessed be God that I have wedded fyve! / Welcome the sixte, whan that evere he shal" (III [D] 44–45), and promise to husband number five, made while she is still married to number four, "If I were wydwe, [he] sholde wedde me / For certeinly, I sey for no

bobance, / Yet was I nevere withouten purveiance / Of marriage . . ." (III [D] 567–71). All quotations from Chaucer's poetry are from *The Riverside Chaucer*, 3rd ed., gen. ed. Larry D. Benson (Boston: Houghton Mifflin, 1987).

18. Marshall Leicester, " 'No Vileyns Word': Social Context and Performance in Chaucer's *Friar's Tale*," *Chaucer Review* 17 (1982): 26.

19. See A. C. Spearing, "The *Canterbury Tales IV:* Exemplum and Fable," in *Cambridge Chaucer Companion*, ed. Boitani and Mann, p. 165.

20. The readings in Hengwrt (Peniarth 392) and Ellesmere, fol. 78v, are the same except that in 1. 1663 Hengwrt gives *this,* Ellesmere *thise.* Since Hengwrt's usual spelling of *these* in Fragment III is *thise,* it seems that here the scribe simply dropped off the final *e* of the adjective. The only MSS in the group of thirteen agreeing with Ellesmere and Hengwrt are Cambridge University Dd 4.24 and Egerton 2726. The only editions in the group of twenty which agree with them are those of Skeat and Robinson.

21. Carruthers, "Letter and Gloss in the Friar's and Summoner's Tales," *Journal of Narrative Technique* 2 (1972): 208–14.

22. For the references to Heywood, Lydgate, and the Parliament-Officer, see Spurgeon, I.xvii, pp. 27, 224.

23. Craik, *Comic Tales of Chaucer*, pp. 53, 99; Derek Pearsall, "The *Canterbury Tales* II: Comedy," in *Cambridge Chaucer Companion*, ed. Boitani and Mann, p. 126.

24. Janette Richardson, "Hunter and Prey: Functional Imagery in Chaucer's 'Friar's Tale,' " *English Miscellany* 12 (1961): 9–20.

25. Richard H. Passon's " 'Entente' in Chaucer's *Friar's Tale*," *Chaucer Review* 2 (1967–68), 166–71, is the best study of the theological effect and purpose of this word, but see also Beichner, "Baiting the Summoner," p. 374.

26. Raymond C. Sutherland, Jr., "A Note on Lines D 1645–1662 of Chaucer's Friar's Tale," *Philological Quarterly* 31 (1952): 436–39, followed by Paul N. Zietlow, "In Defense of the Summoner," *Chaucer Review* 1 (1966–67): 28, and Beichner, "Baiting the Summoner," p. 375; Cawley, "Chaucer's Summoner," pp. 175–76; Mroczkowski, " 'The Friar's Tale,' " pp. 107–20, who has established beyond doubt the tale's affinity with pulpit literature.

27. Rowland, "What Chaucer Did to the Fabliau," p. 211; Beichner, "Baiting the Summoner," pp. 373–75; and Birney, " 'After His Ymage,' " pp. 97–98, have noted the resemblance between the tale and the play.

28. Pearsall, "Comic Tales and Fables," in *The Canterbury Tales*, p. 221.

29 Talbot Donaldson, *Chaucer's Poetry: An Anthology for the Modern Reader* (New York: Ronald Press, 1958), p. 917.

30. Howard, *The Idea of the Canterbury Tales*, pp. 365–68.

31. Paul Zeitlow, "In Defense of the Summoner," pp. 17–19.

32. The concept is obliquely developed throughout *The Idea of the Canterbury Tales*, but is most clearly stated on pp. 386–87. The "idea" develops in the mind of the reader as he moves through the poem.

The Manuscripts and Transmission of Chaucer's *Troilus*

RALPH HANNA III

I first met Don Howard just after Christmas 1965, when he was leaving Riverside for UCLA, and I was a candidate for one of several positions his old department had assigned to replace him. (Even at that early stage in Don's career, it was plain that no straight one-for-one swap could adequately reproduce his acumen, energy, and verve.) Our meeting was particularly interesting because it centered upon a lengthy discussion of what might be termed a submerged interest of Don's, the treatment of textual problems. For amidst all his other efforts at creating a situation of social familiarity with medieval poets, Don was involved and interested in this problem at its most basic level, the production of critical yet available (normalized and carefully glossed) texts for general readers. One particularly impressive monument to this interest, the paperback edition of Chaucer's *Troilus* which Don prepared with Jim Dean, inspires these thoughts.[1] For Don and Jim, I am convinced, did the right thing in resolutely following the readings of those *Troilus* manuscripts which have always been known as group G. In the pages which follow I will survey some heretofore unexamined codicological evidence that underscores the wisdom of their activity.

The propriety of Don and Jim's editorial behavior might not have been apparent to someone reading their book on its first appearance in 1976. For at that time, discussion of the poem had been preempted by the arguments of R. K. Root.[2] Although he did not invent it, Root certainly demonstrated and popularized the idea that *Troilus* manuscripts represent three different versions of the text, which he called A, B, and G. In his great (if fundamentally misleading) edition, Root constructed his text upon the forms offered by the B manuscripts, and his presentation of these matters remained the only argued survey of the textual situation until Barry Windeatt began preparing his edition a decade ago. Root's textual handling remains basic, because evidence for the existence of types A, B, and G is compelling. Not so compelling, however, is Root's decision to follow the readings of type B copies, the production of which I intend to examine here.

Perhaps more than most literary works, no reading text of *Troilus* can be anything other than an eclectic modern hypothesis. None of the surviving manuscripts contains what anyone believes is the full text, except perhaps Huntington HM 114 (Ph), which is widely believed to have obtained that full text by devious (but mechanical and easily explicable) means.[3] The seventeen complete versions that are accorded manuscript status can be divided, following Root, into the three largish groups, ABG, which appears to provide a hopeful basis for discussion. However, among these witnesses only the eight type G copies (one of them, S^1, a conflation with type B) and three scattered manuscripts (Ph of type A, R and the print Cx of type B) provide a continuous and internally consistent version of the text. If the G manuscripts, Ph and RCx are construed to be the three basic forms of the poem, the remaining copies then look as if they change affiliations, apparently willy-nilly. It is this particular problem which I wish to address, to worry why copies present mixed forms of the text, why they are sometimes A and a bit later B, for example. I want to suggest that the transmission of *Troilus* was considerably less straightforward than Root supposed and that the minority B version which he adopted as the genuine form of Chaucer's text was particularly susceptible to some very strange vicissitudes of book-production.

Root's view of the textual situation, of course, involves something like a *stemma codicum*. In his volume on *The Textual Transmission,* he created several diagrammatic presentations designed to show how the surviving copies were derived from Chaucerian materials.[4] The strength of this presentation rests in Root's meticulous and apt description of these lines of descent. But like most genetic editors, Root created his *stemma* to simplify editorial procedures—to use, as simply the diagram which it is, to facilitate choices between variants. I want to consider this *stemma* in a different and more dynamic way.

For Root's *stemma* describes, not a state, but an historical process. Like all genetic editors, Root uses the diagram, from a modern perspective, as a way of moving backward from surviving copies toward a Chaucerian Ur-version. In so doing, he reverses the process by which the *stemma* emerged: the diagram displays that activity in time by which individual scribes received the text, and received it in certain versions, in each case as a unique act in unique circumstances. It is precisely some of these circumstances that I wish to describe.

Root's *stemma* shows us at least four invisible layers of transmission, stages in the history of Chaucer's text. These include Chaucer's fair-copy or foul papers (both surely existed, even though opinions differ on which is the source of the poem we know).[5] The next layer of transmission involved the original scribal copyings behind each version, what are usually considered "the archetypes of all surviving copies." A third invisible layer of the text is formed by the immediate progeny of these post-Chaucerian documents: these I call "lost first-generation derivatives." They, in turn, provided material for those also lost exemplars that were used by the scribes who produced the surviving manuscripts. The last two of these lost layers of textual history, when viewed as a developing textual process, can help to explain why *Troilus* manuscripts appear, from a modern perspective, to shift textual affiliation so often.

Although these textual layers remain invisible in their totality, they are not completely lost to us. Sometimes the surviving manuscripts of the *Troilus*, although they are continuous copies made without apparent hesitation, have imbedded in them features of their predecessors. From these, it is sometimes possible to intuit what those predecessors were like, occasionally in some detail. But the features we intuit from extant copies are, at least initially, not susceptible to exact historical placement: they may belong to the immediate exemplars used by the scribes of those copies or may have emerged at some earlier stage of the text.

In order to consider signs of production in the survivors, there are a few basics we need to consider about producing copies of the *Troilus*. Copying the poem involved certain conventions of presentation, some reflections of physical necessity, others impositions based on the form of the text. First, the *Troilus* is usually transmitted on pages of a reasonably standard size, what we might consider "late medieval quarto." In this format (dependent on the dimensions of "the standard English sheep"), the scribe receives a skin which he can fold twice (a true quarto format in the bibliographical sense, with four leaves from the skin) and end up with a page about $11\frac{1}{4}'' \times 7\frac{3}{4}''$. (Surviving copies are slightly smaller, since the pages have been cut down to some extent in the act of binding.)[6]

Moreover, this space has to accommodate a poem written in rime royale, stanzas of seven lines. In an easily legible writing size of 35–45 lines to the page, a neat scribal norm would have four- or five-stanza pages; nearly all the surviving manuscripts were written in the latter format, although some are written by the line, not the stanza, and have uneven divisions.[7] And, simply as an initial assumption, one can posit a basic (although not necessarily universal) production unit of a quire formed from two skins, eight leaves or sixteen pages. These limits, inherent in the copying process, allow certain rough expectations about how much poem a scribe can get into a basic unit of production:

If the scribe copies:	he rules for:[8]	and produces an eight-leaf-quire with:
4 stanzas/page	31 lines	64 stanzas/448 lines
9 stanzas/folio	35/36 lines	72 stanzas/504 lines
5 stanzas/page	39 lines	80 stanzas/560 lines

| 11 stanzas/leaf | 43/44 lines | 88 stanzas/616 lines |
| 6 stanzas/page | 47 lines | 96 stanzas/672 lines |

Reference to one further scribal habit will complete this summary of production procedures. There is a convention, albeit far from universal, of directing the reader's attention to one of Chaucer's innovations: the *Troilus* is the first English poem with book divisions. Thus scribes often leave a stanza space for the intermediate rubrics which divide Chaucer's text ("Explicit liber primus," "Incipit prologus libri secundi," etc.).

To show the effects of these conventions upon the books which transmit *Troilus,* we can examine, not a manuscript *per se,* but Caxton's *editio princeps* (always accorded manuscript status). Like all copyists in the Middle Ages, Caxton necessarily began with at least one manuscript version of the text. Moreover, his *mise en page* appears inherited from that source: it is the common five stanza per page layout, with rubrics between books occupying the space of a full stanza (as on sig. f 1, for example). But Caxton's edition proves informative because it has a variety of gross and unique mishandlings of the *Troilus* imbedded in a text completely type B. These are sufficient to tell fairly precisely what the immediate source of this first print looked like. Surprisingly, virtually all these mishandlings involve groups of eight stanzas; they thus point toward an exemplar in a format different from most surviving copies and from that which Caxton used in his print.[9]

The first such textual problem occurs at I.449, where Caxton omits a sequence of eight stanzas (through line 504). As an initial hypothesis, we can see what would follow from assuming that these eight stanzas occupied a single leaf which had been lost in Caxton's immediate exemplar. Line 449, the beginning of the omission, falls at the start of stanza 65 of the poem. If Caxton's exemplar had been copied in the four stanza per page format, this stanza 65 should have fallen at the head of the first leaf following a quire of eight folios with eight stanzas per folio (or sixteen pages of four stanzas per page). And the leaf would have contained just the eight stanzas lacking in the print. On this basis, Caxton's exemplar lacked its folio 9.

The next major error in Caxton involves a displacement of the text. Caxton presents I.813–40, four stanzas, before I.785–812, also four stanzas. Line 785 occurs at the opening of stanza 113; that is, it comes after 112 stanzas, or 14×8 stanzas. This section of eight stanzas then should have stood on a single leaf, f. 15, set by Caxton incorrectly, with the text of the verso preceding that of the recto.

Such an error reflects one of two situations. On the one hand, this may be a pure accident: the leaf may have come loose from the binding and may simply have been stuffed back into the manuscript, but reversed. On the other, the persistence of errors involving eight-stanza segments of the poem may suggest that Caxton's compositor was not setting simply from a text unbound (thus broken into constituent quires) but in fact even further dismembered: the bifolia of the source manuscript may have been split into single loose leaves.[10] In any event, the original recto, set as if the verso, had the four stanzas 785–812; and the original verso, set as if the recto, had the four stanzas 813–40.

At I.904–59 a similar textual displacement occurs: lines 904–31, again four stanzas, appear after 932–59, also four stanzas. Line 904 is the start of stanza 130 in modern texts, but in Caxton's text, stanza 129, since like other BG copies, the version lacks a stanza (I.890–96) as the result of an eyeskip. One hundred twenty-eight stanzas again form an exact multiple of the eight stanza per leaf format—16×8; the stanzas would then have appeared on the first leaf of the third quire (f. 17), following two eight-leaf quires of eight stanzas/folio. As in the preceding example, the leaf was loose and single and set by the compositor verso first. Again, the error corresponds exactly to the divisions one would predict in a manuscript of consistent format—that same format which predicts the other errors I have examined. And, of course, this format did not correspond to the one into which Caxton's compositor was setting the text.

The next major problem in Caxton's text occurs at II.246, where eight stanzas, 36–43 of Book II, are missing. In the hypothetical format, with 448 lines or 64 stanzas to the eight-leaf quire, Book I's 155 stanzas (of the full 156) would occupy two full quires (128 stanzas), three full leaves (24 stanzas), and three stanzas on the fourth leaf (f. 20r of Caxton's source). Counting ahead from the end of Book I, Caxton's exemplar could have the form f. 20r end of Book I + explicit instead of fourth stanza, f. 20v incipit instead of a stanza + Book II.stanzas 1–3. (The explicit and incipit might have been split between recto and verso for aesthetic reasons. Having a chapter title at page foot with no following text is still avoided in modern printing.) Folio 21 of the exemplar would then have presented Book II.stanzas 4–11, f. 22 stanzas 12–19, f. 23 stanzas 20–27, f. 24 stanzas 28–35. The missing folio would be the one next following, f. 25, the first of quire 4. So far, every major disruption of Caxton's text corresponds exactly to the limits of the folio in the hypothetical lost manuscript.

The last glitches in Caxton's text occur much later: at III.442–76 the print omits an anomalous five stanzas, and at III.1114–69 omits the eight stanzas which one would expect in this model. In fact, ignoring the odd omission of five stanzas for the moment, the eight omitted stanzas should have stood on the single leaf, f. 72, the eighth and last of quire 9. To continue from II.245 (the end of quire 3 in putative exemplar), in the 64

stanza per quire units, quires of Caxton's source should have ended at II.
693, 1141, 1589, III.273 (24 stanzas from Book II + blank for rubric [f.52r]
+ 39 stanzas from Book III), 721, 1169. . . .

This hypothesis appears to have strong predictive value. Caxton's errors
consistently may be explained as lost or transposed leaves in a four stanza
per page format. But to preserve this hypothesis, one needs an alternative
explanation for the anomalous five-stanza error, the omission of III.442–
76. The coincidence of omissions and pages in the putative format suggests that these five stanzas were present in Caxton's source manuscript.
Without those stanzas, the omission of III.1114–69 would not reflect the
loss of a single folio in the exemplar. Yet Caxton did not print III.stanzas
64–68; in the hypothetical exemplar, these would have appeared on a
single leaf, as the four stanzas on f. 60r and the first stanza of f. 60v (quire
8, leaf 4).

While one cannot be exactly sure how these stanzas were dropped, one
can at least suggest a reasonable psychological mechanism. Leaf boundaries (because they are obvious stopping places) are marvelous times to
take breaks, to shake out fingers numbed with typesetting, to have a cup of
tea, or to just gaze out the window briefly. When Caxton's compositor took
his break after setting f. 59v of his source, it appears that the following
page (f. 60) got turned over. With a logic that is totally human (and thus not
at all logical), the compositor returned directly to his copy somewhere
other than the page-break that he probably expected would remind him
where he was supposed to resume typesetting.

Yet Caxton's compositor did not make this slip all by himself: in this
foulup he had material aid from Chaucer's text. Like all dutiful scribes and
compositors, he had a backup system for finding his place. This was his
key-word, the last word of the copy he had set: to resume his typesetting,
he knew that he had to find this word at the end of a stanza on the open
page. Now the typesetter's key would have been the last word he had set
and the last word in III.441, "disserue"; when he looked down at his copy,
now the verso rather than the recto of f. 60, he saw the first stanza ended
(III.476 in modern editions) with "deuyse". Again with perfectly human
logic, he may not have read the word with care (the two words look similar
enough to be confused in the usual scan procedure everyone uses to read).
Alternatively, the compositor may just have assumed that he had remembered the key-word incorrectly (believing he was disconcerted earlier,
whereas he was in fact only now disconcerted). In any event, he took this
to be his place. He clearly did not turn over the page to see whether
something more suitable was nearby (nor did he read the preceding stanza
III.470–76 to see whether he recalled it as corresponding to something he
had already set in type); he simply resumed his work at III.477 and,
consequently, finessed five stanzas of Chaucer's text. Lest we rush to fault

him for carelessness, we might stop to consider that apparently no one in Caxton's shop read proofs against copy for this section of the text. Or, if someone did, the printshop team decided that the omission didn't matter enough to go to the very serious effort, an insert leaf, necessary to remedy the textual damage.

This reconstruction of printshop behavior can account for the anomalous omission, and it preserves our larger hypothesis of Caxton's eight stanza per leaf exemplar. Moreover, it provides additional support for that hypothesis: this visualization of the lost exemplar not only explains some quite regular patterns of textual disruption in Caxton (an eight-stanza mode) but shows how an exemplar of specified shape might generate other kinds of error as well. As anecdotal material, this reconstruction suggests something about the sometimes erratic procedures of late medieval book production.

This example indicates that one can recover features associated with earlier, invisible portions of textual transmission and can use them to explain features of surviving manuscripts. With Caxton's print, one observes problems in transmitting a single immediately present exemplar. But more perturbing, and more widespread in the tradition of *Troilus,* would appear to be shifts of affiliation. These may perhaps best be explained in terms of exemplar disruption, whereby a scribe shifts from one manuscript to another in his copying. Exemplar disruption of this kind, in fact, may have been far more widespread in the textual transmission than has previously been considered.

For example, one of the more idiosyncratic features of the textual tradition is the behavior of the three manuscripts JRH[4] in Book II. These three copies are at this moment type B (although H[4] is a thorough mess, with at least one ancestral layering produced by simultaneous comparison and copying from two manuscripts of different textual affiliations, and although J will, early in Book IV, wander off to become type A). Suddenly, about 40 percent of the way through Book II, these three texts provide a series of anomalous and completely unconvincing readings which they share with no other existing copy. This textual debility certainly reflects disruption in JRH[4]'s type B source. At this point, the ancestor common to these three copies apparently had to depart from its normal supply of copy; the survivors thus deviate from other type B copies like Caxton's print. Since the three manuscripts diverge from one another elsewhere, this disruption probably occurred in a manuscript antecedent to the immediate exemplars of each, what I have called a "lost first generation copy"; the scribe of each surviving manuscript, then, received this peculiar segment of the text imbedded within his later, "second generation" exemplar.

Now these queer readings begin at II.701, i.e. after Book II, stanza 100. Adding the 155 stanzas of Book I in this version to that figure, one gets 255 total; if to this figure one adds a space corresponding to one stanza for a rubric somewhere (there is no evidence as to whether it fell at the time of the poem or between books), their patch of aberrant readings begins after 256 stanzas. Strikingly, this is 4 × 64 stanzas, or four quires in the four stanza per page format now familiar from Caxton's print.

Because of the point of onset, this change of textual supply looks like some replacement that had to be sought because of the juncture between two quires. As one possible cause (although less likely than a second which will emerge below), one might posit damage at the head of quire 5 in the JRH[4] exemplar. In the nature of things, such damage would have had to be clearly visible, some feature which alerted the scribe of this particular lost manuscript that he had to take drastic measures. He could, for example, have noticed that the catch-word on f. 32v of the exemplar did not match the text on the next leaf. Or there may have been some palpable physical damage—for example, a loose single leaf. In any event, the erratic quality of the text here reveals that the archetypal scribe had to fill a gap in his usual copy by acquiring material from a new and quirky exemplar available to no other scribe in the tradition. (As is thoroughly typical of medieval book production, the availability of two copies did not induce this scribe to undertake any detailed comparison or to adjust readings from one text by reference to the other.)[11]

The point at which this particular group of anomalous readings concludes is also pertinent to the discussion. Conventionally, scholars who describe the affiliations of *Troilus* manuscripts say this aberrancy ceases at II.1113, the last example of all three texts in idiosyncratic agreement.[12] Thereafter, from line 1117 at least, H[4] reverts to readings shared with type A copies. But this manuscript's shift of affiliation very likely represents changes introduced into the archeytpes behind H[4] at a later stage of its development. The scribe of its "second generation" source, which performance included all the readings shared with J and R, simply edited these type B readings out. He did this on an eclectic basis, substituting readings from his second manuscript source, here type A.

H[4]'s return to type A thus is not necessarily a sign that the JR borrowings from a foreign source have ended. In fact, JR still agree in a minor unique reading as late as 1147 and (excluding one possibly convergent agreement in 1143) do not indisputably rejoin other type B copies until they show clear B errors in 1152 and 1155. It seems something more than mere coincidence that an eight-leaf quire in the same format as earlier portions of the JR exemplar (64 stanzas per quire) should have ended at II.1148, just where JR readings "return to normal," as it were.

This example illustrates that one can find traces of lost examplars and use them to explain some kinds of textual deviation. In the case of JRH[4], the scribe of the "first generation archetype" may have had to intrude a quire from a foreign source to correct a textual deficiency. There is no way of knowing how he came up with the fifth quire of text he copied (although given its quality, one should be happy there was no more than a quire of it). But similar analyses offer evidence that the text of *Troilus* may well have routinely circulated, not as the fully articulated and finished literary manuscript, but by the quire.

Armed with the examples of Caxton's print and of JRH[4] deviance, we can scrutinize some other vagaries of *Troilus* manuscripts. The two surviving copies Gg and H[5] share variation between textual types in Books I–III. In them, I.1–II.63 is type B, II.64–1211 is type A with some B readings (although none of the JRH[4] type).[13] From II.1212 until III.399 these copies become type B (and resemble J); at III.400 they switch to type A and remain such to the poem's end. Because these readings are shared by two copies, their source is difficult to pin down: the two scribes may have had access to a single common exemplar, or, as seems more likely, given a good many variations between the two, these shifts of affiliation may reflect scribal behavior in the "first generation archetype" which lies behind the separate exemplars available to each.

Some interesting relationships emerge from an examination of the shifting affiliations of Gg and H[5]. The first two blocks of different text types are of exactly equal lengths, if one ignores possible rubrics (155 stanzas of Book I + 9 of Book II = 164 stanzas, Book II. stanzas 10–173 = 164 stanzas). These blocks of text would appear to have been generated by four quires of 82 stanzas per quire, not a format which could have been consistent and still respected page or folio boundaries but a format roughly equivalent to the five stanza per page form of the text. The first of these 164-stanza blocks, in GgH[5] of type B, also had a type A counterpart: the GgH[5] shift of textual version corresponds to a reversed shift (type A becomes type B) in H[4]. Further, the existence of such an 82-stanza to the quire format for the first generation B exemplar receives some confirmation from J. The portion of text from II.1148, where J ceases to display the deviant readings examined above, to somewhere around IV.438, where the manuscript becomes type A, consists of 410 stanzas (ignoring possible rubrics), or five quires of 82 stanzas each.[14]

In GgH[5], the third batch of the poem, with a return to a type B text, covers 135 stanzas. This segment comprises Book II. stanzas 174–251 [78] + Book III. stanzas 1–57, and is again an awkward figure. It could represent two quires of 67 or 68 stanzas each, again a format roughly equivalent to a regular one, the four stanza per page form. Or it might reflect a situation in which the scribe received non-coincident blocks of copy, ones which had an overlap of material.

But on the basis of this information, the first-generation ancestor of GgH[5] cannot have relied on any single, consistently produced manuscript for copy. The scribe of this ancestor must have received his texts in partial form, almost certainly unbound, and usually in lots of two quires. This type of production occurred, not in an emergency, as may have happened with the deviant JRH⁴ exemplar, but as a result of the scribe's normal copying activity.

Moreover, the archetypal GgH⁵ scribe, although his sources were sometimes of internally consistent formats, is unlikely to have been supplied pieces from a single manuscript source. The apparent variations in format would preclude this alternative. He began his transcription by getting blocks of both A and B texts in comparable formats. But when he resumed copying the textual form with which he started, type B, he apparently received the text in a very different format than on his first encounter. And if my suggestions above about the shape of H⁴ and J's sources through the middle of the poem are correct, the formats of copies behind the exemplars available to these scribes shifted as well.

Two conclusions follow from this analysis. First, the variations in GgH⁵ suggest a reinterpretation of JRH⁴'s quirks. Rather than inferring textual damage, it now appears more likely that the scribe of the JRH⁴ ancestor simply received his text in loose quires which included a single "off" piece from a source utterly unique. Second, this possibility, in conjunction with the variations of format in both GgH⁵ and J exemplars, would indicate that the scribes received batches of copy from what had originally been different manuscripts. GgH⁵'s second batch of B copy was not from a manuscript in the same format as the initial batch of type B, but interestingly enough, GgH⁵'s first batch might, on a format basis, have come from the same manuscript as that also used, later in the poem, by J.

Some thoughts about the situation in which early copying of *Troilus* occurred may help explain these various features. The scribes of none of the first generation copies can have undertaken their transcriptions without knowing that they could finish the job. Thus, knowing they would receive only pieces of the poem at any moment, they must have insured their access to source materials before starting. The evidence is certainly consistent with their having procured the text from a variety of sources, an activity which demonstrably occurred with some early *Canterbury Tales* manuscripts. However, there are compelling reasons for seeing that as an unlikely scenario (save perhaps in the sort of emergency which may have befallen the JRH⁴ archetype). The *Troilus* is a continuous poem, unlike *The Canterbury Tales*. Thus it is difficult to understand how the text could have been derived from various sources which could each provide only fragments and not the whole. It seems more reasonable to assume that, in each case, the whole text came from a single source but in a divided and textually inconsistent form.

If this is so, one should probably visualize some kind of *Troilus* clearing-house, a commercial supplier who provided the poem in sections to individual scribes. The scribe's desire for the whole text was supposed to be a kind of security that he would return the installment he had currently and receive a new one in return. In effect, the supplier was running a lending library, from which batches of text could be dispatched for private copying, perhaps even a great distance away.

For such a process to be feasible, there had to have been fairly consistent demand for the text. And in such a case, the process could only function if the supplier had sufficient copy to meet demand, perhaps two or three full manuscripts of the poem dismembered into constituent quires. Such a supplier could not operate his business profitably if two scribes simultaneously needed the second batch of text (say II.64ff.) and his single copy was "checked out." Such a library of multiple manuscripts to be loaned for copying could function so long as all copies had been arranged to divide the text into roughly comparable units, regardless of distinctions of format. The borrowing scribe would be expected to choose, perhaps at his employer's instruction, the appropriate format for the new book he was copying (as Caxton would later reject the four stanza per page format of his exemplar for a different one). Since fifteenth-century book producers were frequently indifferent to local textual content (we have seen a few examples already) inconsistent versions of the text would pass unnoticed. If one allows that two such clearing-houses might exist, this might well help explain why the surviving type A and B manuscripts of the *Troilus* often show the peculiar fits and starts textual scholars have described.

There are two other split copies of the poem, H² and H³. The textual disruptions in the first of these codices are of a very different (and more easily explicable) nature than those already discussed. The core of this book was written by a single scribe, the individual who copied Ph; he used the same archetype as in his other copying and produced substantially the same pure type A text. However, he did not finish his copy (his text breaks off in mid-quire at IV.196); moreover, the book remained unbound for a protracted period and was subjected to considerable damage (apparently repaired by later scribes who recopied leaves from the original; see note 11).

The major shift of affiliation in the manuscript falls at precisely the point where two later scribes (hands 3 and 4) took up the copying and completed the manuscript from a type B exemplar. Thus, this shift of affiliation is completely fortuitous, a reflection of the later scribes' access to a different exemplar; it provides no evidence, either pro or con, on the form of that exemplar (although the cases of J and H³ suggest that quire breaks well into Book IV could coincide with new partial exemplars). But the shift of affiliation is germane to the discussion, since the manuscript bears no sign that its later continuators were at all aware of, much less interested in, what must have been substantially divergent readings between the exemplar they copied from and the partial copy of *Troilus* they were completing.

H³, a manuscript in need of protracted further study, apparently combines both situations under discussion—a shift of exemplars associated with a change of scribes and other exemplar shifts, which perhaps indicate text supplied by the quire. Hand 1 of the manuscript leaves off in mid-stanza on f. 15: he was copying from a type B exemplar which was not taken up by the scribe who succeeded him (hand 2). This second individual copied all but three pages of the remainder of the *Troilus*. The break on f. 15 (at II.1034, in the 302nd stanza of the poem) seems simply fortuitous, just as that which separates core from recopied leaves and continuations in H², and any discussion of the form of hand 1's archetype is completely speculative.

In H³ the hand 2 continuation is absolutely unique: the scribe managed to acquire, at various times, all three textual types. He thus provides the unique example of what may have been a split archetype, but in any event a fragment, of a type G manuscript. He began by copying this form of the text at II.1034. How far he continued with it is unclear (affiliations are obscured by a heavy, and heretofore unnoted, admixture of type A readings, probably the result of multiple manuscript consultation), but distinctive type G variants appear as late as III.1029. This textual form is succeeded by a section of type B text (first clearly visible in III.1096) and then (at some point after IV.286, certainly by IV.300) by type A. Since the point at which this copyist began was forced on him by departure of hand 1 with his exemplar, the scribe was obviously constrained in his copying and need not have begun his work at any division in the archetypes he had. This fact, in conjunction with difficulties in identifying the end of the type G stint, renders any effort at identifying the forms of his archetypes nearly impossible.

Some evidence allows one to localize the appearance of the split, unbound and lendable exemplars of types A and B. Production of these loose quires must predate the copying of Gg, which probably occurred c. 1415–25 and in a rural setting, northwestern Norfolk.[15] On the basis of this palaeographical dating, booklet archetypes of the *Troilus* were generated, at the latest, during the second decade of the fifteenth century.

One can place this activity pretty securely in London on the evidence of type A copies. There are only two of these which are "complete" (one, H², as I have shown, is a fragment expanded to make a full manuscript of the poem perhaps twenty years after the fact). Type A, as a full and unique textual version, was available only to the single scribe who copied both manuscripts from the same exemplar. He was certainly a professional (a third codex he wrote, Lambeth Palace 491, does not include *Troilus*). Moreover, although he had been trained to write elsewhere, he was working in the London area, perhaps in the 1420s. Proximity and fulltime professionalism may have given him uninterrupted access to his single textual source for type A, as well as to a second complete copy, in this case of type G, from which he corrected Ph. Other than this unique access, type A does not exist except as the odd quires made available to individual scribes. Indeed, one should reformulate Root's conception of the problem: type A should refer only to the archetype available to the scribe of Ph and H[2].

The generation of the other textual types also provides notes of interest. Type G, with the exception of the fragment, in H[3], was never subjected to this particular clearing-house treatment. Although one aberrant codex S[1] (just as H[4]) is derived from an exemplar which used a second manuscript ad lib. along with his received text, every type G copy descends from a single transcription from Chaucer's original (whether foul papers or fair copy).

Moreover, three surviving type G manuscripts (one of them a fragment of a single leaf) very likely predate the split exemplars that circulated by the quire. One of the full copies, Cl, could have been copied as early as 1403–4 (and was certainly copied before 1413). The one-leaf fragment, Windeatt's F11, was produced by the same professional who transcribed the Hengwrt and Ellesmere *Canterbury Tales*. His responsibility for the first of these important codices suggests, at the least, his employment by persons with access to materials directly associated with the poet. His work places the single copying from Chaucerian materials which produced type G no later than 1405 (and perhaps up to a decade earlier). Although the unique lost archetype that underlies all type G copies was a sloppy job, with a number of minor errors (most of them easily corrected through consultation of other copies), its antiquity and the directness of its transmission suggest that one might well wish to privilege this as the Chaucerian form of the text.[16]

Further, type B, as a full and continuous form of the text, can scarcely be said to exist. Virtually all type B copies have emerged from the split archetype system; following my comments about type A above, one should consider, for most of the fifteenth century, these textual portions as "non-PhH[2], non-G" readings. For the exceptions to this statement, strangely, are manuscripts from the very end of the Middle Ages—Caxton's print and R. The latter was produced by four scribes, at least two of whom appear Caxton's near contemporaries. Caxton certainly could have had access to exemplars available in the London book-trade; this and the evidence that I have outlined above for his use of an exemplar of neat and regular format make it fairly clear that a full and consecutive type B archetype could be found. What is not so clear is whether that B archetype, as G certainly does and A probably does, descends from a single copying from Chaucerian sources. I think it is possible to feel less than assured on this score. The B exemplars may have been manuscripts specially executed for precisely the function they served—to be available from a clearing-house on a quire by quire basis. They are conceivably texts produced by consultation and editing of multiple scribal copies (necessarily A and G) available in the London book-trade circa 1410–15.

Our presumptions about books, however much we try to put them aside, have usually been constituted by our sense of modern industrial production. We tend to think about books as they have been pretty much from the dawn of printing: usually predetermined whole entities, planned to a large extent at inception, uniform in structure and in much of the detail, subjected to a certain amount of inspection for accuracy.

One thing which studying the lost exemplars of *Troilus* shows is how foreign such conceptions are to the medieval craft. Making a book in the medieval English vernacular trade was always a touch and go business: the trade, like all medieval industry, was founded on piecework and thus potentially was always decentralized and heavily dependent on nonprofessionals, moonlighters. Moreover, physical decentralization meant that planning was difficult, always subject to accidental disruption of various types. Even initially firm plans could change in response to a patron's whim, an accidental discovery, or a failure of supplies. Further, the conception of the text very likely differed from modern ideas: the producers of many *Troilus* manuscripts may never have seen their desired text *in toto* until they actually completed and reassembled their personal copies. In addition, the books were typically executed with minimal supervision or quality check and with only passing awareness that differences among copies might be a significant matter. To cope with this particularly fluid context, I would suggest taking seriously the rhetorical ploys I have built into my argument—that approaches like game theory may approximate the situation of much vernacular book-production more fully than more sober notions.

Notes

1. See *Geoffrey Chaucer: Troilus and Criseyde and Selected Short Poems* (New York: Signet New American Library, 1976); Don and Jim also edited a volume of selections from *The Canterbury Tales* (New York: New American Library, 1969). In what follows, I depart from past practice in referring to the large flavors of *Troilus* manuscripts by Roman, rather than Greek, sigla.

2. For Root and his textual theories, see my article in *Editing Chaucer: The Great Tradition,* ed. Paul G. Ruggiers (Norman, Okla.: Pilgrim, 1984), pp. 191–205,

285–89, with full references to Root's writings. All citations of the text and manuscript variants come from B. A. Windeatt, *Geoffrey Chaucer: Troilus and Criseyde* (London: Longman, 1984); one should also consult Windeatt's earlier study, "The Text of the *Troilus*," in *Essays on Troilus and Criseyde,* ed. Mary Salu (Cambridge: Brewer, 1979), pp. 1–22.

3. Ph was originally copied as a pure type A text. But the scribe, an inveterate consulter of multiple copies, later corrected his text sporadically against a type G manuscript. In this process, he discovered the three lengthy passages peculiar to types B and G; he copied these on extra sheets that he inserted into his already written quires. I qualify the statement as to whether this is the whole text, since there is one stanza unique to R (following II.1750). I discuss the Ph scribe's activities at some length in "The Scribe of Huntington HM 114," in *Studies in Bibliography* 42 (1989): 120–33.

4. See, for example, Chaucer Society Publications, 1st ser. 99:81, 181, 230, 272.

5. Root, for example, argued that Type A derived from a "published" fair copy but that the archetypal scribes behind types B and G essentially had recourse to foul papers (Chaucer's continuing revision of the text, in the form of corrections to such a type A fair copy); see *Editing Chaucer,* pp. 201–2, for references and discussion.

6. The great majority of the survivors show such dimensions. Thoroughly aberrant is H^3 ($15\frac{1}{2}''$ × $5\frac{3}{4}''$), and H^2 has similar "holster-book" proportions, although more standard vertical dimensions ($10\frac{1}{4}''$ × $5\frac{3}{4}''$). The only other variant copies are Ph, S^2, and H^4, all in simlar "octavo" format (about $8\frac{2}{3}''$ × $5\frac{3}{4}''$). (Ph, for the most part on paper, is plainly a bibliographical quarto, but the vellum wraps for each quire may have been prepared from half-skins.)

7. Again H^3 is an odd man out: it utilizes its long page fully and approximates a nine stanza format. H^1 has six stanzas to the page and the "octavo" H^4 four. Those manuscripts copied by the line generally range from 38 to 45 lines per page.

8. I assume here what the careful copies show, a blank line to separate stanzas (present even in Dg and parts of R, books not copied in a fixed number of stanzas to the page). Manuscripts without such blanks usually assume that an introductory paraph provides sufficient marking of a new stanza.

9. Root noted this fact and surmised the format of pages in Caxton's exemplar, but did not press the matter; see Chaucer Society Publications, 1st ser. 99:8.

10. I am grateful to Christopher de Hamel and Kathleen Scott for suggesting this further dismemberment to me when I read a version of this paper at the University of Victoria's February 1988 conference on manuscripts. I am similarly grateful to Prof. John Tucker of Victoria for allowing me a forum to try out these ideas.

11. One might compare the behavior of one of the scribes of H^2, hand 3. He is plainly to be associated with another scribe, hand 4 of that manuscript, and apparently shared with that copyist a type B exemplar used to complete the abandoned text of H^2. But the manuscript at this point was not simply an atelous fragment: some leaves had apparently become disfigured and needed to be replaced. Hand 3 participated in this procedure, supplying a new outer bifolium for the first quire of the codex (ff. 1 + 8). But in this process, rather than refer to any type B exemplar (assuming such was available for this early textual portion), he appears simply to have replaced the damaged leaves by recopying them: the surviving ff. 1 and 8, in hand 3, show the same type A forms we can tell were in the archetype of the scribe responsible for the fragment.

12. Descriptions of such shifts remain dependent upon Root's positivism—he never examined negative evidence of affiliation and placed the boundaries between textual types at the first or last recorded appearance of the affected manuscripts all agreeing in a lemma. And although Windeatt has surveyed the entire textual tradition anew, he simply chooses to reproduce Root's information; see p. 66.

13. I adjust slightly the usual statement, that the boundary between the Type A and B texts occurs between 1209 and 1210 (my last explicit harping on these problems). This division depends upon the variant 1210 me] god GgH[5]J, very likely an accidental convergent error; the shift between textual versions probably falls between this stanza and the next, where GgH[5] show no sign of a series of distinctive type A readings.

14. Quire 5 of J's B exemplar ended at II.1148. The remainder of Book II consists of 87 stanzas, Book III of 260 stanzas, and the B portions of Book IV of 63 stanzas.

15. This important scribe, engaged in the deliberate gathering of a one-volume *Works,* had access to a succession of outstanding Chaucer archetypes. See M. B. Parkes and Richard Beadle's discussion, volume 3 of *The Poetical Works of Geoffrey Chaucer: A Facsimile of Cambridge Univ. Library MS. Gg.4.27,* 3 vols. (Norman, Okla.: Pilgrim, 1979–80).

16. For the date of Cl, see Jeanne Krochalis's comments at *The Pierpont Morgan Manuscript M.817: A Facsimile* (Norman, Okla.: Pilgrim, 1986), pp. xx–xxi. The Hatfield House fragment (F11) was published by Jackson J. Campbell at *PMLA* 73 (1958): 305–8; A. I. Doyle and Parkes identified its scribe at Parkes and Andrew G. Watson eds., *Medieval Scribes, Manuscripts and Libraries: Essays Presented to N. R. Ker* (London: Scholar, 1978), p. 170. In spite of Campbell's hesitation (p. 307), this leaf is plainly from a type G copy: it has distinctive type G errors in I.808 and 820 and a correct non-type AB reading in 806. (Matters are perhaps complicated by those two occasions—I.824 and 831—where the fragment fails to agree with most type G manuscripts in error; but in each case, other G manuscripts also preserve the correct reading.) Dating the scribe narrowly is hazardous. M. L. Samuels placed this manuscript, on perhaps debatable linguistic grounds, in 1405–6 at *Studies in the Age of Chaucer* 5 (1983): 61–63. The third early type G copy is, of course, Cp; for dating, see Parkes at *Troilus and Criseyde: A facsimile of Corpus Christi College Cambridge MS. 61* (Cambridge: Brewer, 1978), p. 2 (first quarter of the fifteenth century, but with the unargued addition, "contemporary with the earliest datable manuscript," i.e. Cl).

Chaucer's Reticent Merchant

KARLA TAYLOR

I suspect few readers think of Chaucer's Merchant as reticent, yet the climactic scene of his tale owes much to reticence. After describing what happens in the pear-tree with "sodeynly anon this Damyan / Gan pullen up the smok, and in he throng," the Merchant then retreats from his initial bluntness when Januarie too sees "that Damyan his wyf had dressed / In swich manere it may nat been expressed, / But if I wolde speke uncurteisly."[1] Betrayed by the accompanying explicitness, this gesture toward courtesy is really pseudo-reticence; still, its presence at the climax of the tale points toward the large role this rhetorical figure plays in Chaucer's representation of the Merchant. In this essay, I will explore how reticence shapes the relations between narrator and audience both in the Merchant's portrait in the General Prologue, where the importance of the unexpressed first surfaces, and in his Tale. In order to show the oddity of Chaucer's reticent Merchant, I will begin with a more typical use of the figure, from the Ugolino story in Dante's *Inferno*. My choice of example is not accidental, for in outlining the larger implications of Chaucer's narrative address to his audience, I hope also to suggest how his use of reticence responds to Dante.[2]

The figure of reticence depends on the reader's cooperation. Reticence is not saying it all in order to say more, not less, since meaning takes shape as if from within the reader. This is why Ugolino's reticence in *Inferno* 33 is so devastating. His story of imprisonment and death moves by patterned oppositions of grief and hunger, speaking and eating, so that when he ends by saying cryptically "Poscia, più che 'l dolor, poté 'l digiuno" (And then, more than grief, hunger had power),[3] then sinks his teeth again into the nape of the Bishop Ruggieri, his hated companion, it must mean that Ugolino, unable to speak to his children when they were alive, ate them when they were dead. The story is meaningless without this conclusion, but the text does not say it. Instead, it requires us to imagine the ending, and thus to recognize the "bestial segno" (bestial sign [*Inferno* 32.133]) of cannibalism as an imaginative potential within ourselves as well. The effect of reticence is to make Ugolino horrible especially because he is us. We can all break bread with him in our minds.

189

Reticence embodies stylistically the anti-community of Pisa, the "nov-ella Tebe" (modern Thebes [*Inferno* 33.89]) in which all humanity has broken down. Dante represents Ugolino's political betrayal not only by his cannibalism, but also by his inability to speak. For Dante, as for Aristotle, it is through speech that human beings join together in communities; his journey is not only from Egypt to Jerusalem, but also "di Fiorenza in popol giusto" (from Florence to a people just and sane [*Paradiso* 31.39]), the City of God.[4] Ugolino's reticence exiles him from the human com-munity Dante seeks to create in the *Divine Comedy*.

Like Dante's reticence, Chaucer's irony is very much concerned with the human community. On the face of it, the General Prologue establishes Chaucer as one of the fellowship, seeing what thèy see, hearing what they hear and speak, and knowing what they know. His voice is the most complete image we have of the General Prologue society, which finds the Prioress and Monk attractive, sneers at lawyers, and approves of the Friar's sweet English. When Chaucer's expressed opinions match the pilgrims' good opinions of themselves, he both enacts the broader com-plicity of a society that prefers the Friar's easy penance to the more demanding spirituality of the Franciscan ideal, and implicates human social language in the General Prologue's vision of a world grown old. Such a friar couldn't exist without the "frankeleyns" and the "worthy wommen of the toun" (I.216–17), whose idea of honesty corresponds to the Friar's social respectability rather than to the original virtue and chastity of both etymon and order.[5] Here semantic change perfectly en-acts social degeneration. And because Chaucer shares the new meaning of "honest" with the people in the portrait, this aspect of the *General Prologue* voice creates a community between the poet and the society within the text.

But Chaucer's fellowship with the pilgrims also enables him to create a second community, between himself and his audience, at the expense of the first. Mainly with what Jill Mann has called linguistic evidence,[6] Chaucer evokes understandings that differ from his overtly expressed opinions. A good example is the couplet in the Monk's portrait: "He was nat pale as a forpyned goost. / A fat swan loved he best of any roost (I.205–6). Though the lines voice a general social preference for physical vitality, the splendid rhyme of "goost" and "roost" moves us to a different level of understanding. Chaucer concedes to us the authorship of the new under-standing, that fat roasts of any kind ill befit ghostly asceticism.

Chaucer's indirections depend on shared culture, and ask a very high level of cooperation of his audience. The effect of rhyme in this case depends on two kinds of presupposition. First, it assumes as already known the antithesis between "goost" and "roost." This is normal con-versational presupposition, and presumably arises out of a real universe of discourse. Second, it is also fictional, world-creating presupposition, which—even if you didn't already know—actually creates as shared the first kind. Since Chaucer doesn't require you to choose between the two varieties—and hence to expose yourself, if in fact you didn't already know—this seems to me a particularly generous complicity between author and reader. The General Prologue creates a community of shared understanding as if it were merely drawing on a prior state of affairs. Encouraging us to see the pilgrims more wisely than they see themselves, the style of the General Prologue also suggests how poetic language, used as a cooperative exchange of author and audience, might ameliorate the "condiccioun" of a society in crisis. We are being recreated, in both senses of the word.

This we take to be the essence of Chaucerian irony, which we think of as generous and open. Chaucerian irony results from "something missing," for meaning arises not only from what is there, but also from what is not. His irony, then, is a form of reticence: not saying it all in such a way as to say it more meaningfully. It leaves a space for our participation; and consequently the General Prologue is a marvelous example of *confabulatio,* or the conversation of the text.[7] It creates a community of readers who undergo an ethical education by reading; and to this new and superior society—superior, that is, to the anti-community of "singular profit" described *in* the work—Chaucer concedes an enormous authority. This new community of readers comes to share responsibility for an imaginative reconstitution of society, for we are Chaucer's co-equals in the production of meaning.

None of this is particularly new, though I hope I have shifted the ground of discussion from the purely formal with the notion that writing and reading are social acts. I have lingered over it because the General Prologue's conversation between author and reader breaks down in the Merchant's portrait, and later in his tale. And it breaks down because of the stylistic trait I have identified as essentially Chaucerian: reticence.

The reticence of The Merchant's Tale is not, strictly speaking, the rhetorical figure Dante uses in *Inferno* 33. Rather, I single out the extraordinary frequency with which the Merchant cannot or will not say things; this differs from Ugolino's reticence because the Merchant explicitly points out that there are missing parts. This in turn gives us access to the broadest kind of reticence, if I may call it that: the Merchant's habitual refusal to tell us what we need to know in order to follow his bewildering shifts among genres, tones, directions of sympathy and antipathy, and to follow also his pyrotechnic display of an allusiveness so brilliant that it seems designed to go right over any audience's head.[8] The Merchant's refusals evince a peculiar, un-Chaucerian uncooperativeness toward his audience.

Yet his narrative address is related to Chaucer's usual authorial gener-
osity, and indeed it is useful to see it as Chaucer's Ugolino potential.
Shifting responsibility to the audience is central to the aesthetic and
ethical agenda of the *Canterbury Tales,* yet it is not without problems.[9]
The Merchant's Tale explores some of these through characteristics of
style also foreshadowed in the Merchant's portrait. That they are "spoken"
in Chaucer's own voice suggests a kinship between the reticence of General Prologue irony and its darker cousin in The Merchant's Tale.

In the Merchant's portrait, Chaucer shows us a facade in the making. He
presents the Merchant presenting himself, in the language of dress and the
spoken word, as a substantial pillar of the community. The Merchant's
facade of substance is obviously of great value in his financial activities—
"his bargaynes and his chevyssaunce" (I.282) and the "sheeldes" (278) he
exchanges so well—and it is built primarily out of his profitable speech.
"Sownynge alwey th'encrees of his wynnyng" (275), the Merchant con-
verts debt into wealth; this is not just a matter of deceptive appearances,
but a dynamic process in which his speech palpably transforms "is not"
into "is," in a kind of verbal *creatio ex nihilo.*[10] For there can be no doubt
that he is in debt:

> This worthy man ful wel his wit bisette:
> Ther wiste no wight that he was in dette,
> So estatly was he of his governaunce
> With his bargaynes and with his chevyssaunce.
> For sothe he was a worthy man with alle,
> But, sooth to seyn, I noot how men hym calle.

> (279–84)

Here, "For sothe" and "sooth to seyn" are not empty phrases to fill out the
meter; they make explicit the problem that in this portrait language is
antithetical to truth: a means not of knowing, but of not knowing. Most of
the pilgrims are not named, but only in the Merchant's portrait is this
significant; the truth of the Merchant is the absence of his name. We may
imagine this as arising from the Merchant himself—he may be fleeing
creditors, and want to be nameless—or from Chaucer's contempt, which
issues in a conspicuous withholding of identity; but the reason (of which
we cannot in any case be sure) matters less than the dissociation of truth
from what is spoken. Conversely, from the withholding of speech—reticence, that is—the truth emerges.

A second kind of reticence makes the line "There wiste no wight that he
was in dette" more than one of those brief moments of omniscience that
break in on Chaucer's usual pose of limited perspicacity. Despite the
Merchant's profitable speech, "Sownynge alwey th'encrees of his wynnyng," this line expresses not an opinion, but a fact.[11] Its syntax—a verb

of knowing, *witen,* with a *that*-complement in the preterite indicative—presupposes the truth of the complement: whether or not the main clause is negated, whether anyone knows it or not, the Merchant is in debt.[12]

Presupposition distinguishes "new" information from "old" knowledge already shared between speaker and audience. "Ther wiste no wight" is new, now being supposed or asserted for the first time, while "he was in dette" is old background, presupposed rather than asserted. Presupposition reminds us of what we already knew, and confirms the community of shared knowledge between speaker and audience. To the extent that it is new, it is only "renewed"—that is, it merely tells us that this fact, which we already knew, is also relevant here. Presupposition is like saying something again. It is related to reticence because one has not, so to speak, said it the first time.

But Chaucer's use of presupposition here creates a number of problems. For in fact the Merchant's debt is new; we had not known about it before this line. Conversely, the assertion "Ther wiste no wight" is actually old; it only summarizes our prior state of knowledge. Until now, there has been nothing to suggest that the Merchant is in debt, and the Merchant's own testimony that he is not. We are included in the group—everyone—ignorant of the Merchant's debt. And yet, until the second half of the line, we are probably unaware of our membership in that group. With its revelation, what we thought we knew turns out to be precisely what we did not know.

Narratives do use presupposition to create their fictional worlds, and, as in the Monk's portrait, Chaucer often uses this unmarked fictional presupposition. Perhaps my point is only that lines like "Ther wiste no wight that he was in dette" are instances of omniscience on the part of a limited narrator. But omniscience does not quite pin down the oddity of the Merchant's debt. For the Merchant's debt is something different still: presupposition failure.[13] Chaucer's manner of revealing the debt is uncooperative rather than cooperative, socially aggressive rather than tactful. And the line is different only because he brings the verb of knowing to overt expression.

In conversation, presuppositions fail when they are not shared by both speaker and listener; the failure causes one or both to miss signals. Though the reasons for missed signals are varied and complex, they are so common that any community of speakers shares a sure social sense of them. Most missed signals involve at least awkwardness; some a good bit worse. Let me describe a few cases of failed presuppositions in order to suggest what I think is going on in the Merchant's portrait.

Imagine that a teacher says to American college freshmen with average high school educations, "You remember, of course, that Lombardy was associated with tyranny in the late fourteenth century." The teacher here assumes knowledge unlikely to be shared, since, we are told, many students are not even sure when the American civil war took place. The abstruse point she then makes (say, about the political implications of setting in The Merchant's Tale) remains wholly opaque because her students have nothing to remember about Lombard tyrants.

In the most benign case, this is neither intended nor taken as a put-down. The teacher's mistaken assumption can be corrected if the students simply ask questions; knowledge presupposed as already shared thus becomes explicitly new information. Or, the students might remain silent, perhaps condescending to a teacher whom they consider so disconnected from reality that whatever she says is just hot air. What could such a boring pedant possibly say that is worth knowing? But even if the students are trying to cooperate, such a statement cannot help but engender in them a certain shakiness, as well as a heightened dependence on the teacher, when they realize that they have missed something—and, moreover, something the presupposing form of her statement implies they ought to have known. It calls their attention to a hierarchy of knowledge in which they are subordinate.

But what if it *is* intended as a put-down?—if the teacher assumes her students know nothing about Lombard tyrants, but mentions them in the presupposing form that suggests they do? Far from explaining, she only refers to something she never said the first time. Her purpose then is not to teach—to establish common ground in order to bring in new information. Rather, she labels the ground as *not* common, and communicates something like, "Let's get this straight: I know, and you ought to know but don't, about Lombard tyrants." By exposing student ignorance, she calls attention to the hierarchy of knowledge precisely in order to exericse power; I would call this "rank-pulling." Its purpose is to intimidate. If the students recognize the teacher's intentions, they quite properly regard *her* as the tyrant.

I choose examples of conversational failure in the classroom partly because of the inherently unequal social relation in which knowledge can become the basis of power. Something similar obtains when an author creates a fictional world and readers take it in; indeed I started thinking about failures in conversational cooperativeness to explain my own students' response to Dante's authority. When he addresses his readers in *Inferno* 9 as "O voi ch'avete li 'intelletti sani" (You who have sound intellects [line 61]), and expects them to interpret without providing the means for them to do so, they often think he is either a tyrant or a jerk. He has not yet earned their respect and assent. But whether in the classroom or in reading, it seems to me that hierarchies of power are easier to accept when they are not explicitly called to our attention, especially in contexts where people no longer agree about what hierarchies are proper. This is precisely the situation reflected in the General Prologue.

When Chaucer mentions the Merchant's debt as if we already knew about it, the General Prologue complicity—what I have called the conversation of the text—becomes a sham in which the real power relations of author and reader are exposed. We are made awkardly aware of our subordination to the controlling speaker, as Chaucer transforms knowledge presented as if he shared it with us, in complicity against the ignorant pilgrim society, into backhanded domination. This disrupts both communities: first, because Chaucer here clearly distinguishes himself from the pilgrims; and second, because we are suddenly associated with them rather than with the knowing poet. Realizing that we did not know about the debt—and that Chaucer controls whether we are allowed to recognize our ignorance—we are mostly aware that we are at his mercy. He "pulls rank" on us, and so we also become aware that our relationship to him is hierarchical and, at this moment, extremely one-sided. Chaucer retracts his usual concession of authority to the reader, and shows too that he may be capricious in the granting and withholding of knowledge essential to our community with him.

None of this would happen if elsewhere Chaucer did not so invitingly efface his authority. The Merchant's portrait shows that Chaucer could have told us everything all along had he chosen to; the community or conversation of author and reader is as fictive as the General Prologue society itself. The reticent omniscience of the Merchant's portrait is the verso of the reticent openness we usually call Chaucerian irony.

We have our choice. We can bow to Chaucer's authority and become subjects of a rather tyrannical poet who governs at his whim rather than through cooperative interchange, with reciprocal responsibility for meaning; or—if this does not appeal—we can revolt.

I scarcely think my extravagant political metaphor occurs to most readers of the Merchant's portrait. We only feel uncomfortable, unsure of our ground, and hence more than usually reliant on Chaucer's guiding hand. But I have described it in this way because the same effects reappear in The Merchant's Tale as the governing principle of its author-audience relations. That principle is tyranny.

It is no accident that the tale follows The Clerk's Tale, where Walter is the very figure of the tyrant described in late medieval political texts, and as Chaucer himself understood tyrants in the *Legend of Good Women*.[14] Walter's principality, and even Walter himself, are subject entirely to his capricious willfulness; the tale explores what goes awry when a ruler believes the political fiction that there is but one will for king and people. From the beginning Walter follows his own pleasure; and after a brief interlude when his people call him to account to keep the contract of mutual obligation—a feudal mode of government—his pleasure grows more and more singular. He pursues his *delectabilia propria*—"singular profit"—the universal complaint against tyrants, and the universal distinction drawn between tyrants and proper rulers.[15]

The merging of wills Walter requires of Griselda is appropriate only with God, where such union perfects human identity. There is no more beautiful expression of this than Piccarda's in *Paradiso* 3, "E 'n sua voluntade è nostra pace" (And in his will is our peace [line 85]). But with any lesser being, such as a husband or a ruler—despite the common metaphors justifying husbands and kings as stand-ins for God—such union only alienates subjects from themselves and leads them astray. It places them in an untenable position: for merging their wills with that of the ruler obliterates identity defined as individual difference from any other person, and obliterates too the very basis of their subjecthood, which rests on difference from the sovereign. Most medieval political writers counseled prayer (for God can convert sinners) and acquiescence to tyranny; Aquinas argued against deposition, since if it failed, it would only make the tyrant more obdurate in his oppression. But, as we see in The Clerk's Tale, acquiescence also encourages Walter. Griselda, who really does merge her will with Walter's, seems to be an experiment in thought: what would happen if the subject put theory into practice and patiently endured tyranny?

The Clerk's Prologue anticipates the political thread of his tale. The Host reasserts his governance over the tale-telling game, and the Clerk gladly submits, putting himself under the Host's "yerde" and offering to "do yow obeisance, / As fer as resoun axeth, hardily" (IV. 24–25). His obedience, then, parallels Griselda's, but with a reservation she does not make in her vow to Walter. The reservation of "reasonable" obedience argues a different source of authority: the ruled, by whose consent and concession a ruler governs. The Clerk, then, reminds us that the Host's governance derives from the consent of the "compaignye."

My point here is that the language Chaucer uses to mark out relations of literary authority between authors and their audiences is drawn from political discourse, which he elsewhere shows himself thoroughly familiar with *as* political.[16] He then confirms the conjunction of literary and political relations with the tale, in which the Clerk shows the same "reasonable obedience" toward Petrarch, his author, as he shows toward his audience, the Host: over acquiescence combined with a more covert redefinition. Moreover, he extends the line of authority relations by telling a tale that has always tested its readers' willingness to assent. John Ganim has described how the Clerk, by making it hard to accept the official moral of the tale, and then following it with the Envoy, plays with his audience much as Walter plays with Griselda. He requires us to guess at a correct reading of the whole performance without conceding us the authority to do so. His cat-and-mouse game resembles Chaucer's characteristic narrative mode.[17]

We should take note, then, when The Clerk's Tale is followed by yet another tale set in Lombardy, home of tyrants (you remember, of course, the association . . .).[18] Januarie is introduced as one who "folwed ay his bodily delyt / On wommen, ther as was his appetyt" (IV. 1249–50); "delyt" is a defining characteristic of the tyrant. The garden, which Dante had used as the symbolic setting of empire in *De monarchia,* later becomes the space of Januarie's "delit" as he "Shoop hym to lyve ful deliciously. / His housynge, his array, as honestly / To his degree was maked as a kynges" (IV. 2022, 2025–27). These lines come soon after May (in whose gentle heart pity runs freely) is contrasted to tyrants, who have hearts of stone (like Ugolino) and who rejoice in "crueel pryde" (IV. 1993). Also characteristic is Januarie's proclivity to listen to flattery; John of Salisbury had identified flattery as the problem of theocratic kingship most likely to divert it into tyranny.[19]

While none of these details stands alone, together they form a pattern. The manner in which the Merchant tells his tale also enacts the thematic problem of tyranny by deflecting it onto the analogous authority relations between author and audience. The Merchant is, I argue, a tyrannical narrator, who plays tricks with our wills—the faculty of desire in the rational soul.

The Merchant ends his tale by addressing his audience: "Now, goode men, I pray yow to be glad" (IV. 2416). The prayer parallels the question he has just asked of the well-deceived Januarie: "who is glad but he?" (2412). The Merchant's covert association of his audience with the ignorant fool of his tale picks up on the peculiar tricks of the Merchant's portrait, and locates a sense we get even while laughing: there is something to make us squirm behind our enjoyment.[20] The Merchant's spectacular display of narrative power has entertained us; but we have also obscurely been put in our places.

My effort to trace the Merchant's games with his audience's will began with confusion about plot detail: when do the wedding guests leave? It turns out that this banal question is involved with two well-known aspects of the tale: its epic/romantic digressiveness, and the way the narrator plays with sympathy and antipathy toward his characters, aligning himself first with Januarie's point of view, only to shift to May's in such a way as to make Januarie's joy even more fatuous.

The question of the wedding guests involves a basic drive in reading narrative (especially fabliau, with its economy and swift forward motion)—what I would call desire for the plot. By this I mean simply that we want to know what happens next. The most powerful way to arouse this desire is to defer its fulfillment; by delaying what comes next, an author can bring the reader to such a pitch of expectation that, when fulfillment comes, the relief and release are correspondingly greater.

That is just what happens here. This is a wedding, and we actually know what occurs after the guests leave. But the Merchant plays a delaying game; this is one of three places where the tale's digressiveness is most apparent.[21] From the moment the wedding ceremony is concluded, at line 1709, a dense texture of allusion stops the plot in its tracks. For someone whose desire for the plot rules, and who just wants to get on with it, the interruption seems interminable. Knowing what is coming, we are left dangling in suspense as Chaucer skips over the entire terrain of the Western literary tradition: from Orpheus, Amphion, and Thebes to the *Marriage of Mercury and Philology;* from Esther to the Trojan War to the extended apostrophe to Damyan, now also stricken with May's beauty. And the stalled plot *keeps* disappointing. The guests are "haste[d] . . . fro the mete" (IV. 1767) but not out the door, for a few lines later the postprandial dancing and toasting begins (1769–71). The sun goes down— lengthily—and again the guests seem to leave: "For which departed is this lusty route / Fro Januarie" (1800–1801). Januarie plies himself with aphrodisiacs, and, we think, at last we're moving again. But not all have left: "privee freendes" (1813) yet remain, whom Januarie begs to "voyden al this hous in curteys wyse" (1815). The newlyweds are not alone until line 1820: "Out of the chambre hath every wight hym dressed." The deferral has lasted for over one hundred lines (IV. 1709–1820).

The point of the Merchant's elaborate rousing of his audience's narrative desire is to align it with Januarie's parallel desire for May. Januarie, "ravysshed in a traunce" (IV. 1750) by his enchanting bride, is desperate to get rid of his guests, so that he may "manace" May in more than just his "herte" (1752). He too knows what happens next, and is most anxious to get there. The reader's desire for the plot is thus perfectly aligned with Janaurie's desire for May—a desire we already know to be motivated far more by folly and "dotage" than "hoolinesse"—and our fulfillment and his come at the same moment. When the last guests have taken their leave, we find great release in the long delayed fulfillment of desire:

> And Januarie hath faste in armes take
> His fresshe May, his paradys, his make.
> He lulleth hire; he kisseth hire ful ofte . . .

> (IV. 1821–23)

The wait makes us appreciate the tenderness of these lines, but what follows is all the more savage because of them.[22] Though our desire has been for a slightly different object, we too are stung

With thikke brustles of his berd unsofte,
Lyk to the skyn of houndfyssh, sharp as brere—
For he was shave al newe in his manere—
He rubbeth hire about hir tendre face . . .

(IV. 1824–27)

We know that marriage is just the eyewash that allows Januarie to continue following "his bodily delyt / On wommen," but now we are confronted with our own gulling: our desire to get on with this consummation is no less risible than Januarie's. We have been humiliated by our choice, in defiance of everything we know, to share Januarie's desire. And since Januarie remains unaware of his inadequacies (in a parallel to the portrait's tricks with omniscience, May, praising nothing, somehow praises it "nat . . . worth a bene" [IV. 1854]), I would suggest that *we* and specifically our curiosity, are the true targets of the savagery.

The other major digression is the interlude with Pluto and Proserpina. As before, the context defines the purpose of this sequence as, in the main, to arouse and suspend our desire for what comes next. If before we were, willy-nilly, made to identify with Januarie at his most lustful, now we are made to identify with May and Damyan at their most treacherous:

And with that word she saugh wher Damyan
Sat in the bussh, and coughen she bigan,
And with hir fynger signes made she
That Damyan sholde clymbe upon a tree
That charged was with fruyt, and up he wente.
For verraily he knew al hire entente,
And every signe that she koude make,
Wel bet than Januarie, hir owene make,
For in a lettre she hadde toold hym al
Of this matere, how he werchen shal.
And thus I let hym sitte upon the pyrie,
And Januarie and May romynge myrie.

(IV. 2207–18)

Again, we know in general what will happen, and so our narrative desire is aligned with the sexual desire of the characters in the tale. When the long digression begins, with "Bright was the day, and blew the firmament" (IV. 2219), we suffer what might be described as a *lectio interrupta*. Again the digression is one hundred lines long (through 2319); and this time, because Pluto and Proserpina are so garrulous, we really do fear that it will be dilated beyond our patience to bear. Morton Bloomfield has observed how The Merchant's Tale blurs the boundaries among genres as well as between narrator and characters. To these I would add the blurred distinction between characters and audience. We have, so to speak, become Damyans and Mays, impatiently sitting in the pear-tree or waiting for the chance that comes "When tendre youthe hath wedded stoupyng age" (IV. 1738), to leap into the tree from Januarie's obligingly stooped back.

The effect is at once comic and cruel. Even while I am situated in the tale as a treacherous May, my sudden sympathy for the betrayed old Januarie creates an impossible tension. This resembles the alienation from the self engendered when Walter demonstrates his tyranny by requiring Griselda to have no will but his. The Merchant, by playing with his audience—arousing, suspending, and fulfilling our basic desire for the plot so that we become at once treacherous lovers and cuckolded husbands—divides us against ourselves and makes us obscurely aware that we have been drawn into his fiction as subordinate objects, to be manipulated at his will. He is, in short, a tyrannical narrator.

The cruelty emerges when our narrative desire is fulfilled with the union of Damyan and May in the tree. The embellishments and deferrals of romance yield to the bluntness of fabliau when "sodeynly anon this Damyan / Gan pullen up the smok, and in he throng" (IV. 2352–53). The Merchant increases the bluntness by warning us beforehand how "rude" he will be (2351), and withdrawing when Januarie too sees "that Damyan his wyf had dressed / In swich manere it may nat been expressed, / But if I wolde speke uncurteisly" (2361–63). This is the pseudo-reticence I began with, in which the Merchant, by appealing to our polite sensibilities, suggests that "curteisie" is only the phoney covering for a most uncurteis mind. This resembles the difference between saying, "If you can't say anything nice, don't say anything at all," and actually remaining silent. One is polite; the other gestures toward politeness in order to insult and humiliate.

The scene in the tree offers a figure for the Dantean materialization of metaphor that constitutes a kind of poetic plot in the tale: lifting the veil or "smok," the traditional metaphor of allegory as a veil for truth. From "paradys" as a figure for marriage to the literal paradise; from Januarie's ideal wife, malleable as wax, to the literal wax with which May counterfeits the "clikct"; from the personification of "tendre youthe" and "stoupyng age" to Januarie's literally stooped back, the tale borrows the short-circuited allegory of the *Inferno* that Dante exemplifies by Ugolino's reticence.[23] But here, we have to dispense with the beautiful lie of language—the words of the Song of Songs, the figure of marriage as a paradise, and even the "curteisye" that makes it possible for people to live together civilly—in order to get at the underlying truth. The punning rhyme "dressed"/"expressed" associates verbal expression with the clothing Damyan lifts here.[24] Since the veil is lifted in the suggested absence of language—that is, with the Merchant's pseudo-reticence—the tale renews the portrait's opposition of speech and truth.

And the Merchant's truth is that human beings do not differ from other animals. As with Ugolino, the Merchant's reticence is a "bestial segno." All the traditional definitions of humanity—the upright animal; the rational animal; the political and social animal; the image of God—are subverted by the tale's climax.[25] We are instead the stooping animal and the serpent in the tree; and we are defined—as the narrative address to the audience makes clear throughout—like other animals, only by our appetites. And since, as Aristotle wrote, human societies are glued together by the common language that allows us to communicate rationally and to share ethical values, its suggested absence in the Merchant's pseudo-reticence disrupts the social definition of humanity as well. Like tyranny itself, the tyranny of the narrator in The Merchant's Tale destroys the human community.

Though there was a well settled definition of tyranny by the end of the fourteenth century, few political writers offered practical suggestions on what to do about tyrants. Only Marsiglio of Padua and William of Ockham unequivocally proposed deposition, to reassert natural human dignity against the arbitrary will of the tyrant, and to restore the rational, just society that distinguishes people from other animals. When at the end of his tale the Merchant tells us to be as glad as Januarie, he suggests that we should enjoy our own debasement. But as the Clerk says, the world has grown old, and it is hard to find more than two or three Griseldas in every town. Many readers of The Merchant's Tale, perceiving that they have been made into Griseldas, do what she did not: they revolt against the tyranny of the Merchant's word games, and reject the indignities to which he has subjected them.

The problem, then, remains that the Merchant as narrator resembles Chaucer in the General Prologue portrait of the Merchant. I think The Merchant's Tale is Chaucer's experiment in what he would have been if he had chosen to write in the Dantean vein. One of the scores on which Chaucer differs most from Dante is in the quality of narrative authority: Dante's open assertion of authority and open remaking of a "fit audience, though few" in the *Commedia,* as opposed to Chaucer's self-effacement combined with a more covert recreation of his audience in the *Canterbury Tales.* But in The Merchant's Tale, a Chaucerian narrator assumes an authority as strong as Dante's; Chaucer's customary difference may veil something quite different. In his first spectacular digression, the Merchant commands the author of the *Marriage of Mercury and Philology,* "Hoold thou thy pees, thou poete Marcian" (IV. 1732). The line imitates the imperative and the impulse of "Taccia Lucano . . . Taccia . . . Ovidio" at *Inferno* 25.94–99, where Dante vies with the ancient poets.[26] The narrative address of The Merchant's Tale is, I think, meant to silence the Dante in Chaucer, by showing first that Chaucer can vie with Dante on Dante's own ground; second, that the results are antisocial and tyrannical;

and third, that he does not finally want to emulate Dante. Joining this strong authority to the uses of reticence, Chaucer also rewrites the Ugolino cantos, casting Dante himself in the role of the Theban horror and destroyer of communities.

What makes Chaucer different is his considerably less confident attitude toward poetic language. As a skilled *rhetor,* he knows its potential to rewrite its readers; but he also knows and embraces the other side, that it is just so much "eyr ybroken" (*House of Fame* 765). Reading is the province of readers; a poet's authority is conceded to him by his readers as much as the other way around. We can silence a poet very effectively by turning the leaf and choosing another tale—as Chaucer elsewhere invites us to do. Chaucer reckons with the limits this places on his ability to control his audience. The final effect of The Merchant's Tale, then, is to provoke the audience into revolting against the tyrannies to which it has been subjected, and thus embracing, with an educated will, the social recreation—in both senses—that the *Canterbury Tales* proposes.

Notes

1. Merchant's Tale, IV. 2352–53, 2361–63. All references to Chaucer's works are cited from *The Riverside Chaucer,* 3rd ed., gen. ed. Larry D. Benson (Boston: Houghton Mifflin, 1987). These lines are J. S. P. Tatlock's major evidence for the darkness and "obscenity" of the *Merchant's Tale.* See "Chaucer's *Merchant's Tale,*" *Modern Philology* 33 (1936): 367–81.

2. My work on the Dante-Chaucer relation began with a dissertation directed by Donald R. Howard. I wish to acknowledge a more general debt to him for his insistence, in both his writing and his teaching, on the space Chaucer left for the reader's participation, an insistence that awakened my interest in Chaucer's narrative address to his audience.

3. *Inferno* 33.75. All references to the *Commedia* are cited from *Dante: The Divine Comedy,* ed. and trans. Charles S. Singleton, 3 vols. (Princeton: Princeton Univ. Press, 1970–75). For Ugolino's reticence, see John Freccero, "Bestial Sign and Bread of Angels (*Inferno* 32–33)," *Yale Italian Studies* 1 (1977): 53–66.

4. References to the inability or refusal to speak begin with an allusion to *Aeneid* 2.3 ("Infandum, regina, iubes renovare dolorem") at *Inferno* 33.4–6; see also lines 18, 48, 52, and 65. For language as the glue of the human community, see Aristotle, *Politics* 1.1.9. In the *Commedia* the importance of rectified speech is shown particularly by those such as Pier della Vigne and Ulysses, whose sins are depicted as sins of language.

5. See I.246–51, which define honesty as the Friar's particular virtue. The etymon *honestas* usually referred to chastity, as "honest" still could in Middle English. See Norman Davis, et al., *A Chaucer Glossary* (Oxford: Clarendon Press, 1979), p. 76.

6. Jill Mann, *Chaucer and Medieval Estates Satire: The Literature of Social Classes and the General Prologue to the Canterbury Tales* (Cambridge: Cambridge Univ. Press, 1973), esp. pp. 25–36.

7. Glending Olson discusses the importance of *confabulatio* for the roles of

fiction and the relations between tale-tellers and their audiences in *Literature as Recreation in the Later Middle Ages* (Ithaca: Cornell Univ. Press, 1982), pp. 80–89.

8. For the generic shifts of The Merchant's Tale, see Morton W. Bloomfield, *"The Merchant's Tale:* A Tragicomedy of the Neglect of Counsel—The Limits of Art," in *Medieval and Renaissance Studies* 7, ed. Siegfried Wenzel, Proceedings of the Southeastern Institute of Medieval and Renaissance Studies, 1975 (Chapel Hill: Univ. of North Carolina Press, 1978), pp. 37–50; on the disjunctiveness of the narrative, see Robert M. Jordan, "The Non-Dramatic Disunity of the *Merchant's Tale,"* *PMLA* 78 (1963): 293–99; for the shifts in sympathy, see E. T. Donaldson, "The Effect of the Merchant's Tale," in *Speaking of Chaucer* (New York: Norton, 1970), pp. 30–45; for the effect on the reader, see Jay Schleusener, "The Conduct of the *Merchant's Tale," Chaucer Review* 14 (1980): 237–50.

9. See John M. Ganim, "Carnival Voices and the Envoy to the *Clerk's Tale," Chaucer Review* 22 (1987): 112–27 (see esp. pp. 122–24).

10. This was a chief objection to usury in the Middle Ages: the empty parody of divine verbal creation. For an interpretation of the Merchant as a "usurious" narrator, see R. A. Shoaf, *Dante, Chaucer, and the Currency of the Word: Money, Images and Reference in Late Medieval Poetry* (Norman, Okla.: Pilgrim Books, 1983), pp. 185–209.

11. My approach to understanding this line through presupposition thus differs from those of Oscar E. Johnson, "Was Chaucer's Merchant in Debt? A Study in Chaucerian Syntax and Rhetoric," *JEGP* 52 (1953): 50–57, which argues (on what I regard as slender metrical grounds) that he certainly was not; and Gardiner Stillwell, "Chaucer's Merchant: No Debts?," *JEGP* 57 (1958): 192–95, which argues that "if he was in debt, certainly no one knew it" (p. 192). Mann, *Chaucer and Medieval Estates Satire,* pp. 99–103, shows that debt was a regular feature of merchants in estates satire, though she concurs with Stillwell that the debt of Chaucer's merchant is not definitely knowable. Kenneth Cahn, in "Chaucer's Merchants and the Foreign Exchange: An Introduction to Medieval Finance," *Studies in the Age of Chaucer* 2 (1980): 81–119, points out that an exchanger of "sheeldes," a fictional unit of account, would regularly be in debt.

12. The classic semantic definition of presupposition, the operational test that the truth of the complement persists through negation, and the distinction between presupposition and assertion, are P. F. Strawson's, in *Introduction to Logical Theory* (London: Methuen, 1952). There is now general agreement that presuppositions are part of pragmatic rather than exclusively semantic analysis. For a collection of the best work on presuppositions and related problems, see János S. Petöfi and Dorothea Franck, *Präsuppositionen in Philosophie und Linguistik* (Frankfurt am Main: Athenäum, 1973), especially Franck's introduction and the articles by Oswald Ducrot, Charles S. Fillmore, Lauri Karttunen, Paul Kiparsky and Carol Kiparsky, and Robert C. Stalnaker. For application of the concept of presupposition to literature, see Jonathan Culler, *The Pursuit of Signs* (Ithaca: Cornell Univ. Press, 1981), chapter 5 ("Presupposition and Intertextuality"). For earlier stages of English, see Bruce Mitchell, *Old English Syntax* (Oxford: Clarendon Press, 1985), vol. 2, pp. 49–54, 81–84; and Anthony Warner, *Complementation in Middle English and the Methodology of Historical Syntax* (University Park: Pennsylvania State Univ. Press, 1982).

13. See Peter Harder and Christian Kock, *The Theory of Presupposition Failure,* Travaux du cercle linguistique de Copenhagen, XVII (Copenhagen: Akademisk Forlag, 1976). Presuppositions in normal conversations pertain not only to the semantic truth-value of what is literally said, but also to both speaker's and

listener's knowledge about and intentions toward one another. When these are unshared or misunderstood, "presupposition failure" results and communication is impaired. This is what I have called "missed signals"; see below.

14. See esp. the *Legend of Good Women*, G Prologue, 354–76. For tyranny in the Clerk's Tale, see Carol Falvo Heffernan, "Tyranny and Common Profit in the *Clerk's Tale*," *Chaucer Review* 17 (1983): 332–40. For Chaucer's treatment of kings and tyrants in general, see Margaret Schlauch, "Chaucer's Doctrine of Kings and Tyrants," *Speculum* 20 (1945): 133–56, to which I am deeply indebted. David Wallace uses the same materials in his superb discussion of politics, sexuality, and Chaucer's use of Petrarch in The Clerk's Tale in " 'Whan She Translated Was': A Chaucerian Critique of the Petrarchan Academy," in *Literary Practice and Social Change in Britain, 1380–1530,* ed. Lee Patterson (Berkeley: Univ. of California Press, 1990), pp. 156–215.

15. See, for instance, Henry Bracton, *De legibus et consuetudinibus Angliae,* ed. George E. Woodbine, 4 vols. (New Haven: Yale Univ. Press, 1915–40), 2:33, which distinguishes tyrants from proper kings on the basis of *voluntas,* or arbitrary will; and Egidius Romanus, *De Regimine Principum* (Rome, 1482), Book 3, part 2, chap. 6. As Richard Firth Green has established, there were many copies of Egidius's tract in fourteenth-century English book collections, and it was the source for Hoccleve's *Regiment of Princes;* see *Poets and Princepleasers: Literature and the English Court in the Late Middle Ages* (Toronto: Univ. of Toronto Press, 1980), pp. 140–41. For the contrary principle of "Common profit," often invoked by Ricardian writers such as Gower and Chaucer, see Russell A. Peck, *Kingship and Common Profit in Gower's Confessio Amantis* (Carbondale: Southern Illinois Univ. Press, 1978), esp. pp. xi–xxv, 20; and chap. 7, "The Education of a King," pp. 139–59.

16. See, for example, the establishment of the game in the General Prologue, I.777–87 (where the Host suggests the game), 810–18 (where the pilgrims agree to it), and 851–52 (where Chaucer describes the Knight's free assent).

17. In "Carnival Voices," pp. 119–24.

18. For the association of Lombardy and tyranny, see Schlauch, "Chaucer's Doctrine," p. 141, 145–48, following Bartolus de Sassoferrato's mid-14th century *De tyrannia.* Pavia was under the hegemony of the Visconti, the best known of the Lombard tyrants, until 1396. Chaucer describes Bernabo Visconti as the "God of delit and scourge of Lumbardye" in the Monk's Tale, VII 2400. For the cruelty and pride of tyrants, see *Legend of Good Women,* G Prologue 354–76; Monk's Tale, VII.2501, 2508.

19. *Policraticus,* 3.15.

20. This is Schleusener's argument in the "The Conduct of the *Merchant's Tale.*"

21. The first instance of digressiveness is the marriage encomium that begins the tale; I do not consider this because the story as such has not yet gotten going. The third instance is the Pluto-Proserpina interlude, discussed below. These are the three main *loci* of digressiveness discussed in Jordan, "Inorganic Unity," to advance his theory of Chaucer's composition by rhetorical blocs.

22. Donaldson makes this point eloquently in "The Effect of the Merchant's Tale," p. 36.

23. Donaldson, in "The Effect of the Merchant's Tale," cites these materialized metaphors without putting them into an intellectual framework. That framework is evident especially in the *Inferno,* where the principle of *contrapasso* is materialized figures of speech; Bertran de Born's severed head in *Inferno* 28, for

instance, materializes the metaphor of the body politic, here torn asunder as is appropriate for a political schismatic.

24. For "dressed" meaning "clothed," see *Troilus and Criseyde,* II.635, "And eke to see hym in his gere hym dresse." This is admittedly an unusual meaning, but supported by the context of clothing in The Merchant's Tale. See Davis, *Chaucer Glossary,* p. 42.

25. Ovid defines the human being as the upright animal who gazes toward heaven (*Metamorphoses* 1.78–86), a definition echoed in Bartholomaeus Anglicus's *De proprietatibus rerum* 3.1; see John of Trevisa's translation in *On the Properties of Things,* edited by M. C. Seymour et al. 2 vols. (Oxford: Clarendon Press, 1975), I: 90–91. The definition as the animal possessed of a rational soul is probably the most common; see, for example, Trevisa's *On the Properties of Things* 3.13 (1:101–2). The human being (or more specifically, the human rational soul) as the image of God originates in Genesis and is nearly universal in the biblical interpretative tradition. Thomas Aquinas frequently used the Aristotelian definition of man as a political animal (see *Politics* 1.1.9), to which he added social; see, for example, *De Regimine Principum,* 1, chapter 1.

26. This is one of the many oblique imitations of the *Commedia* in The Merchant's Tale. With his reference a few lines above (IV.1716) to Amphion, Chaucer may also allude to *Inferno* 32.1–12 in order to link The Merchant's Tale to the Theban cantos of Ugolino.

Part 3

Medieval Culture and Society

The Literary Uses of the New History

JOHN M. GANIM

As early as *The Three Temptations,* Donald Howard's work revealed a continuing concern with the relation between literature and historiography. In this spirit, this essay explores the importance for Chaucer criticism, and for our idea of medieval literature in general, of the "new history," particularly the social history of popular culture, strongly influenced by anthropological and sociological theory of the late Middle Ages and the Early Renaissance. While the "New Historicism," in its literary application epitomized by the work of Stephen Greenblatt, owes much to the "New History," it is the prior interpretive model of the historians themselves that is my subject here. Its chief practitioners, Emmanuel Le Roy Ladurie, Natalie Davis, Carlo Ginzburg, and others, have worked directly in or in the wake of the *Annales* school, but they also reflect submerged connections to literary theory and narrative discourse, in contrast to the economic and geographic determinism of earlier *Annales* scholars.

The key works of these historians comprise an idiosyncratic and sometimes bizarre catalog of topics and cases. Le Roy Ladurie's *Montaillou* reconstructs the social life of an early fourteenth-century southern French village through the records of an inquisition conducted against a remnant of catharism. Carlo Ginzburg's *The Cheese and the Worms* also uses the records of a heresy trial, this time to reconstitute a tradition of popular beliefs underlying a sixteenth-century northern Italian miller's peculiar theology. Natalie Davis' remarkably original research in a series of books and articles has located apparently sensational events and documents—pardon letters for murderers, the disappearance and return of a sixteenth-century villager to his remarried wife, *charivari,* riots, transvestite revels—in the shifting matrix of early modern French history.[1] Besides this taste for spectacular topics, what these historians also share is a concern with the problematic of deducing ordinary and unofficial popular consciousness from officially mediated records, a concern that impels them as much towards interpretations and texts as towards the reconstruction of events.

There is a certain irony of method here, for these newer historians have learned from literary criticism lessons that literary critics have moved far beyond, and, in moving beyond them, have implicitly or explicitly rejected. At the same time, literary criticism itself has turned to a constellation of disciplines, increasingly self-conscious about their methodology, in an effort to move beyond its own quandaries. Yet the model which informs all of these host disciplines turns out to be the very model of reading and interpretation that literary critics themselves have been seeking to revise. But before turning to these quandaries it might be worth the detour to trace the history of the New History.

I

In reaction to the emphasis on great men, politics, diplomacy and dramatic events typical of the traditional history entrenched in the French academic establishment, Marc Bloch and a group of other French historians founded the now famous journal *Annales*.[2] The history they proposed was one that took account of social structures, long range economic forces, even climate, population statistics and geography. Though Bloch's *Feudal Society* remains one of the standard works known to medievalists in all disciplines, the monument of the *Annales* school (by this time having become the establishment) is Fernand Braudel's astonishing *The Mediterranean*.[3] Here period becomes a subtitle to the primacy of geography, and world-famous battles and personalities take second place to *la longue durée,* the historian's equivalent of geological time.

During the 1950s and 1960s, the chief historians associated with *Annales* became evangelists for new forms of quantification, and celebrated computerization and other forms of mathematical measurement as the primary means to establish the patterns of long-range history.[4] While the fascination with quantification was at least partly the natural result of *Annales'* Napoleonic conquest of all possible forms of historical inquiry, the fetish for quantification must also have had a certain dual set of allegiances. On the one hand it was a way of rejecting the overwhelmingly philosophical and literary interpretative modes of the study of the humanities in France, on the other it was a way of subjecting all aspects of historical and social life to the analyses of the "human sciences." Where scientific models for the humanities in the U.S., for instance, have always been attempts at legitimization and acceptance, even this aspect of the *Annales* agenda had about it a revolutionary quality.

This quality acquired its ideology in the closer association between *Annales* and structuralism. By the late 1940s, *Annales* was associated with Section VI of the École Pratique des Hautes Études, directed first by Lucien Febvre and, after Febvre's death in 1956, by Braudel. Its purpose was to serve as an interdisciplinary center for new ideas in the social sciences, particularly a French sense of the human sciences, or perhaps, what science itself was. Lévi-Strauss was part of Section VI, and Roland Barthes was briefly editor. The promise of a methodology with which all disciplines could be mutually analyzed was profoundly attractive, even if very few articles that literary critics would recognize as "structuralist" appeared in *Annales*. Interestingly, Barthes' essay, "History or Literature," an attack on academic literary criticism as it stood then, and later reprinted in his *Sur Racine*,[5] was published in *Annales*.

Barthes' essay represents an interesting problem, in that its attack on academic, positivist literary history comes very close to becoming an attack on historicism. Academic critics should openly assume the psychology of the authors they write about, said Barthes, or if they seek to place literature historically, they should do away with the study of the author entirely and examine the broader cultural milieu. This apparent ahistoricity is in fact what generated Picard's famous counterattack on the *nouvelle critique,* an attack which, coming from a famous Racine scholar infuriated at Barthes' handling of Racine, was meant to expose the new French criticism, but which had the opposite effect of bringing Barthes to the attention of the world intellectual community. Ironically, part of Picard's attack, suggesting that the secondary referentiality imputed to traditional academic discourse was truer of structuralist discourse, while a foolish rhetorical ploy, does not seem too far off the mark, if in fact the recoil did not do more damage to Picard. But if the essay represented a certain part of Barthes' development that he himself would soon move far beyond, it was perhaps because of his *Annales* chauvinism in defending one of the landmarks of the *Annales* school, Lucien Febvre's study of Rabelais.[6]

Published in 1942, Febvre's book, *The Problem of Unbelief in the Sixteenth Century,* was one of the landmark expeditions of *Annales* history into literary and cultural matters. Febvre's argument is that the modernizing tendency to read Rabelias' humor and satire as evidence of atheism is a mistake. Rather than expressing a sacrilegious and ironic attitude towards the religion of his time, argues Febvre, Rabelais' wordplay and invective is consistent with the nature of belief in sixteenth-century France, which, far from exhibiting the beginnings of modern atheism, reflects the long tradition of learned satire, as well as the place of apparent skepticism in the belief system of the religion of the time. The philosophical and epistemological structures that would even allow atheism to be conceived of had not yet developed, and religious values themselves permeated so many variegated aspects of social and cultural life that it was inseparable from even the most wildly divergent positions.

Febvre, then, ends up with a doubly buttressed historicist position. First of all, he argues that we can only understand Rabelais' humor as it was understood in its time, that the wit and references operate differently then than they do now. Second, he argues further for another level of historicism, that Rabelais can be explained entirely by reference to the mentality of his age, particularly as regards the matrix of religious and social ideas in sixteenth-century France. The result is a Rabelais both more serious and more official than the wildly irreverent Rabelais of modern reception.

Even this second level of historicization would be ordinary, if arguable, in a literary historian. What renders it distinct from positivist literary history is at least partly the utter consistency of historiographic agenda of *Annales* to literary study, so that, for instance, despite the astonishing range of allusion Febvre controls, very little is made of Rabelais' own life or intentions. Indeed, what distinguishes the study from similar studies in England and America in the 1930s through 1950s is the stress on the cultural origin of the work, a stress so thoroughgoing that it seems almost as if his culture, rather than Rabelais, had written the works. The structuralizing impulse which would be the engine of Section VI in the post– World War II period is predicted in a scholarly form apparently indebted to more traditional learning.

For the insistence of Febvre on the absolute historicity of Rabelais' work reveals a problem in the *Annales* school's conception of mentality, which, aside from the question of change, implies that the discourse of the past is the best discourse on the past. In a sense, positivism returns, if not in diplomatic or political history, then in cultural and literary history. *Annales* "literary history," such as it was, while it critiqued the notion of the author and the masterpiece as somehow magically singular, failed to develop a means to include the discourse of the past as part of the past to be analyzed, which in other sorts of history, using techniques such as demography and statistics and geography, it could.

On a superficial level, at least, the totalization of the *Annales* project seems similar to the "area studies" divisions of American academic life. To the degree that these programs interacted with the concerns of the *Annales* school, however, it would seem as if the relatively static conception of interdisciplinary work that area studies practiced was not what the French meant at all, and in general areas retained a pragmatic and generally political orientation even to its social studies, perhaps a mark of their similarity to World War II intelligence research terms, upon which they were modelled. The major example of area studies which predates the postwar period, however, is to the point: the energization of American medievalists in the early days of the Mediaeval Academy.[7] Indeed, to this day American medievalists in most disciplines identify themselves first as medievalists and secondly as historians or critics. Interestingly, the historical contributions of medieval studies had tended towards "official" cultural investigations, in contradistinction to the fascination with the "unofficial" studies of *Annales,* and, again, political, diplomatic, theological and philosophical studies have outnumbered social studies. To the degree that literary studies contributed to the project of medieval studies as a whole, it has tended to serve as evidence, ratification or reflection of the hegemony of theological and philosophical ideas, with the exception of the disputes of the 1950s and 1960s concerning patristic exegesis and the value of the New Criticism.

Although one can find some praise of Ernst Robert Curtius' *European Literature and the Latin Middle Ages*,[8] with its tracing of traditional topics from antiquity to the Middle Ages, none of the *Annales* historians have taken much account of Exegetical criticism as practiced in the U.S., a criticism that presents in its own way *la longue durée*. D. W. Robertson occasionally cites Bloch's *Feudal Society,* especially to support his stress on hierarchy. For *A Preface to Chaucer* claims more than an interpretive key to Chaucer's work, it claims an understanding of how the medieval mind works, and it does so by arguing that people before about the seventeenth century actually had different thought processes than modern people do. Moreover, Robertson argues for a static and consistent tradition of Augustinian scriptural interpretation as the chief poetic hermeneutic from late Antiquity through the later Middle Ages. Despite Robertson's vituperative dismissal of modern criticism, the fact remains that his totalizing systematization of medieval interpretive practices bears certain similarities to structuralist and semiotic efforts, similarities obscured, and finally severed, by his historicist position and his oddly unhistorical idealization of hierarchical social values.

If in fact the earlier *Annales* program imagined by Barthes in *Sur Racine* achieved a coherent working out, it was by a circuitous route. The largely North American agenda of the New Historicism, with its house organ *Representations,* seems almost a self-consciously literary-cultural descendant of *Annales*. Its lack of an officially sponsored institute notwithstanding, however, *Representations* is marked by the thought of its spiritual godfather Foucault. One consequence of that descent is that the structures and the geological pace of *la longue durée* are translated into Foucault's philosophical and political vision, with its pessimistic awareness of the totalizing potential of power. But in fact *mentalité* history was subject to the same pressures that informed Foucault's themes, and already reveals an obsession with the drama of conflicts between hegemonic power and heterodox and idiosyncratic experience.

II

If a change occurs among historians close to *Annales,* manifesting itself in the late 1960s and early 1970s, perhaps in reaction to the events of those years in France, it is a shift in the conception of how to interpret historical data. In place of the stress on structures and impersonal forces, they began to write narrative histories that lay within a single lifetime; in place of large regions and entire continents, they focused on one village or one city. In place of objective, quantifiable data, they sought to recover the ways in which ordinary people imagined and dramatized their lives. While the demographic and economic data of 1950s *Annales* was the necessary backdrop, the emphasis was now on how individuals in society experienced historical change or lack of it. In place of counting, we have reading and interpretation. In place of numbers we have texts. History is now not a landscape, but a language. Interestingly, the turn towards *mentalité* is contemporary with a renewed interest in literature and language on the part of *Annales,* perhaps because by this time it was ensconced in the French research establishment as Section VI, and could recoup the heavily literary and philosophical bias of French intellectual tradition without caving in. Clearly the common impact of structuralist and post-structuralist thinking upon the "human sciences" had something to do with this, but in another way literary criticism and interpretation offered a solution to the problems that historians and other social scientists had run up against, even as literary criticism and theory itself was approaching a crisis under the same pressures.

One of the landmarks of *mentalité* history is Emmanuel Le Roy Ladurie's *Montaillou.* In the early fourteenth century, a stubborn pocket of Cathar heresy still apparently existed in the Pyrenées, long after the military suppression of the Cathar strongholds a century before. An inquisition took place under the direction of Jacques Fournier, Bishop of Pamiers (later Pope Benedict XII). Fournier undertook the task with characteristic thoroughness and zeal, cross-examining dozens of peasants from about 1318 to 1325, whose depositions were recorded (in translation) word for word. The result is an astonishingly detailed record of peasant and village life, thought, and habits. The attractiveness of this record for Le Roy Ladurie is obvious in its detailed evidence, about as unmediated as one could hope for, of peasant life. At the same time, it is the coincidence of the very ordinary, obsessively returned to by the peasants and diligently recorded by the scribes, and the highly unusual and marginal, a dangerous and endangering heresy, that attracts the *Annales* historian.

In one rather obvious respect, *Montaillou* fulfills perfectly the *Annales* agenda, looking backward and forward to a cultural continuum that seems to be impervious to the crises and catastrophes of political history, drawing in great detail the lives and days of an ordinary, even forgotten village and villagers, dramatically foregrounding the heterodox, the singular and suppressed as against the self-justifying record of official documentation. At the same time, it is precisely its mode of presentation, as a narrative (however structurally and topically organized), that both allows and renders problematic its allegiance to this agenda.

Le Roy Ladurie's villagers think and act in ways remarkably like modern French men and women. Le Roy Ladurie highlights this quandary by frequently pointing to differences that seem not to be as distant as one would expect. Even his officials are colored by the tone of post-Napoleonic bureaucratic behavior. Part of the reason for this is the nearly novelistic genre he is seeking to write. In seeking to capture the *mentalité* of his subjects, Le Roy Ladurie comes very close to translating both language and context. His pose, then, is replete with the problems of the anthropologist as well as the historian. (I leave aside the possibility that, consciously or not, *Montaillou* is an allegory, both of the relation of the *midi* to the center, and of resistance against the pressures of collaboration, as per Vichy.) Of course, the anthropologist's task is in some fashion to demystify the urge of the common reader to regard the Other as exotic, and what marks a number of the great anthropological studies is the way in which the Other is represented as utterly mundane.

Anthropology always has had a privileged position within the methodological arsenal of *Annales,* even if only as a metaphor. Marc Bloch's *Feudal Society* reads as much like social anthropology as history. With the increasing prestige of Lévi-Strauss' structural anthropology, the integrated language of anthropology and structuralism began to pepper historical and literary studies. Nevertheless, the search for significance in the structuralist model remains one committed to an objective uncovering of disguised relationships by the investigator. By the late 1960s, however, anthropology was beset by its own crises, ethical, political, methodological. One of the most widely influential movements within the discipline, and one which would influence studies outside it, was the attempt to "read" cultures as one would a text, to understand those cultures on their own terms, in their own context. Clifford Geertz's remarkable essay, "Thick Description," was perhaps the most widely circulated of these rethinkings outside of the discipline, and Geertz's impact on the new historians of popular culture was marked.[9]

Interestingly, however, Geertz's model of reading was close to the model of reading implicit in the New Criticism or perhaps one of its offshoots, such as the concern with reading and performance that one finds in the work of Richard Poirier,[10] or the newly lyrical models of reading one finds in Roland Barthes, who no longer espoused the structural-historical context he asked for in "History or Literature." Geertz was concerned with inventing ways of deducing meanings within the context of a culture, and suggesting the complexities of how those meanings were generated, sometimes through the stated and sometimes through the unstated. This effort was especially compelling to historians who now were concerned with reconstructing and interpreting the experience of people within the great movements of climate and economy that *Annales* had charted.

But the circle of history meeting anthropology meeting literary history occurs in a book partly about ironic circles, Mikhael Bakhtin's *Rabelais and His World* (1968), which, along with his other writings, has had considerable impact on the thinking of historians and anthropologists as well as literary critics.[11] For the center of Bakhtin's argument is a profound engagement with Febvre's *The Problem of Unbelief in the Sixteenth Century,* which was the centerpiece of *Annales* literary study. Bakhtin himself, particularly with his semiotic credentials, begins to affect the generation of historians who come of intellectual age in the full power of *Annales.*

It is precisely this official, serious and historicized Rabelais that Bakhtin takes aim at in his now influential book. In place of a serious Rabelais, he argues for the profundity of laughter. In place of an officially sanctioned text, he points to unofficial and subversive languages. In place of a text that speaks to a learned audience, he offers us a work imbued with, even inseparable from, popular culture. More significantly, however, his model of culture allows for conflict in a way that Febvre's does not, and in so doing politicizes rather than historicizes Rabelais' culture. For Bakhtin, *mentalité* (though he does not use the term) is multivocal, and the various voices use language in signficantly different ways. The temporary inversion of official values in the holiday celebrations of Carnival become, for Bakhtin, the expression of a popular culture which continually replicates and renews itself beneath the strictures of the ruling order.

I have said that Bakhtin politicizes rather than historicizes Rabelais' discourse, and I mean that in a specific way. For Bakhtin, the carnivalesque exists as a historical constant, always lying beneath the surface of official culture, rejuvenating itself by parody and self-parody, ready to break through to the surface whenever possible. Of course, Bakhtin defends his reading of Rabelais by reference to historicization, accusing Febvre of not acknowledging the popular festive sources in medieval culture of the learned traditions Febvre calls upon. But in fact, especially in light of his extension of many of the aspects he locates in Rabelais to other periods and other writers, it is clear that Bakhtin regards the carnivalesque as equivalent to a sort of partisan resistance for *la longue durée.*

III

The most familiar claims for historiography as literary, even the materials of historiography themselves, are found in the work of Hayden White.[12] The historians I am discussing here, however, while they may or may not cite White's work, use literary analysis as another tool of the historian, rather than concerning themselves with what White would regard as the inescapably rhetorical and figurative ways in which history is transmitted. Natalie Davis, for instance, while most explicit about the literary (and anthropological) techniques she is borrowing, at the same time stresses the archival nature of her evidence. In *Fiction in the Archives* (an interesting title, both guarded and provocative at the same time), she details the ways in which literary criticism might be of aid to historians:

> I want to let the "fictional" aspects of these documents be the center of analysis. By "fictional" I do not mean their feigned elements, but rather, using the broader sense of the root word *fingere,* their forming, shaping, and molding elements: the crafting of a narrative.[13]

For Davis, literary analysis is less the nearly deconstructive version that White calls upon than the rhetorically informed formalism of someone like Wayne Booth. Davis keeps a shrewd distance from the assumption that the interaction between history and text renders one on the same plane as the other, the assumption governing much literary New Historicism. The "fiction" of her pardon letters is to be tested against other versions of the same events, as well as against literary models or literary imitations.

Davis' recent work has been concerned in fact with the ways in which ordinary people structure their experience, and the ways in which the larger movements of economy and society are reflected in that experience. As a result, she has been concerned with narrative as a mode, while her earlier work, more influenced by anthropological models, was concerned with symbolic rather than narrative expressions of personal experience. Her important collection of essays, *Society and Culture in Early Modern France,* uncovers a spectacular array of dramatic symbolic activities, and she subtly dissects the historical forces at work in what may have seemed to be erratic popular protests. Records of riots, *charivari,* female symbolic roles, proverbs, carnivalesque celebration are revealed to contain a subtle grammar. While not explicitly structuralist in its interpretations, it is impossible to imagine Davis' work without the model of *Annales,* even if her original essays moved into local and *mentalité* history rather early. More striking is her fascination with the "carnivalesque" theatricality of popular culture, and its uses as historical evidence. For the latter, Davis' guides are not only anthropology and ethnography, but the work of Bakhtin.[14]

Davis offers her own research as a possible source for literary expressions of some of the same themes. Indeed, Davis extends a helping hand to literary critics as often as she borrows from them. She writes "to literary specialists I may have offered a new source for comedy, and perhaps for tragedy, too. C. L. Barber has talked of some of Shakespeare's plays as saturnalia; is Hamlet perhaps a *charivari* of the young against a grotesque and unseemly remarriage, a *charivari* where the effigy of the dead spouse returns, the vicious action is replayed?[15]

Inversely, however, these historians are wary of using literary works as sources precisely because of the problems of mediation that cause literary critics to be wary about too simple relations between literary texts and history. This quandary is even more specific in the case of popular discourses, where a Rabelais, while he might be using the language and images of popular culture, certainly cannot be said to be part of the silent world that these historians seek to make speak.

Bakhtin's highlighting of the circle of popular and elite culture also informs a widely influential exercise in the New History, Carlo Ginzburg's *The Cheese and the Worms: The Cosmos of a Sixteenth-Century Miller.* Ginzburg, interested in the survival of popular religious beliefs, also turns to the records of a heresy trial, this time in Friuli, in Northern Italy. The trial was of a miller, Domenico Scandella, called Menocchio, who refused to stop promulgating his home-grown theory that the world was created spontaneously, through putrefaction, like a cheese. Though Northern Italy was nearly as fertile a field for heterodox beliefs as Southern France, Menocchio seemed to have no direct connection with organized heresies. Nor, though he read and incorporated fragments of his reading into his cosmogony (such as Mandeville), was his peculiar theology a mere pastiche of misunderstood orthodox cultural ideas that trickled down.

Ginzburg argues that the construction of Menocchio's ideas represents an expression of popular ideology, which translates the metaphysical idealism of official, theological teaching into the specifically material experience of peasant life. Moreover, this construction is "not neutral" but is evidence of a submerged cultural and social conflict between official ideology and power, on the one hand, and a largely orally-transmitted unofficial culture on the other. Ginzburg's stress on conflict and strategy distinguishes his position from other approaches. He rejects Mandrou's interpretation of popular literature as an escapist fantasy that obscured actual social relations. (Mandrou assembled popular subliterary writings as a way of reconstructing *mentalité*.) Ginzburg also critiques the late Foucault, who seems to suggest that the powerless can only be described in terms of their oppression, or not described at all. Interestingly, Ginzburg is also hostile to a view of popular culture that would see a "popular religion based on Christ's humanity and poverty, the natural and the supernatural . . . endurance of injustice and revolt against oppression . . . harmoniously fused."[16]

For all his debt to Bakhtin, however, Ginzburg is also critical of Bakhtin's stress on Rabelais as a filter for popular culture. However textual their methods, these historians of popular culture see themselves as moving one step beyond Bakhtin, who uses Rabelais as evidence of the survival of popular culture and also ascribes the power of Rabelais' writing to its contact with that culture. That is, the mediation of the literary text necessarily translates, if it does not in fact appropriate, the discourse of popular culture. I believe that this process is especially central to writers like Chaucer and Boccaccio, poised at the age of print, conflating oral and written languages, rural and urban contexts, alternately fusing and separating popular and elite levels of culture and even marking them as such by virtue of describing them. The model these historians offer is of conflicting discourses within the same text, sometimes with very different political valences.

IV

As an example, what would happen if we took the "Marriage Group" (even the title is redolent of early twentieth-century Ibsenism) and recast it as a version of *charivari?* That is, we could take Davis' suggestion that her research provides a source and consider Chaucer's "marriage tales," particularly the comic ones, as displaced "charivari." The classic form of *charivari* is a village ritual in which the young, usually unmarried bachelors haze the partners of a marriage that somehow disturbs either the values or the sexual ecology of the community. It could also be called upon to mock husbands too famously under the thumb of their wives. Its characteristic form was the hanging of a mock effigy, an incessant "rough music" played upon pots and pans outside the bedroom window, or the pageant-like representation of the virago-like wife, usually in a cross-dressed parodic form of one of the revelers.

Immediately two contradictory pressures are exerted on our conception of the literary problem of the Marriage Group, typical of the bifurcated implications of *Annales* school themes. On the one hand the theme of marriage is apparently placed in the context of a more typically premodern cultural setting, and the sometimes outrageous raillery of the Miller, the Wife of Bath, The Merchant's Tale and The Reeve's Tale acquire a local habitation and a name. Moreover, the terms of the debate, the civil discourse of progressive early twentieth-century America, are recast as the ritualized, almost theatricalized struggles of village life. On the other hand, we find ourselves in a historical quandary. Evidence of medieval *charivari* is rare, with one questionable piece of evidence from the fourteenth century. While there is no reason to suppose that the custom is not older than the records themselves, a certain wariness is in order. More misleading, I think, would be to posit the ritual as a cultural constant, expressing a consistent set of values from the *Roman de Fauvel* to "shivaree" celebrations in modern-day Oklahoma. If any historical study provides a bridge from *Annales* structuralism to the highly contextualized studies of Davis and Ginzburg, it is E. P. Thompson's important 1972 rejoinder to Lévi-Strauss, in which he argues that the brilliant ahistoricized interpretation Lévi-Strauss offers—that Brazilian Indian rituals with their clangerous noise were analogous to the "rough music" and *charivari* in that both protest against a world out of joint—robs the specific culture of its indigenous meanings.[17] The question then is what specific function *charivari*-like activity has in Chaucer, and what the place of its recall in an urban and sophisticated poet means. The answers to these questions touch upon some issues that have superseded the marriage group as the center of Chaucer criticism, specifically the relation between gender and power in Chaucer.

In his fabliau tales, Chaucer does more than adapt the fabliau form. Instead, he grounds it in a local community (a specific village, family and neighbors) and surrounds his plots with values shared both by the characters and by individual characters. (This is less true of The Manciple's Tale, which has certain fabliau-like characteristics, of The Shipman's Tale, which is closer to classic fabliau schematics, and of The Cook's Tale, which is unfinished.) Unlike the world of the French fabliaux, whose unreality in terms of the consequences of action link them to romance as a genre, Chaucer's fabliau tales sometimes rather cruelly encourage identification and sympathy with the characters who are sometimes most harshly treated. The festive action of these tales, then, is more than schematic, but has become part of a cycle within the social world they depict. We find ourselves worrying about what will happen when the tale is over, which is not what the fabliaux normally encourage. Moreover, the female characters in Chaucerian fabliaux are somewhat different than either the silly or impossibly worldly or conniving characters of French fabliaux. Instead, they exhibit a remarkable reticence about motive, so that pleasure, revenge or escape are all equally plausible but never articulated motivations. By allowing the female characters of his fabliau tales a certain inscrutability, Chaucer also allows them a certain freedom. These ambiguities are achieved not only by literary expansion, but by constructing a contrast between setting and ritual that resembles *charivari* activities. Festive structure allows Chaucer a more specific and social perspective regarding the representation of human action, rather than the more mythic or archetypal effect we would expect.

The Wife of Bath, herself referred to by Davis, is another obvious example. For Davis, she represents the carnival image of the "Woman on Top," who, as a fixture of popular festivity, sometimes is presented as only a comic figure symbolizing a social order out of joint, but who in other representations, particularly literary ones, could be assigned more positive, or at least ambiguous meanings. We are faced with conflicting models for the Wife of Bath. One, literate and admonitory, is her undeniable source in *The Romance of the Rose,* the "duenna." Another, however, is her startling analogy in the world of popular theatricality, the "woman on top," the celebratory and satiric image of the woman at the top of the social order, inverting the usual hierarchy so frequently found in carnival festivities and in such celebrations as the Feast of Fools.

The only extended discussion of Chaucer and *charivari* that I am aware of is in Edith Kern's *The Absolute Comic,* in which she argues for an analogy between Davis' description of *charivari* and the action of some of the fabliau tales and the Wife's Prologue.[18] For Kern, the value of the fantasy triumph of "Women on Top" (the title of Davis' chapter) is as a species of the mode she calls the "Absolute Comic," a strain in literary fantasy akin to Bakhtin's "carnivalesque." Kern's effort is to deduce a grammar of the comic, which then takes its place as a generic, thematic or modal constant. Molière, Chaucer, and Rabelais, become prime examples of a mode that stretches as far back as Aristophanes and as far forward as the present century. While attuned to the historical pressures upon the expression of the Absolute Comic, Kern is more interested in it as a constituent of all creative literature.

It is difficult to interpret the Wife as totally satiric, a bundle of anti-feminist clichés, or as totally celebratory, as an exuberant portrait of female protest. This ambiguity is precisely the ambiguity of popular theatrics such as the *charivari,* or the monstrous women of carnival celebrations. These monstrous women represent a second problem, since by all accounts the women in these festivals (until quite late) were not women at all. As Davis observes:

> Sexual inversion in popular festivity differs from that in literature in two ways. Whereas the purely ritual and/or magical element in sexual inversion was present in literature to small degree, it assumed more importance in popular festivities, along with the carnivalesque functions of mocking and unmasking the truth. Whereas sexual inversion in literary and pictorial play more often involved the female taking on the male role or dressing as a man, the festive inversion more often involved the male taking on the role or garb of the woman, that is, the unruly woman.[19]

The nearest festive, nonliterary analogy to the Wife of Bath (except for Noah's Wife in the mystery plays) is not a woman at all, but a man dressed as a woman, saying the things he could not say as a man. As outrageous as the suggestion may be, the Wife of Bath is analogous to the festive performance of a man pretending to be a woman, a transvestite travesty, who is, nevertheless, allowed to express certain truths disallowed to normative characters. While the distinction between literary and festival practice is obviously central, and accounts for the rebellious tone of popular celebration in contrast to its more muted representation of similar themes in literature, Chaucer, I believe, incorporated images of theatrical and festive practices with some regularity.

That the Wife of Bath is an example of transvestite poetics is of course much less shocking than it might seem. Indeed, in its original presentation when Chaucer read it aloud, its very ventriloquism acquired a comic, festive quality. Part of its comedy must have been in self-accusations by the poet as well as in its social criticism. This is not to say that the Wife of Bath is really a man. Rather, the analogy to popular theatricality accounts in some fashion for the ways in which the Wife can alternate between her function as a character with experience, a past, desires and disappoint-ments on the one hand, and a catalogue of antifeminist clichés on the other. Moreover, as a poetic problem, one which he was obviously sen-sitive to judging from the Prologue to the *Legend of Good Women,* Chaucer had to pretend in some fashion to be able to describe how a woman thought and talked and acted (a very different task from the reportage of the General Prologue or the relative silence concerning the inner life of May in The Merchant's Tale or Alisoun in The Miller's Tale). The extended narration of the Wife's Prologue, missing from the Second Nun's or the Prioress's, pretends towards an experience the poet (by definition) does not have, and which he portrays elsewhere, in the con-sciousness of Criseyde, as paradoxically both comprehensible and enig-matic. The incorporation of popular theatricality as a model allows Chaucer to negotiate his dangerous extremes, social satire and subjective experience, autonomous characterization and authorial performance, res-ignation and revolt.

A third example is the form of the General Prologue, which we have interpreted largely in terms of Chaucer's use of previous literary con-vention, or contemporary social thought. But what happens if we think of the form of the General Prologue as akin to the ridings, processions and entries that march through late medieval and early modern cities with so much regularity? While to think of the General Prologue as a "medieval pageant" is a Victorian conception, in a quite specific way its riders and sometimes sober, sometimes exuberant characters literally resemble an urban procession as much as a pilgrimage.

But the urban procession has a long history, from the end of the Middle Ages through the eighteenth century, and some of its features exhibit astonishing longevity in the face of this considerable historical range. In an essay entitled "A Bourgeois Puts His World In Order: The City as a Text," the historian Robert Darnton analyses a description of Montpellier by an eighteenth-century citizen.[20] That title is for our purposes a loaded one, because the very term "bourgeois" has virtually fallen out of Chaucerian circulation under the pressure of questions about the social provenance of

Chaucer's sources and the explanatory force of a perpetually rising middle class. It is also a loaded title because Darnton's documents all date from the eighteenth century. Moreover, the very attempt to locate particular mode of perception as evidenced in historical data and historical documents is itself a problematic undertaking.

Some four hundred years after Chaucer, Darnton's informant reveals a mentality Chaucer may have satirized in a range of portraits such as that of the Man of Law or the Franklin. At the same time, he also reveals a way of organizing things that Chaucer may well have shared, and that reveals not so much an eighteenth-century perspective as a nostalgia for the more clearly demarcated world of an earlier economy and society. His complaints and praise for the city may be evidence of an urban bourgeois perspective similar to the one which Chaucer projects in the General Prologue. As Darnton indicates, the description of the city begins with a description of a procession, one which, however, wildly misstates the relative importance of certain social groups. His text moves from there to a description of the place of estates, and here too the result is a rather savage complaint against the contemporary blurring of social positions. Only when he describes everyday life in the city is he able to accurately capture any consonance between symbolic and actual forms of behavior. But for Darnton's informant, paradoxically, the symbolic is the actual.

Darnton's "bourgeois" describes his procession in ways that still ascribe to traitional organizational forms that we would identify as "medieval," and that in fact tell us something about the organization of processions for some time before. As with most processions, it begins with an armed honor guard. Chaucer begins his "procession" with the Knight, who, we suppose, is in first position by virtue of his nobility. But a slightly different light is shed upon his status if we think of him as akin to an honor guard, symbolically clearing the way and protecting the retinue. We meet the Prioress and the Monk and the Friar taken together in the sequence befitting the regular clergy. But what determines the order of their presentation? The evidence of urban processions suggests that the sequence within such groups depends upon the antiquity of their orders. While we can't tell much about this tradition from Chaucer's text, it does suggest a possible principle behind the grouping. Furthermore, the Merchant and the Man of Law are normally thought to represent the "middle class" or merely gentle pilgrims, not ordinarily explained by medieval political theory. But in processions, and in the descriptions of cities such as Darnton's document provides, the holders of civil office follow the holders of clerical office, so as to establish a connection between the two. My point is that the General Prologue is part of a tradition of urban processional form that exists through the eighteenth century.

More generally, however, the organization of the General Prologue is an expression of a politics, and the ensuing discussions between estates suggest something more than a traditional dissatisfaction with the way things are. Instead, what we observe as the politics of the *Canterbury Tales* is something closer to a bourgeois conception of society as consisting of many levels of various interest groups, theoretically, but not actually, in pursuit of some common goal. If you reduce that vision to a moral, you do get a profoundly traditional complaint comprised of both nostalgia and utopia. But the technique of analysis overwhelms the complaint. This result is very different from the largely clerical and entirely theoretical conception of society as composed of three distinct estates. It pays lip service to this organicist conception, but itself is far more structural in its point of view. On a level of expressed doctrine, Langland and Chaucer and Gower prefer to see things in terms of traditional estates and decry the competiton and grappling for attention of so many different parvenu groups. Indeed, while they accord great respect to tradition, they actually share an early modern urban point of view, aware of a considerable array and shading of various positions.

This of course complicates the sort of distinctions we would like to make between "popular" and "elite" culture or between "official" and "unofficial" positions. Moreover, it tends to undercut both extremely modern conflict models, and extremely traditional hierarchical models. I wouldn't suggest throwing out either of these models on the say so of our poets. For in fact their stress on ranks and distinctions and interest groups represents not a satirical vision or an example of false consciousness. Rather, by considering the organization of the General Prologue as an expression of a very long tradition in urban culture, we can see how Chaucer allows us to locate ways in which *mentalité* can also be defined as ideology.

V

The examples I have cited as possible specific analogues to Chaucerian forms and characters is one obvious use of the New History. But I would argue that it should not be its primary use. In fact, I have purposely bracketed off from my discussion important medieval historians of *mentalité,* such as Jacques Le Goff, precisely to center on method rather than empirical examples. Instead, we might more usefully consider the ways in which the historiography of these studies provide models of cultural assimilation and resistance. For they combine the *Annales* perspective of *la longue durée* with an interest in the specific and the unique, with the inventiveness and improvisational qualities of historical performance. They take the explicit intentions of historical participants as important data, but are not reluctant to subject those intentions to interpretive methods borrowed from current cultural theory. Ritual and myth, narrative self-presentation, rhetoric and performance, these are concepts which literary criticism has grown wary of or weary of, but which now return enlivened by their use in another discipline entirely. That enlivenment comes from a keen sense of cultural politics, of what the social implications are of certain forms and certain performances. These studies suggest that the languages of the past are not inescapably bound by their own limits.

More specifically, these studies provide a model of daring periodization. In place of a Chaucer, say, totally placed in the late fourteenth century, we might think of literary works as sites for long-range cultural forms and perspectives, some of which may stretch far back to classical antiquity, and others of which may in fact be incipient in the works we are discussing. The consequence of such a model is that we would not necessarily explain a work as coherently medieval, as Renaissance, or later in its point of view, but as expressing a possibly conflicting arena of values, in which the literary text in a historical moment becomes a site for cultural events, some of which are evident as powerful traces, and others of which may just be forming themselves in new combinations and reactions.

Notes

1. Emmanuel Le Roy Ladurie, *Montaillou: The Promised Land of Error,* trans. Barbara Bray (New York: Braziller, 1978); Carlo Ginzburg, *The Cheese and the Worms: The Cosmos of a Sixteenth-Century Miller,* trans. John and Anne Tedeschi (Baltimore: The Johns Hopkins Univ. Press, 1980); Natalie Zemon Davis, *Society and Culture in Early Modern France* (Stanford, Calif.: Stanford Univ. Press, 1975); Davis, *The Return of Martin Guerre* (Cambridge: Harvard Univ. Press, 1983); Davis, *Fiction in the Archives: Pardon Tales and Their Tellers in Sixteenth-Century France* (Stanford: Calif.: Stanford Univ. Press, 1987).

2. See Traian Stoianovich, *French Historical Method: The Annales Paradigm* (Ithaca: Cornell Univ. Press, 1976), and Georg G. Iggers, *New Directions in European Historiography* (Middletown, Conn.: Wesleyan Univ. Press, 1975).

3. Bloch, *Feudal Society,* trans. L. A. Manyon (Chicago: Univ. of Chicago Press, 1961); Braudel, *The Mediterranean and the Mediterranean World in the Age of Phillip II,* trans. Sian Reynolds, 2 vols. (New York: Harper, 1972–74).

4. See Le Roy Ladurie, *The Territory of the Historian,* trans. Ben and Sian Reynolds (Chicago: Univ. of Chicago Press, 1979), and François Furet, *In the Workshop of History,* trans. Jonathan Mandelbaum (Chicago: Univ. of Chicago Press, 1984).

5. Barthes, *On Racine,* trans. Richard Howard (New York: Hill and Wang, 1964).

6. Febvre, *The Problem of Unbelief in the Sixteenth Century: The Religion of Rebelais,* trans. Beatrice Gottlieb (Cambridge: Harvard Univ. Press, 1982).

7. See Lee Patterson, *Negotiating the Past: The Historical Understanding of*

Medieval Literature (Madison: Univ. of Wisconsin Press, 1987).

8. Curtius, *European Literature and the Latin Middle Ages,* trans. Willard R. Trask (New York: Pantheon, 1953).

9. Geertz, "Thick Description," in *The Interpretation of Cultures: Selected Essays* (New York: Basic Books, 1973).

10. Poirier, *The Performing Self: Compositions and Decompositions in the Languages of Everyday Life* (New York: Oxford Univ. Press, 1971).

11. Bakhtin, *Rabelais and His World,* trans. Helene Iswalsky (Boston: Massachusetts Institute of Technology Press, 1968).

12. See White, *Tropics of Discourse: Essays in Cultural Criticism* (Baltimore: The Johns Hopkins Univ. Press, 1978), and *The Content of the Form: Narrative Discourse and Historical Representation* (Baltimore: The Johns Hopkins Univ. Press, 1987).

13. Davis, *Fiction in the Archives,* p. 3.

14. Henry Abelove, et al., *Visions of History* (New York: Pantheon, 1983), p. 110.

15. Davis, *Society and Culture in Early Modern France,* p. 123.

16. Ginzburg, *The Cheese and the Worms,* p. xvi.

17. Thompson, " 'Rough Music': le charivari anglais," *Annales* 27 (1972): 285–312. Thompson replies to Lévi-Strauss' *The Raw and the Cooked,* trans. John and Doreen Weightman (New York: Harper, 1969).

18. Kern, *The Absolute Comic* (New York: Columbia Univ. Press, 1980).

19. Davis, *Society and Culture,* p. 136.

20. Darnton, "A Bourgeois Puts His World In Order," *The Great Cat Massacre and Other Episodes in French Cultural History* (New York: Vintage, 1985), pp. 107–43.

Langland's Lives: Reflections on Late-Medieval Religious and Literary Vocabulary

ANNE MIDDLETON

Though Donald Howard is cited nowhere in this essay, he is everywhere in it a tutelary spirit. His lifelong interest in the relations between biographical and poetic forms, in the resources for a poet's invention in the vicissitudes of his own writing life, and in the difficulty of ascertaining the kind of "truth" encoded in the result, represented an imaginative infusion of very traditional critical themes with some very important contemporary ethical and scholarly concerns for medievalists. Herein lay the unifying theme of his diverse scholarly enterprises: his work in cataloguing medieval schemata of the virtues, his studies of pilgrimage, of the "idea" in unfinished work, and of Chaucer's biography. As a friend and mentor as well as in his capacities as scholar and critic, he did much to assure that recent reports of the death of the author would always seem greatly exaggerated. This essay is in honor of his commitment to, and fruitful reflections on, the unity of a life in art.

The objective of my quest here is less a single item of vocabulary than a habit of thought—a habit that has a double existence in *Piers Plowman,* and thus manages to make its inescapable duplicity accessible to the reader as a critical instrument. It is a habit in the double sense that Will gives to this word in the opening lines of the poem: it is the clothing of an idea that makes that idea socially visible and identifies its potential for action, and it is also a virtually automatic and customary practice, deep almost as life, and therefore nearly as inaccessible to critical examination. It is, in fact, precisely this term "life," as a locus of meaning and value and a cultural method for producing these, whose fortunes I hope to outline, in late-medieval social texts generally, and in the special and dislocating senses Langland gives to this habit by assuming it.

"Lives" in late-fourteenth-century discourses are (I am forced to admit) verbal and cultural artifacts that serve many of the same purposes that "lifestyles" do in late-twentieth-century talk. Not, of course, in their particular substance or content: in this respect, the kind of late-medieval

227

"life" that is assigned ethical value and cultural privilege is the polar opposite of that incarnate in the contemporary "lifestyle." But both are compact symbolic messages about a normative social and spiritual ethos inscribed in forms of voluntary bodily performance—even if in contemporary usage the discipline inscribed is likelier to be aerobics or facelifts than fasting and penance. They are similar kinds of semantic fields in that they are neither descriptive nor quite prescriptive of actual individual behavior, but rather a repertoire of the canonical patterns, stories, or scripts that codify aspiration and furnish the decor of its social recognition. They are similar, too, in that one cannot extrapolate from them any image of a differentiated and stable social whole that could be produced by replicating on a massive scale such exemplary individual acts of self-fashioning. As "norms" they are in lived actuality decidedly "abnormal," conspicuously without correlatives on a larger scale in historical experience: both the rarity and the grotesquery of their infrequent incarnation in practice assure their cultural potency.[1] They are, in short, units of ideology—and it is as such, I think, that they particularly interest Langland.

David Aers has of course also argued that Langland is able—at least fitfully, to discern "ideologies" as such.[2] Even if he cannot or will not go so far as the Lollards, for example, in articulating positive alternative models, Langland, according to Aers, exposes to implicit criticism the received standard ways of thinking about social and ecclesiastical order in the fourteenth century by representing them in the narrative as failing to dispose into patterns of social or literary coherence actual contemporary circumstances. In Aers' view it is the "creative imagination" of the poet that penetrates the thickly-encrusted traditional discourses of social order; the writer's armature for this subversive procedure is the direct observation and analysis of contemporary circumstances.

I would argue, however, that for Langland there are no circumstances we can see without interested discourse, and that this assumption is both a conscious and a central premise of his art.[3] He is, in his way, no less "reflexive," in Aers' term, than Chaucer, but as literary scholars we are less practiced in finding the principles of reflexivity in his poetic materials, because they do not lie in the domain of "literature"; my aim here is to suggest how and where one might look for these. Langland's proposed antidote to ideological stasis or impasse is in principle homeopathic: it is more of the same, not observed actuality, that exposes ideological operations to view. The multivocality of the represented world that tears his world apart is also, paradoxically, the only principle of its construction—or of its collective salvation. There is no outside Archimedean point, whether a "view from nowhere," envisioning a "redeemed" language to replace the fallen one that forms the compromised medium of human exchange, or a situation within a somehow prelinguistic here and now of fourteenth century social and material life, that could form a place and rhetorical posture from which the poet can speak. The "life" becomes in Langland's hands at once a literary and ethical category, the basis for his narrative aesthetic of multivocality and repetition.

The term "life" in Middle English—particularly in those writings of spiritual, moral, and institutional edification that are now generally seen to form the immediate substratum of Langland's own expository tech-niques—has two potentially contradictory, and nearly always normative, senses (both now "obsolescent" if not obsolete) that Langland exploits more assiduously than any other writer of the period—and almost always in a way that heightens the sense of opposition between the moral claims the two senses of the term are used to support. This insistent ambiguity of the word in his hands appears to be the reason that both the *OED* and *MED* avoid citing the poem's several memorable occurrences of it in support of any of the several common senses of the word in the fourteenth century: virtually all its interesting uses in the poem are extremely treach-erous. It can mean an ideal pattern or form of living, especially one disposed so as to transcend or minimize the determinative power of mere biological needs; or it can name the means of providing for those needs, either as food or sustenance, or the occupation or craft by which one secures them. It spills over to cover, in other words, some of the terrain of "liflode" (livelihood), a word which in turn is used in a sense that shares some of the former's ideality, as in the "Liflade and Passioun of St. Katherine." It is these two senses that delimit the semantic field that the poet fills with folk. Between them they declare an ambivalent narrative and discursive commitment to the morally representative power of bodily need. As Piers renounces or translates his occupation, he calls that from which he turns his "bely-ioye," or possibly "bilyue" (the latter another term that sustains a comparable duplicity of sense); it is only one of several moments of profound narrative and discursive rupture produced by the troublesome relation between conscience and bodily performance.[4] Latent in the disposition of moral thought and cultural norms around "lives" as distinct from "orders" or "estates" is a historical conflict between two medieval discursive modes for conceiving moral and spiritual order that frames the distinction of voices in Langland's poem. In par-ticular, it supports the argumentative disposition and discontinuous repre-sentation of Will.

In one obvious sense, of course, the meaning of this luminous normative term "life" is the explicit object of both Will's quest and of the critical history of the poem. Not only Will, but most of his informants, tend almost by reflex to conceive and expound his objective as a "life," and further to divert him with the prospect of its bewildering multiplicity of form: Thought, queried about Dowel, offers Will in return knowledge of

"Dowel, Dobet, and Dobest the thridde," and introduces him to his next instructor as seeking "what lyues þei lyuen and what lawe þei usen." In the first half of this century, critical scholarship was similarly diverted, with a quest, and results, that largely re-enacted Will's *paideia* in the middle third of the long versions of the poem. The scholarly quest proceeded on two fronts: to identify the distinction of lives as structural divisions marking the stages of progression in the story of Will's moral and spiritual development—that is, to identify the narrative staging of a succession of Three Lives as the *forma tractatus* of the poem—and, second, to specify a referential content for these terms at the discursive level of the poem, by evacuating and replacing Langland's writing of these terms with triads borrowed from other medieval religious discourses. Of the latter, there proved to be no shortage: finding other triads proved to be less a quest than an exercise in shooting fish in a very full barrel. Both efforts, however, were fruitless, because mistaken in principle. It is now apparent that the so-called Three Lives mean no more than is apparent in their grammatical form: they are three degrees of the same term, set forth in a progressive array of a kind commonly used for rhetorical amplification.

We like to believe that we are now past this distracting and unedifying episode in our interpretive quest. So does Will, and nowhere more than in the final two visions of the poem. But to have arrived at this point—to discover that the copious medieval supply of threefold cultural clothing doesn't quite fit Will's practice, or the structure and method of Langland's poem—is nevertheless to continue to pose the critical task (Will's, the poet's, and ours) in the form of an allegorical narrative, or rather to superimpose one narrative or another so as to translate rather than analyze their assumptions.[5] It is not, however, the narrative of developing "character" but the competing and discontinuous discourses of "lives" that render Will's actions intelligible as a structural device in the poem, and it is by this means that Langland makes visible what Will can only sporadically recognize: the several interests served by the rhetorical schematisms and exhaustive arrays in which the object of his inquiry must be represented. It is a category and strategy of *discours* that Langland turns "lives" back upon their unconscious existence at the level of *histoire*. In this essay I mean to suggest that this process is etched with particular clarity in the final two visions, which present a re-vision, in the form of a discursively recomposed version, of the field of folk presented in the first two visions, but this time disposed not under the sign of the monastic and regal discourses of "estates," but according to the explanation of the world given by mendicant polemic and apologetics.

If the pattern of ideality most conspicuously associated with the contemporary term is "lifestyles of the rich and famous," the form to which most medieval lives claim to aspire is precisely the opposite: that of the poor and ignominious. Born chiefly of the social practices and discursive forms of mendicant spirituality, by the age of Langland the imaginative domain of this notion extends far beyond the professed ideal of any clerical estate, and has come to inform those individual exercises of lay piety—many explicitly fostered by the preaching and teaching missions of the friars—whose orthodox or heterodox valence is particularly difficult to establish in the last decades of the fourteenth century.[6] (The renunciation of funeral pomp, for example, is only one of many that have proved slippery for historians to interpret).[7] It also informs nascent theories of the institutional obligations of the society: how does the premise of communal need—as fact or ideal—determine the exercise of "reason of state"?[8] In the late fourteenth century, the claim to regulate "lowable lives" through an effort to impose an increasingly pervasive calculus of need upon an articulate differentiation of honor or worth that was imagined to be intrinsic or "natural," given rather than relational, became a habit of thought that extended unprecedently deep into the social texts of the laity. Sumptuary laws, the vagrancy legislation of the second Statute of Laborers, and the detailed social and moral cost-accounting of the so-called Lollard Disendowment Bill in the early years of the fifteenth century all attest to this aspiration—even if not to its successful enforcement, which was in each of these cases virtually nil.[9]

The air of unreality that surrounds these late-medieval attempts to recompose lay social practices and institutions in the image of probity that had once defined the ritual purity of the friars does not, however—as is so often assumed in *Piers Plowman* criticism—point to an unfortunate latter-day failing or dilution of an original mendicant ideal, but is present and necessary from its first articulation, intrinsic to its cutting edge as cultural and spiritual self-critique.[10] This edge was soon to be turned upon its inventors. The multivocal vernacular appropriation of mendicant versions of the ideal forms of "life" for self and society provides in the late fourteenth century a classic instance of biting the ideological hand that feeds you, and without this transvaluation of terms neither the 1381 Revolt nor Lollard spirituality and social theory would be intelligible. Langland, I suggest, is the self-appointed recording angel of that development, and the only one among several perceptive witnesses to grasp it as a discursive process. What Langland "sees" (or at any rate makes his narrative enact) through the disposition of textual "voices" is not the shattering of petrified forms by "actuality," but rather the discursive history, the past and the future, of current religious models of self and society; he sees their workings as not only spiritually but historically formative processes. The dense juxtaposition of authoritative voices in the poems heightens one's awareness of their seemingly inevitable frictions, while their apologetic deployment also emphasizes the indissoluble bonds between these ideal models and the specific social formations for which they can be adduced as rationales.

Defining religious probity and social differentiation in terms of the narrative emulation of model "lives," rather than as a totalizing expository array of "orders" or "estates" that together comprise the several functions of a whole organism, is, I have been suggesting, what chiefly distinguishes the explanatory languages of late-medieval spirituality and social theory from those of the high middle ages—or, very loosely speaking, fraternal from monastic forms of spirituality.[11] If, as Georges Duby has proposed, the trifunctional model of the community—and, though he does not develop this correlative, hierarchical and functional models of the inner faculties as well—bespeak their formation in the interests of the Capetian monarchy and Benedictine monasticism, this later model, conceiving of the spiritual fashioning of self and community as the individual emulation of luminous exemplary "lives"—along with its correlative in the representation of the individual's inward forces and resources as a cacaphony of warring voices and claims upon an ever more distractable attention—is intimately bound to urban social formations, and to the practices of devotion and forms of edification, addressed by the mendicant orders.[12] Indeed, these profoundly subjectivizing models of reform are posed, at first in social practice and later in theory, as explicit critiques of these earlier totalizing descriptions of the social body, however much they nevertheless depend on the continued authority of these for the effectiveness of their own oppositional social drama. The injunction to "follow naked the naked Christ"—whether as eremitic, apostolic, or fraternal model—assumes, as the backdrop of its exemplary power to astound and persuade, a settled notion of the proprieties according to each estate in life. It was, however, no accident that the call to a redefined purity of life and communal harmony proposed by St. Francis' personal example was ultimately to issue in the earliest systematic arguments about property and appropriation in European social and economic theory, and, moreover, in the development of new expository forms adequate to the conduct of such argument. Far from a historical irony, it was a historical inevitability, and it is the weaving (the *textualizing*) of this necessity that Langland makes visible in the narrative plotting of the poem.

The new social and spiritual formations of the later middle ages, then, articulate themselves from the beginning through an increasingly sophisticated armature of *oppositional* practices in action, speech, and writing.[13] The rhetorical power of these practices was *by design*, not incidentally, subversive of an antecedent image of social completeness, and they continued to display more openly their deep instability the further they were extended into general social theory. Their authority to exemplify through ritual neediness, and their power to edify through a variety of self-reflexive and affective practices, were secured early from outside and above, by direct papal sanction; in themselves these practices possessed no mediatory rationale that could explain their own categorical imperative.[14] The only image of the social whole restored to probity that could be extrapolated from the emulation of model "lives" on a broad scale was either in the form of such mass social movements as pilgrimage, or apocalyptic. While the latter consequence was embraced only in the more radical quarters of this movement, it is important to recognize that the vision of communal escape into a permanent state of what Victor Turner has called "liminality" is intrinsic to the new subjectivity, and to strategies for the attainment of social purity focused on the universal refashioning of "lives" through individual penitential discipline.[15]

Langland displays this process in both its spiritual *and historical* consequences. At the level of narrative, the historical handing over of regulatory discursive authority from monastic to mendicant spirituality underwrites both the re-vision of plowing as pilgrimage and the unmaking of Piers' occupation.[16] Both Piers and the supplanted discourses that had called him into action are figured thereafter in the poem as absent objects of intense nostalgic longing. Yet they are irrecoverable as social institutions, and can be repossessed only in subjective reiteration, relived in memory and re-enacted through the language of self-modelling: one can never again *find* Piers, still less seat him securely in a position of leadership, but rather only *remember* and desire him. If Holichurche, who views the governance of both self and society under the sign of high-medieval functionalism, is the tutelary genius of Langland's initial vision of the field, and of his first formulation of the kind of reforming poetic project it requires as "estates satire," Conscience is the regulatory subjective authority who in a similar fashion presides over his final re-vision of the field—a field on which now both the defender and the destroyer of Unity are patently the literary creatures of mendicant ethical discourse. The warped and wilful redefinition of each of the cardinal virtues in turn by commune, king, and Need in the final two passus represents the built-in principle of degeneration in late-medieval spiritual discourses with a corrosive historical accuracy as profound as that which Langland had applied in the first two visions to the earlier "estates" discourses. That Conscience, who emerges as the hero of the initial encounter with Meed, or unprincipled reward, should be overcome by guile when the terms that define the field he protects are no longer political but eschatological is not only formally just, completing Langland's massive imitation of Biblical structure, but offers a substantial historical insight as well. A polity evolved from the root premise of a fixed quantity of created goods and returns, and conceiving its objective as the just disposition of these, will not only have a very different institutional shape from one based on the premise of virtually limitless human insufficiency and need: it will also be subject to very different temptations, and inclined to very different forms of rationalization for its exercise of power; Meed and Need are each other's obverse. As Clergie foretold in the Banquet scene where their paths divided, there are fatal limits to Conscience's power to maintain unity when he must operate alone on a field where the symbolic privilege of need, or unprincipled profession of insufficiency, is claimed on every side, in a cacophony of plausible vernacular voices.

If Langland stages the deep history of his own ethical discourses as a narrated *translatio regni* at the end of the first two visions, as plowing yields to pilgrimage, he also envisions prophetically in the last two dreams the immediate future of such apologetic conflict, and the volatile interpretive climate in which his poem was circulated and would continue to be read for the next two hundred years. In the final re-vision of the worldly field under the sign of Scriptural apocalypse, he represents what may have been its specific historical stimulus as the imaginative catalyst for Will's ultimate vision.

In 1371, two Austin friars argued (in Anglo-French) the side of the lay lords against the traditional exemption of ecclesiastical estates from taxation for the king's wars.[17] The arguments they used—based upon reasoning from Gratian's *Decretum* ordinarily applied to the distribution of charitable relief to needy individuals—invoked a favorite fraternal theme: in case of the collective need, the king may take for use what the collective defense requires.[18] As both Aubrey Gwynn and K. B. McFarlane have noted, it was to prove a momentous political transformation of a traditional moral argument, for Wyclif was present to hear it, in what was to be virtually his sole appearance in the arena of political deliberation. The conclusions he drew from it for ecclesiastical polity are, as they say, history.[19]

It was this event, I believe, that gave Langland the idea of ending the penultimate vision of the poem with the king's claim of his right to unlimited appropriation under cover of a cynically redefined *spiritus justicie,* and to present Will's subsequent dream, the final vision of Antichrist, as brought on by Need's slippery application of the friar's favorite tenet as a warrant for appropriation at will. That is, while I wholly endorse Penn Szittya's excellent and thorough recent account of the final two passus, and what they do with traditional fraternal discourses, I believe that fit readers of the 1370s would also be led by the specific terms of the scene to recall, and by the early 1380s deeply to regret, that pivotal moment in 1371 when friars actually taught Wyclif and the Lollards the argument they would come to use in their own increasingly Erastian appeal not merely for taxing clerical properties but, on an extension of the same grounds, for disendowment of all religious orders. It would also turn out to be an argument for turning the unnumbered "lives" of the friars against them in the reformation of a purified commune: the ritually needy mendicant orders would be supplanted by the literally destitute as the legitimate claimants of the surplus of social getting and spending. Here the specific historical substratum for the allegorical events of the passus does not diminish their broad power of symbolic suggestion, but greatly enhances the resonance of Langland's profound critique of the seductive power of mendicant apologetics that pervades the final vision. In exposing the poisonous appeal of their subjective solicitude, he is simultaneously ana-tomizing the treacherous potential of his own poetic language.

From the start, the mendicant discourses of renewed "life" codified practices designed to capture, and to structure, the pious imagination of the laity, and they achieved some of their most spectacular and volatile successes within the last generation of the fourteenth century. The irasci-ble reflex we quickly come to associate with Will in the poem—"*contra, quod I, and comsed to disputen*"—was by no means idiosyncratic, though Langland does more than any writer of his generation to anatomize its destabilizing effects on the field of folk. Within this period, both the orthodox and heretical laity were to show, in a variety of vernacular social texts, what, and how, they had learned from the friars to think, and to say, about the incontrovertible authority of "lives."

A few formal features of what I have characterized as mendicant discourses of subjective self-discovery prove particularly adaptable to oppositional lay uses, and we find them everywhere in late-fourteenth-century literary and social texts. One is the later tendency to dispose difference along horizontal or exfoliating rather than vertical or analog-ically parallel axes of possibility: the *distinctio*, the branching division, and the exhaustive rhetorical array, are the characteristic forms of this late-medieval expository development, just as apposition and the complex rationalized analogy or similitude, particularly of the relations of parts to wholes, are central organizing techniques in the earlier spiritual and ecclesiological explanation characteristic of monastic reform movements. These discursive practices were ultimately explicitly theorized: one must recall here the Scholastic strictures against the validity of analogy in argument, as well as those post-scholastic practices of scriptural interpre-tation and citation which, as Alastair Minnis has shown, demonstrate a well-developed recognition of the mediate *multivocality* of the scriptural text.[20]

These interpretive developments suggest a second way in which—in Langland's poem, as in late-medieval religious discourses generally—the subversive potential of the "life" as a center of spiritual and social idealization is realized formally through an increasingly sophisticated lay poetics and politics of Scriptural citation. The scholastic "discovery" of "voice" and "persona" as categories of analysis in literary theory may be seen in part as a late rationalization of what had long before become a standard style in mendicant and university speech and writing for embedding and redeploying scriptural quotation in argument; these techniques were fundamentally different from citation practices rooted in earlier forms of study of the sacred page. A comparison of nearly any passage of Bernard of Clairvaux with nearly any in Bonaventure will suffice to illustrate the difference. If Bernard's meditative retextualization of Scripture is literally that, a reweaving, a conflating and imagining anew of deep figurative connections between the testimony of disparate passages and "voices," one can virtually see and hear the quotation marks, centuries before their invention, that mark and control the relations among several kinds of witness, between which *distinctiones* are carefully set forth, and dialogic interactions regulated, in Bonaventure's prose.

It is now, thanks to John Alford and Judson Allen, generally accepted that Langland's poem is macaronic in an important rather than incidental sense.[21] In *Piers Plowman,* both have argued, the Latin quotations act as seed-crystals of poetic thought, gathering around themselves a fantastic architecture wherever they are introduced into the supersaturated fluid that is the dream-narrative of allegorical romance. Formerly seen as a kind of authoritative decor, Langland's Latin passages are now widely regarded as principal structural members of his strange vernacular project. What has not yet been fully explored, however, is the eclectic interplay of several distinct historical styles in the way Langland adduces his scriptural materials: the way he, in effect, quotes several different styles of quotation. These, I suggest, parallel the different textual "voices" in which the discourses of ideal "lives" were conducted, and the dialogic tension among these discursive styles in Langland's alternating use of several of them is not only the instrument of his satiric anatomy of his world, but also, in Will's deferred determination of his own mode of "life" and his "craft," enacts the historical terms of struggle among them.

Will as narrative actor is in fact constituted by this war of discursive procedures. He is as deeply a creature of the textual habits that invest and define his endeavor as are the entities he claims to pursue: before he is an ethical everyman, he is, above all, the literate subject, done in the different voices that compose for his culture the authorized versions of selfhood, and the authorized narratives of self-realization. He is not so much a continuous narrative entity as the refractory focal point of the several claims of the social and spiritual discourses of "lives" that both obsess and elude him. It is as they constitute in a dense variety of contemporary vocabularies the *subject* rather than the *object* of inquiry that the habitual cultural recourse to "lives" gives sustained critical power to the fitfully composed narrative, and gives it, for all its discontinuities, immense "depth of field" as a cognitive world. It is as a category and strategy of *discours* that Langland turns Will's hypothetical "lives" back upon their unconscious existence in the culture at the level of *histoire,* and gives Will a diacritical existence in the represented contemporary world. Will's pursuit of a "lowable life" is thus not so much repeatedly humiliated as deconstructed, as "lives" become in Langland's hands instruments of what one astute rubricator in the B-tradition called an "inquisicio," a speculative exploration of the process by which a subject is constituted as inescapably historical, in life as in art.[22]

What George Kane has felicitously called "speculative lives, without historical necessity"—that is, lives provisionally and serially acted out in the authorial *persona*—acquire a theoretical edge: they gain the power to indicate in use their own several origins and interests.[23] Correctly identifying the ideal "life" as the most luminous, central and characteristic organizing idea common to most late-medieval religious vocabularies and treatise forms, Langland sets it in motion as an equally central literary device, the center of the vexed and complex *forma tractandi* of the work. What *persona* or "voice" is in self-consciously fictive writings—as when, for example, the *auctor* in Gower's *Confessio fingens se esse amantem,* "fictively represents himself to be a lover"—Langland suggests, "lives" are in those ethical discourses and social texts that must in all sincerity decline to acknowledge any fictive or hypothetical design, any *invented* status, if they are to maintain in good faith their culturally regulatory integrity—and if his own work, by emulating their terms and gestures, is to claim to deal in truth rather than fable. But the truth Langland tells about these late-medieval ethical and spiritual discourses is not identical to the truth they themselves, each or all, claim to tell.

In its transparent evasions and explicitly threadbare self-justifications, Will's history becomes a palimpsest of the apologetic stories society tells itself about its own origins and composition, and about the forms of selfhood that can be authorized by such schemes. While Will's project as actor in a narrative is to determine his *genre de vie,* it is Langland's project systematically and repeatedly to make his options visible throughout the poem *as apologetic stories*—everywhere consciously perplexing, and everywhere conspicuously ideological, which is to say inseparable from the institutions for which they frame the apologetics. Capturing them within his own poem in their swarming multiplicity, he enables them to speak of their own normally concealed "historical necessity," to show the dead hand of moral *habitus* at work in the world in the form of necessarily conflicting literary strategies and genres, which cannot escape the historical interests they propose to transcend by becoming subjects of literary spectatorship. The "lives they leden" in the world are constituted by the "forme of speche" in which each has been promulgated, and each of these ways of talking about ideality retains to the end its historical specificity. If the subject of the religious discourses Langland captures and retextualizes is the "life" of Dowel, on earth as it is in heaven, the subject of the poem is the combined outrage and salvific necessity of this ceaseless borrowing from those who have gone before us, the deep historicity of the salvific imagination of the self. Langland renders ethical and social recognition as inseparable from textual and literary self-awareness, the acknowledgment of the borrowed and reconstructed character of all late-medieval spiritual discourses.

Judson Allen has claimed that for Langland and many other medieval poets there is no category of "literary" as distinct from "ethical" discourse. To the extent that he meant that medieval writers and readers believed that there were no purely formal pleasures without affective or cognitive effects that had moral consequences, perhaps one must grant the point, while doubting that it greatly distinguishes medieval writings from those of other ages. But it is the specifically unauthorized, provisional, and extra-institutional character of Langland's enterprise—the wholly *gratuitous* and virtually inexplicable aspect of the lifelong imperative to write, and the uncategorizable nature of the result—that becomes the instrument and medium of its truth. It is not the author's appropriation of the clerical habits of literacy—that is, the included scriptural texts and exegetical models for developing them that we have come to see as fundamental to Langland's *inventio* and *dispositio* of his text—that, in the poet's terms secures virtue or value to the poem. Represented as Will's questionable appropriation of a habit to which he has no right, the legitimacy of the cultural claims that Will wishes them to make for him— particularly the implicit notion that they confer on them the right to edify the community—is in the poem repeatedly and properly called into question. What finally validates the poetic enterprise is rather a carefully-staged recognition, by writer and reader, of the inescapability of this social and spiritual condition of lifelong indebtedness—of the thick *textuality* of history—realized in Will's mobile and refractory social and ecclesiological literacy.

Steven Justice has persuasively argued that it is only in collective liturgical enactment, as in the Easter Passus, that Langland can imagine resolving all these competing voices into univocality.[24] I think this is true, but I also think that Langland insists on a difference between liturgical and historical enactment, and that only such a distinction between the forms of repetition each involves can explain why the poem continues past the Easter Passus to a revisitation of the field of the world, and the form that revisitation takes. The truth Langland has to tell is rather about the subject in, and the subject of, history: about the framers and users of these competing traditional ways of thinking, speaking, and living—and how these activities constitute the Christian self and the Christian community. It is in this sense that Langland is the least mystical of writers. Far from envisioning, even if as an unattainable dream, salvation as an escape from, or "redemption" of, a "fallen language" that forms the compromised medium of all human discourse—as in effect a flight from history (a view that several critics have advanced, and I have been among them)—Langland presents humanity's thickly-woven participation in, and incessant repetition of, the words and gestures of their forbears, the historical reliving of historically real model lives—and the simultaneous recognition of this perpetual debtor status—as the form of the only community, or selves, capable of salvation. In this poem, it is not the letter that kills, but the unconsciousness that one is citing or enacting it; the only unforgivable sin is the one that has persuaded itself it is original.

I have tried to outline here an approach to Langland's poetic method that distinguishes its procedures and effects from those of the social and spiritual texts that everywhere pervade it, yet allows us to see the point of asserting that difference, against, on the one hand, attempts to privilege the "literary" as against the "documentary" text as distinctive in nature, and, on the other, the collapsing of both into identical, and authorless, "textuality." For Langland, the constitution of a "life" out of a multitude of voices that precede us and live through us is at once a highly self-conscious poetic method and a way of understanding the created world and its history, the collective memory that forms is "record of treuthe." We will be far closer to understanding Langland's allegorical narrative, I believe, when we understand in what sense it is simultaneously a historical narrative. What gives "depth of field"—the air of cognitive realism—to the poem is the repeated discovery that the treasure one traverses narrative duration to find lies hidden in the discursive field he has been cultivating all along. The "uncreated conscience of the race" is in fact, Langland insists, woven—as well as worn, rent, and mended—every day, like Hawkyn's one cloak, its fabric formed of the common social texts under which people appear to each other and lead, as they put it, their lives. It's always getting dirty, but it's the only one we have.

Notes

1. Cf. Michel Foucault: "When a historically given function is represented in a figure that inverts it, one has an ideological production." From "What is an Author?" in *The Foucault Reader,* edited by Paul Rabinow (New York: Pantheon, 1984), p. 119.

2. David Aers, *Chaucer, Langland, and the Creative Imagination* (London: Routledge and Kegan Paul, 1979), chapters 1–3.

3. The dilemma for a genuinely historically-informed literary criticism, and for

the possibility of literary history, in what may appear with this move to be a reinscription of the pervasive poststructural and cultural-historical "textualization" of all events, experience, and every phenomenon whatever, verbal or otherwise—and a concomitant denial of their material specificity and contingency—is the topic of a recent provocative essay by Gabrielle Spiegel, "History, Historicism, and the Social Logic of the Text," *Speculum* 65 (1990): 59–86, especially pp. 71 and 74. I share Aers' distress at this move and hope to avoid it here, though he might not agree that I have succeeded. See the introduction to his more recent book, *Community, Gender, and Individual Identity: English Writing 1360–1430* (London: Routledge, 1988), for a useful antidote to the *mere* textualization of historical experience. As I do here, he emphasizes the multiplicity of voices and sources of arguments that inform Langland's practice and present him with the necessity of mediating among their incommensurable claims upon him and his society.

4. Most A manuscripts read *liflode* in this line, and this is Skeat's reading; see *The Vision of William concerning Piers the Plowman, in Three Parallel Texts*, edited by W. W. Skeat (London: Oxford Univ. Press, 1986), A.8.103. It is, however, alliteratively deficient, and Kane's edition of A emends to *belyue: Piers Plowman: The A Version*, edited by George Kane (London: Athlone, 1960), A.8.105. The majority of B manuscripts reads *bely ioye* at this point, and so Skeat (B.7.118); the Athlone B-Text emends to *bilyue: Piers Plowman: The B Version*, edited by George Kane and E. Talbot Donaldson (London: Athlone, 1975), B.7.123. The Athlone editors' reading in both instances is a synonym for *liflode* [<OE *biðleofa*] that, perhaps because of its similarity with *bileue*, "belief, faith" seems to have been vanishing from use at the close of the fourteenth century (*OED* s.v. "bylive"); it is precisely this potential ambiguity of the word in A.8/B.7 that seems to have attracted copyists' efforts at clarification in both versions, though with different results. Two further occurrences of the word elsewhere in the poem (Skeat B.19.230/Kane-Donaldson B.19.235 and Skeat C.2.18) are the latest instances cited by the *OED;* in both, as in the controverted reading in A.8/B.7, the word carries the alliteration of the line. A further instance, unique to C, should be added to the list: Skeat C.6.29; there, too, the word is in alliterative position. In the first of these, *liflode* is a variant, appearing in six manuscripts of the first quarter of the fifteenth century and in Crowley's three printings in 1550. Only in Piers' famous renunciation of his occupation in A.8/B.7, however, is its meaning both pivotal to the scene and potentially ambiguous; it is this speech that is cancelled altogether in C, leaving Piers and the priest "jangling" as the dreamer wakes at the end of the Pardon scene. Here it is crucial that we understand Piers as renouncing his occupation, not his faith. The A tradition preserves an early copyist's successful effort to retain the sense *(liflode)* at the expense of the alliteration—one of the commonest scribal responses to words that are intelligible but perceived as unusual or obsolescent; see, in addition to Kane and Kane-Donaldson, Hoyt N. Duggan, "The Shape of the B-Verse in Middle English Alliterative Poetry," *Speculum* 61 (1986): 564–92. The B tradition preserves a coinage, *bely-ioye*, that looks to have entered the line of manuscript transmission at an early stage, probably the result of an effort to construe a word either defaced in the copy-text or already obsolete in the copyist's dialect. *Bely-ioye* maintains the alliteration while it renders at best a blurred and reduced sense of what Piers renounces: it is not the pleasures of bodily sustenance that he here repudiates, but, as the preceding and following lines clearly show, the trade, plowing, by which he obtains it; *(liflode)* incidentally is also used in this period to mean both "daily bread" and the trade or craft by which one earns it. For an objection to the Athlone editor's emendation and Anne Hudson, "Middle English," in *Editing Medieval Texts,* edited by A. G.

Rigg (New York: Garland, 1977), p. 43; as the above account shows, I do not consider the objection warranted.

5. See James Clifford, "On Ethnographic Allegory," in *Written Cultures: The Poetics and Politics of Ethnography*, ed. James Clifford and George E. Marcus (Berkeley and Los Angeles: Univ. of California Press, 1986), pp. 98–121.

6. On the range of views both within and surrounding Lollard practice and belief, and the difficulty in many instances of placing an utterance on the continuum between orthodoxy and heresy, see Anne Hudson, *The Premature Reformation* (Oxford: Clarendon, 1988), passim.

7. See K. B. McFarlane, *Lancastrian Kings and Lollard Knights* (Oxford: Clarendon, 1972), pp. 210–20; Malcolm Vale, *Piety, Charity, and Literacy among the Yorkshire Gentry, 1370–1480* (York: Borthwick Institute, 1976); J. Anthony Tuck, "Carthusian Monks and Lollard Knights: Religious Attitudes at the Court of Richard II," *Studies in the Age of Chaucer*, Proceedings No. 1, 1984: *Reconstructing Chaucer*, ed. Paul Strohm and Thomas J. Heffernan (Knoxville: Univ. of Tennessee Press, 1985), pp. 149–61.

8. In a paper presented at a 1985 Chaucer Division meeting of the MLA, "Exchange and Alienation in the *Shipman's Tale*," Lee Patterson discusses the Aristotelian moral tradition within which scholastic theologians developed the conception of need—human postlapsarian insufficiency or *indigentsia*—as the generative principle of economic as distinct from "natural" value. The "natural" order of value, determined by the position of each thing on the scale of being, is overturned in postlapsarian society by the relation of each thing to the human perceiver's interests; its value becomes its cost—what someone is willing to pay for it. As Patterson summarizes: "As soon as an object enters into the exchange system of the economic order, it loses its natural value and becomes a commodity, an object whose value is determined by the workings of the exchange system itself." I am grateful to him for allowing me to read this paper in typescript.

9. On sumptuary laws, see Claire B. Sponsler, "Society's Image: Estates Literature in Fifteenth-Century England," *Semiotica* 63 (1987): 229–38, 234–5. For the text of the Lollard Disendowment Bill, see *Selections from English Wycliffite Writings*, ed. Anne Hudson (Cambridge: Cambridge Univ. Press, 1978), pp. 135–37 and 203–7; Hudson discusses the bill in *Premature Reformation*, pp. 114–15 and 339–40. The second Statute of Laborers, enacted by the Cambridge Parliament in September 1388, was, despite its initial and quite perfunctory gestures of reaffirmation of the Statute of 1351, in fact largely an anti-vagrancy act; there is no evidence that it was ever widely enforced, though it served as a model for Tudor legislation that was more vigorously applied. I am preparing a monograph on the relation between the social texts that antedate this legislation and the treatment of vagrancy in the C version of *Piers Plowman*.

10. Penn Szittya, *The Antifraternal Tradition in Medieval Literature* (Princeton: Princeton Univ. Press, 1986), makes the point throughout his excellent study that this apologetic warfare was from the beginning a contest between "historical fictions," not a sequence of responses to historical fact; see pp. 6–10.

11. See Lester K. Little, "Pride Goes Before Avarice: Social Change and the Vices in Latin Christendom," *American Historical Review* 76 (1971): 27–29; Lester K. Little and Barbara Rosenwein, "Social Meaning in the Monastic and Mendicant Spiritualities," *Past and Present* 63 (May 1974): 4–32; and Lester K. Little, *Religious Poverty and the Profit Economy* (Ithaca: Cornell Univ. Press, 1978).

12. Georges Duby, *The Three Orders*, trans. Arthur Goldhammer (Chicago: Univ. of Chicago Press, 1980).

13. The notion, and some general axioms about how it works, are borrowed

from Michel de Certeau, *The Practice of Everyday Life,* trans. Steven F. Rendall (Berkeley and Los Angeles: Univ. of Calfornia Press, 1984).

14. St. Francis' insistence that his "rule"—which was no more and no less than a personal (and highly theatrical) *imitatio Christi*—be observed and transmitted "without a gloss," and the virtual institutional untenability of this imperative, were recognized in several quarters during his lifetime, and were immediately refracted in the succession of accounts of his life that were by the saint's own axiom the only form of document that could attest to this rule. My colleague Steven Justice is currently at work on a study of the implications of these developments for the late-medieval formation of narrative as an implicitly argumentative mode; I am indebted to him for many of the thoughts that follow.

15. See Thomas N. Tentler, *Sin and Confession on the Eve of the Reformation* (Princeton: Princeton Univ. Press, 1977), pp. 10–27; John Bossy, "The Social History of Confession in the Age of the Reformation," *Transactions of the Royal Historial Society,* 5th ser., 25 (1975): 21–38, and *Christianity and the West 1400–1700* (Oxford: Oxford Univ. Press, 1985), pp. 45–56. On "liminality," see Victor Turner, *Dramas, Fields and Metaphors: Symbolic Action in Human Society* (Ithaca: Cornell Univ. Press, 1974), esp. chapter 5, "Pilgrimage as Social Process." Caroline Walker Bynum has recently argued that the ritual social process of removing the self from the society's normal forms of social differentiation into a "liminal" state has meaning and utility as a gesture only for a culture's elites, those not already marginalized by prevailing models of social totality; see her essay, "Women's Stories, Women's Symbols: A Critique of Victor Turner's Theory of Liminality," in *Fragmentation and Redemption: Essays on Gender and the Human Body in Medieval Religion* (New York: Zone Books, 1991), pp. 27–51.

16. Elizabeth Kirk, "The Re-Creation of Religious Metaphor: Langland and the Idiom of Fourteenth-Century Religious Discourse," *Yearbook of Langland Studies* 2 (1988): 1–21, argues Landland's originality in transvaluing the plowman from a figure traditionally associated with gross earthliness and the mark of Cain to the bearer of an idea of virtue and leadership.

17. Aubrey Gwynn, *The English Austin Friars* (London: Oxford Univ. Press, 1940), pp. 211–21; K. B. McFarlane, *John Wycliffe and the Beginnings of English Nonconformity* (London: The English University Presses, 1952), pp. 45–6, 58–61.

18. On the law of need in the distribution of poor relief, see Brian Tierney, "The Decretists and the Deserving Poor," *Comparative Studies in Society and History* 1 (1959): 363; and *Medieval Poor Law* (Berkeley and Los Angeles: Univ. of California Press, 1959), chapters 2 and 3.

19. See Hudson, *Premature Reformation,* pp. 338–39.

20. Alastair J. Minnis, *Medieval Theory of Authorship* (London: Scolar, 1984), pp. 118–38, and " 'Authorial Intention' and "Literal Sense' in the Exegetical Theories of Richard Fitzralph and John Wyclif," *Proceedings of the Royal Irish Academy,* 75, sec. C,i (Dublin, 1975).

21. John Alford, "The Role of the Quotations in *Piers Plowman,*" *Speculum* 52 (1977): 80–99; Judson B. Allen, "Langland's Reading and Writing: *Detractor* and the Pardon Passus," *Speculum* 59 (1984): 342–62.

22. On the rubrics, see Robert Adams, "The Reliability of the Rubrics in the B-Text of *Piers Plowman,*" *MÆ* 53 (1985): 208–31.

23. George Kane, *The Autobiographical Fallacy in Chaucer and Langland Studies* (London: B. K. Lewis, 1965), p. 17.

24. Steven Justice, "Irenic Citation: Guillaume de St.-Amour, Friar Ubertino da Casale, and *Piers Plowman,*" read at the International Medieval Congress, Kalamazoo, Michigan, May 1986.

Love and Disorder: A Fifteenth-Century Definition of Love and Some Literary Antecedents

THOMAS C. MOSER, JR.

Aby Warburg's famous remark about God's existing "in detail" has emerged rephrased in some recent discussion about the most profitable approaches to the medieval lyric. Siegfried Wenzel cites William Carlos William's observation that "it is in the minutiae—in the minute organization of the words and their relationship in a composition that the seriousness and value of a work of writing exists." Earlier in the same article Wenzel stresses his feeling "that the evaluative analysis of medieval lyrics must be primarily concerned, not with thought or thought structures, but with language, with the verbal expression of thought or emotion."[1] At the same time, Lee Patterson has argued that in reading Chaucer in particular and any late medieval literature in general the modern audience should understand that "the poem stands within and reflects upon a system of literary conventions and traditions."[2] Patterson takes a lyric fragment of *Troilus and Criseyde* (I.400–406) found in a fifteenth-century treatise for nuns and uses that insertion to construct "one medieval experience of reading Chaucer's" longest poem.[3] In this case Patterson observes the author "survey[ing] the available topoi" and reading *Troilus* as an exemplum that illustrates the "topos of amor and amicitia." His analysis avoids the danger of a strict exegetical interpretation by fixing the reading of Chaucer's poem in a very specific "interpretive context," by offering us simply an individual fifteenth-century attempt to "disambiguate" a complex literary text. He concludes by suggesting one key to the way the medieval poet's mind operates: "we might even be led to argue that late-medieval literary creation operates . . . at the level of form, and that the poet understands his immediate task as being to dispose and vary a range of inherited tropes."[4]

Because Wenzel is primarily concerned with lyric fragments, almost all free-floating or embedded in sermons, he worries about the dangers in modern efforts to reconstruct medieval "contexts," and he stresses a cautious process of literary evaluation that tends to work from the inside

243

out. Patterson comes to his own conclusions about medieval texts by creating a dialogue between a contextualized lyric fragment and the long narrative from which it was lifted. His reworking of the old Curtsian process of topos hunting in essence proposes a search through the literary cosmos for traditions that can be used to pressure meaning from a medieval text, from the outside in.

Modern exegetes of medieval lyric ought, of course, to have it both ways, and, in fact, both of the critics just invoked do. Wenzel works very effectively to locate his lyric subjects in the realm of ideas suggested by the particular manuscript contexts in which they appear, and Patterson pays a great deal of attention to the precise verbal details of the texts he analyses. As modern readers of medieval lyrics, our effort, however imperfectly realized, should be to amplify the conversation between the surviving poetic artifact itself and the larger world of antecedent forms and ideas, to wrest meaning from the old words however we can. My aim in this essay is to examine a short, simple fifteenth-century Middle English lyric, "Y shal say what ynordinat loue is," through the "minutiae" of its language, its unique "verbal expression," while locating the poem in a particular literary and historical context created out of the accumulation of earlier texts. I hope the exercise will permit us if not to reconstruct a contemporary fifteenth-century response, then to see—partially, but in some ways better than the author saw—how the peom's dialectical response to the world of words that spawned it makes the poem what it is.

My lyric subject occupies a small niche in the large history of attempts to define "love," but it also lies along a chain of literary appropriations and rewritings, or at the convergence of several chains, some of whose links may be usefully traced. Such a process of recapturing earlier moments allows us to see a fifteenth-century poet of modest means building on old glosses, rewriting old texts, taking up old language, and renewing it for himself so that it makes sense to him. "Y shal say" stands out from the morass of fifteenth-century Middle English love-lyrics for its direct, vigorous, and emphatic personal voice, for its almost fierce moral *ego,* and for a commanding sense of self that points toward the better religious poetry of the next century. Though verbally aureate, it manages to avoid affectation and, though generically a love definition, it moves beyond a dry recitation of qualities. It is also of interest because it is a translation (as so many Middle English lyrics are) of an earlier Latin poem, a much used fragment of rhetoricized love-lore, whose source and approximate course of transmission can be traced.

The lyric appears uniquely on the final leaf of a fifteenth-century manuscript, Copenhagen Thott 110 in the Royal Library, that contains three treatises composed by the thirteenth-century Italian judge Albertanus of Brescia, and was first published in 1939 by Carleton Brown under the invented title of "Inordinate Love Defined."[5] Since then it has been reprinted occasionally, but not, to my knowledge, commented on at any length. It goes as follows:

Y shall say what ynordinat loue ys:
The furyosite and wodnes of mynde,
A instynguyble brennyng fawtyng blys,
A grete hungre ynsaciat to fynde,
A dowcet ylle, a yvell swetness blynde,
A ryght wonderfulle sugred swete erroure,
Wyth-owte labor rest, contrary to kynde,
Or wyth-owte quyete to haue huge laboure.

Written in the manuscript above these eight lines of rough decasyllables (number [4] in this essay's appendix) is the pair of regular Latin elegaic couplets (number [3] in appendix) that the poet translated in creating his poem:

Dicam quid sit Amor: Amor est insania mentis,
Ardor inextinctus, insaciata fames,
Dulce malum, mala dulcedo, dulcissimus error,
Absque labore quies, absque quiete labor.

[I will say what love is: love is a madness of the mind,
An inextinguishable burning, an insatiable hunger,
A sweet evil, an evil sweetest error,
Rest without labor, labor without rest.]

The remainder of the page contains a one-line Latin proverb (designated [1] in appendix), a Middle English rhyme-royal stanza that expounds on the proverb (2), and two Middle English quatrains (5) and (6). At the foot appears an *ex libris* placing the manuscript in the possession of a "brother Nicholas Barkley" and subsequently in that of his nephew "brother Nicholas London." The first four items seem to be written in a single hand, items (5) and (6) and the first part of the *ex libris* in a second hand, and the final words in a third. Together the six literary fragments form something like a clerical soliloquy on reason and unreason—the first pair listing four causes of madness in men and the second pair apparently providing commentary on the observation in item (2): "bokys . . . Sayn that wymen maketh men most to madde." Later, another hand (and voice) came along (presumably Nicholas Barkley) to add a third pair of fragments that shift the argument to invoke the unreason that is faith in Christian mysteries. While quatrain (5) (like "Y Shall Say") appears to be unattested elsewhere, items (2) and (5) are quite common in fifteenth-century manuscripts and have been attributed to John Lydgate and Reginald Pecock respectively.[6]

As a whole, this little discussion of human *ratio* forms an appropriate coda to a book of spiritual treatises written by a famous jurist.

The four Latin lines that constitute (3) form part of the vast and various body of relatively independent, short, aphoristic Latin poems which crop up constantly in medieval collections of lyrics, in sermons and treatises, on margins and end leaves.[7] In his book on the Middle English poems in the *Fasciculus morum,* Wenzel stresses the "tendency to summarize doctrine in verse form which flourished in the twelfth and thirteenth centuries," and the generation or so on either side of the year 1200 was the breeding ground for these summary love definitions as well. Yet despite the vast numbers of Latin aphorisms in circulation, pithy love definitions per se were apparently not very common; a handful of short verses seems to have constituted the most popular of them, at least for English manuscripts.

Two of these poems, the two most frequently evident and both beginning "Nescio quid sit amor," seem to have begun life separately and then, as time passed came increasingly to be written together:

"(A)Nescio quid sit amor nec amoris sentio nodum
          Set scio quis amat nescit habere modum.

[I do not know what love is, nor do I feel the knot of love,
But I know that whoever loves knows no measure.]

(B) Nescio quid sit amor nec amo nec amor nec amavi
          Sed scio, si quis amat, uritur igne gravi.

[I do not know what love is, I do not love, nor am I loved, nor have I loved,
But I know that if anyone loves he is burned by a painful flame.]

The verses show up first as independent distichs, one in a late twelfth-century French manuscript and the other in a thirteenth-century. Italian, but by the fourteenth century are found quite often as a pair.[8] A third love definition (C), "Amor est quedam," appears much less commonly than (A) and (B) and seems to have originated sometime in the thirteenth century.

(C) Amor est quedam mentis insania
          Que vagum hominem ducit per devia
          Sitit delicias et bibit tristia
          Crebris doloribus commiscens gaudia.

[Love is a certain madness of the mind
Which leads the wandering man by side roads.
He thirsts for delights and drinks sadness,
Mixing frequent sorrows with joys.]

Its earliest poetic version occurs as page filler in Bodleian MS Douce 139, from the late thirteenth century, but it also appears (in an altered form) as part of two medical treatises on love sickness—one of them perhaps older than the Douce manuscript. So, in the prologue to an anomalous version of Peter of Spain's commentary on the *Viaticum,* composed in Siena around 1250, we find (C) sandwiched anonymously between two much earlier medical love definitions from Avicenna and Constantinus Africanus; and a later medical writer, Bernard of Gordon, uses a truncated prose version of it to conclude a discussion of *amor hereos* he wrote in Montpellier in 1303. In the fifteenth century, the scribe of Trinity College Cambridge MS 0.2.5 included (A), (B) and (C) together on the same page as part of a series of love definitions.[9] As for "Dicam quid sit," the source of our Middle English lyric, it can be traced to John of Garland's encyclopedic, 6600 line-long *Epithalamium Beate Marie Virginis,* written around the year 1230. It was thence extracted almost immediately and translated by Richard Fournival into French prose. Subsequently it roamed the nooks and crannies of Latin culture until our fifteenth-century poet, probably unconscious of its source, translated the fragment again, this time into Middle English.[10]

Why did the four lines of neat Ovidian elegiacs knocked loose from John of Garland's poem prove to be so attractive? At the rhetorical level—in their terminology, their exploitation of tropes, their appropriation of the form of classical love verse, their reworking of an essentially Ovidian model—the couplets epitomize what the twelfth- and early thirteenth-century *aetas Ovidiana* sought aesthetically in its poetry. "Dicam quid sit" is a poem that sounds something like Ovid, but could not actually be his. The love language of the distichs, first of all, has a very mongrel parentage. Love as *labor, error,* and above all *ardor* are apparently common notions in Ovid and in others, even if not phrased or conceived exactly as here;[11] likewise if love never appears as *insania mentis* in Ovid, he frequently talks of *insanos amores.*[12] Love as *fames,* however, was *not* Ovidian and seems likely to be a postclassical usage, even though *fames* was used broadly for other sorts of greedy desires.[13] Similarly, love can be classically *dulcis* (especially in Ovid), but love's oxymoronic collocation with *malus* and *dulcis* doesn't happen in Ovid and probably not elsewhere.[14] Other terms in the four lines had only a very restricted use in classical literature. Both *inexstinctus* and *insaciata* turn out to be rare words before the Middle Ages, the former restricted entirely to a few instances in Ovid (who uses it of *libido* as well as *ignis*); only Statius and Prudentius use them adjectivally.[15]

The same hybrid quality occurs in the poem's manipulation of tropes. Classical poetry used the oxymoron sparingly and only rarely to characterize love's contradictions (the *Ad Herennium* does not even list it among the major figures of speech),[16] but that trope and the rhetorical play of carefully balanced syntax with emotional imbalance became one of the central medieval ways of talking about the experience of love. In response to their own ambivalent reaction to the disordering power of any strong passion, especially love, medieval writers adopted a trope that both expressed (through contradiction) and controlled (through rigid parallelism) a dangerous fact of human existence. Rhetorically, then, the four lines represent a classical trope of modest status, expanded, played with, reconstituted out of medieval Ovidianisms. So the crucial *amor* of line one appears consecutively with different stresses (x ' and ' ') as if to point up its variability. The first two lines, each carefully balanced around the caesura, contain a triplet of modifiers beginning with *in-* whose use introduces the topos of inexpressibility or unsurpassability (an unhealthy mind causes unquenchable hunger and fire), which leads thence to a double oxymoron and its result ("sweet evil" plus "evil sweetness" equals "most sweet error") that makes use of three different forms of the word *dulcis* (the trope of "transplacement"); in the last line the two hemiepes neatly mirror each other ("transplacing" *labor* and *quies*) to produce another double oxymoron.

From the mid-twelfth century on, oxymoronic language like that in "Dicam quid sit" appears regularly in Latin and vernacular literature—in lyrics of the troubadours and trouvères, in Walter of Chatillon, Jean de Meun, Petrarch, Chaucer, and Gower.[17] The *locus classicus* for twelfth-century love definitions, and a key to understanding medieval love language, is Alain de Lille's *De Planctu Naturae* and the closely related "Vix nodosum valeo," by the same writer.[18] The sort of ambivalent wordplay taken up in these two works to discuss the power of erotic attraction provides both terms and method for later writers; sections of both works are worth pausing over for a moment to provide a fuller sense of Alain's Neoplatonic justifications for eros, justifications constantly undercut by the author's own fears.

John of Garland's "Dicam quid sit," in fact, is almost a miniature of the *De Planctu*'s fifth meter and the prose prologue leading up to it. At this point in Alain's long prosimetron Natura has introduced herself to the poet and explained her mediating function, as God's handmaiden, between the divine and the sublunar. "Thus on the table of comparison," she asserts, "we can find three degrees of power and they are termed the *superlative* power of God, the *comparative* power of Nature, and the *positive* power of man."[19] The platonic and grammatical hierarchy she sketches that runs between cosmos and earth is complicated by the existence of further subdivisions between Natura: Venus, a "subdelegate" of Natura along with her spouse, Hymenaeus; and Venus' son, Cupido, who in turn takes orders from his mother. This simple ideal, whose effect is to explain the genealogical relationship between God's originary creative act and human art and human sexual reproduction, has been perverted by Venus (we learn later) who, against Natura's wishes, took a lover, Antigenius, and produced an evil double for Cupido, Jocus. Venus' ability to be corrupted and the existence of a dark twin for her son both reveal the poet's uneasy attitude about human desire. On the one hand, Alain feels compelled to promote procreative human sexual activity as a sublunar reflection of God's own creative impulse; on the other, he recognizes desire's inherent ability to tend either to good or to evil. In sum, however he appears at a given moment in the *De Planctu,* Cupido always contains his opposite and the opposite always threatens to emerge. This danger makes Cupido's power, in Alain's words, "antiphrastic," able to turn a word's meaning backwards, forcing opposites to exist simultaneously; and any human attempt to understand desire only leads one into an "inextricable labyrinth."

Just prior to the fifth meter, Lady Natura thus promises she will teach her pupil about love, a thing incommunicable, a "rem immonstrabilem" and "inexplicabilem:"

> Either by describing with reliable descriptions or defining with regular definitions, I will demonstrate the *indemonstrable,* extricate the *inextricable,* although it is not bound in submission to any nature, does not abide an investigation by reason and thus cannot be stamped with the stamp of any one description.
> Let the following, then, be set forth as a delimiting of the unlimited, let this emerge as an explication of a nature that is *inexplicable,* let this be regarded as knowledge of the unknown, let this be brought forward as a doctrine on the unknowable.[20]

Natura's attempt to define Cupido's nature produces a welter of oxymorononic and semi-oxymoronic formulations that define *amor.*

> Love is peace joined to hatred, loyalty to treachery, hope to fear and madness blended with reason. It is sweet shipwreck, light burden, pleasing Charybdis, sound debility, *insatiate hunger,* hungry satiety, thirst when filled with water, deceptive pleasure, happy sadness, *joy full of sorrow, delightful misfortune, unfortunate delight,* sweetness bitter to its own taste. Its odor is savoury, its savor is insipid. . . . Does not Desire, performing many miracles, *to use antiphrasis,* change the shapes of all mankind?[21]

Natura recognizes the inconsistency in her attitude toward her own metaphysical grandson and insists that the poet "not be surprised . . . [if] I have interjected some items of censure despite the fact that [Cupido] is connected with me by a certain bond of true consanguinity." In self-justification she invokes a distinction that again points up the instability inherent to the grammar of Cupido: "I bring no charge of dishonourable conduct against the basic nature of Desire, if it restrains itself with the bridle of moderation, . . ."[22] Thus love, for Alain, involves at once the simple question of its aim (i.e. the end towards which it is directed) and degree (whether it is controlled and moderated sufficiently), but the relationship between these two qualities remains obscure.[23]

Alain's anxious short poem "Vix noddosum valeo" deals with a very different love problem from the *De Planctu,* but begins with a series of formulations that were probably also familiar to John of Garland. Here, instead of writing a philosophical treatise to promote sexual activity aimed at reproduction and to criticize all other sexual acts, Alain aims to convince men that virgins are more worthy of seduction than are married women. It takes Alain thirty-six lines to arrive at his subject matter and that space is largely devoted to an exposé of Venus's power of inversion, her ability to create unnatural oppositions—she is a knot impossible to untie and, he puns, a monster undemonsterable:

> Vix nodosum ualeo nodum denodare
> Et indemonstrabile monstrum demonstrare
> Unde uolens Veneris uultum denudare
> Que naturas hominum uult denaturare.

> [I can scarcely untie the knotty knot and give a demonstration of an indemonstrable monstrosity—why Venus, who is ready to denature man's nature, is willing to reveal her face.][24]

This introduction merges into a long string of oxymorons that recalls the same moment in the *De Planctu:*

> *Dulce malum amor est et dulcor amarus,*
> Inimica caritas, inimicus carus,
> Ignara prudentia, sapiens ignarus,
> Preauara largitas, largiens auarus . . . ,
> Sitiens ebrietas, sitis debriata,
> Saties famelica, *fames satiata,*
> Virtuosum uicium, uirtus uiciata,
> *Inquietum gaudium, requies ingrata.*

> [*Love is a sweet evil and bitter sweetness,* a hostile love, an unfriendly friend, an ignorant wisdom, a wise ignoramus, miserly generosity, generous miser. . . . She is thirsty drunkenness, drunken thirst, hungry fulness, *full hunger,* virtuous vice, virtue gone vicious, *restless joy, joyless rest.*][25]

Despite the criticism of Venus, Alain comes not to condemn her utterly, but to limit where man may appropriately place his love:

> Sicut bruma gratior dies est estiua
> Floreque decrepito rosa primitiua,
> Sic matrone Venus est quasi positiua
> Cum Venus uirguncule sit superlatiua.

Floret Venus uirginis nondum deflorata,
Cum sit nuce uilior Venus triturata.

[Just as a Summer's day is more pleasing than one in Winter and the first rose than a withered flower, so the love of a matron is, so to speak, positive while the love of a young maiden is superlative. The love of a maiden blooms un-deflowered, while a love that has been threshed is more worthless than a nut.][26]

Venus remains a worthy, if suspect, power so long as she stays within the strict bonds of Natura's laws.[27]

Whether or not he was actually a student of Alain de Lille, John of Garland stands as an intellectual heir to Alain and near the end of the line of twelfth-century Neoplatonic poets. Alain constitutes for John, in large part, the poetic filter through which passed the Ovidian language and the rhetorical notions manifest in "Dicam quid sit." The four lines John wrote that provide the basis for "Y Shal Say" take the oxymoronic language Alain used ambiguously to describe Amor and Venus in the *De Planctu* and the "Vix nodosum" and place it in an unambiguous situation strongly reminiscent of the psychomachia that concludes Alain's *Anticlaudianus.*[28] "Dicam quid sit" constitutes a fragment of a prudential conflagration in which Modesty overcomes Amor in single combat during a battle that occurs at the court of Christ and the Virgin.[29] The distich immediately following "dicam quid sit" in the *Epithalamium* has the wicked person-ified *Amor* singing her own *exsequiale carmen oloris*—her funeral swan-song. John of Garland wants his definition of love to be perfectly plain: *amor* in this context is the *Venus scelestia,* the bad Venus and opposite of *Pudicitia,* who abandoned Natura's norms and mated with Antigenius. Like the evil Venus conquered by the Novus Homo in the *Anticlaudianus,* Amor must be overthrown; not merely a grammatical disruption, she is a form of madness and disease—"insania mentis."

Yet most of the descriptive language of the lyric fragment does not seem to have been expressly marked for medieval writers as suitable only for a condemnation of love. When Richard of Fournival takes over the passage a few years later for his *Consaus d'Amours,* he disambiguates the fragment in his own way to help define a sort of love he wants to explain and defend—the love "par amours" of one person for another of the opposite sex, originating in "boine volont," which alone is the source of all other loves. The shift from Latin to the vernacular signals a shift in audience: where Alain de Lille and John of Garland wrote for male clerics, Richard addresses his little treatise to his uncloistered and marriageable sister. Love may be good or bad ("en bien et en mal"), but only good love has any interest for the writer. And though love wields great power and threatens great difficulty and even disease, it remains a good thing if approached properly. Richard stresses repeatedly that since this matter is the root of all other virtues and all other loves it should be learned by heart ("de cuer escoute"), citing master John of Garland by name as one who defines and describes love in this way:

> Ceste maniere d'amour, selonc ce que je puis savoir, par maistre Jehan de Garlande et par les conditions ki sont en li, se definist et descrist en tele maniere: "Amours est une foursenerie de pensee, fus sans estaindre, fains sans soeler, dous mals, boine douchours, plaisans folie, travaus sans repos, et repos san travel." Par ceste descripsion, ki tant est mervelleuse et diverse, poés vous savoir que il covient grant soutilleté a cele amour maintenir.

> [This manner of love, as far as I can tell according to Master John of Garland and to the attributes he cites, is defined and described in this way: "Love is a madness of the mind, an unquenchable fire, a hunger without satisfaction, a sweet evil, a good sweetness, plaisant folly, work without rest, and rest without work." By this description, which is so marvellous and diverse, you may know that it requires great subtlety to maintain his love.][30]

In the margin of Paris, MS B.N. f. fr. 25566 (the only copy of the treatise) have been added the four Latin lines and John's name. Clearly the translation is about as close to the original as Richard could make it, except for the substitution of "plaisans folie" in place of the only unequivocally negative assertion in the Latin ("gratissimus error"), the substitution of "boine douchours" for "mala dulcedo" (which ruins the oxymoron), and for the use of the far less pointed "foursenerie" for "insania." With some minor alterations, John of Garland's swan song of a justly murdered love becomes to Richard's mind a "marvellous" and "diverse" indication of the "great subtlety" needed to maintain this virtuous "amor enracine." His explication of these lines from his near contemporary point up how thoroughly he has reread John of Garland. Love is a "foursenerie de pensee" because love does what it likes, striking people without regard to rank: "con li solaus, ki luist aussi bien sur .j. fumier ke sur .j. rosier" (Like the sun, which shines as readily on a dung heap as on a rose bush). Love is an oxymoron by nature, but not an error, merely a "plaisans folie" because it shows so many "diverses contenances."[31]

All four of the Latin love definitions I have discussed—"Dicam quid sit," (A), (B), and (C)—sooner or later found Middle English translators. Siegfried Wenzel's study of Middle English verses in Latin sermons has made clear the enormous debt owed to Latin prose and poetry by the early Middle English lyric. "We must," he writes, "think of the clerics and preachers of the high Middle Ages as immensely eager to formulate an observation . . . in a verse that is often pithy, witty, and even punning." Medieval English preachers in search of "punch lines in verse" took over key passages from the Bible and liturgy, from hymns and prayers, from stories venerable and contemporary, translating them into English verse.

The habit of including such aphoristic translations in sermons seems to have "begun well before 1300," though most of the surviving texts are later, and waned by the 1550s. "It is worth noting," Wenzel concludes, "that in later fifteenth-century English prose texts one frequently misses verses at precisely those places where one finds them in fourteenth-century sermons and sermon handbooks.[32] "Dicam quid sit" and its late Middle English rendering take their places toward the close of this long tradition of translating pithy Latin verses into English. At the same time the later poem, not surprisingly for the fifteenth century, is far more expansive and latinate than any of the earlier Middle English translations of love definitions.

Alan de Lille, John of Garland, and Richard Fournival in turn each took the same essential vocabulary and rhetorical strategy in defining love and turned it to different ends. Even if our anonymous fifteenth-century poet knew none of this, I suspect it was anxiety over the ambiguity built into the popular distichs that most directly informed his Middle English translation of "Dicam quid sit amor," along with a pedantic desire to straighten things out and get them right, to call things by their real names.[33] In the process of expansion, the poet of "Y shall say" experiments with the aureate diction of the period, Englishing Latin polysyllables almost verbatim, doubling the number of lines, and turning a pair of elagiac couplets into what is almost a rhyme-royal stanza. By expanding the four lines into eight roomy, if uneven, decasyllables and by using a stanzaic rhyme-pattern, he gave himself space to work and closed off the open-ended structure of the distich, making the process of translation into an occasion for linguistic play and experimentation, creating noun-pairs, using a few odd words, adding qualifying adjectives and explanatory phrases in an effort at moral clarification.

The expansion of the simple Latin *amor,* in the first line, to *inordinat love,* sets in train all subsequent rewriting. Like much medieval love-language, the exegetical use of "inordinate" has its roots in the Song of Songs, in this case when the *Sponsa* declares in 2.4–5:

Introduxit me in cellam vinariam;
Ordinavit in me charitatem.
Fulcite me floribus,
Stipate me malis,
Quia amore langueo.

In establishing the terms of the long medieval discussion of love and disorder Augustine played a central role. For him, Adam and Eve's ordered affections in Eden provided the model of perfect love; just as they felt no hunger and thirst there, and labor and rest were in balance, so the love between them was prefectly harmonious until their disobedience cast

them into disorder. Since the fall, humanity has had to employ the poor
forces of reason to keep in check a will beset by threatening passions,
among them *amor*. Passions exist that they might be reined in and turned
to good use under the aegis of Christian wisdom.[34] The particular passion
of "love" is complicated because of its terminology: Scripture employs the
words *amor, dilectio,* and *caritas* synonymously and uses all three *in bono*
and *in malo*. *Amor* must thus be defined by its direction as well as by its
need for moderation by reason:

> The right will is, therefore, well-directed love, and the wrong will is ill-directed
> love. Love, then, yearning to have what is loved, is desire. . . . Now these
> motions are evil if the love is evil; good if the love is good.[35]

Twelfth-century theologians like Bernard of Clairvaux heard Augustine's
distinctions when they explicated the passions of the Song of Songs.
Properly ordered love, for Bernard, is a controlled and moderated passion
directed towards God and away from the things of the earth. Tempering the
natural upwelling of emotion, the good person will turn it away from the
transitory and towards the eternal:

> Da mihi hominem, qui ante omnia quidem ex toto se diligat Deum. . . . atque in
> hunc modum ad caetera quaeque Dei ordinato intendat amore, despiciens
> terram, suspiciens coelum, utens hoc mundo tanquam non utens. . . .
>
> [Give me the man who wholly loves God before all else. . . . and in this way
> turns to the things of God through ordered love, despising the earth and trusting
> heaven, using the world and not using it. . . .][36]

Bernard's younger contemporary, Richard of St. Victor, also follows Augustine in distinguishing between the good and the bad manifestations
possible of a number of human emotions. When he analyzes "amor" by
itself in his treatise *De IV gradibus violentiae charitatis,* he sets up twin,
four-stage systems based on the object—carnal or spiritual—of the passion, in a sort of rough parallel to the two Cupidos of the *De Planctu*. Each
of the four consecutive and increasingly profound stages of loving God he
outlines—*insuperabilis, inseparabilis, singularis,* and finally *insatiabilis*—has a disordered double in the trajectory of fleshly love.
Richard's observation that what seems to be essentially *the same* desire
may operate in mirrored opposition to itself provides a theological basis
for the oxymoronic formulation of love definitions. The word *amor,* as a
word, contains its own obverse.

The mystical ruminations produced by Bernard and Richard provide a
ground for the ecstatic spirituality of the fourteenth-century English hermit Richard Rolle and it is perhaps most directly through his influence that
our fifteenth-century translator came to rewrite the thirteenth-century

distichs as he did. Writing near the end of his life for a woman recluse just beginning her enclosure, Rolle offers a three-part scale of love that repeats Richard of St. Victor's *gradus,* omits the final stage:

> Thre degrees of lufe I sal tell þe, for I walde þat þou moght wyn to þe heest. The fyrst degre es called insuperabel; þe secund, inseparabel; þe thyrd es syngulere.[37]

A little later in the same treatise, in chapter 10, a catechism of questions about the love of God, occurs what may be the first recorded use of "inordinat" in English:

> þe fyrst askyng es: What is lufe? And I answer: Luf es a byrnand yernyng in God, with a wonderfull delyte and sykernes. God es lyght and byrnyng. . . . Lufe es a st[i]ryng of þe saule, for to luf God for hymself, and all other thyng for God; þe whilk lufe, when it es ordayned in God, it dose away all inordinate lufe in any thyng þat es noght gude. Bot al dedely syn es inordynate lufe in a thyng þat es noght; þan lufe puttes out al dedely syn.[38]

Though the tone of "Y shal say" is much starker than the ecstatic prose of Rolle's treatise, both works depend on the old discussion of love's double nature and both writers felt the usefulness and accuracy of the term *inordinat.*

Inordinat, in the most orderly "Y shal say," comes to mean not "excessive," but "disordered," discordant with the rest of the cosmos, and in this sense the Middle English poet really understood his sources. Having declared himself, he unfolds the rest of his translation through an accretion of word pairs and clarifying phrases. Because he follows the basic pattern of the Latin, the syntax remains essentially that of the original, yet the overpowering "antiphrastic" thrust of the Latin rhetoric becomes dissipated in the process of expansion. For the tightly packed rhetorical play that characterizes the Latin, the Middle English translator substitutes a greater verbal richness and precision. And by rejecting the older aesthetic, he ends up with more powerful poetry.

He begins by splitting and doubling the "insania" of "insania mentis" into the more modern and latinate "furyosite," plus the old Anglo-Saxon "wodnes," echoing Chaucer, who, in *Anelida and Arcite,* described Mars as "furious and wod." The *MED*'s only record of the noun *furiosite,* here again with *wodnes,* is contained in the medical textbook of Guy of Chauliac (translated circa 1425) and used technically of the leper's state of mind and the itching caused by scrofulous. These astrological or medical uses of the paired terms suggest that the poet of "Y shal say" is seeking an almost scientific precision of expression. To render "ardor inextinctus," he invents "instynguyble" (the *MED*'s only citation), ignoring the more common "inextinguyble" used first by Lydgate circa 1420 as a synonym for "unquenchable"; and to counter the courtly cliche of the lover's ecstasy he qualifies that term with "fawtyng blys," or lacking happiness. Whatever bliss there is, it is not found in this sort of conflagration. "Fames" in line four of the English becomes a "great hunger"; the "ynsaciat" that the poet retains constitutes only the second recorded instance of the word's use. As a whole, the stanza builds toward the long, rolling, tactile condemnation of line six—the expansion of "dulcissimus error"[39] into a whole verse of its own: "A ryght wonderfulle sugred swete erroure." At this point the poet abandons antiphrastic symmetry in order to divide the Latin "dulce" between "dowcet" (another fifteenth-century coinage) and two versions of the much older, germanic "sweet," adding a synesthetic "blynde" to "yvell swetness" that recalls the iconography of the blindfolded Cupid as well as more general moral blindness. In the final two verses he once more gives up the symmetry of the Latin as he sorts out the complexities of the labor and rest oxymoron. His solution is to split the two halves with a qualification that makes explicit what the Latin, if read moralistically, implies. Again (as with "furyosite"/ "wodnes" and "dowcet"/"swete") he doubles a crucial term into synonyms: disordered love goes against nature ("contrary to kynde") because it collapses verbal oppositions; it is an "erroure" because it destroys the natural and necessary distinction between rest and labor, because it breaks apart the divinely established order of the cosmos as ought to be revealed in human conduct and in human grammar.

"Y shal say" stands at the end of a long tradition of Latin poems and a long train of thought about love—from Ovid, to Alain in the twelfth century and John in the thirteenth, down to a didactic Englishman at the close of the Middle Ages. As modern readers and archaeologists of thoughts we set about the inherently imperfect task of suggesting possibilities. The poems' manuscript context offers clues about the scribe's notions of what the poem meant to him at the moment when he thought to include the lyric on the page he was writing; the presence of a Latin original provides a concrete sense of linguistic and literary history behind the Middle English verse; the minute verbal details of both versions serve as signposts, ambiguous and (like the Scarecrow in Oz) pointing backwards and forwards at once, but still significantly suggesting the noumenal world of ideas that inform the work. Some of these ideas would have been consciously present for the poet, others merely ghosts. What this poem offers, finally, is something appropriate to its age, and felt only at an intellectual remove in the rhetorical tortuousness of the old original, but something with which Alain and John could have agreed. To quote John Ganim on another fifteenth-century topic, the English version gives a sense of "fixity, a conciseness, and a structure that implies an equally

fixed and reliable moral order . . . a clear moral message . . . an antidote
to a century of excess or defect."[40]

Notes

1. Siegfried Wenzel, "Poets, Preachers, and the Plight of Literary Critics,"
Speculum 60 (1985): 351.
2. Lee Patterson, *Negotiating the Past* (Madison: Univ. of Wisconsin Press,
1987), p. 150.
3. Patterson, *Negotiating,* p. 116.
4. Ibid., pp. 148–50.
5. *Religious Lyrics of the Fifteenth-Century,* ed. Carleton Brown (Oxford:
Clarendon, 1939), p. 2897, with the note: "Occurs only in the MS.; not heretofore
printed" (p. 350). The three works by Albertanus of Brescia are *De doctrina
dicendi et tacendi, De consolacione et consiliis,* and *De amore et dilectione Dei.*
The second of these, in its French translation, provided Chaucer with the source
for the *Melibee.* The MS must have been in England by the fifteenth century; in the
eighteenth century it came into the library of Francis Wise at Trinity College
Oxford. See Ellen Jørgensen, *Catalogus Codicum Latinorum Medii Aevi*
(Copenhagen: Glydendalia, 1926), pp. 67–68.
6. See appendix for a transcription of the page. For (1) and (2), Francis Lee
Utley, *The Crooked Rib* (Columbus: Ohio State Univ. Press, 1944), pp. 311–13,
records sixteen MS sources, the earliest being John Shirley's MS Ashmole 49
(1447–56), where the Middle English poem is attributed to Lydgate. Utley suggests
an ultimate source for the Latin proverb in the Vulgate's 3 Esdras, 3–4. Stow prints
the poem in his 1561 edition of Chaucer's works and attributes it to Chaucer. Poem
(6) appears in various forms and in some MSS with a Latin quatrain:

> Hoc mens ipsa stupet quod non sua ratio cernet
> Quo modo virgo pia genetrix sit sancta Maria
> Ac Deus almus homo sed credat ratio miro
> Namque fides superest cum perfida ratio subsit.

Poem (6) also appears on the last flyleaf of Cambridge MS Corpus Christi College
78 (s.XV) with the following:

> Sensus miratur que racio dicere nescit
> Quo modo Virgo parit et homo factus deus extat
> Desere quod sentis verum mirabile credas
> Namque fides prestat fidei tua racio cedit
> Vel.   Desere persuasum credens mirabile verum
> Namque fides prestat fidei quoque racio cedit.

At the end of his edition of Reginald Pecock's *The Repressor of Over Much
Blaming of the Clergy,* Rolls Series 19.2 (London: Longman, 1860), Churchill
Babington prints an extract from Thomas Gascoigne's fifteenth century *Dic-
tionarium Theologicum.* In the extract Gascoigne claims Pecock—Oxford scholar,
logician, and bishop of Chichester—recited the poem (6) when he was publicly
compelled to abjure certain heretical doctrines.
7. Some idea of the scope of the genre can be gotten by glancing through a few
of the nearly thirty-five thousand entries in Hans Walther's collection of Latin

proverbs and sentences. See *Proverbia Sententiaeque Latinitatis Medii Aevi: Lateinisches Sprichwörter und Sentenzen des Mittelalters,* 5 vols. (Göttingen: Vandenhoeck and Ruprecht, 1963–69). Cited here as *Sprichtwörter.* See also his *Initia carminum ac versorum medii aevi posterioris latinorum* (Göttingen: Vandenhoeck and Ruprecht, 1959). Cited here as *Initia.*

8. Poem (A) is listed as *Initia* 11741 and *Sprichwörter* 16532. Its earliest appearance seems to be in MS. B.N. 6765, fol. 61 (s.XIIex), where it can be found without (B) as part of a collection of anonymous proverbs and aphorisms among poems attributable to Serlo of Wilton (fols. 56–60 and 62v–63v). B. Hauréau, *Notices et extraits de quelques manuscrits latins de la Bibliothèque Nationale,* 6 vols. (Paris: Klincksieck, 1890–93), 1, 317 says (A) is found "plusieurs fois" in other MSS, notably B.N. 8427, fol. 18.

MSS Oxford, Jesus 39 and Oxford, Bodleian, Laud Misc. 99 also contain (A), where it is quoted and translated in the course of the *Disce mori.* The anonymous author of the treatise attributes the distich to "þe poete Ovide, *De arte amandi.*" See Patterson, *Negotiating,* p. 124 and n. The Middle English version is as follows:

> I wote not what is love,
> Ne I feele not þe knot,
> But I wote þat who so loveth
> Kepeth no more manere þan dooth a sotte.

Poem (B) is listed as *Initia* 11740 and *Sprichwörter* 16531. It appears, apparently alone, in B.N. 11341, fol. 110 (s.XII/XIII). The MS is not discussed in Hauréau; perhaps the earliest occurrence.

At fol. 17v in the National Library of Scotland, Advocates Library MS 18.7.21, (1372)—i.e. John of Grimstone's Preaching Book—(A) appears written as one poem with (B) and with a Middle English translation (*Index* and *Supplement* 1337). See Utley, *The Crooked Rib,* p. 31; and G. R. Owst, *Literature and Pulpit in Medieval England,* 2nd ed. (Oxford: Blackwell, 1961), p. 21. Edward Wilson, *A Descriptive Index of the English Lyrics in John of Grimstone's Preaching Book* (Oxford: Blackwell, 1973), p. 5, cites the poem:

> I ne wot quat is love,
> Ne i ne love ne lovede nouth;
> But wel i wot wo so lovet
> He brennet harde in his þouth. +

> I ne wot quat is love,
> Ne love me never bond;
> But wel I wot wo so lovet
> Reste havet he non.

+ Owst and Utley print "youth;" Wilson corrects to þouth."

9. I am very grateful to Mary F. Wack for bringing the two medical treatises to my attention. See her *Lovesickness in the Middle Ages: The Viaticum and its Commentaries* (Philadelphia: Univ. of Pennsylvania Press, 1990).

(C) is not listed in either *Initia* or *Sprichwörter.* C. T. Onions, "Amor Est Quedam Mentis Insania" (*Bodleian Quarterly Record* iv.41 [1924], 114), published the poem from Oxford Bodleian Douce 139, fol. 157 (x.XIII) along with the following translations:

> Amur est une pensee enragee
> Ke le vdif humme meyne par veie deueye.

Ke a soyf de delices e ne beyt ke tristesces
& od souuens dolurs medle sa tristesce.
Loue is a selkud wodenesse
þat þe idel mon ledeth by wildernesse
þat þurstes of wilfulscipe and drinket sowenesse.
And with lomful sorwes menget his blithnesse.

In line 4 Onions substitutes *tristesce* for MS *liesse* ("happiness"). M. Dominica
Legge, *Anglo-Norman Literature and Its Background* (Oxford: Clarendon Press,
1963), pp. 338–39, quotes the Anglo-Norman version of the poem from Paul Meyer,
"Mélanges de Poésie Anglo-Normande," *Romania* 4(1875): 382–84 and, with
Meyer, omits the fourth line.

The older medical version of (C) occurs in Peter of Spain, *Questiones Super
Viaticum,* Siena, circa 1250, anomalous B-version, found in Rome, Vat.pal.lat.
1166, fol. 8 (s.XIII/XIV):

Circa primum sic procedimus et potest ab Avicenna talis diffinitio extrahi: Amor est
melancolica sollicitudo mentis cum profunditatione cogitationem in qua figitur mens
propter pulchritudinem et dispositionem ad [????] et dicitur melancolica propter acciden-
cia in quibus comitat cum melancolia. Vel aliter et diffinitur sic: *Amor est mentis insania
qua vagatur animus per inania crebris doloribus permiscens gaudia.* Constantinus autem
in pantegni sic diffinit in capitulo de melancolia libro xxo: Amor est confidencia anime
suspicionis in re amata et cogitationis in eadem assiduitas.

Bernard de Gordon, *Practica dicta lilium medicine* Lyons, 1574, p. 218, composed
in 1303 in Montpellier, also contains the poem:

ultimo intelligendum, quod ista passio pulcherrimo modo potest describi sic: *amor est
mentis insania, qui animus vagatur per maniam cerebri, doloribus permiscens gaudia.*

The fifteenth-century MS Cambridge, Trinity College 0.2.5, p. 52 contains a
somewhat garbled version of (C), plus (A) and (B):

Quid est amor? Mentis insania
Vagum animum ducens per inania
Stitit delicias bibit tristitias crebris
Doloribus sua mistens gaudia.

For still other versions of this definition see Gian Battista Speroni, "Il 'Consaus
D'Amours' di Richard de Fournival," *Medioevo Romanzo* 1(1974): 217–78, 250n.

10. John of Garland's text is quoted from British Library MS. Cotton Claudius
A.x., fol. 55v, in L. J. Paetow, *Morale Scolarium of John of Garland,* Memoirs of
the University of California, 4 (1927): 114. The quotation found in MS Thott 110
differs from the text of the Cotton Claudius MS only in the substitution of "sit" for
"est" in the first line and "dulcissimus" for "gratissimus" in the third:

Dicam quid est amor. Amor est insania mentis,
Ardor inextinctus, insatiata fames,
Dulce malum, mala dulcedo, gratissimus error,
Absque labore quies, absque quiete labor.
Hoc est prodigium, cum luctu gaudia miscens,
Exsequiale canit carmen oloris amor.

[I will say what love is. Love is a madness of the mind, an inextinguishable burning, an
insatiable hunger, a sweet evil, and evil sweetness, a very great error, rest without labor,

labor without rest. This is a prodigy, mixing joy with sorrow, love sings its funeral swan-song.]

The *Epithalamium* is also found in at least two other manuscripts: Oxford, Bodleian, Digby 65 and Library of Kersall Cell (Lancastershire) MS 4, now in Chetham's Library, Manchester. Evelyn Faye Wilson discusses the entire *Epithalamium* in her unpublished doctoral dissertation "A Study of the Epithalamium in the Middle Ages: an Introduction to the *Epithalamium Beate Marie Virginis* of John of Garland" (University of California, Berkeley, 1930).

11. See especially the *Ars Amatoria,* where the labor of love is often implicitly compared to the poet's labor of writing the poem; e.g. "Hoc opus, hic labor est, primo sine munere iungi" (1.453; other instances of love labor include 1.35–37 and 3.787). For "error" see *Heroides* 7, 109, Dido's letter to Aeneas; for "ardor" (as a verb at least) see *Amores* 1.9.33: "ardet in abducta Briseide magnus Achilles."

12. See *Ars Amatoria* 1.371–72:

Tum de te narret, tum persuadentia verba
Addat, et insano iuret amore mori. . . .

See also 2.563 and *Heroides* 15.176. There are numerous non-Ovidian examples as well, e.g. Propertius, *Elegies* 2.34.25: "Lynceus ipse meus seros insanit amores."

13. Ovid never uses *fames* in either *Amores* or *Ars Amatoria* and the *Thesaurus Linguae Latinae* records no examples of *fames* tied to *amor,* though *fames* is generally used as a synonym for all sorts of excessive lusts.

14. See for example *Ars Amatoria* 2.478–80, in which love is a "sweet act":

Constiterant uno femina virque loco;
Quid facerent, ipsi nullo didicere magistro:
Arte Venus nulla dulce peregit opus.

In two instances Ovid comes close to the "dulce malum" oxymoron: "inpia sub dulci melle venena latent" (*Amores* 1.8.104), and "usque adeo dulce puella malum est" (*Amores* 2.9.26). Patterson, *Negotiating,* p. 122 n. 6, cites these and several other medieval examples of "dulce venenum," as well as Alain de Lille and John of Garland (Patterson, *Negotiating,* p. 139 n. 60).

15. *Inextinctus* seems in the classical period to have been an entirely Ovidian term: the *Thesaurus Linguae Latinae* cites only Ovid's use of it before Paulinus of Nola picks up the term. Ovid employs it of *ignis* (*Fasti* 6.297) and of *libido* (*Fasti* 1.413). *Insatiata* appears very rarely and no earlier than Statius (*Thebiad* 6.305) and Prudentius (*Psychomachia* 478), though other forms of the word (e.g. *insatiabiliter* and *insatiabilis*) may be found in Cicero, Juvenal, Pliny, Tacitus, and elsewhere.

16. *Rhetorica ad Herennium* comes closest to the idea of the oxymoron in describing *contentio* (4.15.21) and *commutatio* (4.28.39). Geoffrey of Vinsauf's *Poetria Nova* does not discuss the oxymoron either, but comes closest in describing the "two-fold mode" of making statements. See *Three Medieval Rhetorical Arts,* trans. James J. Murphy (Berkeley: University of California Press, 1971), p. 57 n. 50.

17. For the troubadours and trouvères see Frederick Goldin, trans. *Lyrics of the Troubadours and Trouvères* (Garden City, N.Y.: Anchor Books, 1973), pp. 99, 181, 287, 355, 371. For Walter of Chatillon, see *Die Lieder Walters von Chatillon in der Handschrift 351 von St. Omer,* ed. Karl Strecker (Berlin: Weidmann, 1992), pp. 42–

43. Poem 25, *Hymnus auf dem Amor,* includes a series of oxymoronic formulations in vv. 5–7:

> 5. Amor, tua mollicies
>   declinat in contrarium
>   tua blanditur rabies,
>   tuum mel fit absintium.
> 6. Tu saturis esuries,
>   siti peruris ebrium,
>   per abrupta planities,
>   per plana precipitium.
> 7. Amor, tua duricies
>   vertitur in remedium,
>   ludus, tuus est series,
>   tuus labor est ocium.

Jean de Meun adapts Alain de Lille's oxymorons in his *ars amatoria, Roman de la Rose* 4263–4310 (Patterson, *Negotiating,* p. 139 n. 60). For Chaucer and Petrarch one need only cite Chaucer's translation of Petrarch's Sonnet in Vita 88 ("S'amor non è") in *Troilus and Criseyde,* I.400–420. G. C. Macaulay prints a poem under the heading "Carmen quod Iohannes Gower super amoris multiplici varietate sub compendio metrice composuit" which begins with a series of oxymorons:

> Est amor in glosa pax bellica, lis pietosa,
> Accio famosa, vaga sors, vis imperiosa,
> Pugna quietosa, victoria perniciosa,
> Regula viscosa, scola deuia, lex capitosa,
> Gloria dampnosa, flens risus et ira iocosa, . . .

See *The Complete Works of John Gower,* 4 vols. (Oxford: Clarendon, 1899–1902), 4: 359.

18. Nikolaus M. Häring, ed., "Alain de Lille, *De Planctu Naturae,*" *Studi Medievali,* 3rd ser., 19 (1978): 797–879; James J. Sheridan, trans., *Alan of Lille: The Plaint of Nature* (Toronto: Pontifical Institue of Mediaeval Studies, 1980). Nikolaus M. Häring, ed., "The Poem Vix nodosum by Alan of Lille," *Medioevo* 3 (1977): 165–85. "Vix nodosum" is often found appended to the *De Planctu* in MSS.

19. Sheridan, *Plaint,* p. 126.

20. Ibid., p. 148.

21. Ibid., p. 149–50.

22. Ibid., p. 154.

23. The rhetorical status Amor/Venus achieves as an oxymoron is reflected in Alain's use of the trope in the *Anticlaudianus* to describe God (James J. Sheridan, trans., *Alan of Lille: Anticlaudianus or the Good and Perfect Man* [Toronto: Pontifical Institute of Mediaeval Studies, 1973]), in Book V, and Fortune, in Book VIII.

24. English and Latin texts are both from Häring, "Vix nodosum," pp. 167, 178. The monster/demonster pun is found in Cicero's *De Divinatione* I.42.

25. Häring, "Vix nodosum," pp. 67–68 and 179–80.

26. Ibid., pp. 68 and 181.

27. Ibid., p. 182, where Venus is declared to be under the "lex" of "nature principe" even though she has the power to break Natura's laws.

28. In Alain's elaborate allegorical battle staged in books 8 and 9 of the *Anti-*

claudianus Venus is one of the major vices the Novus Homo must overcome in his struggle for identity. He kills her, without the direct aid of any of the personifications who support him, by following customary advice: he flees while he shoots an arrow at her. Excess, not Venus, however, is seen as the "outstanding figure in the battle and the beginning and origin of the entire war" (Sheridan, *Anticlaudianus,* p. 212).

29. The text is quoted by L. J. Paetow, *Morale Scolarium,* p. 114, and in E. F. Wilson, "The Epithalamium," pp. 320–21. My translation.

30. Speroni, "Il 'Consaus'," p. 249–50.

31. Ibid., p. 251–52.

32. Siegfried Wenzel, *Verses in Sermons: Fasciculus Morum and its Middle English Poems* (Cambridge, Mass.: Mediaeval Academy of America, 1978), pp. 88 and 94–98.

33. Wenzel, *Verses,* p. 81, comments on the "pattern of glossing expansion" he finds in Middle English verse translation of biblical Latin. Often the "Latin material expanded to include . . . the moral application or interpretation of the biblical text."

34. *City of God* 9.7. For a discussion of "ordinate" and "inordinate" love in other contexts, see H. B. Willson, "*Amor Inordinata* in Hartmann's 'Gregorius,'" *Speculum* 41 (1966): 86–104.

35. *City of God* 14.8. Philip Schaff, ed., *St Augustine's City of God and Christian Doctrine* (Grand Rapids, Mich.: Wm. B. Eerdmans, 1956), p. 267.

36. *Sermones in Cantica, PL* 183. col. 1024. For more strictly allegorical readings of Song of Songs 2,4–5, see Honorius of Autun, *Expositio in Cantica PL* 172. cols. 585–88 and Alain de Lille, *Elucidatio in Cantica PL* 210. col. 66.

37. Hope Emily Allen, ed., *English Writings of Richard Rolle* (Oxford: Clarendon Press, 1931), p. 104.

38. Allen, *English Writings,* p. 109.

39. This is a very logical shift from the "gratissimus" of the original (as contained in MS. B.L. Cotton Claudius A.x).

40. John M. Ganim, *Style and Consciousness in Middle English Narrative* (Princeton: Princeton Univ. Press, 1983), p. 123.

Qui insatuat hoie; hoi es euac. ssciã. et bniñ

Worshyp wymmen wyne and olde ache
causeth men to fone for lacke of resoure
Age causeth dulnes ~~ And betuye
Worshyp causeth chaunge of condicion
Exercise of wyne blyndeth discord
And all bodys that en poetis made or wolde
Seyn that wymmen makyth men most to madde

Dicã qd sit Amor. Amor est infama mentf
Ardor inuotnetq. insaciata fumes
Dulce malu. mali dulcedo. dulcissmj error
Absq labor ideo. absq quiete labor

Y shall sey what y no dynett lone ys
The purposite and se dnes of vnpide
A instynernyble bienyng salutyng blys
A quete ysmezee. vnsicant to fynde
A douicet ysle. a pett stre ness blynde
A rysht wonderfille sacred swete error
owyth owte labor rest. cotzary to kynde
Or wyth owte quyete. to haue huge labor

He ys qnycke that smyth deds
And also flessh that smyth blode
He ys one that smyth moo
And very god that smyth nott so
Wytt hath wonder that reason nott can
Tell hongh mayde ys modyr & god ys man
lett be thy Reason lett be thy wondyr
ffor feyth ys a bobo. and reason ys tender

fiñ

Iste liber constat Me Barkley. Oz postea ptm A
Ad frem Nicho London psem fine affinis dñi sosio
sus filius naturals

Copenhagen, Royal Library ms Thott 110 fol. 163r (reproduced by permission).

Appendix

Copenhagen MS. Thott 110, fol.163r (15th century)

(1) Quatuor infatuant hominem: honor, etas, femina, et vinum

(2) Worship wymen wyne and olde age
Causeth men to fonde for lacke of reson
Age causeth dulnes and dotage
Worship causeth change of condicion
Excersice of wyne blyndeth discrec[i]on
And all bokys that ever poetis made or radde
Sayn that wymen maketh men most to madde

(3) Dicam quid sit amor, Amor est insania mentis
Ardor inextinctus, insaciata fames
Dulce malum, mala dulcedo, dulcissimus error
Absque labore quies, absque quiete labor

(4) Y shall say what ynordynat loue ys
The furyosite, and wodnes of mynde
A instynguyble brennyng fawtyng blys
A grete hungre, ynsaciat to fynde
A doucet ylle, a yvell swetnesse blynde
A ryght wonderfulle sugred swete errour
Wyth owte labor rest, contrary to kynde
Or wyth owte quyete, to haue huge labour

(5) he ys quycke that semyth dede
And also flecsh that semyth brede
he ys one that semyth moo
And very god that semyth nott soo

(6) Wytt hathe wonder that reason nott can
Tell hough mayde ys modyr and god ys man,
lett be thy reason lett be thy wondyr,
ffor feythe ys a bove, and reason ys under

> frati
Yste liber constat / Nicolao Barkley. Sed postea pertinet
Ad fratrem Nicholaum london prefati fratris affinem idest sororis
sue filium naturalem.

"About Her": Margery Kempe's Book of Feeling and Working

SUE ELLEN HOLBROOK

When Donald Howard, for his book *Writers and Pilgrims,* turned in 1980 to Margery Kempe's book for the story of the pilgrimage Kempe made from England to Jerusalem, he was disappointed by what he saw. "There is not in her book a scintilla of traveller's curiosity, so we get no bananas, giraffes, or elephants from Margery; not even descriptions of the shrines." Evidently, he had hoped for a tale told by someone with an attractive personality to delight the reader with observations of "distant places," "strange customs," and fellow travelers. But to Howard's mind, Kempe's book is not about her pilgrimages at all—"It is about her." Worse, it was not a "her" he liked: "for she was quite mad—an incurable hysteric with a large paranoid trend." And so, finding that it "offers little that is useful to our purposes," he dismissed the book of Margery Kempe.[1]

In finding Margery Kempe's book to be "about her," Howard is one of many readers in the last half-century to see it as an account of a life. Some share his disgruntlement, but others, even those few who accept the designation "hysteric," such as Hope Phyllis Weissman and Nancy Partner,[2] are less dismissive. In the light of the gender-conscious studies of the last decade, we may find much, rather than little, "that is useful to our purposes." After all, less than a handful of writers known to us from fifteenth-century England are female, and Margery Kempe is the one we know most about. Although we have some archival records, the document that tells us most about Kempe is her book.

It is what Margery Kempe's book tells us about itself, as well as about her, that provides the subject here. My focus is on what I believe to be a foregrounded theme in the text, whether approached as social document or literary work: producing a book of revelations. One of the book's several themes, this one is *a piece* with certain others that relate gender with language in this book. Yet, even with such work pertinent to this topic as Janel Mueller's, Karma Lochrie's, and my own,[3] Kempe's story about writing her revelations has hardly received its due, partly because more ground needs breaking, partly because there is controversy over whether Kempe is the author of a book about herself, and partly because references to making a book tend to be read as background information for an editor's preface rather than as a piece of a textual pattern.

The theme of making a book of "feeling and working" has many aspects, of which some that have been controversial, neglected, or misunderstood will occupy us here. First, we will acknowledge the text's presentation of what has become Book I as a treatise of spiritual guidance "written" by a priest. Second, we will examine the relationship of this priest's two prologues to each other, and then redefine the character of Kempe's authorship. Third, we will consider the book Kempe could have written but declined to, reflect on the danger associated with composing what has become Book I, and then, to see the nature of Kempe's book of revelations more clearly, note briefly how Book I differs from Book II and also how sixteenth-century readers responded to the book of Margery Kempe. Finally, we will return to the attraction of autobiographical readings. The implications of the points to be raised are relevant to the life of Margery Kempe as well as to the book of Margery Kempe. Moreover, some discussion of these points will illumine, I hope, two views unnecessarily obscured by present-day tendencies to look at Margery Kempe's book as autobiography: Margery Kempe as a writer and her book as a treatise with theological content.

"the boke of Margerie Kempe de Lynn"

Although, for reasons to be reviewed later, Margery Kempe's book is generally thought of today as autobiography—indeed, the first autobiography in English,[4] the single manuscript version of the book we have presents itself differently. In the extant manuscript (British Library Additional MS 61823), enscribed by one Salthouse probably not long after 1440,[5] this work begins as a treatise: "Here begynnyth a schort tretys and a comfortabyl" (1). This incipit opens a prologue of five pages by a priest who identifies himself as having written "þis boke," which is followed by another prologue, also by the priest, of about one page; both bear the date 1436. These prologues are followed by eighty-nine chapters (102 folios) brought to a close by the priest's explicit, explaining that he has reached the end of the copy of the treatise from which he has been working. The rubric *"secundus liber"* announces a second book, which turns out to be a continuation initiated by the priest and not referred to as a treatise. In the first of its ten chapters (13 folios), the priest, giving the date as 1438, explains that he will write of events not included in the previous book. The tenth chapter ends with an "Amen." On the next page come prayers attributed to Kempe's use. These are followed by the signature of the manuscript's copyist: "Ihesu mercy quod Salthows."

Nowhere in the Salthouse manuscript does the priest have a name; most of the references to him are in the third person, as "the priest" (or "he") "who wrote this book." Similarly, nowhere in the manuscript does this priest name Margery Kempe as the author of the book he is writing. Within the narrative of Book I, her name does appear in direct address: fifteen times as Margery by friendly figures speaking to her and once as the daughter of John Brunham, Mayor of Lynn, by the Bishop of Worcester. In the continuation, the narrator uses her name just once, there in indirect address ". . . sum dissolute personys, supposyng it was Mar. Kempe of Lynne, seydyn . . ." (II:9, 243). However, the primary term for Kempe throughout the prologues, both books, and the prayers is not her name but "this creature," accompanied therefore by the third-person singular pronouns "she," "her," "herself."[6]

The manuscript text, then, does not present Margery Kempe as an autobiographer, one who tells "my" story in a first-person voice. Rather, the text resounds with many voices: we hear the voice of this creature, the voices of the Lord Jesus Christ, his mother, St. Elizabeth, and the many men and women with whom Kempe interacts, and the discourse of figures in stories and books that Kempe and others quote and paraphrase. We have, furthermore, the voice of a writer, self-consciously contributing information, testimonial, and commentary both about the book he is writing and the events related within that book. And, we have the voice of a narrator, framing episodes, connecting events into a story, carrying the story forward. At times the narrative voice and Kempe's indirect address blend; at times the narrator and the writer share the same voice.

The effects of the third-person narrative style and the pervasive use of the term "this creature" make Kempe's book a text about her, not by her. More specifically, the text is about what this creature, the narrator, and the priest call her revelations and manner of living. The revelations, a term used synonymously with "feelings," are her direct experiences with her Lord Jesus Christ, his mother, and other saints, experiences that come in her contemplation, a term used synonymously with "meditation." Her manner, or form, of living refers both to the content of these revelations and accompanying sensory phenomena and also to practices through which she increases in grace as a contemplative—what we now call a mystic (a term not used in the text). Her revelations and manner of living are threaded by the common theme of contrition and compassion for the Lord Jesus Christ; they make her an example to other Christians of the grace the Lord works in creatures who love him compassionately. The purpose of the book is to give through the example of this creature comfort and guidance to Christians to increase their compassion and awareness of the Saviour's love. When we describe it in its own terms, then, Margery Kempe's book is a treatise, followed by a continuation, both written by a priest about the revelations and manner of living of a creature in whom the Lord Jesus Christ worked his grace.

To acknowledge that Margery Kempe's book is written by a priest is at first disquieting. It seems to give Kempe's words away to male authority. Even if we hasten to substitute "transcribed" for "written" and "scribe" or "amanuensis" for "writer," we may have to see, as several scholars have,[7] that the words on the leaves—not to mention arrangement, themes, details, artistry—are as much his as hers. Nevertheless, by looking at the book in its own proclaimed terms, we will come to understand the particular conditions of its production. Rather than rob Margery Kempe of composing a book, we will uncover a story of the power of literacy in the lives of the disenfranchised.

Writing a Book

References to the making of the book arise periodically throughout the Salthouse version. Not surprisingly, the most informative passages include the prologues to Book I. Beginnings of works, like endings, are conventional places for announcements of purpose, audience, source, identity, and so on. The double prologues to Book I, however, are remarkable not only for their pertinent details but also for their relationship to each other, a relationship that has gone unexamined. The longer prologue is not simply an addition; it is an expansion of the shorter one, and the differences reveal a transformation in the priest's perception of Margery Kempe's project.

The longer of the two prologues is the one we come upon first. It sets out the treatise's audience (p. 1, l. 2), purpose (p. 1, ll. 1–12), and subject matter (p. 1, l. 14–p. 3, l. 15), declares the revelations authentic (p. 3, ll. 8–20), and recounts the circumstances of the book's formation (p. 3, l. 20–p. 5). By his own attestation, the priest composed it in 1436 soon after the shorter prologue, which he dates the "day after Mary Magdalen's day."[8] He tells us that after writing a quire, he wrote another prologue (now the first) in order to express more fully what was in the original prologue, which he had written while strangely unable to see well enough to make his letters or to mend his pen:

> When þe prest began fyrst to wryten on þis booke, hys eyn myssyd so þat he myght not se to make hys lettyr nor mygth se to mend hys penne. Alle oþer thyng he mygth se wel a-now. He sett a peyr of spectacles on hys nose, & þan [it] wast wel wers þan it was be-for. He compleyned to þe creatur of hys dysese. Sche seyd his enmy had envye at hys good dede & wold lett hym yf he mygth & bad hym do as wel as God wold зeue hym grace & not levyn. Whan he cam a-geyn to hys booke, he myth se as wel, hym thowt, as euyr he dede be-for be day-

lyth & be candel-lygth boþe. & for þis cause,whan he had wretyn a qwayr, he addyd a leef þerto, and þan wrot he þis proym to expressyn mor openly þan doth þe next folwyng, whech was wretyn er þan þis. Anno domini m[10]. cccc. xxxvi. (5)

Upon comparing the two prologues, we discover that the "more open expression" of the new prologue means that the priest has expanded the original by providing more details, new information, and also a different perspective. The expanded prologue retains the pieces of information presented by the original prologue, but follows a somewhat different order. Only the expanded prologue refers to the creature's tears and weeping (p. 2, ll. 20–24, p. 3, l. 3, p. 4, ll. 21–22) and to the series of people she consulted to make sure she was not suffering illusions and deceit (p. 3, ll. 8–20). Whereas the original prologue uses only the appellation "our Lord," and that only twice, the expanded prologue makes the terms "Savior," "Christ," "Jesus," and "Holy Ghost" prominent (six instances of combinations of "savior," "Christ," and "Jesus" and eight of "Holy Ghost" as well as eight of "our Lord" alone and five of "God"). Like the original, the expanded prologue presents the priest and the creature in the third person without names, but it revises the vocabulary that describes the contents of the treatise: the treatise is no longer an account of "tribulations" (used twice in the original prologue) as well as "feelings" (used once), but an account of "feelings" and "revelations," "devotions of high meditations," "high contemplations," "speeches," "dalliance," "secret things," and of a "form of living." The creature is no longer merely "drawn" by various afflictions in the grammar of passivity; rather, the Lord Christ Jesus "moves" her.

Furthermore, although both prologues refer to reading and writing the "treatise," the expanded version makes the term "book" prominent, using it fourteen times (in contrast to once in the original prologue). Whereas the original prologue does not indicate by whom or why this treatise should be read, the expanded prologue offers the treatise as an account of Christ's work to comfort and instruct "sinful wretches."

Finally, instead of the original prologue's ten lines about Kempe's first writer and "a" priest (about one-fourth of the whole prologue), the expanded prologue gives seventy-one lines to the book's genesis (about two-thirds of the whole): we learn of three writers (not just two), the first two of whom are secular and the third and only adequate one a priest. We learn of this priest's three tries before being able to write as asked. We learn of a miraculous gradual clarification brought about by this creature as her prayers first enable the priest to read the copy she gave him and second enable him to write a version of it.

Some of the information presented by the expanded account of the book's writing does not exist in the original prologue, and most of it does not exist at all within the chapters of Books I and II: namely, that several clerics offered to write a book of her revelations with their own hands (the original specifies a White Friar), that God finally commanded her to do so (also in the original prologue), that at first she could find no writer (not in the original) and then had first the man whose copy turned out to be unintelligible (also in the original) and second another man who tried to revise the first copy but could not (not in the original), and that at last, with Kempe's help (not in the original), the priest was able both to lead the first writer's copy of her book and to write the book. Evidently, from Kempe's knowledge or his own, the priest has brought forward this extratextual information.

The synopsis of the subject matter, on the other hand, does come directly from the text within Book I. In places the synopsis is so close a paraphrase or a quotation as to suggest that the writer had just finished the relevant chapters. However, the priest makes no mention of Kempe's examinations as a heretic, of her pilgrimages, of her husband, of her white clothing, of her difficulties with a certain Friar Preacher in Lynn, of the content and form of the revelations other than that they included proph- ecies ("secret things that would befall afterwards"), of the healings and conversions to virtue she brought about, or the signs of her grace other than tears—her vocal cries, for instance, go unmentioned. When we trace both the matter and the language the priest uses in telling us what the treatise is about, we discover that the expanded prologue draws selec- tively but largely on Book I:1–18 for its synopsis and perspective on the treatise's purpose and worth. If we accept the priest's statement that he had written a quire before he made the new prologue, we can estimate that he might indeed have copied the equivalent of the first eighteen or so chapters.[9]

By comparing the two prologues, then, we discover that the priest has re-oriented his understanding of the treatise from one about tribulations to a book about revelations inspired by the Holy Ghost, which learned clerics could well have written before now. After four years and three tries at writing this book, the priest "sees" what to do. Taken in human terms, Kempe's frustrating search for a writer and the priest's tepid false starts and mysterious eye trouble, even with spectacles on his nose, may strike us as fictional exaggration setting the right atmosphere for a book of divine encounters or as an amusing anecdote about the perils of the illiterate. But both the metaphor and the sequence are excruciatingly apt. The expanded prologue demonstrates a transformation that is all part of the story, a story that preserves for priests, not lay writers, authority over the legible word. That Margery Kempe knew how to use that authority to legitimate her book will become apparent as we pursue the questions of who wrote what and how.

From the various passages that refer to the book's evolution, several points emerge to suggest an ampler picture of authorship than the usual one implied by the assertion that Kempe was an illiterate woman who dictated to scribes.[10] First, let us distinguish, as the book does, between the "treatise" that the priest copied into "this little book" beginning in 1436 and *"secundus liber,"* the continuation that he took upon himself to write in 1438. The treatise is framed by references to its making: the priest's two prologues at the beginning and descriptions of its writing in the final two chapters. This treatise is the book at stake, and the suggestive points about its authorship are the following.

One, it is Kempe who selected the experiences to include and the order for them, and who insists on telling them as she remembers them. In chapter 83, Kempe explains that she did not always remember everything about her revelations long after experiencing them (201–2). Unlike Catherine of Siena and Birgitta of Sweden, each of whom had her revelation recorded at the time of its occurrence,[11] Kempe worked entirely from memory. Her writer recorded matters in the order of this remembering process. The original prologue simply says that the priest began to write "aftyr þe informacyon of þis creatur" (6), but the expanded prologue contains this passage: "Thys boke is not wretyn in ordyr, euery thyng aftyr oþer as it wer don, but lych as þe mater cam to þe creatur in mend whan it schuld be wretyn, for it was so long er it was wretyn þat sche had for-getyn þe tyme & þe ordyr whan thyngys befellyn. And þerfor sche dede no þing wryten but þat sche knew rygth wel for very trewth" (5).

Two, it is Kempe who helps with the revision by correcting it against her knowledge of what the text should say. When the priest is finally able to read the first version before beginning the work of writing it over, "he red it ouyr be-forn þis creatur euery word, sche sum-tym helpyng where ony difficulte was" (5).

Three, it is Kempe who decides to write the book. All the momentous decisions in this book pertain to revelations and manner of living and therefore are formulated in terms of the Lord's directives; just so this one: "And many ȝerys aftyr sche was bodyn in hyr spyrit for to wrytyn," says the original prologue (6); "Aftyrward, whan it plesyd ower Lord, he comawnded hyr & chargyd hir þat sche xuld don wryten hyr felyngys & reuelacyons & þe forme of her leuyng," says the expanded prologue (3–4). What is significant is the explanation that precedes this reference to the onset of the book's writing: Kempe's refusal of offers made earlier. According to the original prologue, "þis creatur had greet cownsel for to don wryten hir tribulacyons & hir felingys, and a Whyte Frer proferyd hir to wryten frely yf sche wold. And sche was warnyd in hyr spyrit þat sche xuld not wryte so sone" (6). According to the expanded prologue, it is "worthy & worshepful clerkys" who opportune her, but she refuses even

those who "proferyd hir to wrytyn hyr felyngys wyth her owen handys, &
sche wold not consentyn in no wey, for sche was comawndyd in hir sowle
þat sche schuld not wrytyn so soone" (3). The moment at which Kempe
decided to write is referred to only in the priest's prologues; it did not
become the topic of a colloquy described in the text. But, in an encounter
we will consider again in the next section, her refusal to write the book
upon someone else's prompting, namely that of Bishop Philip Repyngton
in 1413, is described: "He . . . commendyd gretly hir felyngys & hir
contemplacyons, seyyng þei wer hy maters & ful deuowt maters & en-
spyred of þe Holy Gost, cownselyng hir sadly þat hir felyngys schuld be
wrteyn. & sche seyd þat it was Goddys wyl þat thei schuld be wretyn so
soon, ne þei wer wretyn xx ᴣer aftyr & mor" (34).

Finally, it is Kempe who organized the book's production. She searched
for, housed, paid, or otherwise prevailed upon writers. According to the
expanded prologue (4–5), when she decided the time was right, it turned
out that at first she had "no writer þat wold fulfyllyn hyr desyr ne ᴣeue
credens to hir felingys." The first writer she found was living in Germany;
exactly how he learned of her desire for a writer is not specified, but he
comes "wyth hys wyfe & hys goodys & dwellyd wyth þe forseyd creatur
tyl he had wretyn as mech as sche wold tellyn hym for þe tym þat þey wer
to-gydder." Chapter 88 also describes this writer working with Kempe in
her chamber at home (216).

After his death, she "communed" with the priest, someone she felt
"gret affecyon to," and "browt hym þe boke to redyn." Unable to read it
because the language was neither good English nor good German and
because the handwriting was so poor, the priest nevertheless promised
"þat if he cowd redyn it he wolde copyn it owt & wrytyn it betyr wyth
good wylle." The priest, however, procrastinated because he was too
cowardly to be associated with her during this period, when her weeping
was causing people to say evil things about her. She "cryed often on hym"
during the next four or so years. But imploration was not enough. In
chapter 24, in a story that has gone unappreciated, amusing yet appalling
in what it displays about power, the priest admits that he actually threatened not to write her book if she did not forecast the consequences of
various things, and afraid that he would not, she does something she
normally will not do, deliver prophecies on demand:

The prest whech wrot þis boke for to preuyn þis creaturys felyngys many tymes
& dyuers tymes he askyd hir qwestyons & demawndys of thyngys þat wer for to
komyn, vn-seker & vncerteyn as þat tyme to any creatur what xuld be þe ende,
preyng hir, þei sche wer loth & not wylly to do swech thyngys, for to prey to
God þerfor & wetyn, what owyr Lord wold visiten hir wyth deuocyon, what
xuld be þe ende, and trewly wyth-owtyn any feynyng tellyn hym how sche felt,
& ellys wold he not gladlych a wretyn þe boke. And so þis creatur, sumdel for

drede þat he wold ellys not a folwyd hir entent for to wryten þis boke, com-
pellyd, dede as he preyd hir. . . . (55)

When asking and even prophecying failed, Kempe approached a third
writer "a good man" the priest recommended as someone familiar with
the first scribe's writing. To this man she paid "a grett summe of good for
hys labowr" and also asked him not to reveal the book while she was alive.
But even money does not work; this scribe managed to write only "a-bowt
a leef" because the book was so badly written. Finally, the priest felt guilty
about reneging on his promise "to wrytyn þis boke, зyf he mygth com to
þe redyng þerof," so, at his request, she "gat a-geyn þe book & browt it to
þe preste." This time she did not rely on an affectionate relationship, on
requests and implorations, on prophecies, or on money. She purchased his
services all right, but through prayer: "preyng hym to hys good wyl, and
sche schuld prey to God for hym & purchasyn hym grace to reden it &
wryteyn it also." As we have seen in our discussion of the expanded
prologue, this contract succeeds.

In these several ways—deciding when to have the book made, selecting
the material, overseeing the revision, and organizing the production
through a variety of resources and contractual arrangements—the text
represents Margery Kempe as the chief maker of the book: she is its writer
in the essential modern sense of the word.

Of "felyng & werkyng"

A layer in the evolution of the book that became the treatise lies folded
in the story of Margery Kempe's visit with Philip Repyngton, the Bishop of
Lincoln, in August 1413. Repyngton is one in a series of "goddys
seruawntys" and "many worthy clerkys, doctorys of dyuynty, & bach-
elers" whom Kempe visits in order to discern whether her revelations are
authentic (I:12, p. 25). While she is with Repyngton, she also asks him to
authenticate the vow of celibacy she and her husband had made between
them on Midsummer Eve; moreover, she wants Repyngton to give her
permission to wear a mantle, ring, and white clothes, presumably to mark
her change in status from a wife in a sexual relationship with her husband
to a wife who is celibate. Repyngton authenticates her revelations and the
contract of celibacy, but instead of permission for the mantle, ring, and
white clothes, he gives her money, advises her to wait until she is better
known, and sends her on to ask a higher authority, the Archbishop of
Canterbury. Nevertheless, despite his caution, in the earlier course of their
private discussion, as we have heard, he urges Kempe to have her "feelings" written.

What did Repyngton, who had once had to abjure his Lollard beliefs and who at the time of Kempe's visit was clearly nervous about the white clothing, suppose a book of Kempe's revelations would be like? He approved of her revelations and of her responses to his learned counselors (see pp. 34–35), but was not a man to take risks.[12] An experiment in hypothesizing what the Bishop's book would have contained will keep our eyes on the theology of Kempe's experiences and also make two other points: it underscores Kempe's reticence to publicize her revelations, and it reminds us that the book ultimately to come to us was not inevitable in form, content, or even existence.

To uncover the experiences that might have appealed to Repyngton, we need to reconstruct the chronology of events occurring during the years before Margery and John Kempe visit him; this reconstruction shows the following: Kempe has experienced two or three of the sensory phenomena she later has: a melody (which marks her conversion, chapter 3); weeping (first tears of compunction, then of compassion), and possibly a burning sensation (the "ardor of love" mentioned in chapter 13). She has been the subject of a miracle of healing (chapter 9); she has witnessed a marvel in conjunction with a revelation about the book of Birgitta of Sweden (chapter 20); and she has had some colloquies with the Lord and Mary, prophetic revelations, and visions. Among the several oral divine communiques and dialogues, she has been commanded to leave off her hair shirt, fast, and receive meditations (chapter 5), been assured that she is a pillar of the church (chapter 13), and been guaranteed that the Lord loves her as much as maidens (chapter 22). The prophetic revelations (or premonitions) have been about women and men in the community (chapters 18–19, 23), pertaining in several instances to who is going to live or die.

Most important, perhaps, are the visions, that is, revelations in a distinctly pictorial mode. We have descriptions of eight belonging to the time preceding Kempe's visit with Repyngton. Kempe's very first revelation is a vision of the Lord Jesus Christ, who "aperyd . . . in lyknesse of a man," sitting on her bedside, clad in purple silk, and then stepping up into the air (chapter 1, p. 8). At a later time, she has a sequence of meditations in which she sees St. Anne give birth to Mary, goes with Mary (pregnant with God) and Joseph to Elizabeth, sees Elizabeth give birth to John the Baptist, goes with Mary to Bethlehem for the birth of Jesus and the arrival of the three wise men, and finally accompanies the holy family into Egypt (chapters 6–7). During this sequence, she participates in Anne's service, taking charge of Mary until the Mother of God is twelve, and then acts as Mary's handmaid, making detailed arrangements for lodging and the care of the baby. Finally, Kempe describes in a sequence five other detailed visions that belong to these early years (the last of which seems to belong to the end of the sequence just iterated): namely, an angel bearing the Book of Life in which Kempe's name is written at the foot of the Trinity, the Lord Jesus Christ being scourged, the Lord's body being cut by a knife, the Lord standing so near her that she is able to touch his toes, and Our Lady showing her baby Jesus (chapter 85).

Although spoken revelations, notably the dialogues, seem to dominate Book I, especially in those portions concerned with events during and after Kempe's pilgrimage to Jerusalem and Rome, visual revelations are also described or mentioned (with words referring to sight) throughout this book, including the portions presenting the post-Jerusalem period (see chapters 59, 73, 74, 78–81, 82). However, the earliest sequence described (chapters 6–7) and the latest (chapter 78–81) differ in content. Whereas the sequences described extensively in chapters 78–81, which are accompanied by vocal cries as well as tears, narrate the Passion, the earliest sequence concentrates on the Annunciation and Nativity, or holy motherhood.[13] During the pre-Jerusalem period, of course, Kempe was still bearing children,[14] a fact conditioning her form of empathetic participation.

According to the text, Kempe's early and "less subtle" spiritual understanding, which focused on the Manhood of Christ, is succeeded by a higher understanding of the Godhead, which first occurs in Rome in her marriage to God (chapter 35). It is not clear, however, that all of the revelations in the post-Jerusalem and post-Rome period, whether seen or spoken, signify the "subtle and more high" understanding of the Godhead. Nevertheless, it is clear that at the time Kempe speaks with Repyngton, she has achieved just the lesser understanding, the Manhood of Christ.

When Kempe "shows" Repyngton "hyr medytacyons, & hy contemplacyons, & oþer secret thyngys boþe of qwyk & of ded as owyr Lord schewyd to hir sowle" (pp. 33–34), we may be certain from the language that he hears about the prophetic revelations, those pertaining to who lived and who died, "of quick and of dead." These, however, are too local for the Bishop of Lincoln to deem of interest to a wider readership—no popes and kings here, just widows and priests in Lynn. More likely, Repyngton is taken with the visions of the Manhood of Christ in which Kempe has imagined her participation. If such visions had been recorded in 1413, by learned doctors of the church, as the prologues claim they could have been, Kempe's book of feelings would have been quite different from the treatise she finally composed. This early book of feelings would not have described the vocal cries, which so disturbed Kempe's community. There would have been no account of the sacred (or profane) experiences of Kempe's pilgrimage to the Holy Land, such as the astonishing, if not unique, marriage to the Lord. Nor would there have been descriptions of the trial and persecution for heresy and the controversy stirred by the Friar Preacher in Lynn. And there would not have been the extensive colloquies. Instead the Bishop's book of Margery's feelings would have displayed only empathetic visual meditations on the Manhood of Christ accompanied by tears of compassion. Such visual meditations were in the Bonaventurean mode promoted by Nicholas Love's *Mirror of the Life of Christ*. Such tears, however noisome to neighbors, were a conventional sign of grace: tears are the one manifestation of religious enthusiasm allowed by the author of the *Chastising of God's Children*.[15] Such a book might have been quite useful to cautious men like Repyngton.

By saying no to a bishop, Margery Kempe may have missed a chance to have her divine revelations become the subject of learned doctors whose prose record might even have been in Latin. The motivation behind her refusal was evidently fear of spiritual deceit (and political manipulation). Eventually, she became convinced that her feelings were authentic, yet the conditions in which the book finally began were pervaded with secrecy. Her sense of danger demands notice.

Before Kempe composed her book of feelings, many people had seen her weep, heard her cry, conversed with her about holy matters, known of her premonitions, and been affected by her acts of reform and healing. But only to a select few had she shown openly or in part her high contemplations. By making a book of her revelations, however, she was making public what she had kept secret for thirty-five or more years—not that old sin she never did confess to us (chapter 1), but the feelings and workings that were her visions and dalliances. Indeed, the information in the expanded prologue that she exacted a promise from the middle scribe not to reveal her book while she was alive indicates that while she was first writing the book, she did so in secret.[16]

By matching the expanded prologue's references with the chapters narrating the relevant period, we see that Kempe undertakes the project in an atmosphere of suspicion and divided community. Her search for a writer probably begins circa 1425, during the controversy fired by the Friar Preacher (chapter 61–69) and fanned as well no doubt by the prosecution of heretics in Norfolk.[17] Despite the loyalty of her principal confessor, Robert Springold, and also Master Alan, Kempe has been segregated from the rest of the community, forced to worship in isolation, and prevented from hearing sermons. By his superior's orders, even Master Alan has been prohibited from communicating with her (chapter 69). By the mid-1420s Kempe's vocal cries have ceased, but the parishoners and some of the clergy continue to be hostile, now calling her a hypocrite because she no longer cries. In this atmosphere of linguistic oppression, secrecy is an appropriate precaution.

As the text has displayed in a series of cycles, Margery Kempe sought to understand spiritual matters, to study them, to become informed by the reading and hearing of such matters, to discuss them, to communicate them, and ultimately to write of them. But she lived in a time and place and was of a gender and a class that gave expressions of desire for such understanding the potential for heresy. Her practice of wearing white clothes and travelling without her husband brought suspicion of other heresy. Her tears, cries, and other physical manifestations brought suspicion of diabolic possession, disease, and hypocrisy. Her knowledge of spiritual matters and adamant teaching of others brought accusations of heretical Lollardy and risk to her life. What would a book of her revelations bring?

Margery Kempe's book of feeling and working did emerge from secrecy to a reading public. Although little understood, the second book is one sign of this triumph; its nature also throws the first book into relief. In the prologue to *secundus liber,* the priest defines his stance as the initiator of a continuation, begun in 1438 on the Feast of St. Vital Martyr, i.e., 28 April probably to celebrate the admission of Margery Kempe to the Trinity Guild in Lynn on 13 April 1438. His source is Kempe's spoken account, and his subject is "sweche grace as owr Lord wrowt in hys sympyl creatur" (I:1, p. 221). This grace is primarily prophetic revelations and secondarily the gift of tears, and the priest displays these signs of grace in two stories having the chronological and thematic tie of "coming home in safety." The continuation differs from the treatise in several ways, of which we should particularly note the absence of descriptions of visual meditations and the absence of extended revelations in which we hear Kempe in colloquy with the Lord, Mary, or other saints. It is especially in those colloquies, or "dalliances," that the treatise set forth the issues of, for instance, the discernment of spirits, the conduct by which to achieve a meditative state, the distinction between contemplations on Christ's Manhood and on the Godhead, the meaning of the Trinity, what possibility for holiness there is for married, child-bearing women, and the meaning of the sensory phenomena. The contrast between the signs of grace in the continuation and those in the treatise ought to become of interest as research widens on the content and form of Kempe's revelations. For instance, the extant organization of the two books in the Salthouse manuscript may or may not reflect a steady chronological pattern to Kempe's spiritual development,[18] but the text does report or display changes in that experience. Thus, both as our hypothetical reconstruction of Bishop Philip Repyngton's book and as the priest's continuation indicate, a book produced at a different moment in Kempe's life might well have been quite different from the book she eventually brought forth.

The book Margery Kempe did give to her contemporaries elicited serious and diverse interest both among the enclosed and unenclosed. One source testifying to its impact is the set of red annotations made on the Salthouse manuscript itself by a Carthusian monk working in the priory of Mount Grace in Yorkshire after 1527. This annotator provides an abundant series of responses (running throughout both books) that include the problem of being a contemplative when one is also a wife, the passionate quality and marital form of Kempe's spiritual relationship to the Lord, the visions and all the sensory manifestations of communion with God, and the similarity between Kempe's experiences and those of Father Richard Methley of Mount Grace, Prior John Norton also of Mount Grace, and Richard Rolle of Hampole. This annotator clearly found the enthusiastic devotion of a particular woman attractive.[19]

Another testimonial to the reception of Margery Kempe's book is the short version of it published by Wynkyn de Worde circa 1501, which provides a wholly divergent reading. Called in the incipit "a shorte treatyse of contemplacyon taught by our lorde Jhesu cryste / or taken out of the boke of Margerie Kempe de Lynn," this text consists of an arrangement of painstakingly chosen passages from Book I that presents the following point: women should turn away from willing martyrdom, acts of penance, or other violent and public demonstrations of their love of Christ and instead commune with Christ in silence through the forms of thought and private prayer, tears of compassion, and endurance of rebuke in patience. The compiler of the "shorte treatyse of contemplacyon" seems to have wanted to show that despite its radical and enthusiastic themes, Book I contained a message from which he thought laywomen and their religious counsellors would benefit. Wynkyn de Worde, setting up his new press in London, evidently saw the utility of this treatise for his readers. He issued it by itself as a practical manual for contemplation in a quarto format with a woodcut of the Crucifixion; among his publications it has a niche with vernacular books about the contemplative life and especially with books, in English or Latin, related to the vital mysticism represented by the Carthusians and Bridgettines.[20] Henry Pepwell also perceived such utility when in 1521 he issued an anthology of contemplative treatises in which Kempe stands side by side with Walter Hilton and Catherine of Siena.

"& of hir-selfe þt had al þis tretys in felyng & werkyng"

The short treatise of contemplation taken from the book of Margery Kempe of Lynn, in the version published by de Worde and then Pepwell, gives us a visionary woman author to reclaim and a vernacular devotional text to study. With the recovery of the Salthouse manuscript, we also have an account of a life. For medieval readers, that account was still a treatise of contemplation, but since 1936, when the owner of the manuscript, W.

Butler-Bowden, published a modernized version, readers have approached Margery Kempe's book as autobiography or biography. Alternation between calling it "biography" and "autobiography" depends on issues of generic definition, authorial proprietorship, or veracity, that is, in general, how scholars resolve the problem of Kempe's scribes.[21] Whether they view it as biography or autobiography, the chief characteristics that readers respond to include the relative amount of social, even personal, information and quotidian detail; the fact that there is a story line with ample and vivid dialogue between people (and not just Kempe and the Lord) and accounts of events in profane time and space; the retrospective cast to the narrative (for she speaks about the past as she remembers it from a point in the present); and the fact that every event told involves Kempe. More important, especially to feminist readers, the book has also seemed to be autobiography because it is concerned with explaining, or at least displaying, the development of the speaking subject's identity or of her inner life.

Feminists have inherited the claim, probably from R. W. Chambers, whose interest was a nationalistic one in the English language, that *The Book of Margery Kempe* is biography or autobiography and the first in English.[22] To label a devotional treatise a "memoir" or "autobiography" can trivialize it. However, the recent feminist interest in autobiography is motivated differently. For feminists reacting to the surge of modernist interest in men's autobiography among literary critics in the 1970s, *The Book of Margery Kempe* comes readily to hand, as the work of Mary Mason and Domna Stanton exemplifies.[23] Furthermore, as part of the revalorization of social constructs of the feminine, there is a feminist interest in theorizing the personal. The concreteness and focus on herself that have repelled some earlier readers of Kempe's book now make it an attractive object of study. Adding women's writings to the canon, finding a tradition of women's writing, exploring differences between men's and women's writing, studying representations of femininity in texts by women as well as by men, locating stories of "strong" women, locating medieval women at all—for all these transformative activities in the academy *The Book of Margery Kempe* does great service.[24]

Yet, a book so richly autobiographical as this one has an ambiguous status as an object of scholarly occupation: is it the book or the life that engages us? Historians claim Margery Kempe for themselves, letting textual representation melt away, leaving only facts. If Kempe were not so effective a story teller and if she and her priest-writer had not found so many particulars about her life to be relevant to the record of her feeling and working, we might be less taken with the autobiographical cast. But the long version of Margery Kempe's book is not just a repository of facts for social and literary historians. The relationship between a life as lived and a life as recalled, narrated, and arranged in a book is an intricate and fascinating one. Elizabeth Petroff's anthology provides the beginning context for comparative work among visionary women writers that an earlier feminist, Hope Emily Allen, had hoped to see a half-century ago, while the work of Hope Phyllis Weissman, Sheila Delaney, David Wallace, Janel Mueller, and David Aers,[25] among others, indicates a variety of fruitful explicatory approaches to the patterning and style of the text in relation to the life. As we continue to explore the relationship between the style of the text and of the life as well as the style of the text and its ideas (or theology), with diverse, possibly even contradictory approaches, we should be able to move beyond the declaration that *The Book of Margery Kempe* is the first autobiography in English. By itself that is a fact of minimal interest, valuable information only so long as "autobiography" or "English" is what we are looking for. It does, however, form a starting point for asking how self-representation in written words works or how this book, which tells us so much about *itself,* came to be "the first autobiography" in English, and how it was that a merchant-class woman could be not only its subject but its author.

By concentrating on the theme of producing a book of revelations, I have tried in this essay to direct our attention to Margery Kempe as someone more than a gifted raconteur who led an adventurous life or a case study in hysteria, to Margery Kempe as a writer, a female writer in a context bound by John Gerson's dictum that "All words and works of women must be held suspect."[26] Such questions as how in this context Kempe was able to develop a discourse for talking about the love of God remain for future exploration. Here my argument has been, in part, that producing a book of her revelations—not just receiving them, not even just sharing them with authorities or a few special people in conversation— became extremely important to Margery Kempe, that it was a daring act and a difficult one, but through the use of a range of resources in combination with fortuitous circumstances, she did succeed. There are many instances of the frustration and then the empowerment of language in the book of Margery Kempe, of which the book's own story is one.

Notes

1. Donald R. Howard, *Writers and Pilgrims* (Berkeley and Los Angeles: Univ. of California Press, 1980), pp. 35, 28, 34–35.
2. Phyllis Hope Weissman, "Margery Kempe in Jerusalem: *Hysterica Compassio* in the Late Middle Ages," in *Acts of Interpretation: The Text in Its Contexts, 700–1600; Essays on Medieval and Renaissance Literature in Honor of E. Talbot Donaldson,* ed. Mary J. Carruthers and Elizabeth D. Kirk (Norman, Okla.: Pilgrim Books, 1982), pp. 201–17; Nancy Partner, " 'And Most of All for Inordinate Love': Desire and Denial in *The Book of Margery Kempe,*" in *Gender*

and the Moral Order in Medieval Society, ed. Thelma S. Fenster. *Thought* 64 (September 1989): 254–67.

3. Janel M. Mueller, "Autobiography of a New 'Creatur': Female Spirituality, Selfhood, and Authorship in *The Book of Margery Kempe*," in *Women in the Middle Ages and the Renaissance: Literary and Historical Perspectives,* ed. Mary Beth Rose (Syracuse, N.Y.: Syracuse Univ. Press, 1986), pp. 155–71; Karma Lochrie, "The Book of Margery Kempe: The Marginal Woman's Quest for Literary Authority," *Journal of Medieval and Renaissance Studies* 16 (1986): 33–55; Sue Ellen Holbrook, "Order and Coherence in *The Book of Margery Kempe,*" in *Worlds of Medieval Women: Creativity, Influence, and Imagination,* ed. Constance H. Berman, Charles W. Connell, and Judith Rice Rothschild (Morgantown: West Virginia Univ. Press, 1985), 97–110.

4. See, for example, R. W. Chambers, introduction to *The Book of Margery Kempe,* ed. W. Butler-Bowden (1936; reprinted, World's Classics, 1954) ("The book is a biography, or autobiography," p. xv); David Knowles, *The Religious Orders in England* vol. 2 (1955; reprinted, Cambridge: Cambridge Univ. Press, 1979), who calls it "her autobiography"; Joan Goulianos, ed. *By a Woman writt: Literature from Six Centuries by and about Women* (Indianapolis: Bobbs-Merrill, 1973) ("It is the first known extant autobiography in English," p. 3); Clarissa W. Atkinson, *Mystic and Pilgrim: the* Book *and the World of Margery Kempe* (Ithaca: Cornell Univ. Press, 1983) ("Hers is the first autobiography in English," p. 36); Jonathan Z. Kamholtz and Robin Sheets, "Women Writers and the Survey of English Literature: A Proposal and Annotated Bibliography for Teachers," *College English* 46 (1984): 278–300, who call it an "autobiography of contemporary of Juliana who copes with politics, social class, and a husband as well as mysticism," p. 289; and Elizabeth Alvida Petroff, ed. *Medieval Women's Visionary Literature* (New York: Oxford Univ. Press, 1986) ("She invented the first autobiography in English," p. 301).

5. On Salthouse (possibly from Lynn) and the date of the manuscript, see Sanford Brown Meech and Hope Emily Allen, eds. *The Book of Margery Kempe,* EETS O.S. 212 (1940; reprinted, London: Oxford Univ. Press, 1961), pp. xxxiii–xxxv. Citations will be to this edition. The manuscript does not bear a title.

6. The third person and the epithet "this creature" may be Kempe's own usage as she dictated (as assumed, for example, by Susan Dickman, "Margery Kempe and the Continental Tradition of the Pious Woman," in *The Medieval Mystical Tradition in England,* edited by Marion Glasscoe [Cambridge: D. S. Brewer, 1984], pp. 150–68 and Atkinson, *Mystic and Pilgrim,* p. 21). But Kempe may have composed in the first person; the third-person may be the conversion of scribes. Vestigial first-person singular pronouns occur (pp. 4, 14, 44, and 230). Meech and Allen assume that these instances of "I" are Kempe speaking, but in context they are as likely to be the writer's, most certainly so on page 4, which is part of the first prologue. Two instances of first-person plural are also suggestive: one (p. 34) is obviously Margery Kempe's, but the other (p. 71) could well be the writer's.

7. Meech and Allen, *The Book of Margery Kempe;* William Matthews, ed., *Later Medieval English Prose* (New York: Appleton-Century-Crofts, 1963); Hirsch, "Author and Scribe in *The Book of Margery Kempe,*" *Medium Aevum* 44 (1975): 145–47; Anthony Goodman, "The Piety of John Brunham's Daughter of Lynn," in *Medieval Women,* edited by Derek Baker (Oxford: Basil Blackwell, 1978), pp. 347–58; and Atkinson, *Mystic and Pilgrim.*

8. Atkinson is mistaken in thinking the priest writes this prologue when he "began to write Book II at Margery's dictation" (*Mystic and Pilgrim,* p. 30).

Mueller, "Autobiography of a New 'Creatur'," assumes the "preface" was written by the first scribe, whom she assumes died in 1436 (p. 55), but the wording of the first prologue assigns the prologues to the priest; the first writer was not a priest at all, for he had a wife and child (p. 4).

9. In the Salthouse manuscript, the first (expanded) prologue occupies two-and-a-half leaves (five pages), not one. The length of the text through chapter 18 could be sufficient for a quire (technically, 12 or 16 folios). We should note, in this regard, that as of chapter 16, Lynn, previously designated as "N." for *nomen* (name), is named explicitly for the first time, and that chapter 18 looks as if it should end before the first widow story (p. 45, 1.2). Some change in the priest's activity may be indicated.

10. For presumptions of Kempe's illiteracy, see, for example, Anthony Goodman, "The Piety of John Brunham's Daughter of Lynn"; Atkinson, *Mystic and Pilgrim*, pp. 13, 18, but also 25; and David Wallace, "Mystics and Followers in Siena and East Anglia: A Study in Taxonomy, Class, and Cultural Mediation," in *The Medieval Mystical Tradition in England*, ed. Marion Glasscoe (Cambridge: D. S. Brewer, 1984), p. 184. Elsewhere I will present evidence for a revised conception of Kempe's state of literacy.

11. Catherine of Siena's secretaries took down in Italian the words she spoke in Tuscan while she was receiving her revelation; see Phyllis Hodgson and Gabriel M. Liegey, eds., *The Orcherd of Syon*, EETS. O.S. 258 (London: Oxford Univ. Press, 1966), pp. vi–vii. Birgitta of Sweden, using Swedish, either wrote her revelation down for herself or dictated it immediately after receiving it. A confessor then translated the Swedish into Latin and read it over to her; a copy was then sent to the person who occasioned the revelation, and a copy was also recorded in a book (Alfonso's redaction); see Sancta Birgitta, *Revelaciones Book I*, ed. Carl-Gustaf Undhagen (Stockholm: Almquist and Wiksell International, 1977), pp. 2–25.

12. On Repyngton, see Meech and Allen, *Book of Margery Kempe*, pp. 273–74, n. 33/24–25.

13. The vision beginning in chapter 82 occurs on Purification Day and belongs in content to the early emphasis on holy motherhood, but because of the vocal cries described, it belongs in chronology to the decade after Jerusalem. The sequence in chapter 85 includes three scenes that belong to the Passion. One of them includes the details that "And þan cam on wyth a baselard-knyfe to hir syght & kytt þat precyows body al on long in þe brest." Both that vision and the one that follows, in which Kempe sees Christ so near her that she touches his toes, resemble in perspective two illuminations in the Hours of Catharine of Cleves, namely, the Saturday Mass of the Virgin, in which Mary watches the Crucifixion, and the Ascension for the Vespers hour in the Hours of the Virgin sequence, in which Mary looks up at Christ's feet, which are just above her head. It is the Marian perspective that is notable.

14. Using a psychohistorical approach, Weissman argues that at Jerusalem Kempe's spiritual experience is being realized as childbirth—weeping, writhing, and loud cries are the accompaniments of labor ("Margery Kempe in Jerusalem," pp. 210–15).

15. On tears in *The Chastising of God's Children*, which was composed circa 1382, apparently for a particular house of religious women, see Joyce Bazire and Eric Colledge, eds., *The Chastising of God's Children* (Oxford: Oxford Univ. Press, 1957), p. 60. According to the editors of Julian of Norwich's *Book of Showings*, Julian's words to Kempe repeat the first chapter of *The Chastising of God's Children* (*A Book of Showings to the Anchoress Julian of Norwich*, ed. Eric

Colledge and James Walsh [Toronto: Pontifical Institute of Medieval Studies, 1978], pp. 36–37); citing Paul and Jerome, Julian assures Kempe that tears come from the Holy Ghost and not evil spirits (chapter 18, pp. 42–43).

On meditation on the Passion as "the heart of Margery Kempe's spirituality," the influence on Kempe of the *Meditationes Vitae Christi,* especially in Love's English translation, and "the polemic against Lollard teaching" that Love's translation provided, see Wallace, "Mystics and Followers," pp. 179–82. Denise Despres, "Franciscan Spirituality: Margery Kempe and Visual Meditation," *Mystics Quarterly* 12 (1986): 12–18, also situates Kempe in the Franciscan tradition of imaginative meditation for laypeople, which placed "imaginative visualization and extemporaneous creation of sacred scenes" in the narrative framework of Christ's life (13, 15).

16. The anonymity that prevails in Kempe's book may be influenced by the secrecy in which she kept her revelations and first wrote her book. Indeed, the secrecy may condition the minimalism and unspecificity that Mueller notes in the design of the early blocks of narrative in Kempe's "autobiography."

17. Evidence for the date of Kempe's search is too complex to be summarized here, but an important indicator is Kempe's cries. When Kempe is writing, she no longer has her vocal cries (see, e.g., chapter 89, p. 219); their cessation occurs during certain events that date to the early 1420s, such as the fire in Lynn and Wavering's sermon. On heretics in Norfolk in the mid-1420s, see M. D. Lambert, *Medieval Heresy: Popular Movements from Bogomil to Hus* (London: Edward Arnold, 1977), Appendix D.

18. See John C. Hirsch, "Author and Scribe in *The Book of Margery Kempe"*; Holbrook, "Order and Coherence"; Mueller, "Autobiography of a New 'Creatur'"; Petroff, *Medieval Women's Visionary Literature.*

19. See Holbrook, "Margery Kempe and Wynkyn de Worde," in *The Medieval Mystical Tradition in England,* Exeter Symposium IV, ed. Marion Glasscoe (Cambridge: D. S. Brewer, 1987), pp. 27–46.

20. Ibid.

21. See, for example, Wayne Shumaker, *English Autobiography: Its Emergence, Materials, and Form* (Berkeley and Los Angeles: Univ. of California Press, 1954), pp. 12–13; Matthews, *Later Medieval English Prose,* p. 41, "Author and Scribe," p. 147–48; Goodman, "The Piety of John Brunham's Daughter of Lynn," p. 349; Atkinson, *Mystic and Pilgrim,* p. 30.

22. In his introduction to *The Book of Margery Kempe* in the modernized version made by the owner of the manuscript, W. Butler-Bowden (which preceded the Meech and Allen edition for the EETS), Chambers refers to the book as "a biography, or autobiography" (p. xv) but also as "a continuous biography" (p. xvii), and asserts that its "great interest" is that "it is our first extant prose narrative in English on a large scale" (p. xvii). Butler-Bowden's prefatory note openly treats *The Book of Margery Kempe* as autobiography.

23. Mary Grimley Mason and Carol Hurd Green, eds., *Journeys: Autobiographical Writings by Women* (Boston: G. K. Hall, 1979); Mason, "The Other Voice: Autobiographies of Women Writers," in *Autobiography: Essays Theoretical and Critical,* ed. James Olney (Princeton: Princeton Univ. Press, 1980), pp. 207–35; and Domna C. Stanton, "Autogynography: Is the Subject Different?" in *Female Autograph,* ed. Stanton (Chicago: Univ of Chicago Press, 1984), pp. 3–20.

24. On the problems and attractions of the very notion of "finding a female tradition," see Mary Eagleton, ed., *Feminist Literary Theory: A Reader* (Oxford: Basil Blackwell, 1986), pp. 1–4; on the various "plots" in feminist theoretical

activities in general, see Paula A. Treichler, "Teaching Feminist Theory," in *Theory in the Classroom,* ed. Cary Nelson (Urbana: Univ. of Illinois Press, 1986), pp. 57–128; on feminist interest in autobiography, see Stanton, "Autogynography: Is the Subject Different?"

25. Weissman, "Margery Kempe in Jerusalem"; Sheila Delany, *Writing Woman* (New York: Schocken, 1983); Wallace, "Mystics and Followers"; Mueller, "Autobiography of a New 'Creatur' "; David Aers, *Community, Gender, and Individual Identity* (London: Routledge, 1988).

26. Hodgson, *"The Orcherd of Syon,"* p. 238.

Scriptura Rescripta: The (Ab)use of the Bible by Medieval Writers

GEORGE H. BROWN

It is now a truism that for most medieval writers, as for most people of the time, the Bible stood paramount as an inexhaustible source of wisdom, history, narrative and fact. It was the potent authority, recognized by all and known well by many, which could be called upon in nearly any context for authorization, sanction, justification, and confirmation. In summarizing the consensus of scholars about the pervading influence of the Bible in every aspect of medieval culture, Lawrence Besserman resorts to simile:

> To begin by trying to assess the place of the Bible in medieval culture is like trying to apprehend the oxygen in the air we breathe. In the liturgy, in proverbs and idioms of common speech, in the language of the law and of political thought, through dramatic performances in churchyards and in village squares, in the art of the cathedrals and of parish churches, for the high born and low born alike, the Bible was everywhere; it was a constant component of the mental life of medieval men and women. Throughout the European Middle Ages it was regarded as the sole irrefutably true source of history, wisdom, and doctrine, a guide to proper actions and procedures in all the domains of human endeavor.[1]

The careful reader of medieval literature recognizes that the Bible influences the text in various degrees of proximity and remoteness. Even when it is not directly cited or quoted, it forms a matrix and serves as a referent. In John Fleming's clever characterization, it serves as "supertext," not "subtext," in medieval "intertextuality."[2]

The influence of the Bible is indisputable. What is problematic, however, is not so much the medieval reverence paid to the Bible as the medieval irreverence paid to it. The supertext in a variety of ways was frequently turned to other uses: imitation, satire, parody. So, with Fleming, "we search for canons by which we can hope to adjudicate complex literary relationships that include, in one and the same instance, deference if not servility on the one hand and an assertive competitiveness on the other."[3] Medieval writers, for whom the Bible was "a constant component," not only treat the Bible with great reverence but also with marked irreverence and "assertive competitiveness": parody, whimsy, scatalogical allusion, misappropriation, witty burlesque, and a host of other improprieties. Such appropriation of the sacred to the mundane might well seem to the modern reader abuse, mockery, and even blasphemy. We might also expect the orthodox and pious readers of the Middle Ages and the church authorities to condemn such use as sacrilegious. That is not the case.

First, let us turn to the writer passionately studied and elucidated by Donald Howard, Geoffrey Chaucer, the familiar author whose works have been intensely scrutinized for biblical use and allusion. Readers of Chaucer and Chaucerian criticism have come more and more to recognize his extensive and adroit use of the Bible.[4] Chaucer's biblical quotations and allusions number more than seven hundred;[5] they serve his literature in various ways: to prove a proposition, to reinforce a statement, to enhance some personage, to criticize a rascal's life or actions, to heighten the farce or deepen the pathos. Chaucer's religious stance before the Bible is both complex and simple. Although he does not possess the theological profundity of Dante, he shows serious interest in sophisticated theological issues, such as providence and predestination (in The Knight's Tale, The Nun's Priest's Tale, and in *Troilus and Criseyde*). By contrast, he sometimes displays an unaffected simple piety, such as that expressed in *The ABC to the Virgin*.[6] The childlike devotion in that little poem indeed resembles the sentiments expressed by the critically maligned Prioress of the *Canterbury Tales*, as in her Prologue she recites and glosses Psalm 8, a psalm especially familiar to both religious and laity in the Little Office of the Blessed Virgin.

Although Chaucer could employ a scriptural text to support an argument as well as any other medieval writer, his really extraordinary artistry is manifested in his use of clipped, well-chosen biblical reference and allusion.[7] The Canterbury Tales are replete with both manifest and concealed biblical references. We may note as apt but quite typical of medieval exegetical practice his use of Jeremiah 6.16 at the beginning of The Parson's Tale, which elevates the Canterbury prilgrimage to the allegorical journey to the heavenly Jerusalem. The venerable trope furthers the pilgrimage theme of the *Tales*. But we are astonished by the ingenuity, irony, and boldness of the allusions in the General Prologue, the biblical echoes in The Miller's Tale, the perversely adapted citations in The Wife of Bath's Prologue, and the parody of the Song of Songs in The Merchant's Tale. Every church-goer in fourteenth century England would have been aware that the "olde lewed words" that Januarie fervidly addresses to the adulterous May were from the Canticle attributed to Solomon, frequently applied to Christ's Spouse, the Church, and with equal frequency to the Holy Spirit's beloved, Mary.[8] Januarie's salacious usurpation of the love song, therefore, not only offends traditional Christian exegesis but also makes bedfellows of the Virgin Mary and the Venusian May. Modern commentators point out this amusingly irreverent application in a comic fabliau arises from the disillusioned Merchant's soured view of every noble ideal, especially marriage.[9] What commentators have *not* confronted is why Chaucer and his audience could innocently chuckle at an outrageously blasphemous utterance. Apparently his and their enjoyment is as uncritical of such *turpiloquium* as ours—or even less so, since no one in Chaucer's day, including Chaucer himself, accused him of blasphemy. He was pretty hard on himself in his *retracciouns* at the end of the *Canterbury Tales,* but there his remorse is expressed for "translacions and enditynges of worldly vanitees," as well as "the tales of Caunterbury, thilke that sownen into synne" and "many a song and many a leccherous lay" (X.1084–86); there is certainly no specific mention of his play with Scripture.

Although, like his contemporaries, Chaucer uses amplification, *expolitio, ecphrasis,* and other expansionary devices to fulfill his narrative purposes, by contrast he also packs a far-reaching critique into a concise allusion or brief reference. Many scholars have demonstrated how Chaucer's insertion of a seemingly casual detail about a physical deformity, an emblematic characteristic of one of the pilgrims, or an apparently off-hand reference to some historic event like the Peasant's Revolt of 1381 expresses essential and often profound meanings for the text. The same is true for Chaucer's scriptural references and allusions.[10] Some of these allusions involve simple wordplay, as when Friar John in The Summoner's Tale accuses the secular clergy of gluttony and drunkenness, so that "Whan they for soules seye the psalm of Davit: / Lo, 'buf!' they seye, *'cor meum eructavit!'* " (III.1933–34), playing upon the literal meaning of *eructare,* "to belch."[11] Some references, however, involve a great, even a gross contradiction to the original biblical text, so that although Nicholas sings *"Angelus ad Virginem"* in The Miller's Tale (I.3216), his Annunciation to Alisoun is hardly Gabriel's to the Virgin Mary.[12] Dame Alice of Bath brazenly identifies herself with the barley bread with which "Oure Lord Jhesu refresshed many a man" (III.146).[13] Perhaps the least funny but most powerful inversion of the New Testament in the *Canterbury Tales* is the Pardoner's travesty of the Eucharist in his story, with the sordid *agape* of bread and poisoned wine consumed by two members of the unholy Trinity after the sacrificial death of the third.[14] The Pardoner's exemplum offers a specimen of the way Chaucer can use a biblical motif to provide a hellish contrast rather than a pious comparison. Chaucer can even use Scripture for a scatological joke: his parody of the Pentecost event in The Summoner's Tale (III.2243–86), first by the typological contrast to Moses, who sees God's posterior, and Elijah, who restores the widow's son to life, with Friar John, who receives the gift from Thomas's backside and pretends to give eternal life to the wife's dead child by his prayers; and then by the descent and distribution of the fiery *flatus* as a fart divided amongst the twelve fraternal disciples and their prior. This egregious example demonstrates Chaucer's willingness to parody, even to travesty, Holy Scripture; but he does it with the artistic purpose of creating the Summoner's exegetically sophisticated satirical attack on the Friar. Ian Lancashire argues that "Chaucer does not mock the Bible but creates an intolerable, comic gap between the sacred roles John and Thomas assume, and the wretchedly profane performance that results."[15] Another wildly irreverent Chaucerian comparison is set up by the Host's angry accusation against the Pardoner:

> "Thou woldest make me kisse thyn olde breech,
> And swere it were a relyk of a seint
> Though it were with thy fundement depeint!"

(VI. 948–50)

In fact, one pair of foul old hair breeches belonged to Saint Thomas à Becket and were displayed as the relic of the saint for the pilgrims' homage in Canterbury cathedral, to which Chaucer's pilgrims were wending.[16]

How can a medieval poet so biblically devout that he penned *The ABC* to the Virgin Mary, so theologically serious that he frequently treats the question of God's predestination and foreknowledge, and so morally sensitive that he composes a lengthy treatise on penance to finish the *Canterbury Tales,* also engage in satire, parody, and profanation of the Bible? One might respond by pointing out that it is not usually Chaucer but one of Chaucer's characters who so abuses Scripture.[17] The reply to that is that Chaucer the artist is ultimately responsible for creating the character who parodies Scripture, and Chaucer the author is the immediate source of the parodies of the Garden of Eden, of the Eucharist, and of Pentecost in his text. Chaucer is, after all, a great parodist of sacred and profane literature: of the Bible, of the liturgy, of Dante's *Divine Comedy* in the *House of Fame,* of medieval romance in *Sir Thopas;* indeed, parody and witty imitation are characteristic of most of his writings.[18]

Satire, mockery, and farce are all legitimate for moral and artistic ends. But are the means to those ends, when they entail parody of Scripture, legitimate for the medieval artist? It is noteworthy that no recorded contemporary, ecclesiastic or lay, voiced any objection to Chaucer's artistic profanation of Scripture. It is even more noteworthy that no authority, ecclesiastic or lay, objected to any authors' parodic use of the Bible.

Indeed, I have chosen Chaucer to lead into my topic because he well illustrates a common phenomenon throughout English and European medieval literature: nothing is too sacred to be exempt from parody, travesty, and scurrility; the more sacred, the greater the parody. Some of the finest satiric pieces are burlesques of the gospels, such as the droll attack on papal venality, the *Evangelium secundum marcas argenti et auri* [*The Gospel according to Marks Silver and Gold*] and the *Passio domini nostri pape Romanorum secundum marcam argenti et auri* [*The Passion of Our Lord the Pope of the Romans according to Mark of Silver and Gold*].[19] If the sacred mystery of the Eucharist in which Christ comes as salvific food to man was not exempt from parody by a Christian society, as the various *missae potatorum* demonstrate, then nothing could be or was. The transformations are clever but sacrilegious. The psalm-text recited at the beginning of Mass, "Introibo ad altare Dei / Ad Deum qui laetificat iuventutem meam. / Confiteor Deo omnipotenti . . ." [I shall go unto the altar of God, / to God who gladdens my youth. / I confess to almighty God . . .] becomes "Introibo ad altare Bacchi / Ad eum qui letificat cor hominis. / Confiteor reo Bacho omnepotanti . . ." [I shall go unto the altar of Bacchus, / To him who gladdens man's heart. / I confess to almighty Bacchus . . .] and the "Pater noster, qui es in caelis . . ." [Our Father, who art in heaven . . .] changes into "Potus noster, qui es in cypho," [Our drink, which art in goblet . . .], et cetera.[20] Furthermore, the parodies, witty travesties, and burlesques were not just the product of vagabond students; the most respected Christian poets, indeed prelates of the Church, created them.

What is the explanation for orthodox writers' using Scripture beyond its formal exegetical bounds? First, Christian writers of every age, from the Fathers of the Church to contemporary ecclesiastics, have felt entitled to use a Scriptural text, separated from context, for establishing some thesis, giving it sanction, and wrapping it in divine authority. In this they are doing what the New Testament writers did to the Old Testament authority. This is what Dante in the *Divine Comedy* did most extraordinarily to the Bible and the liturgy. This is what lesser authors did ordinarily throughout the Middle Ages. Sometimes the stretched literal or allegorical interpretations amount to mimetic parodies.

Second, Scripture was used often in polemic and satirical pieces, especially during periods crying for reform, in the eleventh century led by Peter Damiani, in the twelfth century led by Bernard of Clairvaux, in the thirteenth and fourteenth centuries by the clerics of the universities, and in the sixteenth and seventeenth centuries by leaders of the Reformation and Counter Reformation. In the heat of battle against various evils, the venality of the papal curia or the vices of simoniacal bishops, clergy fought fire with fire, text with text. They contorted the biblical or liturgical text by parody to mock the false users of the genuine text.

Third, in medieval literature parody and parodic allusion remained subject to the authority of the original text, never totally usurping the Bible's sacral domain. The Middle Ages observed a certain decorum about where perversions of the biblical text could be tolerated. John Alford has pointed out that other artistic media besides literature confirm such a hierarchical relationship: within a single church, for instance, one will see such parodic distortions in the misericords of the choir but not in the stained glass or monumental sculptures of the portals. Similarly, in a fine manuscript, such as a book of hours, one observes the obvious subordination of the marginal drolleries to the main illustrative program.[21] Biblical parody occupied a similarly important but marginal status vis-a-vis biblical exegesis.

Fourth, one might argue that parody also arose out of deep human urge to resist and mock authority, covertly or openly. Parody is a manifestation of the human spirit against dominion. Parody of the divine word in medieval Christianity is but a component of a larger cultural phenomenon. In ancient Greece, dramatic productions were part of official state worship, in which the tragedies were followed immediately by the satyr plays and the comedies. The gods who were treated with awe and respect in the tragedy became scurrilous, sordid, farting, belching, lecherous rogues in the satyr plays. As René Girard has stressed, the sacred and the violations of the sacred are close concomitants in society.[22] Against the mind's will to order, the body has its imperatives. Bakhtin has explained that literalness, as the respectable and official dialect of the elite, is opposed by parody; the privileged text of the official language is countered by the unofficial language of parody.[23] And as writers from Euripides to Freud have elucidated, under the sacred runs the sexual. A striking iconographic example of this is the decorated manuscript letter Q beginning the gospel of Luke ("Quoniam quidem multi conati sunt ordinare narrationem . . ."), in the shape of female pudenda.[24] This may not seem so outrageously improbable if we recollect the Wife of Bath's pun on the same word: "I hadde the beste *quoniam* myghte be" (III. 608). The Latin word formed the basis for many clerical jokes. Giraldis Cambrensis tells of the chaplain charged with concubinage defending himself before the ecclesiastical tribunal solely with texts from the Psalms, "Quoniam bona est" (Psalm 108.21) and "Dilexi quoniam" (Psalm 114.1), and so on.[25] The poem, "de concubinis sacerdotum" contains the stanza:

O quam dolor anxius, quam tormentum grave
  nobis est dimittere *quoniam* suave;
  hoc, Romane pontifex, statuisto prave:
  ne in tanto crimine morieris [moriaris?] cave.[26]

[O how troubling a sorrow, how grave a torment
  It is for us to put aside our sweet *quoniam;*
  This, Roman pontifex, you have decreed wickedly:
  Be careful lest you die in so great a crime.]

Use of Scripture for a profane, erotic purpose can also have the effect of not so much demeaning the Bible as elevating the secular work, conferring on it some of the status of the privileged text. Clifford Geertz has noted that among Arabic-speaking peoples, the poets

> turn the tongue of God [the Quran] to ends of their own, which if not quite sacrilege, borders on it; but at the same time they display its incomparable power, which if not quite worship, approaches it. Poetry, rivaled only by architecture, became the cardinal fine art in Islamic civilization, and especially the Arabic-speaking part of it, while treading the edge of the gravest form of blasphemy.[27]

In a somewhat analogous way, medieval European authors both honor and parody sacred Scripture. The lyric, for example, by employing terms and images from the Bible, liturgy, and devotion adorn woman, both Mary and Alisoun, with sacral vestiture. Medieval authors are adept at transferring these hieratic images. In the *Book of the Duchess,* Chaucer says of the Duchess, who is aptly named Blanche, that her throat "semed a round tour of yvoyre" (946), a nice borrowing from the Song of Songs' "collum tuum sicut turris eburnea," customarily applied to the Virgin Mary, as in the Litany of Loreto. The Duchess is also a "chef myrour," from the *speculum sine macula* of Wisdom 7.26, likewise attributed to Mary.[28]

In Greek civilization, the genre of parody evolved early and flourished;[29] however, authors who wrote the sacred and the serious did not usually do the comic and scurrilous (as Plato has Socrates remark in the *Symposium*). Apuleius pleaded in his defense against the charge of composing immoral love poems that serious Latin poets were known to have written some lascivious verse;[30] but as a rule the sacred and profane were kept distinct in Latin literature, at least to the extent that Latin authors did not let the genres of serious and light literature mingle. In medieval literature notable authors used the Scripture in both soberly sacred and parodically satirical ways, sometimes, as in Chaucer and Langland, in the same generic work. This reflects, I want to suggest, the medieval writers' attitude toward the privileged text. Moreover, this playing free with Scripture did not occur only after the rise of scholasticism and the universities in the twelfth century: we have interesting examples from far earlier than that.

I pass over earlier Germanic vernacular literatures, which take liberties with the biblical text but usually in a quite serious mode, to note first the amusing Carolingian Latin romp, the *Cena Cypriani*.[31] The beginning of the poem is a take-off on the Marriage Feast of Cana. Invited by a certain king named Johel, all the important and many of the lesser figures of the Old and New Testament arrive to feast, and each sits down on his or her emblem: Eve on a figleaf, Cain on a plow, Abel on a milkpail, Noah on the ark, and so on. The food and wines are also proper to each guest. Jesus, for instance, drinks "passus," i.e., *sec,* pressed from dried grapes— fittingly, of course, because he who gave his blood to drink under the form of wine, "*passus* et sepultus est." After the feast, Johel sends everyone back to his and her appointed place and state: Jesus to teaching, Noah to drunkenness, Job to his sorrow, etcetera. The king then calls them back to bring appropriate gifts: Abraham a ram, Samson a lion, Joseph, grain. Finally the king sends each to his torment: John to decapitation, Adam to exile, Susanna to accusation, and so on.

The *Cena Cypriani* enjoyed a wide circulation, as the many extant manuscripts and various versions and imitations attest. The Carolingians, as Paul Lehmann observed, characteristically judged the piece neither foolish nor blasphemous.[32] Notable for my thesis is the fact that one version was composed by no less a respected and orthodox theologian than Hrabanus Maurus, "der," as Paul Lehmann remarks, "ein dogmentreur strengkirchlicher Mann war" (*Parodie* 14). Along with his version of the *Cena,* Hrabanus sent in 859 a dedicatory letter to King Lothar II. He emphasized the usefulness of the piece as Bible lore but also offers it "ad iocunditatem," for entertainment.

Throughout its long history biblical parody, even in its extreme manifestations, was not only practiced but condoned by ecclesiastical authority. Clerics preached against every conceivable religious abuse: swearing and cursing, violation of churches and nuns, simony and nepotism, and a host of other offenses called "blasphemia," "turpiloquium," and "vaniloquium." But I know of no patristic condemnation of parodies of sacred Scripture (even though such travesties existed from at least the sixth century),[33] I know of no ecclesiastical condemnation or censure, either by church council, synod, or episcopal court. Protests by defensive ecclesiastics against scurrilous attacks are frequent, but the complaints, such as W. Bothewald's invective against Walter Mapes, do not include abuse of Scriptural citations.[34]

During the bloomtime of the Schools, the twelfth and thirteenth centuries, biblical parody attained its most luxuriant forms, notably in the *Carmina Burana* and the *Cambridge Songs.*[35] These and works such as the biblical burlesque, the *Apocalypse of Golias,* and the many so-called "goliardic" poems are clerical products. We tend to forget that collections such as the *Cambridge Songs* are anthologies that contain both impeccably religious poems of biblical piety and, cheek by jowl, scabrous, lascivious, and funny biblical and liturgical burlesques. Thus, in the Cambridge songs, a penitential alphabetical poem, whose refrain is "Adtende homo, quia pulvis es / et pulverem reverteris" (#18), from Genesis 3.19 and Ash Wednesday liturgy, is separated by a page or two from the infamous "snowchild" fabliau, "Modus Liebinc"; an ecclesiastical allegory invoking the Song of Songs (#25) lies next to an erotic "Invitatio Amicae" using the same Song of Songs (#27).

We may look at the other arts for a similar ambivalence. For instance, the Gregorian chant introit "Haec dies"—from Psalm 117, verse 24, "Haec est dies quam fecit Deus, exultémus et laetemur in ea," used for the Easter liturgy—formed the basis of a hymn to the Blessed Virgin and a love song to Maid Marian.[36]

Vernacular poets like Jean de Meun, Chrétien de Troyes,[37] Dante, and Chaucer likewise engage in biblical borrowing for both orthodox and parodic purposes. As in much else, Dante is a special case. The intertextual relationship between the Bible and the *Divine Comedy* is especially complex not only because the Bible is cited or alluded to more often than any other text—even Virgil's *Aeneid*—but also because, as in Charles Singleton's insightful phrase, Dante chose to "*imitate* God's way of writing."[38] Dante's use of the Bible has been classified into six categories by Christopher Kleinhenz:

> There are essentially six types of biblical reference in the *Comedy:* 1) exact citation of the Latin text; 2) slightly modified citation of the Latin text; 3) incomplete citation of the Latin text. Categories four through six are the same as these except that they comprise those citations in an Italian translation of paraphrase.[39]

It is in the areas of "slightly modified citation" and "incomplete citation" where Dante extends the meaning of the biblical text for his own purposes. Within each category, each use of the text is quite distinctive and sometimes surprising, in nearly every instance polysemous and multireferential. There is also a further extension of the biblical authority in the Dantean text:

> In addition to these six types of verbal citation, there is another large and more difficult to define category of biblical reference in the *Comedy,* namely Dante's imitative prophetic voice which permeates the poem and gives it its special tone and character. (p. 229)

Deeply convinced of the sacral power of the Word, Dante despised the frivolous substitutions and perversion of the text by mendicant preachers. In *Paradiso* XXIX.109–17, Beatrice remarks bitingly:

> Non disse Cristo al suo primo convento:
>   'Andate, e predicate al mondo ciance';
>   ma diede lor verace fondamento;
> e quel tanto sonò ne le sue guance,
>   sì ch'a pugnar per accender la fede
>   de l'Evangelio fero scudo e lance.
> Ora si va con motti e con iscede

a predicare, e pur che ben si rida,
gonfia il cappuccio e più non si richiede.

[Christ did not say to his first company, 'Go and preach idle stories to the world,' but he gave to them the true foundation; and that alone sounded on their lips, so that to fight for kindling of the faith they made shield and lance of the Gospel. Now men go forth to preach with jest and buffooneries, and so there be only a good laugh, the cowl puffs up and nothing more is asked.][40]

Despite this condemnation, this most serious and exalted poet himself makes something close to parodic use of Scripture. In the *Inferno,* as is fitting, the biblical text appears least often;[41] when it is used, it, like so much in hell, may appear *torta,* twisted and perverted. Thus, in the notorious *crux* in *Inferno* VIII.43–45, after the pilgrim has rebuked Filippo Argenti, Virgil pushes the filthy shade away from Phlegyas's ferryboat, and then:

Lo collo poi con le bracchia me cinse;
   basciommi 'l volto e disse: "Alma sdegnosa,
   benedetta colei che 'n te s'incinse!"

[Then he put his arms about my neck, kissed my face, and said, "Indignant soul, blessed is she who bore you!"][42]

Most commentators believe that by having these words that were addressed to Christ in Luke 11.27 addressed to Dante, Virgil is paying Dante a fine compliment. Kleinhenz argues that "what the critics have failed to consider is *the rest of the biblical allusion,* for this suggests that Virgil's praise is wrong, and consequently, that Dante's reaction to Filippo Argenti in this canto is equally wrong." Since Jesus rejects the compliment as inappropriate, the compliment is equally inappropriate for Dante (p. 233). In any case, no matter how the critics interpret the *crux,* the fact is that by use of the biblical text Dante is identified with Christ. This is serious parody.

In the larger arena of the whole *Comedy,* Dante is not only Jesus, he is God, who "judges the living and the dead." He insists at least that as God's scribe his creation is God's own, for, in Singleton's famous dictum, "the fiction of the *Divine Comedy* is that it is not a fiction."[43] Robert Hollander adds another element to the complex portrait of the artist:

His Dante also creates a fiction that presents itself as a true account, but at the same time contrives to let the reader know that his work is "precisely fictional." What this amounts to is a "Theologus Dantes" with a sense of humor, one who gives away his poetical enterprise by staring down the reader in the midst of what can only be taken as a bold-faced lie. . . .
   This portrait of the artist as "Theologus-Poeta" stands somewhere between a pious perception of Dante as *scriba Dei* and Croce's purely literary genius. It

gives us a poet who writes in imitation of God in order to establish the authority of Christian poetry in the face of theological attack; who lies in order to tell the truth; who is supremely conscious of the tight rope he walks between the world of discourse and another.[44]

Peter Hawkins concludes his brilliant analysis of *Purgatorio* XXIX, which examines Dante's reworking the Bible to square its vision with his own, by remarking

> Dante may have been a theologian with a sense of humor, occasionally demythologizing his own myth (as Hollander suggests). On the other hand, he is always a comedian in earnest, whose stakes are not ultimately the admiration of his readers but, rather, their conversion.[45]

No matter how much self-referentiality is present in the *Comedy* and how much insistence on it as a product of poetic creation, the fact is that "Dante presents himself at the end of a line, the author of a poem which is, so to speak, a third testament" (p. 85). In the detail about the number of wings on the four living animals, he not only identifies himself with St. John the Divine in Revelation but boldly asserts "Giovanni è meco" (*Purgatorio* XXIX.105)—not "I am with John," but "John is with me"! (p. 86). Such an assertion of authority goes far beyond mimesis, parody, or intertextuality. To some, it might seem the greatest abuse of Scripture; to most, it is breathtaking—and true.

Dante's (ab)use of Scripture represents an extreme case. For most authors the Bible represented the supreme text to be quoted, cited, used and even parodied. The entire culture, including the Church, accepted such practice without dissent. Within the same genre, even with the same work, both orthodox exegetical use and playful parody were tolerated. The importance of understanding the medieval rationale for doing both exegesis and parody in the same work is well exemplified by the history of criticism on *The Second Shepherds' Play*. In a bold farce the Wakefield master in this popular Nativity play comically literalizes the figure of the *Agnus Dei* by having Mak and his wife Gyll wrap a stolen lamb in swaddling clothes and pretend that it is their child in the cradle. The visit of the shepherds forms a comic parallel with their visit to the swaddled Child, the Lamb of God, at the end of the play. Until the magisterial article, "Symbol and Structure in the *Secunda Pastorum*," by Lawrence Ross, the play was considered a lively farce of 754 lines to which the playwright attached a legitimating ending of a hundred lines describing the adoration of the shepherds. That, according to Albert Baugh, made it "an artistic absurdity."[46] However, Ross demonstrated that the literal data in the first part are charged with religious symbolism: the peasant gifts of ball, bird, and bob of cherries are as iconographically laden as the bound lamb that is to be consumed; the two parts of the play, parody and typological event, are truly analogous actions, in which there is the further symbolism tokened by recovery of the stolen sheep as the recovery of lost sheep by the divine Shepherd (Matthew 18.11, John 10.10). The Bible furnishes the basis of the historical and liturgical Nativity but also the parodic, or better said, mimetic action of the English mystery play. The parodic use of Scripture by medieval writers has seemed to some modern critics a manifestation of a coarse naïveté, which A. P. Rossiter characterizes:

> A strangely comprehensive two-ways-facingness brings together in medieval art the remote, the transcendental, the noble, the vulgar, the gross and the base; often switching abruptly from the one to the other, from pathos to brutality, or from reverence to blasphemy. (p. 53)

> A travesty is effected by nearly-exact parallelism [in the *Secunda Pastorum*], of lines in what Euclid called 'opposite senses'. Clowning and adoration are laid together, like the mystery and boorishness in Breugel's *Adoration of the Magi*, or mystery and surrounding nescience in others of his pictures. We are left to wrestle with uncombinable antinomies of the medieval mind: for these immiscible juxtapositions constantly imply two contradictory schemes of values, two diverse spirits; one standing for reverence, awe, nobility, pathos, sympathy; the other for mockery, blasphemy, baseness, meanness or spite, *Schadenfreude,* and derision. (72)[47]

That may be eloquent, but is it right? Here is a critic working out of his own aesthetic system; but Lawrence Ross, a scholar better educated in medieval culture and religious sensibility, has furnished a healthy corrective. Perhaps to call the many medieval uses of Scripture for other than strictly exegetical and pious purposes parody, travesty, pastiche, or burlesque already censoriously prejudges the practice and blocks an aesthetic comprehension of the works.

The fact that Chaucer engages in literal and parodic use of the biblical text within the same work does not make him a rare Menippean satirist or an impious profaner. Just as it is wrong to call him a Wycliffite because, along with many another orthodox writer of the fourteenth century, he is critical of religious abuses, so it is also wrong to accuse him of being a religious skeptic or blasphemer because he is sometimes impudently playful with the Bible. Although he is unique as a masterly creator, a great satirist and ironist, he shares a penchant for biblical parody with many other good Christian writers of the Middle Ages.

Notes

1. Lawrence Besserman, *Chaucer and the Bible: A Critical Review of Research, Indexes, and Bibliography* (New York and London: Garland, 1988) p. 4.

2. John V. Fleming, *Reason and the Lover* (Princeton: Princeton Univ. Press, 1984), pp. 69–70; quoted in Besserman, *Chaucer and the Bible,* p. 28. Besserman claims that "The Bible, appropriately implied but left unnamed, is of course Fleming's main example of a 'supertext' in the *Roman.*" That may be so, but in this instance Fleming is actually talking about Boethius's *Consolatio* as a supertext for Jean's *Roman* and the *Roman* as a supertext for Chaucer, for "we see him 'translating' Jean de Meun on virtually every page he wrote" (p. 70).

3. Fleming, *Reason and the Lover,* p. 70. Besserman maintains that "when the Bible is at issue, [Fleming] proves over and over again that the relationship of these writers toward their 'supertexts'—Jean de Meun and Chaucer in the present context—was uniformly one of 'deference and servility' " (*Chaucer and the Bible,* p. 28).

4. See the essays in David Lyle Jeffrey, ed., *Chaucer and the Scriptural Tradition* (Ottawa: Univ. of Ottawa Press, 1984). Earlier important studies, frequently cited by the writers in that volume, include Grace W. Landrum, "Chaucer's Use of the Vulgate," *PMLA* 39 (1924): 75–100, and W. Meredith Thompson, "Chaucer's Translation of the Bible," in *English and Medieval Studies Presented to J. R. R. Tolkien,* ed. Norman Davis and C. L. Wrenn (London: Allen & Unwin, 1962), pp. 183–99, and D. W. Robertson, Jr., *A Preface to Chaucer* (Princeton: Princeton Univ. Press, 1962; rpt. 1969), pp. 317–31. More recently, see Lawrence Besserman's *Chaucer and the Bible,* especially his "Research on Chaucer and the Bible: A Critical Review," pp. 15–17, and his bibliography, pp. 389–432.

5. "The total number of Chaucer's biblical allusions (were there any significance to this information in itself) is hard to come by because of the large number of doubtful cases and the wide range of types of allusion (from shadowy parallels, to echoes of phrasing, to sustained direct quotation), but the few hundred referred to by Thompson (1962), the six-hundred-or-so references listed by Skeat (1894), and even the seven hundred-and-thirty cited by Landrum (1924, 98–99) are clearly on the low side" (Besserman, *Chaucer and the Bible,* p. 51).

6. The fact that *The ABC* is a skillful translation of a prayer by Guillaume de Guilleville does not cast doubt on Chaucer's own piety but rather by his care, adaptation, and phrasing asserts it.

7. For detailed references, see, in *Chaucer and Scriptural Tradition,* ed. Jeffrey: Chauncey Wood, "Artistic Intention and Chaucer's Use of Scriptural Allusion," pp. 35–46, Edmund Reiss, "Biblical Parody: Chaucer's 'Distortions' of Scripture," pp. 47–61, and Lawrence Besserman, "*Glossynge is a Glorious Thyng:* Chaucer's Biblical Exegesis," pp. 67–73. See also his extensive index in *Chaucer and the Bible,* pp. 55–304.

8. See Friedrich Ohly, *Hoheliedstudien: Grundzuge einer Geschichte der Hohleidsauslegung des Abendlandes bis zum 1200* (Wiesbaden: F. Steiner 1958); Douglas Wurtele, "The Blasphemy of Chaucer's Merchant," *Annuale Mediaevale* 21 (1981); 91–110, esp. 94–106.

9. See James I. Wimsatt, "Chaucer and the Canticle of Canticles," in *Chaucer the Love Poet,* ed. Jerome Mitchell and William Provost (Athens: Univ. of Georgia Press, 1973), pp. 66–90; Kenneth A. Bleeth, "The Image of Paradise in the *Merchant's Tale,*" in *The Learned and the Lewed,* ed. Larry D. Benson (Cambridge: Harvard Univ. Press, 1974), pp. 45–60; Douglas Wurtele, "Ironical Resonances in the *Merchant's Tale,*" *Chaucer Review* 13 (1978/79): 66–79, and Wurtele, "The Blasphemy of Chaucer's Merchant," cited above.

10. See the introduction and explanatory notes in *The Riverside Chaucer,* 3rd ed., gen. ed. Larry D. Benson (Boston: Houghton Mifflin, 1987), and the notes to, for example, lines 468 (the "gat-toothed" Wife), 565 (the Miller's "baggepipe"), 634

(the Summoner's garlic and leeks). See also the Explanatory Notes to III. 1934 and 1980 (p. 878), and IV. 2138–48 (pp. 888–89). Edmund Reiss, "Biblical Parody," pp. 49, 51, summarizes the discoveries of Chaucerian biblical parody made and commented on by many scholars, and concludes: "Along with the straightforward citations of Scripture and those where incongruity is possible are scores—if not hundreds—of others that clearly alter, pervert, or in some way misapply the biblical original."

11. Paul E. Beichner has demonstrated from a number of authorities (including Cassiodorus, Rufinus, and Bruno the Carthusian) that "commentators on *Psalm* xliv had made it impossible for their mediaeval readers to be unaware of the literal root meaning of *eructavit*" in connection with Psalm (136); he concludes the survey with the often quoted couplet by Peter Riga:

Non alleluia ructare sed allia norunt;
Plus in salmone quam Salomone legunt.

[They know how to bring up not "alleluia" but garlic;
They select more in salmon (or the Salmon Tavern) than they read in Solomon.]

(*"Non Alleluia Ructare," Mediaeval Studies* 18 (1956): 135–44)

12. See W. F. Bolton, "The 'Miller's Tale': An Interpretation," *Mediaeval Studies* 24 (1962): 83–94; Reiss, "Biblical Parody," p. 51.

13. For the identification of the *barly-breed,* see Christine Hilary's note to III 144–45, with citations, in *The Riverside Chaucer,* p. 866.

14. See Robert E. Nichols, Jr., "The Pardoner's Ale and Cake," *PMLA* 82 (1967): 498–504; Rodney Delasanta, "Sacrament and Sacrifice in the *Pardoner's Tale,"* *Annuale Mediaevale* 14 (1973): 42–52; Janet Adelman, "That We May Leere Som Wit," in *Twentieth Century Interpretations of the Pardoner's Tale,* ed. Dewey R. Faulkner (Englewood Cliffs, N.J.: Prentice-Hall, 1973), pp. 96–106.

15. Ian Lancashire, "Moses, Elijah and the Back Parts of God: Satiric Scatology in Chaucer's *Summoner's Tale,"* *Mosaic* 14 (1981): 17–30, at 22. Less convincing is Roy Peter Clark's attempt to equate Thomas with the apostle Thomas, in "Doubting Thomas in Chaucer's *Summoner's Tale," Chaucer Review* 11 (1976–77): 164–78. For the iconographic parody of the Pentecostal descent, see the articles by Levitan, Levy, Clark, and Szittya cited by Janette Richardson in *The Riverside Chaucer,* note to III 2255, p. 879.

16. See Daniel Knapp, "The Relyk of a Saint: A Gloss on Chaucer's Pilgrimage," *ELH* 39 (1972): 1–26.

17. As D. W. Robertson observed in his classic *A Preface to Chaucer,* p. 317: "There are a number of exegetes in Chaucer's *Canterbury Tales,* some casually so and some professionally. Among the more prominent are the wife of Bath, the friar in the *Summoner's Tale,* the pardoner, and the parson. Of these, the first is hopelessly carnal and literal, the second is an arrant hypocrite, the third is aware of the spirit but defies it, and the last is, from a fourteenth-century point of view, altogether admirable."

18. An attempt to characterize Chaucer as a Menippean satirist was mounted by F. Anne Payne, *Chaucer and Menippean Satire* (Madison: Univ. of Wisconsin Press, 1981).

19. Texts in Paul Lehmann, *Die Parodie im Mittelalter,* 2nd ed. (Stuttgart: Hiersemann, 1963) pp. 183–88; commentary, pp. 33–41. See also John A. Yunk, *The Lineage of Lady Mede: The Development of Mediaeval Venality Satire* (Notre Dame, Ind.: Univ. of Notre Dame Press, 1963), pp. 76–78.

20. Lehmann, *Parodie,* 233, 240, 249; see also sections 16–24, pp. 233–57.

21. I owe this astute observation to Prof. John Alford, commenting on a draft of this essay. If I had started with his perception, this essay would have very likely taken another form.

22. See, for example, René Girard, *Things Hidden since the Foundation of the World,* trans. Stephen Bann and Michael Meteer (Stanford, Calif.: Stanford Univ. Press, 1987); *The Scapegoat,* trans. Diane Freccero (Baltimore: The Johns Hopkins Univ. Press, 1986); *Violence and the Sacred,* trans. Patrick Gregory (Baltimore: The Johns Hopkins Univ. Press, 1977.)

23. Mikhail Bakhtin, *The Dialogic Imagination: Four Essays by M. M. Bakhtin,* ed. and trans. Michael Holquist and Caryl Emerson (Austin: Univ. of Texas Press, 1981), pp. 296–97, 381–84; cited in Joseph Dane, *Parody* (Norman: University of Oklahoma, 1988), p. 8.

24. The late Prof. Robert Kaske brought this to my attention some years ago.

25. *Giraldi Cambrensis Opera,* ed. J. S. Brewer, Rolls Series 21, 8 vols. (London: Longman, 1861–91), 2: 345–46. See also Thomas D. Hill, "A Note on *Flamenca,* line 2294," *Romance Notes* 7 (1965): 81 and n. 4.

26. "De concubinis sacerdotum," lines 25–28, in *The Latin Poems Commonly Attributed to Walter Mapes,* ed. Thomas Wright, Camden Society 16 (London: Nichols, 1841), p. 172. See also F. J. E. Raby, *A History of Secular Latin Poetry,* 2nd ed. (Oxford: Clarendon, 1957), 2: 225. Raby comments: "We must regard this [*quoniam*] as a noun, and need not, as F. Lot (in *Les poésies des Goliards,* p. 127, note 1) suggests, alter it to 'quod est tam suave.' 'Quoniam suave' refers clearly to the priest's wife" (p. 225 n. 2).

27. Clifford Geertz, "Art as a Cultural System," *MLN* 91 (1976): 1490.

28. See Colin Wilcockson's note to line 946 in *The Riverside Chaucer,* p. 974.

29. See Dane, *Parody,* pp. 17–64; A. S. Martin, *On Parody* (New York: Holt, 1896), pp. 1–3.

30. *Apulei Apologia,* ed. H. Butler and A. S. Owen (Oxford: Clarendon, 1914; reprint, Hildesheim: Olms, 1967), pp. 9–12, and the notes, pp. 23–33.

31. Text in *Monumenta Germaniae historica, Poetarum latinorum medii aevi* 4.2, ed. Karl Strecker (Berlin: Weidmann, 1914), pp. 857–98.

32. As Lehmann says: "Charakteristischerweise haben die karolingischen Gelehrten das Werk weder für töricht gehalten, was moderne Forscher taten, noch für blasphematorisch, was nicht überraschen würde" (*Die Parodie,* p. 14).

33. For example, the *Dialogue between Hadrian and Epictetus; Ioca monachorum; Solomon and Marcolphus:* cited in Lehmann, *Die Parodie,* pp. 10–11.

34. Printed in *The Latin Poems Commonly Attributed to Walter Mapes,* ed. Wright, Appendix IV, p. xxxv.

35. *Carmina Burana,* ed. Alphons Hilka and Otto Schumann, 2 vols. (Heidelberg: Winter, 1930), especially I:301 (#180), 304 (#181); *Carmina Cantabrigiensia,* ed. Karl Strecker, 2nd ed., *Monumenta Germaniae historica, Scriptores rerum germanicarum* 40 (Berlin: Weidmann, 1955). Peter Dronke, "The Song of Songs and Medieval Love-Lyric," in *The Bible and Medieval Culture,* ed. W. Lourdaux and D. Verhulst (Leuven: Leuven Univ. Press, 1979), pp. 236–62, after discussing the influence on the Song of Songs on a number of lyrics, argues convincingly that the lyric "Iam, dulcis amica, venito," "survives in two deliberately distinct versions, and that these versions should not be conflated, . . . because the one makes itself open especially to the sacred potential of the language in the love-dialogue, and the other to the profane" (p. 244; see also p. 249).

36. In addition, see Adrienne F. Block, *Early French Parody Noel,* Studies in

Musicology 36, 2 vols. (Ann Arbor, Mich.: UMI, 1983). In musical terminology, "parody" means the use of a piece of music for another text or the substitution of a new text for a piece of music, called *imitatio* in the Middle Ages; later it gets another term, *contrafactum*. See Wolfgang Steinecke, *Die Parodie in der Musik* (Wolfenbuttel: Moseler, 1934; reprinted 1970).

37. Chrétien De Troyes' scriptural allusions are particularly challenging for the literary critic. For instance, in *Le Chevalier de la Charrete (Lancelot)*, ed. Mario Roques (Paris: Champion, 1963), lines 1829–1949, Lancelot mimetically enacts a harrowing of hell. D. D. R. Owen has analyzed the account, but he is perplexed: "Why Chrétien should suggest this equation between Lancelot and Christ is puzzling. Is it in order to increase his hero's stature in our eyes, or through its very incongruity to make him appear the more ridiculous? At least we can be sure that here, as in the similar equation in *Cligés*, Chrétien intended no blasphemy" (Chrétien de Troyes, *Arthurian Romances*, trans. with intro. and notes by D. D. R. Owen [London: Dent, 1987]), pp. 512–13. See also *Le Chevalier au Lion (Yvain)*, ed. Mario Roques [Paris: Champion, 1960], 4385–4411 (alluding to the Woman Taken in Adultery, John 8.3–11), and 5771–5807 (in which Yvain the savior-knight, compared to Christ in glory, is given an "almost divine aura," Owen, p. 520).

38. Charles S. Singleton, *Dante Studies 1: Commedia: Elements of Structure* (Cambridge: Harvard Univ. Press, 1954), p. 15.

39. Christopher Kleinhenz, "Dante and the Bible: Intertextual Approaches to the *Divine Comedy*," *Italica* 63 (1986): 226. For a list of many past studies that consider Dante and the Bible, see p. 235 n. 2. See also Kleinhenz, "The Poetics of Citation: Dante's *Divina Commedia* and the Bible," in *Italiana 1988: Selected Papers from the Proceedings of the Fifth Annual Conference of The American Association of Teachers of Italian, Nov. 18–20, 1988*, ed. Albert N. Mancini, Paolo A. Giordano, and Anthony J. Tamburri (River Forest, Il.: Rosary College, 1990), pp. 1–21.

40. Text and translation from Dante Alighieri, *The Divine Comedy*, tr. Charles S. Singleton, vol. 3: *Paradiso*, Bollingen Series 80 (Princeton: Princeton Univ. Press, 1975), pp. 330–31.

41. "Nella *Commedia* si devono distinguere le singole parti. *L' Inferno*, come era da attendarsi, e il più povero di riferimenti biblici" [In the *Comedy* one must differentiate the individual parts. The *Inferno*. as one would expect, is the most poor in biblical references], *Enciclopedia Dantesca* (Rome: Istituto della Enciclopedia Italiana, 1970), s.v. Bibbia, I:626. For additional references to studies on Dante and the Bible see Angelo Penna's bibliography, p. 629.

42. *The Divine Comedy*, trans. Singleton, I. *Inferno*, 80–81.

43. Charles S. Singleton, "The Irreducible Dove," *Comparative Literature* 9 (1957): 129.

44. Peter S. Hawkins, "Scripts for the Pageant: Dante and the Bible," *Stanford Literature Review* 5 (1988): 76–77, referring to Robert Hollander, "Dante Theologus-Poeta," *Studies in Dante* (Ravenna: Longo, 1980), p. 86.

45. Hawkins, "Scripts for the Pageant," p. 91. See also his "Resurrecting the Word: Dante and the Bible," *Religion and Literature* 16 (1984): 59–71.

46. Albert C. Baugh, *A Literary History of England* (New York: Appleton-Century-Crofts, 1948), p. 273. For Ross's study, see *Comparative Drama* 1 (1967–68): 122–43.

47. A. P. Rossiter, *English Drama from Early Times to the Elizabethans* (London: Hutchinson, 1950), pp. 53, 72; Ross, "Symbol and Structure," pp. 142–43.

The Bodies of Jews in the Late Middle Ages

STEVEN F. KRUGER

The miracle of Chaucer's Prioress's Tale is manifestly physical, involving as its central fact the dead-but-not-dead body of the tale's "litel clergeon" (VII.503).[1] That body, subjected to violence and degradation—cut open and thrown into "a wardrobe . . . Where as thise Jewes purgen hire entraille" (572–73)—remains, through the miraculous intervention of the Virgin Mary, undefiled and functionally whole. In the filthy "pit" (571, 606) "Ther he with throte ykorven lay upright" (611), the "innocent" (566, 608) is described by images not of defilement and injury but of purity and intactness. The boy becomes not a butchered child but "This gemme of chastite, this emeraude, / And eek of martirdom the ruby bright" (609–10).[2] Indeed, the mutilated body is finally translated from its place of violent degradation to one of honor and safety: "And in a tombe of marbul stones cleere / Enclosen they his litel body sweete" (681–82).

Bodily injury and intactness are among the tale's central concerns. As Chaucer repeatedly emphasizes, despite the nature of his injury, the slit throat that should make speech physically impossible, the boy sings out loud and clear, in a voice powerful enough to make his surroundings respond with their own sound: "Ther he with throte ykorven lay upright, / He *Alma redemptoris* gan to synge / So loude that al the place gan to rynge" (611–13). The abbot of the tale explicitly recognizes the paradoxical relation between the boy's singing and the injury that makes singing impossible: "Tel me what is thy cause for to synge, / Sith that thy throte is kut to my semynge?" (647–48). And the boy responds (in a speech whose very existence is miraculous) by recognizing both the real, radical nature of his injury—"My throte is kut unto my nekke boon, / . . . and as by wey of kynde / I sholde have dyed, ye, longe tyme agon" (649–51)—and the physical capacity that miraculously survives that injury—"Yet may I synge *O Alma* loude and cleere" (655). The miracle of the boy's singing of course involves an intrusion of the supernatural into the world, but that intrusion, Mary's intercession, itself takes place in the realm of the physical:

And whan that I my lyf sholde forlete,
To me she cam, and bad me for to synge

301

This anthem verraily in my deyynge,
As ye han herd, and what that I hadde songe,
Me thoughte she leyde a greyn upon my tonge.

                                                                (658–62)

The "me thoughte" here may leave room for doubt about the actual
physical quality of Mary's intervention, but when the abbot pulls out the
boy's tongue and takes "awey the greyn" (671), all such doubt must vanish.

The emphasis on the physical in The Prioress's Tale is not unusual in
late-medieval religious writing. Indeed, as Caroline Bynum has forcefully
argued, late-medieval spirituality, especially women's spirituality, is intimately tied up with the physical, with food and with flesh; the body often
serves as a locus for the immanent workings of divinity.[3] While such a
valuation of body might seem to contradict the truisms with which, in
shorthand, we tend to define medieval Christian attitudes toward body—
body is the prison of soul; the flesh battles the spirit and the spirit the
flesh[4]—it should not surprise us. Christianity is, after all, grounded in the
marriage of flesh and spirit, the incarnation of a bodiless divinity and the
concomitant spiritualization of his flesh. The Incarnation, the Virgin Birth,
the Immaculate Conception, transubstantiation, resurrection, all involve
body as much as spirit.

The miracles of the later Middle Ages often parallel the originary mysteries of Christianity; the divine often shows itself in the physical—for
instance, in the workings of relics, pieces of body in which saintliness
somehow inheres. In late-medieval literature, saints' lives and related
genres (such as the "miracle of the Virgin" of which The Prioress's Tale is
an example) are especially apt to focus attention on bodies dedicated and
sacrificed to religious ends and on bodies miraculously preserved. Thus,
Chaucer's own life of St. Cecilia, The Second Nun's Tale, is a story of
voluntary, wedded chastity that includes two beheadings (398), a fatal
flagellation (405–6), and a scene of extended torment. St. Cecilia is boiled
"in a bath of flambes rede" (515), yet remains "al coold," feeling "no wo"
(521). Smitten three times in the neck, "half deed, with hir nekke ycorven
there" (533), she, like the Prioress's "litel clergeon," yet lives on, "And
nevere cessed hem the feith to teche / That she hadde fostred . . ." (538–
39). Here, as in The Prioress's Tale, the story's central miracle allows an
intactness of body despite violent attempts to destroy that intactness.

A recognition of the intimate involvement of body in late-medieval
spirituality need not, however, negate our sense that medieval Christiantiy
also deeply distrusts body, often indeed depicting body as a prison, as
rebel to reason and spirit, as a force that must be controlled, denied, even
sometimes destroyed. Bynum is, I believe, right "that medieval asceticism
should not be understood as rooted in dualism, in a radical sense of spirit
opposed to or entrapped by body": "late medieval asceticism was an effort

to plumb and to realize all the possibilities of the flesh. . . . They were not rebelling against or torturing their flesh out of guilt over its capabilities so much as using the possibilities of its full sensual and affective range to soar ever closer to God." But medieval attitudes toward body are not revealed only in the ascetical practices that "arose in a religious world whose central ritual was the coming of God into food as macerated flesh."[5] Indeed, strikingly opposed to a theology centered in the positive valuation of suffering body are the frequent late-medieval attempts to repudiate *certain* human bodies as animal-like, disgusting, contaminating. Woman's bodies, which might be intimately involved in the approach to God, were also treated as possessing abhorrent flesh:

> A woman is an imperfect creature excited by a thousand foul passions, abominable even to remember, let alone to speak of. . . . No other creature is less clean than woman: the pig, even when he is most wallowed in mud, is not as foul as they. If perhaps someone would deny this, let him consider their childbearing; let him search the secret places where they in shame hide the horrible instruments they employ to take away their superfluous humors.[6]

Leprous bodies, though they might also become part of spiritual practices,[7] were nonetheless segregated from society, treated as already dead.[8] Lepers were seen "as the most repellent, the most dangerous and most desolate of creatures, representing the last degree of human degradation."[9] Less ambivalently treated (because never incorporated into Christian spirituality) were the bodies of male homosexuals and of Jews. Late-medieval law sometimes classed homosexual intercourse alongside intercourse with animals (and with Jews) and sentenced those guilty to live burial;[10] Aquinas "compared homosexual acts . . . with violent or disgusting acts of the most shocking type, like cannibalism, bestiality, or eating dirt."[11] And Jews were often seen as the possessors of diseased and debased bodies:

> . . . the Jew suffered . . . from certain peculiar and secret afflictions that were especially characteristic of him, and which did not normally trouble Christians. . . . Most often mentioned among these ailments was that of menstruation, which the men as well as the women among the Jews were supposed to experience;[12] close seconds, in point of frequency of mention, were copious hemorrhages and hemorrhoids (all involving loss of blood). Among the great variety of these maladies were included quincy, scrofula, a marked pallor, various mysterious skin diseases, and sores that gave forth a malodorous flux.[13]

Even more disturbingly, Jews were depicted as destroying other (Christian) bodies and using body parts (especially blood) to heal their own diseases and to perform magical acts.[14] Partially in consequence of such myths, Jewish bodies were often themselves seen as the prime targets of violence.[15]

Bodies marginal to, and persecuted by, late-medieval society and Christianity deserve our close attention in the larger reassessment of medieval attitudes toward body that is currently in progress.[16] Here, as part of that reassessment, I would like to concentrate attention especially on the bodies of Jews, and in particular on the treatment of those bodies in two late-medieval English literary texts—Chaucer's Prioress's Tale[17] and the Croxton *Play of the Sacrament*—that closely link the corruptions of Jewish body to Christian bodily miracles. In doing so, I hope to clarify the relation between the positive valuation of body in late-medieval spirituality and the attack on body often present in the treatment of Jews.

I. Tortured and Torturing

In The Second Nun's Tale, violence works in only one direction, against the persecuted Christian minority. All the tale's victims are Christians; the pagan oppressors, so long as they remain pagan, are never subjected to physical torment.[18] Indeed, the tale dramatizes the opposition between Christian victim and pagan tormentor by showing us several violent pagans who convert to Christianity and who, as a result, become themselves the victims of torment. Valerian at first threatens violence against his wife Cecilia if, as he suspects, she loves "another man" (167)—"Right with this swerd thanne wol I sle yow bothe" (168). When, however, he is convinced of Cecilia's faithfulness and holiness, he takes on her religion and with that religion "the palm of martirdom" (240): he is beheaded for his faith (393–99). In a similar way, Maximus, an officer of the Roman prefect Almachius, and the often Roman "tormentoures" (373, 376) are converted by Christian "prechyng" (375): "They [the Christians] gonnen fro the tormentours to reve, / And fro Maxime, and fro his folk echone, / The false feith, to trowe in God allone" (376–78). Maximus, in his turn, becomes a Christian preacher, and as a result himself suffers an excruciating death: "And with his word [he] converted many a wight; / For which Almachius dide hym so bete / With whippe of leed till he his lif gan lete" (404–6). On the other hand, the tale's central villain, Almachius, remains a pagan, and (although his power erodes) he never himself becomes a victim of violence.

The Second Nun's Tale depicts a "former age" of primitive Christianity in which all Christians, even the pope ("Men sholde hym brennen in a fyr so reed / If he were founde" [313–14]), are potentially Christlike victims of torment that brings with itself clear rewards—salvation ("Hir soules wenten to the Kyng of grace" [399]) and the demonstration of divine immanence (in the miracle of Cecilia's supernatural survival). The death and survival of the "clergeon" in The Prioress's Tale similarly make manifest divine care for the Christian martyr; Mary directly promises the boy's salvation: "My litel child, now wol I fecche thee, / Whan that the greyn is fro thy tonge ytake. / Be nat agast; I wol thee nat forsake" (667–69).

But the Christianity of The Prioress's Tale is less pristine than that of The Second Nun's Tale and the workings of violence in its world less clearcut. Whereas, in The Second Nun's Tale, the whole Christian community is directly endangered by its oppressors and the solidarity of that community in Christian suffering is shown by a series of martyrdoms, the Church in The Prioress's Tale is powerful and its identity with the little boy's suffering is demonstrated not by direct physical endangerment but in a more symbolic mode. The leader of the Christian community, the abbot, seeing the "wonder" of the boy's death (673), in a vicarious experience of physical disability, "fil al plat upon the grounde, / And stille he lay as he had been ybounde" (675–76). The abbot's community follows suit: "The covent eek lay on the pavement /Wepynge, and herying Christes mooder deere" (677–78). In this physical and emotional reaction, the larger Christian community shows itself to be in sympathetic unity with the suffering martyr, a unity that the narrator, in part through her invocation of the English martyr Hugh,[19] wishfully extends to include both herself and her audience: "Ther he [the clergeon] is now, God leve us for to meete!" (683); "O yonge Hugh of Lyncoln . . . Preye eek for us, we synful folk unstable" (684, 687). Indeed outside the tale proper, we see the miracle's effect upon a Christian community of listeners (Chaucer's pilgrims), an effect less severe than but similar to that felt by the "covent" within the tale: "Whan seyd was al this miracle, every man / As sobre was that wonder was to se" (691–92).

The powerful Church thus escapes a relentless reiteration of real bodily suffering even as it identifies with and soberly celebrates that suffering. Furthermore, its power allows the Christian community to move actively (and violently) against its "oppressors." Here, physical torment does not work, as in The Second Nun's Tale, in only one direction. The Jewish "persecutors" are (like the Christians persecuted in The Second Nun's Tale) in the minority. The "Jewerye" exists "*Amonges* Cristene folk" (489; emphasis mine), surrounded by Christianity, and it survives only through the patronage of a non-Jew: "Sustened by a lord of that contree / For foule usure and lucre of vileynye" (490–91). The Jewish crime against the "clergeon" is punished and punished with a physical violence designed as direct retribution for the injuries to which the Christian body has been subjected:

With torment and with shameful deeth echon,
This provost dooth thise Jewes for to sterve

That of this mordre wiste, and that anon.
He nolde no swich cursednesse observe.
"Yvele shal have that yvele wol deserve";
Therfore with wilde hors he dide hem drawe,
And after that he heng hem by the lawe.

(628–34)

"Torment" and "shameful deeth" clearly compensate here for the tale's earlier murder and defilement.

The suffering of the "litel clergeon" thus provides not only an occasion for the miraculous incursion of divinity into the realm of body and not only a demonstration of how the suffering Christian body may serve as a focal point for the feelings of the larger community. It also provides the opportunity for a Christian attack on bodies perceived and treated as radically different from the "innocent" body of the little boy. At the heart of The Prioress's Tale is an opposition between the Christian body, attacked but preserved, and the Jewish body, foul (purging its "entraille" [573]), attacking innocence, justly destroyed. And this opposition occurs not just at the level of the individual body. The punishment of the Jews is more than simply "just compensation" for a discrete crime, more than the old law "yvele" for "yvele" (632): not only the one "homycide" (567) directly responsible for the boy's death, nor only those Jews who "conspired / This innocent out of this world to chace" (565–66), but all "this Jewes . . . That of this mordre wiste" (629–30) suffer painful and shameful execution. The action of the one "cursed Jew" (570) who commits the murder is presented not as an individual act but as part of a conspiracy that bears communal responsibility. While, when the crime is first described, we see the singular "homycide" killing the boy and casting his body into a pit (570–71), immediately afterward the description of the action is broadened to suggest communal guilt—"I seye that in a wardrobe *they* hym threwe" (572; emphasis mine). And the conclusion of the tale broadens Jewish culpability even further, leaving the particular crime and its exotic, Asian setting behind to find "cursed Jewes" closer to home:[20] "O yonge Hugh of Lyncoln, slayn also / With cursed Jewes, as it is notable, / For it is but a litel while ago" (684–86). The crime against one Christian body takes on wide implications, is seen as part of a larger Jewish threat, and, as a consequence, the corporate punishment imposed is "shown" to be justified. After all, Jews are communally "cursed": "Oure firste foo, the serpent Sathanas . . . hath in Jues herte his waspes nest" (558–59).

Ultimately, then, in Chaucer's tale, both individual suffering and individual guilt become corporate. Christians take on the suffering of the martyred child (and concomitantly they hope for a salvation like his); "cursed Jewes" suffer the punishment earned by the singular "cursed" "homycide" (570, 567). But while the relation between "clergeon" and "homycide" is clear—it is the archetypal relation between strong and weak, oppressor and victim[21]—the extension of that relation into the larger Jewish and Christian communities complicates matters. As we have seen, the Christian community does not simply suffer but also inflicts suffering.[22] The Jewish community not only makes the little boy a martyr but is itself victimized. Each community acts as both persecutor and persecuted, and, interestingly, both are, at least at one point, described in similar terms. The Jews, as they approach their "torment and . . . shameful deeth" (628), are bound (". . . the Jewes leet he bynde" [620]); similarly, the abbot, suffering along with the young Christian martyr and with his larger community, "lay as he had ben ybounde" (676).

I do not want to suggest that our sympathies, when we read The Prioress's Tale, are meant to be divided between Christians and Jews (though the modern reader, recognizing the tale's anti-Semitism, often does have a divided reaction). At least in the Prioress's presentation of events, the Jews are clear villains. However, even as it makes strong distinctions between "cursed," Satanic Jews and Christians who are "hooly" (642), "or elles oghte be" (643), the tale brings together the two opposed religions—by showing both to be tormentors of bodies as well as the possessors of tormented bodies and by (linguistically) binding together the "bound" bodies of Christians and Jews. As a result, the final picture of body in The Prioress's Tale is a complex one in which the role of both tormented and tormentor are simultaneously validated (as these roles are played by Christians) and repudiated (as they are represented by Jews). If the primary function of the Christian body is to suffer humbly and patiently in unity with the suffering, crucified Christ (a role Bynum identifies as central to late-medieval spirituality), that body, at least as it shows itself in the powerful, corporate body of the Church, also refuses to suffer, identifying its enemies and moving to inflict suffering on them. If the Jewish body is primarily a menace to Christian innocence, it is a menace easily contained, tormented, destroyed.

The introduction of Jewish bodies into a tale like the Prioress's thus allows for the enactment of a complex and deeply ambivalent Christian valuation of body. On the one hand, the weakness and vulnerability of the human body is placed center stage; in its very capacity for being wounded, body makes possible union with the humanity-divinity of the suffering Christ who stands at the origin of Christianity. But Christianity, at least as it is depicted in Chaucer's tale, is unwilling to embrace wholeheartedly the suffering body. Vulnerability is not in itself to be valued; indeed, as it shows itself in Jewish bodies, it is to be taken advantage of, and body itself is to be extirpated. Christianity moves—even as it celebrates the miracle of the little boy's martyrdom and shows itself in solidarity with his suffering—to assert its own power, the *in*vulnerability of its corporate body, and to prove that power by victimizing the bodies of "cursed Jewes." It follows a path not taken by the crucified Christ and not accessible to the early Christian martyrs, availing itself of worldly power to impose punishment on criminal (Jewish) bodies. Thus, the Prioress's Tale presents us with bodies that are, as they suffer, both to be embraced and cast aside, and, as they cause suffering, both to be praised and anathematized.

II. Holy and Corrupt Body

In The Prioress's Tale, the miraculous mutilated body, preserved and celebrated as "This gemme of chastite, this emeraude" (609), lies starkly beside those "cursed" bodies that must "purgen hire entraille" (573), bodies drawn and hung (633–34), bodies thankfully destroyed. Hallowed and corrupted bodies stand together and work upon each other: Jews kill and defile the Christian "innocent," ironically making possible the miracle that preserves him and that binds the Christian community with the primal, redemptive suffering of Christ; Christians, even as they suffer vicariously with the martyred boy and praise the miracle that attends his suffering, bind, debase, and eliminate the Jewish bodies ultimately "responsible" for the miraculous events.

The complex relation between Christian and Jewish, corrupt and holy, bodies that we thus see in Chaucer's *Prioress's Tale* appears often in late-medieval literature and reveals, I believe, crucial elements of medieval attitudes toward both Jews and body. The late fifteenth-century Croxton *Play of the Sacrament*[23] is especially interesting as an expression of those attitudes in that it explicitly connects the holy body at the heart of Christian worship—Christ as he is made ever-immanent in the Eucharist—to those bodies that stand outside Christianity and attack it.

In this play, the immediate didactic purpose of which is to argue the truth of Christian doctrine concerning the Eucharist and transubstantiation,[24] Christian body is represented by the consecrated host, illicitly purchased and then tortured by Jews. Here, as in The Prioress's Tale, the Jews are cast in the role of tormentors and the torment they inflict is again visited back upon their own bodies. In some ways, the treatment of Jews in the play is more subtle and less violent than in Chaucer's tale: though punished, the Jews are not finally destroyed, and Jewish perfidy is less absolutely opposed to Christian purity than it might be.[25] The Jews do not act alone in their defilement of the host: Christian sin aids them. The Christian merchant Aristorye, after offering some weak resistance, agrees to steal the consecrated wafer and sell it to the Jewish merchant Jonathas (274–335). Indeed, even before the Jewish plot to torment the host is introduced, the play establishes an affinity between Aristorye and

Jonathas: in a long, boastful speech (81–124),[26] Aristorye claims repeatedly to be "[a] merchaunte mighty" (90), "most mighty of silver and of
gold" (87), "a merchante most [of] might . . . In Eraclea is non[e] suche"
(85–86), and Jonathas introduces himself with similar boasts (149–204)—
"I am chefe merchaunte of Jewes, I tell yow, by right" (196), "In Eraclea is
noon so moche of might" (194).

These opening speeches, however, also serve to differentiate the two
characters, and thus they begin to delineate Jewish and Christian roles in
the play. Although, as soon as Aristorye begins speaking, he shows himself
to be proud and avaricious, he also reveals his awareness of the Christian
deity: "Now Crist, that is our Creatour, from shame he cure us" (81); "All
I thank God of his grace, for he it me sent" (118). On the other hand,
Jonathas worships not Christ but "almighty Machomet" (149), and he
quickly institutes the play's central action by issuing a direct challenge to
Christianity:

> The beleve of thes[e] Cristen men is false, as I wene,
> For the[y] beleve on a cake—me think it is onkind—
> And all they seye how the prest dothe it bind,
> And by the might of his word make it flessh and blode—
> And thus by a conceite the[y] wolde make us blind—
> And how that it shuld be He that deyed upon the rode.
>
> (199–204)

Christians may behave badly: as he himself is aware, Aristorye, in selling
"Christ's body" to the Jews, commits a grave sin analogous to Judas's
betrayal of Christ:

> For, and I unto the chirche yede,
> And preste or clerke might me aspye,
> To the bisshope they wolde go tell that dede,
> And apeche me of [h]eresye.
>
> (299–302)

Still, the Christian merchant remains a believer. He is finally not the
instigator of "heresy," nor is he fully privy to the evil intentions of the
Jews. In persuading Aristorye to procure the host, Jonathas whitewashes
his "entent" (291), making no mention of the plan to torment Christ's
body:

> Sir, the entent is, if I might knowe or undertake
> If that he were God all-might;
> Of all my mis I woll amende make
> And doon him wourshepe bothe day and night.
>
> (291–94)

Aristorye remains innocent of the most heinous part of the Jewish plot; Christians, though implicated through Aristorye in the crime at the play's center, remain finally peripheral to that crime, remote from the actual scene of torment.

On the other hand, Jonathas and the four Jews who serve him are from the very beginning intent on violence, prepared to torment the host. Jonathas is not, as Bevington argues, "*simply* a type of skeptic who considers the Christian dogma of the mass to be rationally indefensible,"[27] though skepticism indeed provides one of the two explicitly stated motivations for Jewish procurement of the host:

> Yea, I dare sey feythfully that ther feyth [is fals]:
> That was never He that on Calvery was kild!
> Or in bred for to be blode, it is ontrewe als.
> But yet with ther wiles they wold we were wild.
>
> (213–16)

But even as they state their disbelief in the host's sentience, the Jews of the Croxton *Play* express the desire to cause it physical and emotional distress:

> I swer by my grete god, and ellis mote I nat cheve,
> But wightly the[r]on wold I be wreke!
>
> (211–12)

> Yea, I am mighty Malchus,[28] that boldly am bild.
> That brede for to bete biggly am I bent!
> Onys out of ther handys and it might be exiled,
> To helpe castyn it in care wold I consent.
>
> (217–20)

The play does not seem concerned that the two motivations the Jews thus provide for their actions are contradictory (in the Middle Ages, Jewish attitudes toward Christian doctrine were often believed in fact to be self-contradictory—Jews knew the truth of Christianity even though they perversely insisted on denying it).[29] The Jews of the Croxton *Play* both boldly deny transubstantiation and act as though they believe in its truth: when Jonathas finally has the host in his possession, he refers to it skeptically as "this bred that make us thus blind" (388),[30] but he also addresses the host as if it were indeed a person: "Now in this clothe I shall the[e] covere, / That no wight shall the[e] see" (383–84).

The Jews' double reasons for stealing the host continue to motivate their actions once they have it in their possession. Their skepticism shows itself in a careful consideration of the "mervelows" (394) claims of Christian doctrine. Jonathas describes the establishment of the Eucharistic meal at the Last Supper (397–408), and his four Jewish companions discuss other aspects of the Christian "heresy" (415, 424): the Annunciation and Virgin Birth (409–16), Christ's Resurrection and Ascension (417–24), the descent of the Holy Ghost on Pentecost (425–32), and finally the Last Judgement (433–40). Throughout this extended summary of Christian doctrine, the Jewish expositors remain deeply skeptical, concluding that the "entent" of these teachings is "To turne us from owr beleve" (439), and reiterating the desire to test the host (442–43).

The Jews do, however, accept one bit of Christian doctrine:

> There [in Bosra] stainyd were his clothys—this may we belefe,
> This may we know—there had he grefe,
> For owr old bookys verify thus:
> Thereon he was jugett to be hangyd as a thefe—
> "*Tinctis [de] Bosra vestibus.*"[31]
>
> (444–48)

This evocation of the historical violence against Christ serves as a bridge between the Jews' skeptical review of doctrine and the expression of their other, more malicious, intentions for the host. Jason proposes "a conceit good" (450)—"Iff that this be he that on Calvery was mad[e] red . . . Surely with owr daggars we shall ses on this bredde, / And so with clowtys we shall know if he have eny blood" (449–52)—and his companions respond to this suggestion with enthusiastic violence:

> *Jasdon.* . . . with owr strokys we shall fray him as he was on the rood,
> That he was on-don[e] with grett repreve.
> *Masphat.* Yea, I pray yow, smite ye in the middys of the cake,
> And so shall we smite theron woundys five!
> We will not spare to wirke it wrake
> To prove in this brede if ther be eny life.
>
> (455–60)

While the Jews are still concerned with disposing doctrinal claims ("if he have eny blood," "if ther be eny life"), they also express their belief in the host's sentience, in its capacity to suffer "wrake."

With these Jewish threats of violence begins the play's central action, the reenactment of the historical torment of Christ on the body of the host. The Jews' first actions economically evoke the buffeting and scourging of Christ (see lines 468 and 476) along with the five wounds of the Crucifixion:

> *Malchus.* Yea, goo we to, than, and take owr space,
> And looke owr daggarys be sharpe and kene!
> And when eche man a stroke smitte hase,
> In the midyll part thereof owr mastere shall bene.
> *Jonathas.* When ye have all smityn, my stroke shal be sene:
> With this same daggere that is so stif and strong

In the middys of this print I thinke for to prene!
On[e] lashe I shall him lende or it be long.
  Here shall the four Jewys prik ther daggerys in four
  quarters, thus say[i]ng:

Jason. Have at it! Have at it, with all my might!
This side I hope for to sese!
Jasdon. And I shall with this blade so bright
This othere side freshely afeze!
Masphat. And I yow plight I shall him not please,
For with this punche I shall him prike!
Malchus. And with this augur I shall him not ease:
Anothere buffett shall he likke!

Jonathas. Now am I bold with bataile him to bleyke,
This midle part all for to prene,
A stowte stroke also for to strike:
In the middys it shal be sene!

                                                        (461–80)

Like the "homycide" of The Prioress's Tale, the Jews here act in an attempt to destroy the physical integrity of an innocent, holy body. But, as also in Chaucer's tale, the Christian body resists disintegration, and Jewish violence is finally visited back upon the Jews themselves, demonstrating simultaneously the corruptibility of their unholy bodies and the miraculous vitality of the sanctified body of Christ.

As soon as Jonathas delivers the fifth wound to the center of the host, it, to the Jews' horror, begins to bleed:

Ah, owt, owt, harrow! What devill is this?
Of this wirk I am on were!
It bledith as it were woode, iwis!
But if ye helpe, I shall dispaire!

                                                        (481–84)

Bleeding, for any normal body a sign of the loss of physical wholeness, here paradoxically proves the host's life—a life that the remainder of the play's action will demonstrate to be ultimately inviolate. Like the blood shed in Christ's crucifixion, the blood of the host is both a sign of wounding and token of life—both a result of Jewish violence and a proof of the fundamental impotence of that violence, which succeeds in its goal of wounding only to prove what it wants to suppress, the truth of Christianity.

Indeed, from this point on, the Jews' skepticism about the Eucharist is no longer an issue in the play: Jonathas and his companions now know with certainty "if he have eny blood" (452). But while the Jews can no longer rationally challenge Christian dogma, their violent attack on the host does not end so easily. Indeed, in an attempt to stop the disturbing Eucharistic bleeding, they intensify their violence. Jason calls for fire and a cauldron of oil (485–86), and Jasdon promises to "helpe it were in cast, / All the three howrys for to boile" (487–88);[32] Masphat and Malchus set up a furnace and cauldron (489–96). But when Jonathas tries to "bring that ilke cak[e] / And throwe it in" (497–98), violence begins to turn back upon itself. Masphat earlier promised to "wirke [the host] wrake" (459), but now, as Jonathas announces, "it werketh me wrake" (499). The violated host clings stubbornly to Jonathas's hand:

> I may not avoid it owt of my hond!
> I wille goo drenche me in a lake.
> And in woodnesse I ginne to wake!
> I renne, I lepe over this lond!
>   *Her[e] he renneth wood, with the [h]ost in his hond.*
>
> (500–503)

Jewish violence here begins to destroy Jewish minds and threaten Jewish bodies. The proposed boiling of the host leads instead to Jonathas's proposed drowning.

That the torment of Christian body results instead in the destruction of Jews is made absolutely clear and literal in the play's next scene. The crazed Jonathas is physically restrained by his companions (504–7), and, in the play's second reenactment of the Crucifixion, the clinging host is nailed to a post:

> Here is an hamer and nailys thre, I s[e]ye.
> Liffte up his armys, felawe[s], on hey,
> Whill I drive thes[e] nailes, I yow praye,
> With strong strokys fast.
>
> (508–11)

Of course, since Jonathas's hand is attached to the host, it too is nailed to the post. Here, the tortured and torturer are almost merged with each other; the Jews, in crucifying Christ, guarantee for themselves a kind of crucifixion.

Jonathas's fellows now try to free him by pulling him away from the host; they succeed, however, only in pulling him away from his own hand:

> *Masphat.* Now set on, felouse, with maine and might,
> And pluke his armes awey in fight!
>   [*They try to pull Jonathas from the host.*]
> W[h]at? I se he twicche, felouse, aright!
> Alas, balys breweth right badde!
>   *Here shall thay pluke the arme, and the hand shall hang*
>   *still with the sacrament.*

Malchas. Alas, alas, what devill is this?
Now hat[h] he but oon hand, iwis!

(512–17)

The dismembered Jewish "mayster" (518) and his companions, routed by their victim, now retreat for a time from the scene of torture and of their own humiliation.

At this point, the play moves briefly away from its concentration on the Eucharist to introduce two new characters, the physician "Mayster Brendiche of Braban" (533) and his servant Colle. The scene that follows is often treated as a comic interpolation having little to do with the main action, but, in its emphasis on the body and bodily rebellions, it clearly has thematic connections to the remainder of the play:[33]

All manar of men that have any siknes,
To Master Brentberecly loke that yow redresse!
What disease or siknesse that ever ye have,
He will never leve yow till ye be in yow[r] grave.
Who hat[h] the canker, the collike, or the laxe,
The tercian, the quartan, or the brynni[n]g axs;
For wormys, for gnawing, grindi[n]g in the wombe or in the boldyro;
All maner red eyn, bleryd eyn, and the miegrim also;
For hedache, bonache, and therto the tothache;
The colt-evill, and the brostyn men he will undertak[e],
All tho that [have] the poose, the sneke, or the tyseke.
Thow[g]h a man w[e]re right heyle, he cowd soone make him sek[e]!
Inquire to the colkote, for ther is his logging . . .

(608–20)

Colle and Master Brendiche thus comically bring to our attention all the ills to which flesh is heir and all the ways in which the physician of the flesh can intensify those ills. As the scene draws to its close, Jonathas's wound is explicitly associated with all the "hurtys" and "hermes" (637) that receive medical attention. Colle suggests that the good doctor make him a patient: "Here is a Jewe, hight Jonathas, / Hath lost his right hond" (628–29).

Jonathas, however, concerned to keep his dismemberment under wraps (see lines 520–24 and 638–45), violently refuses the physician's advances:

Avoide, fealows, I love not yowr bable! [*To his servants.*]
Brushe them hens bothe, and that anon!
Giff them there reward that they were gone!
  *Here shall the four Jewys bett away the leche and his
  man.*

(649–51)

Having, in the physician episode, kept body prominently in the foreground, the play now returns to its central problem—the Jewish treatment of the host and the host's effect on Jewish body—with a vengeance. In action that parodies the deposition of Christ's crucified body, the Jews "pluck owt the nailys" (658, 662) and cover the host "in a clothe" (659).

But, instead of burial, the crucified body and attached hand now receive more torment. The cauldron, prepared earlier, is finally put to use:

> *Jason.* . . . into the cawdron I will it cast.
> *Jasdon.* And I shall with this daggere so stowte
> Putt it down that it might plawe,
> And steare the clothe rounde abowte
> That nothing thereof shal be rawe.
> *Masphat.* And I shall manly, with all my might,
> Make the fire to blase and brenne,
> And sett thereundere suche a light
> That it shall make it right thinne.
>
> (664–72)

The torture of the host now necessarily also entails Jewish self-torture. And despite the new trial to which it is subjected, the host remains miraculously intact, continuing to prove its vitality by means of copious bleeding:

> Owt and harow, what devill is herein?
> All this oile waxith redde as blood,
> And owt of the cawdron it beginnith to rin!
> I am so aferd I am nere woode.
>
> (673–76)

On the other hand, Jewish flesh is destroyed—"The hand is soden, the fleshe from the bonys" (706)—finally becoming separable from the host, but not before it is has lost its own substance.

Confounded, the Jews nonetheless do not halt their violent attacks on the integrity of the host. To "stanche his bleding chere" (687), they prepare a red-hot oven (683–84), and, handling the host with self-protective care, they cast it into the oven:

> I shall with thes[e] pinsonys, withowt dowt,
> Shake this cake owt of this clothe,
> And to the ovyn I shall it rowte
> And stoppe him thow[gh] he be loth.
>
> (701–4)

In a final attempt to overcome the wafer, the Jews enclose it in a sealed structure (reminiscent of Christ's tomb) and try to bake the life out of it:

> I stoppe this ovyn, withowtyn dowte;

> With clay I clome it uppe right fast,
> That non[e] heat shall cum owtte.
> I trow there shall he hete and drye in hast!
>
> (709–12)

This last-ditch attempt of course also fails. In the most "mervelows case" (716) yet, "This ovyn b[l]edith owt on every side" (714) and finally "ginnith to rive asundre" (715). The prison/tomb constructed to contain the host (like Hell faced by the power of the crucified Christ) loses its own physical integrity. And now not only does the host maintain its wholeness and ability to bleed, it is miraculously transformed into "an image" of Christ himself, "with woundys bleding" (712, 716).

The Jews are now confronted by incontrovertible proof of the host's identity with Christ, and (as if the bleeding image itself were not enough) Christ addresses the Jews directly, interrogating their motives in what is a condemnation of all Jewish disbelief:

> Why blaspheme yow me? Why do ye thus?
> Why put yow me to a newe tormentry,
> And I died for yow on the crosse?
> Why considere not yow what I did crye?
> While that I was with yow, ye ded me velanye.
> Why remembere ye nott my bittere chaunce,
> How yowr kinne did me avance
> For claiming of min[e] enheritaunce?
> I shew yow the streitnesse of my grevaunce,
> And all to meve yow to my mercy.
>
> (731–40)

Faced directly by the body of Christ that they have been tormenting, the Jews suddenly convert, begging forgiveness for their misdeeds (741–61). They recognize finally that their violence presents a true danger not to Christ but to themselves: "Lord, I have offendyd the[e] in many a sundry wise. / That stickith at my hart as hard as a core" (758–59). As Christ himself makes explicit to Jonathas, Jewish pain and dismemberment result from the Jews' own attempts to inflict pain:

> Ser Jonathas, on thin[e] hand thow art but lame,
> And this thorow[gh] thin[e] own cruelnesse.
> For thin[e] hurt thou mayest thyselfe blame:
> Thow woldist preve thy powre me to oppresse.
>
> (770–73)

Now, however, that Jonathas has given up the will "to oppresse" and "mekely" begs for "mercy" (745), his body can be restored. Christ recognizes the Jew's "grete contricion" (775) and miraculously heals him:

Go to the cawdron—thy care shal be the lesse—
And towche thin[e] hand, to thy salvacion.
  Here shall ser Jonathas put his hand into the cawdron,
  and it shal be [w]hole again . . .

(776–77)

This final bodily miracle dramatizes what is the central point of much of the play's action. Corruption of body attends disbelief, attacking those who presume to attack the fabric of Christianity; wholeness of body, on the other hand, comes with true belief. No matter how battered or wounded, the body of Christ, the host of the Eucharist, and those who partake of that body (even the newly converted Jonathas), can never lose their essential integrity and life.

Appropriately enough, the Croxton *Play* ends with a long communal ritual in which the chastened Jews are accepted into the body of the Christian community and that community reaffirms its intimate connection to the suffering but living body of Christ. The bishop, informed by Jonathas about what has happened, leads his people to *"the Jewys howse"* (813), where Christ's image, "A child appering with wondys blody" (804), remains. There, as in The Prioress's Tale, the martyr's suffering is felt vicariously in the body of the Church:

O Jhesu, fili Dei,
How this painfull Passion rancheth mine[e] hart!
Lord, I crye to the[e], *miserere mei,*
From this rufull sight thou wilt reverte!
Lord, we all, with sorowys smert,
For this unlefull work we live in langowr.

(814–19)

In response to the bishop's prayer for "grace," "marcy," and "peté," "the im[a]ge change[s] again into brede" (820–25), and the bishop now leads a community wholly unified in its dedication to the Eucharistic ritual:

Now will I take this holy sacrament
With humble hart and gret devocion,
And all we will gon with on[e] consent
And beare it to chirche with sole[m]pne procession.
Now folow me all and summe!
And all tho that bene here, both more and lesse,
This holy song, *O sacrum convivium,*
Lett us sing all with grett swetnesse.

(834–41)

"All" are finally united in "devocion" to the Eucharist. Aristorye repents and confesses that he "sold our Lordys body for lucre of mony" (902); he receives an appropriate penance, "nevermore for to bye nore sell" (915). The bishop bids him, in recompense for what he has helped do to Christ's body: "Chastis[e] thy body as I shall the[e] tell, / With fasting and pray[i]ng and othere good wirk" (916–17). The Jews, who have already received their bodily penance, recapitulate, in a confessional mode, their crimes against the host (932–47) and pray for "a generall absolucion" (930) and "to be christenyd" (950). The bishop complies; Jonathas promises "Owr wickyd living for to restore . . . Never to offend as we have don before" (965–67); and the play ends with praise of Christ.

III. Conclusion

In the Croxton *Play of the Sacrament,* body thus shows itself to be, at one and the same time, wonderfully invulnerable and horribly corruptible. The body of the host and of Christ—passive, wounded, bloodied—is finally shown to be inviolate, uncontainable, capable of a miraculous healing. Jewish body, powerfully violent, succeeds ultimately in attacking only itself; it disintegrates and can only become whole by ceasing to be Jewish. These two kinds of body exist, as in The Prioress's Tale, in intimate connection to each other. The violence of Jewish body makes possible the miraculous suffering and survival of the host; the miracles of Christian body lead inexorably to Jewish dismemberment and disintegration. The images of hand and host crucified as one, of "bread" and "bone" boiled together, vividly depict the inseparability of the two kinds of body—one holy, tortured, yet vital; the other corrupt and violent, powerful, yet falling to pieces.

The intimate linking of Christian bodily miracles to the violence of Jews and to the dismemberment and disintegration of their bodies betrays an intense ambivalence in the late Middle Ages about body itself. On the one hand, as Bynum has shown, body—attacked, stabbed, boiled, baked, yet miraculously intact, alive, and enlivening—stands at the center of Christian ritual. This is the body of the crucified Christ, of the Eucharist, of the Christian martyrs and their relics, of the devout ascetic. But late-medieval Christianity does not simply embrace the bodies that link it to the archetypal body of Christ. Even as it celebrates the miraculous virtues of its own beleaguered bodies, it finds bodies to attack—the strange bodies of Jews, bodies suffering from "peculiar and secret afflictions,"[34] bodies broken but in no way to be identified with the broken body of Christ.

The relation of Jewish bodies to the bodies of Christian ritual is complex, as the complicated interactions between them in both The Prioress's Tale and the Croxton *Play of the Sacrament* show. Any attempt fully to explain that relation must take into account a broader range of historical, cultural, and literary material than I can here. I will only present one tentative suggestion. It is as though the deep involvement of medieval Christianity in body—the consumption of blood and flesh in the mass; the faith in the power of relics; the focusing of attention on food and on bodily exudings[35]—creates a correspondingly deep *nervousness* about body. Are these rituals and beliefs primitive, magical, even cannibalistic? Of course, such a question cannot be directly asked by Christians about the central ritual of Christianity. But anxiety can be projected outward, onto foreign bodies. Jews who needed to drink the blood of Christian innocents to be made whole; Jews who destroyed bodies for their own primitive, magical rituals and who were, in turn, dismembered—these could be imagined, created, and controlled.

Notes

1. Chaucer quotations are from *The Riverside Chaucer,* 3rd ed., gen. ed. Larry D. Benson (Boston: Houghton Mifflin, 1987).

2. As we see in a poem like *Pearl,* gemstones are often in the Middle Ages emblems of purity and completeness.

3. See Caroline Walker Bynum's recent work, especially *Jesus as Mother: Studies in the Spirituality of the High Middle Ages* (Berkeley and Los Angeles: Univ. of California Press, 1982), pp. 110–265; "Women Mystics and Eucharistic Devotion in the Thirteenth Century," *Women's Studies* 11 (1984): 179–214; "'. . . And Women His Humanity': Female Imagery in the Religious Writing of the Later Middle Ages," in *Gender and Religion: On the Complexity of Symbols,* ed. Caroline Walker Bynum, Stevan Harrell, and Paula Richman (Boston: Beacon Press, 1986), pp. 257–88; and *Holy Feast and Holy Fast: The Religious Significance of Food to Medieval Women* (Berkeley and Los Angeles: Univ. of California Press, 1987).

4. Contributing importantly to such negative evaluations of the worth of body are Neoplatonic and Biblical (especially Pauline) traditions. See, for instance, Macrobius, *Commentary on the Dream of Scipio,* trans. William Harris Stahl (New York: Columbia Univ. Press, 1952), 1.11.3 and Galatians 5.17.

5. Bynum, *Holy Feast and Holy Fast,* pp. 294–95.

6. Giovanni Boccaccio, *The Corbaccio,* trans. Anthony K. Cassell (Urbana: Univ. of Illinois Press, 1975), p. 24. The misogyny of Boccaccio's *Corbaccio* even goes so far as to deny the Virgin Mary a real female body: ". . . that only Bride of the Holy Spirit was such an undefiled, virtuous being, so pure and full of grace, and so completely remote from every corporeal and spiritual uncleanness, that in respect to the others, it is as if She were not composed of natural elements but were formed of a quintessence fit to be the dwelling place and hostelry for the Son of God, Who, wishing to become flesh for our salvation, prepared Her for Himself *ab eterno* as a worthy abode for such and so great a King, in order not to come and inhabit the pigsty of modern womanhood" (pp. 32–33). Such a view, of course, is related to the controversial doctrine of the Immaculate Conception.

7. Bynum, *Holy Feast and Holy Fast,* p. 209.

8. R. I. Moore, *The Formation of a Persecuting Society: Power and Deviance in Western Europe 950–1250* (Oxford: Basil Blackwell, 1987), pp. 58–59.

9. Moore, *The Formation of a Persecuting Society,* p. 60. It is, of course, the

very repellent, degraded quality of the leper's body that allows it to play a part in Christian spirituality, in the embracing of suffering flesh that is Christ. Still, leprosy is not only embraced but vigorously pushed away. For more on medieval ambivalence about leprosy, see Moore, *The Formation of a Persecuting Society*, pp. 60–61. For a full treatment of medieval attitudes toward leprosy, see Saul N. Brody, *The Disease of the Soul: Leprosy in Medieval Literature* (Ithaca: Cornell Univ. Press, 1974).

10. John Boswell, *Christianity, Social Tolerance, and Homosexuality: Gay People in Western Europe from the Beginning of the Christian Era to the Fourteenth Century* (Chicago and London: Univ. of Chicago Press, 1980), p. 292.

11. Boswell, *Christianity, Social Tolerance, and Homosexuality*, p. 329. See further Boswell's treatment of the late-medieval "rise of intolerance," pp. 269–334; and see Moore's brief discussion, *The Formation of a Persecuting Society*, pp. 91–94.

12. For more on the myth of male menstruation among Jews, see Joshua Trachtenberg, *The Devil and the Jews: The Medieval Conception of the Jew and its Relation to Modern Anti-Semitism* (Philadelphia: The Jewish Publication Society of America, 1983), pp. 149 and 228 n.27; Léon Poliakov, *Histoire d l'anti-semitisme: Du Christ aux juifs de cour*, vol. I (Paris: Calmann-Lévy, 1955), p. 160; and Sander L. Gilman, *Jewish Self-Hatred: Anti-Semitism and the Hidden Language of the Jews*, (Baltimore and London: The Johns Hopkins Univ. Press, 1986), pp. 74–75 and 403 n.13.

13. Trachtenberg, *The Devil and the Jews*, p. 50.

14. Ibid., pp. 50–51, 140–55. Also see Poliakov, *Histoire de l'antisemitisme*, p. 160; and Gilman, *Jewish Self-Hatred*, p. 75.

15. See, for instance, Guibert of Nogent's description of a massacre of Jews associated with the First Crusade, *Self and Society in Medieval France: The Memoirs of Abbot Guibert of Nogent (1064?–c. 1125)*, ed. by John F. Benton, trans. C. C. Swinton Bland [revised by Benton] (New York: Harper & Row, 1970), pp. 134–35; and see Cecil Roth, *A History of the Jews in England*, 3rd ed. (Oxford: Clarendon Press, 1964), for descriptions of anti-Jewish violence at London in 1189, 1215, and 1263 (pp. 19–20, 36, 61–62) and at York in 1190 (pp. 22–24, 272).

We could, of course, multiply the instances of marginalized groups treated, in the late Middle Ages, as in possession of degraded bodies. See, for instance, Moore's discussion of heretics, *The Formation of a Persecuting Society*, esp. pp. 60–65, for the suggestion that heretics, Jews, and lepers all resemble each other "in being associated with flesh, stench and putrefaction, in exceptional sexual voracity and endowment, and in the menace which they presented in consequence to the wives and children of honest Christians" (p. 64); and see Moore's brief discussion of female prostitutes, pp. 94–98.

16. Bynum's work has been especially important in bringing body to our renewed attention; see the references in note 3 above. Recent work on medieval medicine also reflects a deep interest in the treatment of body; see, for instance, Danielle Jacquart and Claude Thomasset, *Sexuality and Medicine in the Middle Ages*, trans. Matthew Adamson (Princeton: Princeton Univ. Press, 1988); and Mary F. Wack, *Lovesickness in the Middle Ages* (Philadelphia: Univ. of Pennsylvania Press, 1990). All this work takes its place in a more general renewal of interest in the body's historical and literary importance. See, for instance, Peter Brown, *The Body and Society: Men, Women and Sexual Renunciation in Early Christianity* (New York: Columbia Univ. Press, 1988) and see Elaine Scarry, *The Body in Pain: The Making an Unmaking of the World* (New York and Oxford: Oxford Univ. Press, 1985).

17. For an overview of the critical issues involved in reading the *Prioress's Tale,* see Florence H. Ridley, *The Prioress and the Critics,* University of California Publications: English Studies 30 (Berkeley and Los Angeles: Univ. of California Press, 1965). For various treatments of the tale's anti-Semitism, see R. J. Schoeck, "Chaucer's Prioress: Mercy and Tender Heart," *The Bridge: A Yearbook of Judaeo-Christian Studies* 2 (1956): 239–55 (reprinted in *Chaucer Criticism,* ed. Richard J. Schoeck and Jerome Taylor, vol. I [Notre Dame, Ind.: Univ. of Notre Dame Press, 1960], pp. 245–58); Sherman Hawkins, "Chaucer's Prioress and the Sacrifice of Praise," *JEGP* 63 (1964): 599–624; Ridley, *The Prioress;* Edward H. Kelly, "By Mouth of Innocentz: The Prioress Vindicated," *PLL* 5 (1969): 362–74; Albert B. Friedman, "The *Prioress's Tale* and Chaucer's Anti-Semitism," *ChauR* 9 (1974): 118–29; John C. Hirsch, "Reopening the *Prioress's Tale,*" *ChauR* 10 (1975): 30–45; Hardy Long Frank, "Chaucer's Prioress and the Blessed Virgin," *ChauR* 13 (1979): 346–62; and John Archer, "The Structure of Anti-Semitism in the *Prioress's Tale,*" *ChauR* 19 (1984): 46–54. Friedman suggests that anti-Semitism is largely "incidental" to the tale (p. 127), as does Frank (p. 358). Hawkins claims that "Anti-Semitism in the usual sense is quite beside the point" (p. 604); see Archer's brief reply (p. 46). I believe that the tale displays a deep anti-Semitism, manifested largely on the ground of the body.

18. Interestingly, toward the tale's beginning, Cecilia warns her new husband, Valerian, that the angel who guards her will execute him if he insists on having sex with her: "And if that he may feelen, out of drede, / That ye me touche, or love in vileynye, / He right anon wol sle yow with the dede, / And in youre yowthe thus ye shullen dye . . ." (155–58). However, at no point in the tale do divine powers actually move to save Christians from martyrdom.

19. On Hugh of Lincoln, see Gavin I. Langmuir, "The Knight's Tale of Young Hugh of Lincoln," *Speculum* 47 (1972): 459–82.

20. This move is especially interesting in light of the absence of Jews from fourteenth-century England. The threat that is thus made present to Chaucer's audience is immediately (indeed, preemptively) contained or negated (by the explusion of 1290), just as the Jewish threat within the tale is eliminated as soon as it is revealed.

21. In the statement, "The blood out crieth on youre cursed dede" (VII.578), Chaucer invokes the archetypal biblical account of victimization, Cain's murder of Abel. Compare Genesis 4.10: "dixitque ad eum: quid fecisti? vox sanguinis fratris tui clamat ad me de terra" [And He [God] said to him: "What have you done? The voice of your brother's blood cries out to me from the earth"] (my translation). See Archer, "The Structure of Anti-Semitism:" (p. 48). The line also perhaps calls to mind the (Jewish) crowd's response to Pilate, Matthew 27.25: "et respondens universus populus dixit: sanguis eius super nos et super filios nostros" [and the whole people responding said: "Let his blood be on us and on our children"] (my translation).

22. Perhaps the problem of a suffering Christianity that nonetheless holds power and itself inflicts suffering is meant to be minimized in the tale by the serparation of the roles of abbot (sufferer) and provost (punisher). See Kelly's suggestion that the provost is, in fact, a non-Christian, "gentile" authority ("By Mouth of Innocentz," p. 368). However, any separation between religious and secular authority is mitigated by the provost's explicit association with Christian piety at the very moment he moves to punish the Jews: "He cam anon withouten tariyng, / And herieth Crist that is of hevene kyng, / And eek his mooder, honour of mankynde, / And after that the Jewes leet he bynde" (VII.617–20). See Howard's comments on the "Chaucerian irony" of this passage—"which underscores the

travesty of justice that takes place" (Donald R. Howard, *The Idea of the Canterbury Tales* [Berkeley and Los Angeles: Univ. of California Press, 1976], p. 277.)

23. In *Medieval Drama,* ed. David Bevington (Boston: Houghton Mifflin Company, 1975), pp. 754–88.

24. Cecilia Cutts, in "The Croxton Play: An Anti-Lollard Piece," *MLQ* 5 (1944): 45–60, argues that "the play was a deliberate piece of anti-Lollard propaganda composed and presented for the purpose of strengthening the faith of the people in the face of heretic teachings and influences" (p. 45). Sister Nicholas Maltman, in "Meaning and Art in the Croxton *Play of the Sacrament,*" *ELH* 41 (1974): 149–64, sees the play's "purpose [as] the clear, accurate, vivid statement of the meaning of the Blessed Sacrament" (p. 149): "The impulse behind the play was undoubtedly pastoral and didactic; the message of the play is doctrinal, its matrix liturgical, and its tone serious" (p. 162). Richard L. Homan, in "Devotional Themes in the Violence and Humor of the *Play of the Sacrament,*" *Comparative Drama* 20 (1986–87): 327–40, suggests that the play, concerned with "man's sinfulness, the Passion, the Eucharist, and Christ as child and as conqueror," is written "in the manner of serious devotional art" (p. 339). Indeed, G. R. Owst, in *Literature and Pulpit in Medieval England* (Cambridge: Cambridge University Press, 1933), proposes that "the Croxton drama of *The Sacrament* suffices . . . to show how a favourite pulpit story setting forth the miraculous virtues of the Host could be dramatized . . . direct from the preacher's notebook" (p. 490).

25. Indeed, critics have consistently denied the anti-Semitism of the *Play of the Sacrament*. See Cutts "The Croxton Play"; Maltman "Meaning and Art"; and David Bevington, *Tudor Drama and Politics: A Critical Approach to Topical Meaning* (Cambridge: Harvard Univ. Press, 1968), pp. 38–39. Homan, "Devotional Themes," concludes, more nervously, that, while it "derives from two especially odious articles of anti-Semitism," the play finally "addresses concerns important to the Christian community of fifteenth-century England . . . not in the manner of anti-Semitic ridicule but in the manner of serious devotional art" (339). While I would not want to deny the play's "serious devotional" intent, neither should we ignore what is manifestly anti-Semitic in it. To assume, as the play does, that human beings can be redeemed only through Christianity is in itself anti-Semitic. Further, as the following discussion will show, the depiction of the Jews, although milder than it might be, remains deeply troubling, particularly in its treatment of Jewish body.

26. "The Banns" occupy the first eighty lines of text.

27. Bevington, *Tudor Drama and Politics*, p. 38 (emphasis mine).

28. It is perhaps significant that one of the Jewish captors and tormentors of the host is named Malchus (the play's other Jews are Jonathas, Jason, Jasdon, and Masphat). Malchus is, in John's gospel account of the betrayal of Jesus, the high priest's servant whose right ear is cut off by Simon Peter (John 18.10). The association of bodily dismemberment with the betrayal of Christ, thus present in the brief account of the Biblical Malchus, is, as I will show, a central theme of the Croxton *Play*.

29. See Trachtenberg, *The Devil and the Jews*, pp. 15 and 17.

30. Compare line 203: "And thus by a conceite the[y] wolde make us blind."

31. See Isaiah 63.1, typically read as a prophecy of Christ's Crucifixion: "quis est iste qui venit de Edom tinctis vestibus de Bosra" [who is this who comes from Edom, in dyed garments from Bosra] (my translation). The Jews here adopt a Christian reading of the Old Testament, and their own words thus challenge their skepticism about Christian doctrine.

32. The "three howrys" here (and the "thre galons of oile clere" later in the

passage [493]) call to mind the three days between Christ's Crucifixion and Resurrection, during which time Christ harrows the "furnace" and "cauldron" of Hell. The Harrowing and Resurrection are evoked again later in the play.

33. See also the readings of Maltman, "Meaning and Art," pp. 153–54, and Homan, "Devotional Themes," pp. 332–35. Maltman's proposal that Brendiche— "the quack, who gives ointment and potions that bring the patient not to life but to the grave"—stands here in opposition to "Christ the true physician" (p. 153), is especially attractive, given Christ's role in the following sections of the play.

34. Trachtenberg, *The Devil and the Jews,* p. 50.

35. See Bynum, *Holy Feast and Holy Fast.*

Contributors

GEORGE H. BROWN is professor of English and (by courtesy) Classics at Stanford University, where he directs the Medieval Studies Program. An internationally acclaimed scholar of Anglo-Saxon and Anglo-Latin literature, he is recipient of a number of fellowships and honors. He is president of the Medieval Association of the Pacific and officer in several other organizations. In addition to serving as editor, he has produced many articles, reviews, bibliographies, and a book on *Bede the Venerable* (1987). He is currently finishing a book on Alcuin and working on another, *The Language of Love in the Middle Ages.*

ALFRED DAVID is professor of English at Indiana University. He is author of *The Strumpet Muse: Art and Morals in Chaucer's Poetry* (1976), co-editor of *The Minor Poems, Part One* for the Chaucer Variorum (1982), editor of *The Romaunt of the Rose* in *The Riverside Chaucer,* and one of the editors of *The Norton Anthology of English Literature.* He is currently serving as president of the New Chaucer Society.

JAMES M. DEAN is associate professor of English at the University of Delaware. He is the author of *The World Grown Old in Later Medieval Literature* (1992) and co-editor (with Donald R. Howard) of *The Canterbury Tales: A Selection* and *Troilus and Criseyde and Selected Short Poems.* He is currently completing a book-length study of Ricardian literature.

JOHN M. FYLER is professor of English at Tufts University. He has published a book on *Chaucer and Ovid* (1979) and a number of articles on Chaucer and other medieval authors and texts; and he has edited the *House of Fame* for *The Riverside Chaucer.* He has been an ACLS and Guggenheim Fellow, and has served as chair of the English Department at Tufts. He is currently interested in theories of language in the Middle Ages and medieval biblical commentaries.

JOHN M. GANIM is professor of English at the University of California at Riverside. He is author of *Style and Consciousness in Middle English Narrative* (1983) and *Chaucerian Theatricality* (1990). In 1990 he was a fellow at the Center for Ideas in Society.

RALPH HANNA III is professor of English at the University of California at Riverside. He edited *The Awntyrs of Arthure at the Terne Wathelyne* (1967), *The Ellesmere Manuscript of Chaucer's Canterbury Tales: A Working Facsimile* (1989). He has published *A Handlist of Manuscripts Con-*

taining Middle English in the Henry E. Huntington Library (1984) and numerous essays on textual editing and other medieval subjects.

R. W. HANNING is professor of English and Comparative Literature at Columbia University. His publications include *The Vision of History in Early Britain* (1966), *The Individual in Twelfth-Century Romance* (1977), a translation of *The Lais of Marie de France* (with Joan Ferrante), and essays on a range of medieval and Renaissance subjects. He is currently completing a book on the interaction of verbal and social constructions in Chaucer's *Canterbury Tales.*

SUE ELLEN HOLBROOK is associate professor of English at Southern Connecticut State College. She has published articles on Margery of Kempe, Malory's *Le Morte Darthur,* and punctuation in Caxton's text. She has directed three seminars on Malory for the NEH and is vice-president of the Consortium for the Teaching of the Middle Ages (TEAMS).

SHERRON E. KNOPP is professor of English at Williams College. She has published articles on a variety of classical and medieval topics: Catullus, Gottfried von Strassburg, the *Roman de la Rose,* Chaucer, and Arthurian romance. Her essay on Virginia Woolfe's *Orlando* (*PMLA* 1988) won the Crompton-Noll Award of the Gay and Lesbian Caucus of the MLA in 1989. She is currently working on a book about Chaucer and medieval poetic theory, called *Chaucer and the Dilemmas of Fiction,* which was supported in 1986–87 by an NEH Fellowship for College Teachers.

STEVEN F. KRUGER is assistant professor of English at Queens College, CUNY. He has published articles in *Speculum* and *The Chaucer Review,* and his book, *Dreaming in the Middle Ages,* is forthcoming. His dissertation from Stanford University (1988) was awarded the Alden Prize. He is currently writing on the medieval depiction of Jews, gay men, and other marginalized groups; and he is beginning a project that will examine the treatment of AIDS in novels of the past ten years.

ANNE MIDDLETON is professor of English and former department chair at the University of California at Berkeley. Her publications include essays on Chaucer, Langland, and the formation of vernacular writing vocations and public voices in the later fourteenth century. She is currently preparing a book on Langland, vernacular authorship, and the category of the literary as represented in late fourteenth century and late twentieth century critical discourses.

THOMAS C. MOSER, JR. is assistant professor of English at the University of Maryland at College Park. He has published articles on Middle English lyrics, medieval hymns, Chaucer and music, and William of Conches. In 1991 he was a fellow of the University of Maryland Research Center for Arts and Humanities, where he worked on a book on the erotic Latin lyric in the twelfth century.

GLENDING OLSON, professor of English at Cleveland State University, has written *Literature as Recreation in the Later Middle Ages* (1982) and a number of articles on medieval literary theory and on Chaucer. With V. A. Kolve he edited *The Canterbury Tales: Nine Tales and the General Prologue* (1989). He has held ACLS, NEH, and Guggenheim grants. His current work is a book-length study of the game in the *Canterbury Tales*.

LEE PATTERSON is professor of English at Duke University. Author of *Negotiating the Past* (1987) and *Chaucer and the Subject of History* (1991), he has held fellowships from the NEH and the Guggenheim and Rockefeller Foundations. He is currently at work on a book about the history of modernity from 1350–1525.

FLORENCE H. RIDLEY, professor of English Language and Literature at the University of California, Los Angeles, is author of a number of books and articles in the fields of Chaucerian and medieval Scottish studies, including *The Prioress and the Critics* (1965), "The Middle Scots Poets" section for *A Manual of the Writings in Middle English 1050–1500*, vol. 4 (1973), and editions of the works of Gawain Douglas and of William Dunbar. She has served on the boards or councils of the New Chaucer Society, the International Association of University Professors of English, and the Medieval Academy of America. She is a Fellow of the Medieval Academy.

PAUL STROHM is professor of English and former department chair at Indiana University. He is author of *Social Chaucer* (1989).

KARLA TAYLOR is associate professor of English and graduate chair at the University of Michigan. She is the author of *Chaucer Reads The Divine Comedy* (1989) and of articles on Chaucer and Dante.

CHRISTIAN K. ZACHER is professor of English and Director of the Center for Medieval and Renaissance Studies at The Ohio State University. His publications include *Critical Studies of Sir Gawain and the Green Knight* (co-edited with Donald R. Howard, 1968), *Curiosity and Pilgrimage: The Literature of Discovery in Fourteenth-Century England* (1976), and the section on "Travel and Geographical Writings" in *A Manual of the Writings in Middle English 1050–1500*, volume 7 (1986). Since 1990 he has served as executive director of the New Chaucer Society.

Bibliography of Howard's Published Works

Books

College Workbook of Composition. Boston: D. C. Heath, 1960.

The Three Temptations: Medieval Man in Search of the World. Princeton: Princeton University Press, 1966.

(With Christian Zacher) *Critical Studies of Sir Gawain and the Green Knight* (editor). Notre Dame, Ind.: University of Notre Dame Press, 1968. Reprinted 1972.

Geoffrey Chaucer. *The Canterbury Tales, A Selection* (editor). New York: Signet, 1969.

Lothario dei Segni (Pope Innocent III). *On the Misery of the Human Condition: De miseria humane conditionis.* Translated with an introduction with Mary Dietz. Indianapolis: Bobbs-Merrill, 1969.

(With James Dean) Geoffrey Chaucer. *Troilus and Criseyde and Selected Short Poems* (editor). New York: Signet, 1976.

The Idea of the Canterbury Tales. Berkeley and Los Angeles: University of California Press, 1976.

(With Morton W. Bloomfield, Bertrand-Georges Guyot and Thyra B. Kabealo) *Incipits of Latin Works on the Virtues and Vices, 1100–1500 A.D.* Cambridge, Mass.: Medieval Academy of America, 1979.

Writers and Pilgrims: Medieval Pilgrimage Narratives and Their Posterity. Berkeley and Los Angeles: University of California Press, 1980.

Chaucer: His Life, His Works, His World. New York: E. P. Dutton, 1987. (Published in Great Britain as *Chaucer and the Medieval World.* London: Weidenfeld and Nicolson, 1987.)

Short Story

"The Black Suit." *The University of Kansas Review* 26 (1959): 47–56.

Articles

"Milton's Satan and the Augustinian Tradition." In *Renaissance Papers,* edited by Allan H. Gilbert 11–23. Columbia: University of South Carolina Press, 1954.

"Thomas's 'In My Craft or Sullen Art'." *The Explicator* 12, no. 4 (February 1954).

"Hamlet and the Contempt of the World." *South Atlantic Quarterly* 58 (1959): 167–75.

"The Conclusion of the Marriage Group: Chaucer and the Human Condition." *Modern Philology* 57 (1960): 223–32.

"A New Manuscript of Petrarch's *De vita solitaria:* Vatican Lat. 5151." *Manuscripta* 5 (1961): 169–170.

"Thirty New Manuscripts of Pope Innocent III's *De miseria humanae conditionis* ('De contemptu mundi')." *Manuscripta* 7 (1963): 31–35.

"Structure and Symmetry in *Sir Gawain.*" *Speculum* 39 (1964): 425–33. (Reprinted in: *Sir Gawain and Pearl,* edited by Robert J. Blanch, 1966; *Twentieth-Century Interpretations of Sir Gawain and the Green Knight,* edited by Denton Fox, 1968; *Critical Studies of Sir Gawain,* edited with Christian Zacher, 1968.)

"Chaucer the Man." *PMLA* 80 (September 1965): 337–43. (Reprinted in *Chaucer's Mind and Art by D. S. Brewer and Others: Essays,* edited by A. C. Cawley, 1969.)

"Literature and Sexuality: Book III of Chaucer's *Troilus.*" *Massachusetts Review* 8 (1967): 442–56.

"Experience, Language, and Consciousness: *Troilus and Criseyde,* II, 596–931." In *Medieval Literature and Folklore Studies: Essays in Honor of Francis Lee Utley,* edited by Jerome Mandel and Bruce Rosenberg, 173–92. New Brunswick, N.J.: Rutgers University Press, 1970. (Reprinted in *Chaucer's Troilus: Essays in Criticism,* edited by Stephen A. Barney, 1980.)

"Sir Gawain and the Green Knight." In *Recent Middle English Scholarship and Criticism: Survey and Desiderata,* edited by J. Burke Severs, 29–54. Pittsburgh: Duquesne University Press, 1971.

"The World of Mandeville's Travels." *Yearbook of English Studies* 1 (1971): 1–17.

"*The Canterbury Tales:* Memory and Form." *ELH* 38, no. 3 (1972): 319–28.

"Lexicography and the Silence of the Past." In *New Aspects of Lexicography: Literary Criticism, Intellectual History, Social Change,* edited by Howard D. Weinbrot, 3–16, 171–73. Carbondale: Southern Illinois University Press, 1972.

"Medieval Poems and Medieval Society." *Medievalia et Humanistica: Studies in Medieval and Renaissance Culture,* n.s. 3 (1972): 99–115.

"Renaissance World-Alienation." In *The Darker Vision of the Renaissance: Beyond the Fields of Reason,* edited by Robert S. Kinsman, 47–75. Berkeley and Los Angeles: University of California Press, 1974.

"Flying Through Space: Chaucer and Milton." In *Milton and the Line of Vision,* edited by Joseph Anthony Wittreich, 3–23. Madison: University of Wisconsin Press, 1975.

"Chaucer's Idea of an Idea." *Essays & Studies* 29 (1976): 39–55.

"The Humane Writing Teacher." In *Getting It On Paper: Materials from a Conference on Student Literacy,* edited by Elizabeth R. Hatcher, 79–88. Towson: Towson State University, 1976.

"The Poet as a Person." *University Publishing* (Summer 1978): 12–13.

"Fiction and Religion in Boccaccio and Chaucer." *Journal of The American Academy of Religion* 47, Supplement (1979): 307–28. (Part of a symposium on "Religion and Literature: The Convergence of Approaches," sponsored by Drew University.)

"The Four Medievalisms." *University Publishing* (Spring 1980): 5–6.

"The Idea of a Chaucer Course." In *Approaches to Teaching Chaucer's Canter-*

bury Tales, edited by Joseph Gibaldi, 57–62. New York: Modern Language Association of America, 1980.

"Thwarted Sexuality in Chaucer's Works." *Florilegium: Carleton University Annual Papers on Classical Antiquity and The Middle Ages* 3 (1981): 243–49.

"The Philosophies in Chaucer's *Troilus.*" In *the Wisdom of Poetry: Essays in Early English Literature in Honor of Morton W. Bloomfield,* edited by Larry D. Benson and Siegfried Wenzel, 151–72. Kalamazoo, Mich.: Medieval Institute Publications, 1982.

"Chaucer: The Life and Its Work." *Chaucer Newsletter* 5 (1983): 1–3.

Reviews

Howard Schultz. *Milton and Forbidden Knowledge.* In *Seventeenth-Century News* (Winter 1955): 43–45.

Dylan Thomas, *A Child's Christmas in Wales* and *Poetry;* John Malcolm Brinnan, *Dylan Thomas in America: An Intimate Journal,* "Then I Slept." In *Renascence* 9 (Winter 1956): 91–96.

R. A. Durr. *On the Mystical Poetry of Henry Vaughn.* In *Speculum* 39 (1964): 137–40.

B. F. Huppé and D. W. Robertson, Jr. *Fruyt and Chaf: Studies in Chaucer's Allegories.* In *Speculum* 39 (1964): 537–41.

C. W. Jones. *The St. Nicholas Liturgy and Its Literary Relationships.* In *Speculum* 39 (1964): 706–7.

J. A. Burrow. *A Reading of Sir Gawain and the Green Knight.* In *Speculum* 42 (1967): 518–21.

John Gardner. *The Complete Works of the Gawain Poet.* In *Speculum* 42 (1967): 149–52.

Siegfried Wenzel. *The Sin of Sloth: Acedia in Medieval Thought and Literature.* In *Speculum* 43 (1968): 758–61.

Paul T. Thurston. *Artistic Ambivalence in Chaucer's Knight's Tale.* In *Modern Language Quarterly* 31 (1970): 112–15.

A. C. Spearing. *The Gawain Poet: A Critical Survey.* In *Speculum* 47 (1972): 548–51.

Michael Means. *The Consolation Genre in Medieval English Literature.* In *MLR* 72 (1977): 653–55.

Robert B. Burlin. *Chaucerian Fiction.* In *JEGP* 77 (1978): 267–70.

Penelope B. R. Doob. *Nebuchadnezzar's Children: Conventions of Madness in Middle English Literature.* In *Modern Philology* 76 (1978): 63–66.

Robert Hollander. *Boccaccio's Two Venuses.* In *Renaissance Quarterly* 31 (1978): 604–8.

Barbara Nolan. *The Gothic Visionary Perspective.* In *Criticism* 20 (1978): 423–26.

W. A. Davenport. *The Art of the Gawain Poet.* In *Speculum* 54 (1979): 561–64.

Joy H. Potter, *Five Frames for the Decameron;* Judith P. Serafini-Sauli, *Giovanni Boccaccio.* In *Renaissance Quarterly* 36 (1983): 410–12.

Jean Richard. *Les récits de voyages et de pèlerinages.* In *Speculum* 58 (1983): 558–59.

John Ganim. *Style and Consciousness in Middle English Narrative*. In *Criticism* 27, no. 2 (Spring 1985): 203–7.

George Kane. *Chaucer*. In *Studies in the Age of Chaucer* 8 (1986): 209–10.

Charity Cannon Willard. *Christine de Pizan, Her Life and Works*. In *Renaissance Quarterly* 39 (1986): 69–70.

Index

331